# Milestones in Mass Communication Research

## MEDIA EFFECTS

### THIRD EDITION

D0226360

**Shearon A. Lowery**
*Department of Sociology and Anthropology*
*Florida International University*

**Melvin L. DeFleur**
*School of Mass Communication and Public Relations*
*Boston University*

**Longman** *Publishers USA*

**Milestones in Mass Communication
Research: Media Effects, Third Edition**

Copyright © 1995 by Longman Publishers USA.
All rights reserved.
No part of this publication may be reproduced,
stored in a retrieval system, or transmitted
in any form or by any means, electronic, mechanical,
photocopying, recording, or otherwise,
without the prior permission of the publisher.

Longman, 10 Bank Street, White Plains, N.Y. 10606

Associated companies:
Longman Group Ltd., London
Longman Cheshire Pty., Melbourne
Longman Paul Pty., Auckland
Copp Clark Longman Ltd., Toronto

Executive editor: Pamela Gordon
Assistant editor: Hillary Henderson
Production editor: Linda Moser
Cover design: Edward Smith Design, Inc.
Production supervisor: Richard Bretan

**Library of Congress Cataloging-in-Publication Data**
Lowery, Shearon.
    Milestones in mass communication research : media effects /
Shearon A. Lowery, Melvin L. DeFleur.—3rd ed.
        p.   cm.
    Includes bibliographical references and index.
    ISBN 0-8013-1437-2
    1. Mass media.   2. Mass society.   I. DeFleur, Melvin L. (Melvin
Lawrence), 1923-.   II. Title.
HM258.L68   1994
302.23—dc20                                          94-3707
                                                     CIP

1 2 3 4 5 6 7 8 9 10-CRS-9897969594

# Contents

# Foreword

Today the field of communication study has reached a level of growth and maturity in the United States and in other nations that leads scholars and students to look back at their past in order to understand their future. Of the approximately one million bachelors' degrees awarded annually by universities in the United States, 50,000 (5 percent) are in various fields of communication. This number represents a doubling in the past 10 years. Since communication study was institutionalized in American universities somewhat prior to 1960, about 2,000 departments and schools of communication have been established. There is no more important innovation in American universities in the past century.*

The vision for communication study formed during the World War II years among a set of leading social scientists who were then working for Federal agencies during the emergency. Wilbur Schramm, on leave from the University of Iowa to work for the Office of Facts and Figures (and its successor agency, the Office of War Information), returned to his university in 1943 to launch the world's first Ph.D. program in "communication." Thus he implemented the vision that had been created in the nation's capital. This event was a turning point in the evolution of the field of communication study.

*Milestones in Mass Communication Research,* Third Edition, tells an important history of this growth of communication study, beginning with the famous Payne Fund studies of the effects of movies on children, carried out by sociologists,

---

* Everett M. Rogers, *A History of Communication Study: A Biographical Approach* (New York: Free Press, 1994).

psychologists, and educational researchers around 1930. About half of the 14 milestones in this book were conducted prior to 1960, the somewhat arbitrary date of the beginning of university departments and schools of communication. These early studies of mass communication were conducted by sociologists, social psychologists, and political scientists, and formed the intellectual basis for later students and scholars of communication. Several other histories of communication study focus on the early communication scholars who carried out these investigations, emphasizing the historical context in which they operated, rather than the substantive content of what these pioneering researchers actually found.

*Milestones in Mass Communication Research* takes quite a different approach to this history of mass communication research. A distinctive aspect of this text is that it organizes the history of our field by "milestones." What is a milestone? The term derives from the stone markers placed along ancient roads like the Romans' Appian Way to inform travelers of how far they had come and thus how far they had yet to go to reach their eventual goal. The 14 milestones featured here provide the reader with a scholarly roadmap of the path taken by mass communication research. For the new student of mass communication, the present book answers such questions as Where did we come from? How did we get here? Where are we? Where are we going? I have used the first and second editions of *Milestones* in my courses at Stanford University, the University of Southern California, and at the University of New Mexico. I found my students very interested in these classics. *Milestones* presents our past in an interesting and effective manner, so that the reader grasps the multidisciplinary foundations from which mass communication research has emerged.

## FOCUS ON MEDIA EFFECTS

The main focus in the 14 milestone studies is upon mass media *effects*. Mass communication research has been dominated by an effects-orientation over the 60-year period covered by this book. This concern with media effects is guided by a one-way model of mass communication, originally proposed by Claude E. Shannon's *A Mathematical Theory of Communication* (University of Illinois Press, 1949). This one-way model came on the intellectual scene about halfway through the sequence of the milestones detailed here, but it fit well with the existing concerns of mass communication scholars. The mass media in a nation like the United States reach such huge audiences with such rapidity that any observer of these mass media (and many laypeople) believe in strong media effects. Much of the funding for mass communication research has come from research sponsors who are primarily interested in media effects issues. Given this dominant orientation toward determining media effects, the Shannon model was interpreted by mass communication scholars into an effects framework (even though that interpretation of his model was not intended by Shannon).

## ADVANCES IN THE EPISTEMOLOGY OF MASS COMMUNICATION RESEARCH

The 60-year era spanned by the 14 milestones was punctuated by important methodological advances that allowed mass communication scholars to study the effects question with greater precision. Survey design, multivariate statistical methods, and new measurement techniques were incorporated in scholarly studies of media effects. Paul F. Lazarsfeld, one of the main founders of mass communication science, in the *People's Choice* study (chapter 4 herein) utilized a panel design with 600 research interviews each month for six months prior to the 1940 presidential election. The panel design allowed scholars to trace changes in voting intentions due to mass media influences. The mass media had relatively weak effects in the political campaign (we should remember that the Erie County, Ohio study was conducted in the pre-television days, and the project's results might be different today).

The 14 milestone studies of media effects are empirical, quantitative social science investigations, carried out in the mainline academic tradition of North American functionalist theory. These 14 soundings in the academic river of mass communication research illustrate the nature and directions of multidisciplinary social science research in the United States, as it grew in size and scientific sophistication across the six recent decades. Halfway through this period, about the time that the Shannon model appeared, the first Ph.D. degrees in mass communication were awarded, first at the University of Iowa, then at the University of Illinois, at Stanford, and soon thereafter at many other research universities.

Once mass communication research became institutionalized in university departments, schools, and research institutes, the field began to display greater consistency, and moved toward becoming a discipline. Communication scientists today have their own scholarly journals, scientific associations, textbooks, and other trappings of a discipline. Many contributions to mass communication research continue to be made by sociologists and other social scientists, and communication science remains open to intellectual contributions by many scholars who were trained in other fields. No other social science discipline today is so open to external intellectual influences as is communication study.

Communication scholars have displayed (in the topics they select to study) a certain degree of *technological determinism,* the belief that technology is a cause of social change in society. Most American mass communication scientists are probably "soft" technological determinists, believing that communication technology is *one* cause, along with others, of social change in American society.

The focus on children in certain of the milestone studies suggests that mass communication scholars often regard media effects with a critical stance, looking for possibly harmful impacts (like those of television violence on children's aggressive behavior). Certainly, critics of mass communication research cannot accuse these scholars of assuming that media effects are usually positive for the audience individuals under study.

## THE MILESTONES OF MASS
## COMMUNICATION RESEARCH

Most of the milestones chapters in this book have appeared in the two previous editions of *Milestones in Mass Communication Research* but are updated here. Two new chapters have been added. Chapter 5 concerns an important theoretical perspective, uses and gratifications, that began in the 1930s and 1940s with studies of daytime (radio) soap operas. Chapter 6 analyzes research on the diffusion of innovations, a research front that began around 1940 with a classic study of the diffusion of hybrid seed corn in Iowa. Since then, over 5,000 investigations of the diffusion of new ideas have been carried out.

What have the mass communication studies told us about media effects? For example, the television effects research shows little support for a catharsis effect, that TV violence purges the viewer of aggressive tendencies. Support *is* provided for a social learning model of television effects; viewers may identify with television roles and thus learn certain of the behaviors depicted in television programs. At least for some individuals, such modeling leads to television effects on behavior.

An important topic for mass communication research in recent years centers on an indirect media effect, which is covered in chapter 12 (The Agenda-Setting Function of the Press). This field of research began with an investigation by Max McCombs and Donald Shaw of the 1968 U.S. presidential election. These scholars, then at the University of North Carolina, found that the mass media influenced the relative importance that the public attached to various political issues. In the two decades since the McCombs-Shaw research was published, over 300 studies of the agenda-setting process have been completed. This research provides evidence that the media play an important role in influencing what the public *thinks about,* even though the media may not determine *what we think.* The scope of the original McCombs-Shaw research has been widened to explore (1) how the media agenda is set and (2) how the public agenda (that is, what the public thinks are the most important issues) influences the policy agenda (what public officials and politician think are the most important issues). This indirect effect of the mass media was stimulated, in large part, by mass communication scholars' search for media effects (and their general inability to find strong media effects of a direct nature in the methodologically sophisticated research of the 1950s and 1960s). Perhaps mass communication researchers will investigate other types of indirect media effects in the future.

The 14 milestones in this book represent a sampling of the outstanding breakthrough discoveries in mass communication research over the past six decades. Additional milestone chapters undoubtedly remain to be "written" by future investigators.

Everett M. Rogers
University of New Mexico

# Preface

After more than six decades of empirical research on the process and effects of mass communication, consensus remains incomplete among media scholars as to exactly what makes up the intellectual heritage of their discipline. It is clear, however, that the dominant mode of inquiry—the major methodology—that has been moving the cutting edge of that discipline forward is quantitative research conducted within the theoretical perspectives and methodologies of social science. Other modes of analysis are obviously important. Interpretive qualitative studies often reveal subtle influences on the nature, functions, and consequences of mass communication that could not be understood from quantitative studies alone. Critical perspectives call attention to power relationships between communicators and their audiences that every thoughtful citizen needs to examine. However, it is the accumulation of quantitative research completed within the guidelines of the scientific method that has made the most significant contribution to our emerging understanding of the process and effects of mass communication.

That conclusion has guided the selection of studies to include in *Milestones in Mass Communication Research,* particularly in the present third edition. Moreover, the studies selected form a pattern that is more than the sum of its parts. That is, in a rough and often unplanned way, the research on media issues summarized in the various chapters has led to the formulation, assessment, and refinement of an increasingly rich body of theory. Admittedly, the relationship between theory and research in mass communication has seldom fit the tightly articulated model described in textbooks. Nevertheless, the significant studies of the past have helped lead the way to an accumulation of theories explaining the nature, functions, and influences of our major mass media. To understand how particular studies contributed to the development of theory, it is necessary to look backward to see what was studied and what was discovered. For that reason, the final chapter of this third edition briefly notes ways in which one or more of the milestone studies have contributed to ten specific theories that have been under development by media scholars.

Such a retrospective view of a series of seminal studies provides the major organizing framework of this book. Following discussion of the general nature of the society in which mass communication began, the initial chapter sets the stage with a discussion of the logical foundations of communication research and the role of quantitative procedures. The body of the work reviews 14 specific projects that have been conducted within a developing scientific perspective that has matured over time. Finally, in a nontechnical way, the last chapter links the studies to ten theories that have been proposed and investigated during the last six decades.

How were these 14 projects selected? Several criteria were used, as outlined in detail in chapter 1. One criterion was *theoretical significance*—some studies brought about new ways of thinking about the process and effects of mass communication. Another was *methodology*. At least a few projects developed or made use of innovative strategies that truly advanced the capacity of researchers to investigate the role and consequences of the media for individuals and society. A third criterion, used in part, was *scope*. Most of the studies and projects included in the book were large scale, involving thousands of subjects. However, scope in itself was not enough. Some of the milestones selected were actually of relatively small scale. In spite of this they are included because, in retrospect, they played a major role as turning points in the development of a particular explanatory perspective on the functions, process, or effects of the media.

Unfortunately, selection also implies exclusion. The gatekeeping process exercised by the authors, based on the above criteria, resulted in the exclusion of many worthwhile studies that made contribution to the development of the field. Fortunately, however, most are available in professional journals and can be identified and accessed via on-line information retrieval of electronic databases. In contrast, many of the works reviewed in the present book are not easily obtained in that they are reported in long–out-of-print books, multivolume publications, or complex government documents.

As in any area of scholarship, the most thorough and informative way to understand the methods, findings, and implications of a complex project is to review its original report. It should be kept in mind that the chapters of the present book are merely *summaries* of what was done and found. As such, they can serve only as secondary sources. At the same time, an attempt was made throughout to convey as much of the original report as possible, retaining the conceptual framework and general outline of each while focusing on the main issues and conclusions. Inevitably, however, any summary cannot reveal the richness of the full research report as presented by its original authors.

Why was a third edition necessary? Simply put, as scholarship advances, older studies come to be seen in a new light—sometimes as having had a previously unsuspected but significant influence on developments in the field or as having turned out to be dead ends. Thus, looking backward in a process of constant reassessment provides fresh insights into the intellectual roots of the discipline. By so doing, the study of the process and effects of mass communication remains a dynamic discipline, in which generalizations, causal explanations, and theoretical predictions are constantly under assessment and revision.

For the above reasons, this third edition of *Milestones in Mass Communication Research* presents some totally new chapters, substantial revisions of several carried over from previous editions, and others that remain virtually unchanged. In addition, the authors have made an effort to make the book more accessible to undergraduate students. When the book was first prepared, it was written for an audience consisting mainly of upper division and graduate students, primarily from the social sciences. More and more, however, the book is being used in communication departments and schools offering undergraduate courses dealing with mass communication theory and research. To make the material more suitable for such users, careful attention has been given to such matters as definition of terms, explanations of research designs and methods, and avoidance of unnecessary social science or statistical jargon.

More specifically, the third edition contains the following changes: Chapter 1 has been shortened and rewritten. It now provides an introduction explaining why research is important. It lays out the criteria for selecting the milestones, and it sets forth a point-of-departure theory that came to be abandoned and replaced as research began and continued. Overall it shows how the media, public concerns about their influences, and the ability to conduct related research all came together earlier in this century to provide the foundation for a new discipline of mass communication research.

Chapters 2, 3, and 4 are essentially unchanged from previous editions. These chapters discuss three very important pre–World War II investigations that provided a solid beginning for the new field of media research. These were the Payne Fund studies of the influence of movies on children (chapter 2), Cantril's investigation of public response to the *War of the Worlds* broadcast (chapter 3), and the classic *People's Choice* research on the role of the media in the 1940 presidential election (chapter 4).

Chapter 5 is completely new. It shows the origins of the uses and gratifications perspective on media audiences. The foundation study of ways in which thousands of listeners made use of and received enjoyment from the daily radio soap operas provided a turning point in scholarly thinking about the behavior of media audiences.

Chapter 6 is also completely new. It shows how a relatively obscure study of Iowa corn farmers, and the way they took up a new kind of seed, led to a theory of the adoption of innovation. In today's era of the information superhighway and numerous other dazzling media innovations, the process by which people come to accept and adopt new technologies is central to the field of media studies.

Chapters 7, 8, and 9 are carried over from previous editions with only minor changes. The film studies of World War II (chapter 7) remain important in cautioning all of us against overestimating the degree to which seeing a movie can produce fundamental changes in people's beliefs, attitudes, and values. The Yale program of attitude studies (chapter 8) remains important in that it was a seminal series of experiments from which came many concepts and generalizations about the process and effects of communication that continue to guide thinking and research. The role of personal influence (chapter 9) is still important in understanding that the mass communication process includes not only direct exposure to messages but a flow of word-of-mouth information from media to opinion leaders and then on to secondary audiences.

Chapter 10, on Project Revere, has been revised. In particular, it places that research effort into a context of cold war concerns that even the investigators and authors at the time did not suspect. Leaflets remain a mass medium of last resort, able to reach audiences when contact by other means is out of the question. Moreover, in view of recent disclosures about the Mark-Ultra research sponsored by the CIA, this study takes on more dramatic dimensions.

Chapters 12, 13, and 14 have been edited in only minor ways. The theory of the agenda-setting function of the press (chapter 12) has become widely researched since it was introduced in the study discussed. The report of the President's Commission on the Causes and Prevention of Violence (chapter 13) and its assessment of the amount of violence on television provided the foundation for theories linking people's beliefs about their society with degree of exposure to televised portrayals of that society. The Report to the Surgeon General (chapter 14) remains a classic and large-scale effort by social scientists to understand the link between violence portrayed on television and aggressive behavior on the part of children and adolescents.

Chapter 15 consolidates what were two long chapters on Ten Years of Progress in the second edition into a single, more concise chapter. It now has a more central focus on televised portrayals of violence and children's aggressive behavior, which remains high on today's agenda of public concern.

Finally, chapter 16 is new. It provides a summary of the major findings of each milestone project in concise form. Equally important, it identifies in a very basic way ten specific theories of mass communication that either emerged from one or more of the milestones or were significantly influenced by them.

Generally, then, this third edition focuses somewhat more on emerging theories than did previous editions. It includes additional studies that have come to be recognized as milestones in that they contributed to theory development, and it emphasizes the value of accumulating a strong base of quantitative empirical research as a foundation for understanding the process and effects of mass communication. Above all, it makes accessible to students at least part of the intellectual heritage of the discipline of mass communication by summarizing a number of remarkable research efforts by which brilliant investigators made major contributions to this increasingly important area of knowledge.

## ACKNOWLEDGMENTS

We are grateful to the following individuals who reviewed the manuscript and provided helpful suggestions:

Benita Dilley, University of Colorado
Carol Glynn, Cornell University

Margaret Haefner, Illinois State University
Ernest Hakanen, Drexel University
Doug McLeod, University of Delaware
Jerry Morgan Medley, Auburn University
Ron Milavsky, University of Connecticut
James Sneegas, Southwest Missouri State University

# chapter 1

# Research as a Basis for Understanding Mass Communication

There are many frameworks within which the mass media can be studied. For some scholars, the media are seen as the major mode of transmission of popular culture to massive audiences. For the student of politics, the media are viewed as critical in shaping the nature of public opinion and central to the process of selecting candidates. For the critical cultural theorist, the media are examined as tools by which powerful corporations who own or control them manipulate the public for their own gain. For the commercial world of the media industries, such variables as audience size and composition, and people's preferences for particular categories of content, are the significant issues influencing profit. For religious leaders, the media are often seen as a menace that threatens moral values. For parents, mass communication seems to pose a threat to their children through its emphasis on crime and violence.

The reason the media can be viewed from many perspectives in today's world is that they play an important part in each of our lives and in every one of our nation's major social institutions. This has led many kinds of academics— anthropologists, psychologists, sociologists, political scientists, educators, and so on—to study them within a *research* perspective. Thus, each discipline provides a viewpoint from which to investigate, as Harold Lasswell put it, "who says what to whom in which channel with what effect?"[1] Perhaps the only part of the academy that has shown relatively little interest in the central role of the media in contemporary society is the historians. Typically, they develop their analyses of the flow of events without much mention in their textbooks of newspapers, magazines, film, radio, or television.

But in spite of the diversity of attention paid to mass communications by various members of the academy and other groups, a critical question has yet to be answered fully with objective evidence. The question is, *What do mass communications actually do to us,* both individually and collectively? Are the mass media powerful influences that command the attention of every eye and ear? Do the messages that they bring us deeply influence our feelings, shape our ideas, and channel our actions, good or bad? Or are they merely interesting diversions, conveyors of fun, puffery, and glitz—channels of information whose messages have only limited influence on what we feel, think, and do?

Scholars from the social sciences and from communications studies have persistently addressed that central question for more than six decades. They have done so within a quantitative (and sometimes qualitative) research perspective. For the most part, their strategies of investigation have been based on a model of inquiry adopted from classical physical science. That perspective focuses on *empirical evidence*—observations made with the senses and analyzed within an objective numerical and probability framework. It is those classic investigations produced by that group between the late 1920s and the early 1980s on which the present book focuses.

The summary of each milestone in this book presents an overview of the problems investigated in the project, the methods used, and the major conclusions reached concerning various aspects of the process and effects of mass communication. Some of the milestones are groups of related studies; others are single projects.

## HOW THE MILESTONES WERE SELECTED

How were the specific studies included in the book selected? The first criterion was that they had to be *historically* important. This could be the case for several reasons: Some provided an initial look at an aspect of the process and effects of mass communication that later developed into a significant concern of the field (e.g., chapters 2, 4, 5, 9, and 12).

Several of the selections served as pivotal points in the *theoretical* development of the field. That is, their findings led to a turn away from an earlier perspective on how the media influence people and suggested new ways of thinking about the process (chapters 3, 6, 7, 8, and 11). Others addressed major questions still under active investigation (chapters 13, 14, and 15).

A second criterion that aided in the selection in some cases was the *methodology* used in the project. At least a few of the studies were included not only because they met one or both of the above criteria but also because they offered a model of mass communication research at a sophisticated level. These included panel survey designs, laboratory-type simulations, and field experiments (chapters 4, 7, 8, 10, and 15).

Most represent *large-scale* projects, although that is not universally true. At times a small study goes almost unnoticed when it is first published but later takes on a much larger significance when it is discovered that it was the first that focused on a truly important aspect of mass communication, or did so in a new way. Therefore, at least two of the milestones included had their origins in relatively small investigations (chapters 6 and 12).

Generally, then, some combination of multiple criteria—historical, theoretical, methodological, and overall scope—was used that in the opinion of the authors identified a project or series of studies as important in one or more ways in the development of the field of mass communication research. Not everyone will agree with the final list. Nevertheless, the 14 studies, projects, or series summarized in the chapters that follow provide a reasonably representative guide to important investigations that have shaped the field.

More of the milestones appeared early (1930s through 1950s) in the development of mass communication as a discipline than appeared in later decades (1960s through 1980s). That is understandable because in many ways the classic early studies structured the concerns of the field for those that followed. Thus, most of the problems and issues that were first explored in the milestone studies remain central to researchers today.

Each of these studies is presented within its own historical context. That is, an attempt has been made to explain the general issues of the times that were important considerations having some influence on decisions to fund and conduct the project. What that context shows is that research is as much a political process as it is a scientific endeavor. Few of the studies presented were conducted solely because the investigators were struck with intellectual curiosity in the middle of the night. In virtually every case, some powerful group—a media industry, a military service, the Congress, a philanthropic foundation, or a large government agency—had some stake in the outcome. This led them to sponsor the study or project and provide the funds needed for the research. This does not mean that the investigators in any way "slanted" the results. The ethics of science and the process of self-policing among colleagues are such that these actions would be very unlikely.

The principal organizing framework within the book is sequential through time. However, it is approximate rather than precise. The reason is that it is not always easy to identify exactly a specific point in time when a project was initiated, conducted, or completed. Only the dates when the results were published can be precisely fixed. However, that can be misleading because in some cases there were lengthy delays between completion of the project and publication of the results. The overall period represented by the studies selected extends from the late 1920s to the early 1980s. For example, some of the investigations included in the Payne Fund studies (chapter 2) began in 1929, others in 1930 and 1931. Some reports on parts of the project appeared in 1933, but the last report was not published until 1935. Similarly, voter choice research (chapter 4) was conducted during the presidential election campaign of 1940. However, the book *The People's Choice* did not appear until 1948.[2] Thus, the order in which the chapters appear in this book is basically sequential through time, with some overlap in a few cases.

The authors make no claim that the full story of research objectives, methodology, and theory development in mass communication is represented by the studies summarized. The book is intended to be primarily a historical account of specific investigations rather than a developmental conceptual analysis. That is, each of the research projects discussed provided in one way or another an important project in the development of the field. Many have since become identified as the seminal studies that resulted in a body of accumulated research on a particular issue, process, or topic. However, the book does not attempt to trace out all of the consequences of each study in terms of later research done within the perspectives that it opened or confirmed. That would be a Jovian task requiring a separate volume for virtually every milestone included.

Few of the milestones of mass communication research summarized in this book have been flawlessly conducted. There is little doubt that the study of media influences has always been a very difficult undertaking at best. It was even more difficult as research began than it is now. Looking back with 20/20 hindsight makes it clear that some of the earlier studies were obviously characterized by many methodological shortcomings. They were completed at times when the techniques and requirements of research on human behavior, including communication, were not as fully developed as they are today. Nevertheless, they show how the field initially came into being—sometimes haltingly at first but with greater sophistication as methodology improved.

Generally, then, each chapter in the book addresses an important area of research on a particular medium or on some significant aspect of the process and effects of mass communication. Each chapter places the seminal research in a context of the times in which it was done; it explains how the research was conducted; it summarized what was found; and it indicates what it contributed to the search for understanding about the actual power of the mass media to influence us, both personally and socially.

## THE UNSYSTEMATIC PROGRESSION
## OF MASS COMMUNICATION RESEARCH

In an ideal world, science would proceed very systematically to accomplish its twin goals of discovering new knowledge and accumulating a body of well-verified understandings. In such an ideal world, some studies would press forward the cutting edge of theory and method whereas others would replicate and confirm earlier findings. Such an ideal science would be self-policing, and the generalizations accumulated would be both reliable and valid. Unfortunately, things never work out so neatly in the real world of scientific investigation. Studies in almost every field are undertaken for a bewildering variety of reasons, ranging from the trivial to the profound. Some are done simply because an investigator is interested in the topic and manages somehow to round up the necessary funds. Others are demanded by a deeply concerned public, which gets the attention of politicians who supply the needed funds. Others are almost byproducts of ongoing and continuously funded research programs originally designed for other purposes. And so it goes. Because of the many motivations for conducting research, the accumulation of knowledge is often haphazard and frustratingly uncoordinated.

Research on mass communication has been particularly unsystematic. It has never been a precisely defined field, and those who have studied the media in the past have come from several different disciplines. One consequence is that researchers have seldom developed their research efforts in a "programmatic" manner (where each new study follows leads uncovered by those done earlier). Second, researchers have seldom been willing to abandon a conclusion on the grounds that someone else's data failed to support it. And third, many investigations of the effects of the media have been carried out mainly because some group or part of the public wanted answers to policy questions and there was a substantial amount of money available for the purpose of finding those answers. Such research seldom leads to theoretically significant results. In other words, media research did not move forward in a neat, orderly, and efficient manner following an ideal model of science. Our selection of milestone studies clearly reflects this.

But in spite of the unsystematic accumulation of research on the process and effects of mass communication, earlier studies did have at least *some* influence on later ones. Thus, the milestones selected represent an intellectual heritage of the field as it developed and as it exists now. The selections will show that there has been an increase in the sophistication of the questions addressed and in the methods and techniques used in their study. There has also been a continuing development of theories that can explain various aspects of mass communications and their influences.

## CONCEPTUALIZING MASS SOCIETY

An essential beginning point for understanding the history of research on the process and effects of mass communication is to gain a thorough understanding of the term *mass society.* It is from this concept that came such terms as "mass" audience, "mass" media, and of course, "mass" communication. Only after the nature of this rather complex concept has been clarified can early thinking about the influences of the media be understood. The first empirical studies of the media were founded on a conception of mass society that was current in the early years of the century. Then, as psychologists and sociologists moved away from that interpretation to very different conceptions of human nature and the social order, new ways of thinking about the process and effects of mass communication had to be developed. Thus, there is a close relationship between prevailing theories of both human psychological functioning and the structure of society and the kinds of projects that are undertaken by communications researchers seeking to understand the effects of mass communication. We begin, therefore, with the conceptualization of mass society that provided the intellectual foundation of the earliest milestones in mass communication research.

The term *mass*, as used in "mass" society, does not refer merely to large numbers. Many so-called mass societies happen to have large populations.

However, the underlying features that distinguish this type of society from other forms (e.g., traditional society) have to do with the relationships between their members rather than the size of their populations. This idea of mass as a form of societal organization emerged from a century and a half of theoretical analyses by a number of pioneer social scientists. It remains important in the public's beliefs about the power and influence of the media.

The concept of mass society emerged from the study of fundamental social changes that took place in society over the last two centuries. These changes altered drastically the relationships that members of society have with others as they carry on their everyday lives. The changes were subtle, complex, and profound. It is not easy to capture their essential nature in a brief review. However, we can begin by summarizing the master trends that shaped the emerging mass society.

## The Master Trends

Prior to the late eighteenth century, Western society was what sociologists call "traditional" in its organization. It was changing only slowly. People remained rooted to the land, and agriculture was almost everyone's principal preoccupation. The production of goods from wood, metal, leather, and cloth was in the hands of individual artisans and craftsmen. There were a few cottage industries and entrepreneurs, but no factories and no vast systems for distribution and consumption of manufactured products. Water, wind, and muscle were the sources of power used to operate the few machines that existed.

In terms of social organization, people were tied to each other through family and kinship, loyalties to local rulers, or through deeply established beliefs, customs, and traditions that guided their behavior in almost all aspects of social life. Communication between people was, for the vast majority, a matter of word-of-mouth. Books were being printed, but only a few people were sufficiently affluent or literate to use them. Early forms of the newspaper had appeared in some cities, but they played little part in the daily affairs of the population at large.

By the end of the eighteenth century, major changes that would drastically restructure this traditional type of society were beginning. The development and spread of mass communication would be part of those changes, but almost every aspect of social life was to undergo alteration. In retrospect, we can identify three master trends that were, and continue to be, at the heart of the change from traditional to modern society. These are *industrialization, urbanization,* and *modernization.* As a new society was developing, each of these trends had a profound influence on social relationships, material culture, social norms, and the thoughtways of individuals.

*Industrialization.*    Generally speaking, the Industrial Revolution began as the eighteenth century came to a close. It was not a sudden transition but a gradual acceleration of processes of change that had begun much earlier. The idea of producing goods for entrepreneurs to market was well established in Europe long before the mid-1700s. Developments in science and engineering were about to yield new power sources and machinery. The next major step was to combine investment capital with the new machines that could spin, weave, grind, stamp, and cut with a stamina and precision that no craftsman could match. With these devices replacing human hands and muscles, goods could be produced far more rapidly, uniformly, and cheaply than ever before. Steam power derived from wood or coal soon replaced other sources of energy and transformed one industry after another.

Such applications spread through the Western world all during the nineteenth century, and soon a great variety of manufactured goods were being produced. The social significance of this process is that it greatly changed relationships between people in terms of their work. Earlier, human beings made things for each other. The artisan or craftsman performed or controlled all phases of the production process, from assembling raw materials to selling the finished product to the customer. In the new industrial order, the process of production was divided into a host of mini-steps, with machines doing most of the more demanding tasks. The human being became a kind of appendage to the machine, working at the machine's pace, feeding it raw products, or taking its finished goods away to be marketed by impersonal systems to unknown customers. In his classic analysis, Marx maintained that this system resulted in serious *alienation* of the industrial worker, not only from the work itself but from other people and even from himself.[3]

The industrial labor force required people with minimal skills who could be hired for minimal pay. They had to be free from traditional obligations to lands and landlords so that they could work when they were needed. In England, much earlier, many peasants had been evicted from their farms by the Enclosure Acts; they constituted just such a pool of free labor. It became clear quite early that using such workers was better than using slaves (who were available at the time). Even though the workers had to be paid, they could be dismissed in slack periods, which in the long run minimized the costs of production. In other countries there were somewhat similar poorly educated and unskilled populations that could make up an industrial labor force. In the United States, immigrants who had been driven out of other countries were welcomed as they entered at the "bottom of the ladder" in the mines, mills, and factories. Even many of those who went first to the farms later migrated to towns and cities to become part of the new labor force.

Two additional elements were especially significant in shaping the emerging social order. These were the *factory system* and the *corporation*. The factory system was a direct result of the economic advantages of "shop production." This meant housing the machinery, labor, and stages of the manufacturing process under one roof. Plants were located, logically enough, where materials, labor, and transportation could easily come together. The social significance of the early factory system was that new communities developed around the sites—communities with no history or traditions of their own. They drew their residents from diverse sources. Social relationships in such areas, even outside the plant, tended to be culturally rootless and personally anonymous.

As factories, marketing enterprises, transportation systems, and financial institutions grew larger, the importance of the corporation became increasingly clear. Corporations, as legal entities for sharing risks and protecting shareholders from personal liability, had existed prior to industrialization, but it was the spread of this form of sociolegal organization that made the industrial society possible. The majority of early factories were often financed by a single individual, or at most by a few partners or a family. But as industrial and commercial activities increased in scope, larger and larger amounts of capital were required. Through the sale of shares, it was possible to obtain funds from hundreds or even thousands of owners willing to risk their capital for a proportionate part of the profits.

The significance of the development of the corporate structure and the great expansion in the size of industrial-commercial groups is that they brought a new dependence on *bureaucracy* as a form of social organization. A small group can be informal and depend upon intuitive understanding of its rules and tasks in order to achieve its goals. A group of thousands, designed to achieve the goals of a factory, a retail chain, or even a newspaper, must be far more impersonal in its structure. Groups organized as bureaucracies are deliberately designed to achieve clear-cut goals in a rational and efficient manner. Aside from all of the bad jokes about bumbling bureaucrats and snarls of red tape, bureaucracy, in principle, is the most effective way in which large-scale social enterprises can be conducted. A bureaucratic group has written rules; the activities of each person's position are carefully set forth; patterns of power and authority are clearly defined; the system of rewards and punishments is specified in contractual agreements. There are no real alternatives to this form of social organization for enterprises of large scope. For this reason, we live in an age of bureaucracy. All large-scale activities in contemporary society—manufacturing, commercial, educational, military, religious, sports, medical, and recreational—are carried out by groups that are bureaucratically organized. About the only exceptions are our families and friends.

Needless to say, the new types of human relationships resulting from the growth of bureaucracy were very different from the older forms based on friendship, kinship, or traditional loyalty. As the traditional society gave way to the industrial order, the bonds that united people were based less and less on such sentiments and more and more on the impersonal obligations of the legal contract.[4] People still had families and friends, but the increasingly mobile, differentiated, and bureaucratized society was one that tended to reduce close personal ties between people rather than strengthen them.

**Urbanization.**    The social controls that traditional people exercise over each other decline sharply with the changes mentioned. People's customs and other rules for behavior give way to more formal means of control through civil law and criminal justice systems with police, courts, and penal institutions. Deviant behavior becomes increasingly common as the older rules lose their force. The second master trend that has played a part in the emergence of mass society is *urbanization*. Defined very simply, urbanization is a process by which an increasing proportion of the population of a given area live in towns and cities. In the history of humankind, it is a relatively recent phenomenon. While human life in various forms goes back 4 million years, people have been city dwellers for only a short part of that time. For example, the first known cities were established a mere 7,000 years ago.[5] We think of Europe today as highly urbanized. However, 150 years ago it was still overwhelmingly rural. As late as the beginning of the nineteenth century, only 3 percent of the world's people lived in communities of 5,000 or more.[6] Today, urbanization is one of the most significant trends of modern life. Even in the New World, cities reach 20 million or more (e.g., Mexico City). Dozens of cities in the United States have exceeded 1 million inhabitants. Today, less than 2 percent of the U.S. population is still in farming, and only about a quarter of the population lives in rural areas. These trends are very much in evidence in other parts of the globe. Some countries are considerably more urbanized than the United States.

This explosion in urban growth began and kept pace with the Industrial Revolution. But while the two master trends are closely linked, they are not simply different ways of looking at the same thing. In many areas, urbanization has proceeded without industrialization. Other areas have become industrialized without significant changes in the proportion of the population that is urban. The social significance of urbanization is that it changes the quality of life. Above all, it *brings unlike people together.* In the early days of industrialization, uprooted farm people were drawn to the new factory towns to seek work. They were joined there by others from different parts of the country and by people from the slums of established cities. These people did not relate to each other easily because of their social and psychological differences. Whereas the earlier rural and traditional social order was based on clear conceptions of the rules of social behavior, life in the new cities was characterized by a confusion of the rules, customs, and traditions, a condition called *anomie.*

The process of bringing unlike people together was accelerated greatly in the United States by heavy immigration from other lands. Not only were rural people going to the city to seek their fortunes, but millions of foreigners were arriving to enter at the bottom of the social ladder. The population of the United States grew very rapidly during the late nineteenth and early twentieth centuries as national policy sought to fill vacant land. A veritable tidal wave of immigration brought poorly educated and economically deprived people to the new world. Emma Lazarus's words inscribed at the base of the Statue of Liberty capture the essential characteristics of this inflow of humanity:

Give me your tired, your poor,
Your huddled masses yearning to breathe free,
The wretched refuse of your teeming shore,
Send these, the homeless, tempest-tost to me:
I lift my lamp beside the golden door.

And so they came. They poured in from northern, southern, and eastern Europe; from Asia and Africa; and from dozens of lands to the south. They settled mainly in the cities, entered at the bottom of the labor force, and began their struggle upward. They spoke different languages, followed different customs, and subscribed to different values. They developed prejudices toward each other; called each other bad names; discriminated against each other; and sometimes fought each other in the streets. All the while, those who had arrived earlier deplored and rejected the later arrivals. The end product was what Auguste Comte had called "a multitude of separate corporations."[7] They split up into enclaves where language and customs could be maintained and where dislike and distrust of "the others" could be kept alive. Emotion and sentiment became more significant than reason and rationality in decisions about behavior. As time went on, many of those who had entered at the bottom did move up the social ladder. The majority did not. The industrial labor force, its related commercial activities, and the opportunities provided by public education provided the basis for upward mobility for some and social differentiation for all. Urbanization, in other words, created great *differences* between people. These differences provided no basis for the older and traditional bonds, based on loyalty, trust, and fealty, to develop again and keep people together. The new social order was what Ferdinand Tönnies called the *Gesellschaft.*[8] Trust was replaced by *distrust.* In a society of distrust, the contract rather than the handshake becomes the principal basis for regulating obligations between people.

*Modernization.*    As industrialization and urbanization continued, the lifestyles of the inhabitants of modern societies underwent change. Hundreds and even thousands of *innovations* were adopted. Inventive people designed machines for every conceivable purpose. By the turn of the century, the industrial order was producing an incredible array of devices that the ordinary family could purchase and use. These ranged from basics, such as tools and clothing, to the exotic, such as ointments for bust development or electric devices guaranteed to restore hair on bald heads. Mechanical innovations—indoor plumbing, central heat, the automobile, refrigeration, electric lights, and so on—had an impact on every aspect of life. Not only were the objects of everyday use undergoing change, but the very rhythm and meaning of life were different. Time scheduling assumed a new importance. Work, play, meals, education, and even worship started and stopped according to the clock.

Industrialization and urbanization had already created differences between people. Modernization was a force toward even greater distinctions. Material lifestyles, based on consumption of the products of the new industries, were quite different at each level in the stratification system. Rich people had always lived differently from poor people, but the emerging industrial order brought a tremendous new diversity of goods. Those at the highest economic level could engage in conspicuous consumption and surround themselves with amenities never dreamed of by the affluent in more traditional societies.

Many of these new products served as status symbols and were adopted as quickly as possible by those who could afford them. Those lower in the system looked on with envy or used the new time-payment plans to acquire what they could. Between the economic elite at the top and the destitute poor at the bottom stretched numerous middle levels identified mainly by their patterns of consumption of the goods of modern society. In this way, modernization created another basis for social differentiation in addition to those stemming from regional, ethnic, and religious sources.

The process of modernization is closely linked with the growth of the mass media. Populations undergoing modernization increase not only their consumption of goods but also their use of print, film, and broadcast media. Generally, they undergo a corresponding increase in literacy, which has an influence on their perceptions and participation in government.[9]

Modern societies, then, are media-dependent societies. Their populations make use of the media for achieving a great many goals that are handled differently in the traditional society. The media provide information critical to economic, political, religious, and educational decisions in ways that are totally different from those of preindustrial societies. This flow of information further breaks people away from traditional ways of life and thrusts them into constantly changing ways of thinking about family obligations, sexual mores, basic values, and other central features of human existence.

## Contemporary Society as Mass Society

Our review of the master trends underlying the transition from traditional to contemporary society has emphasized increases in *social differentiation* and *psychological isolation* in urban-industrial populations brought about by such factors as bureaucracy, contracts, migration, stratification, and the spread of innovation. It is said that all of these individual and social forces have worked to set people apart far more than to bring them together. The master trends, in one form or another, led social theorists of the last century to conceptualize the urban-industrial society as a *mass* society. The term *mass* in this context refers not to numbers but to a distinctive pattern of social organization, more precisely, a process of changing social organization that occurs when industrialization, urbanization, and modernization increasingly modify the social order. In other words, "mass" society emerges when the following changes take place:

1. Social differentiation in the society *increases* because of the growing division of labor, the bureaucratization of human groups, the mixing of unlike populations, and differential patterns of consumption.
2. The effectiveness of informal social controls *erodes* as the influence of traditional norms and values declines, leading to increases in the incidence of deviant behavior.
3. The use of formal social controls (the contract, civil law, and criminal justice systems) *rises* as the new impersonal society develops.

4. Conflicts *increase* because of social differences between people with opposing values and lifestyles.
5. Open and easy communication as a basis of social solidarity between people becomes *more difficult* because of social differentiation, impersonality and distrust due to psychological alienation, the breakdown of meaningful social ties, and increasing anomie among the members.
6. Because of all of these changes, people in modern society become increasingly *dependent* on mass communication to obtain information they need.

Does this theoretical description provide an accurate picture of society today? Clearly it does not. There is much more to contemporary society than this portrayal of people psychologically and socially isolated from each other. Yet, the idea remains important. The concept of mass society is significant for the study of the media for two reasons. First, in spite of the fact that the theoretical picture it provides of contemporary society is overdrawn, we can recognize at least some of these trends around us. We *have* undergone industrialization, urbanization, and modernization. Life in contemporary society is very different because of these changes from what it was in the "good old days" of traditional society. The ideas embedded in the conceptualization of mass society do provide an understanding of at least some of the features of life in the urban-industrial social order. But more important, it was this conceptualization of mass society that dominated the thinking of those intellectuals who were first concerned about the effects of the new mass media.

As each new medium came into the society and was adopted for widespread use, there was an increasing level of concern about the influences of the mass communication process. As the newspapers and, later, films and broadcasting were increasingly criticized for their presumed undesirable influences, the idea that members of the mass society could easily be controlled by powerful media troubled the critics.

## THE MAGIC BULLET THEORY AS A POINT OF DEPARTURE

The sociological theory of mass society sketched above and current at the beginning of the twentieth century provided a systematic picture of the nature of the social order and of the ways in which individuals related to each other. However, it said little about the individual human being from a psychological point of view. Nevertheless, there were widely accepted theories in psychology that addressed this issue. As the century began, just before the new film and broadcast media arrived, psychologists had very definite and clear conceptions of the nature of human nature. These were to play an important part in the way that they visualized the relationship between media and mass. Those conceptions were heavily influenced by the evolutionary perspectives of Charles Darwin.

Before Darwin published *The Origin of Species* (in 1854), thinking about the nature of human nature emphasized *religious* interpretations. Human beings were said to be unique "rational" creatures formed in the image of God. The choices people made in their behavior were interpreted within a framework of original sin, good versus evil, and commitments to religious commandments. They were expected to make rational choices within the norms set by religious scriptures in order to achieve salvation. After Darwin, scientific thinking began to stress a very different conception of the human being based on the importance of inheritance and biology as causes of human behavior.

Influenced by this genetic perspective, behavioral scientists of the time rejected interpretations of human beings as rational creatures and stressed the *animal* side of human nature. They assumed that there was continuity between the behavior of higher animals and that of human beings. For example, animals within a particular species presumably all behaved in more or less the same way because of their *uniform inherited instincts* (derived from their evolutionary history). It was assumed, therefore, that human beings were also uniformly controlled by their biologically based instincts and that they would react more or less uniformly to whatever stimuli (situations confronting them) came along. Under this conception of human nature, responses made by human beings to stimuli were thought to be shaped by instincts over which people lacked rational control or by other unconscious processes that were also inherited but not guided by intellect.

This view of human nature was compounded with the theory of mass society set forth earlier. From this combination, a *theory of mass communication* seemed to follow. While it was never articulated systematically at the time, it came in later years to be known by the colorful name the "magic bullet" theory. In retrospect, it brings together the basic understandings of human nature and the social order that prevailed at the end of the nineteenth century. Those conceptions continued to be regarded as valid well into the twentieth century.

The magic bullet theory was a frightening view of the power of mass communication. It portrayed media audiences as composed of irrational creatures guided more or less uniformly by their instincts. They lived in a mass society with limited meaningful social contacts with each other and a deep dependency on information received from the mass media. Because of these personal and social conditions, they could presumably be swayed and controlled by cleverly designed mass communication messages. It was this vision of the process and effects of mass communication that led people early in the century to believe that those who controlled the media could effectively control the public. For this reason, propaganda was thought to be extremely effective; there was little doubt that people could not resist mass advertising; and the use of media by demagogues to control the political process was a matter of deep concern.

If the conditions of the mass society and the instinctual basis of behavior were true, it would follow logically that a media message would reach every eye and ear in the same way, like a symbolic "bullet," immediately bringing about the same changes of thought and behavior in the entire audience. Briefly stated, the basic propositions of the magic bullet theory are the following:

1. People in "mass" society lead *socially isolated lives* with very limited social controls exerted over each other because they are from diverse origins and do not share a unifying set of norms, values, and beliefs.
2. Like all animals, human beings are endowed at birth with a *uniform set of instincts* that guide their ways of responding to the world around them.
3. Because people's actions are not influenced by social ties and are guided by uniform instincts, individuals attend to events (such as media messages) *in similar ways.*
4. People's inherited human nature and their isolated social condition lead them to *receive and interpret* media messages in a uniform way.
5. Thus, media messages are like symbolic "bullets," striking every eye and ear, and resulting in effects on thought and behavior that are *direct, immediate, uniform,* and therefore *powerful.*

Again, this theory was never formulated in such a systematic way at the time. But when its development is examined in retrospect, it is clear that the social scientists who began studying the process and effects of mass communication within a scientific framework entertained the theory's basic assumptions. It was also the view of the general public. Thus, most people early in the twentieth century, when film and broadcasting were relatively new, thought that the media were powerful, manipulative, and therefore dangerous. It was within this guiding framework that empirical research on the influences of mass communications was to begin.

## THE DEVELOPMENT OF THE TOOLS OF RESEARCH

By the 1920s, each of our contemporary media—print, film, and broadcasting— had become a reality, at least in its preliminary form. People regularly received newspapers and magazines, and they could go to the movies and receive broad-cast signals on receivers in their homes. While these media have increased greatly in sophistication today, they clearly were part of the everyday lives of citizens by the end of the decade following World War I. Prior to the 1920s, however, there was little in the way of systematic investigation of the *effects* of mass communication within what we would today call a scientific perspective. There was a great deal being written about the media. Most intellectuals of the nine-teenth century denounced them at one time or another for their presumed destructive effects on the social order. Such critical claims continued in the twentieth century (and continue still). But these claims were just that—claims. Until well into the present century, it was not possible to approach the issue of media influences within a framework of objective, quantitative analysis where conclusions were based on value-free criteria. That is, it was not until scientific methods were available that research findings could replace speculation, accusation, and undocumented conclusions in the discussion of media effects. The development of those scientific methods did not come quickly or easily. They were part of the more general development of the social and behavioral sciences.

## The Logical Foundations of Communication Research

Communication research is an extension of the methodology and theory-building strategies of the social and behavioral sciences. These in turn rest heavily upon the underlying logical strategies of the physical and biological sciences. Early in the nineteenth century, it became clear to many scholars concerned about human individual and social behavior that the research strategies of the physical sciences offered hope for the future in understanding people. Those research strategies were leading to great success in developing reliable and valid knowledge in such fields as physics, chemistry, and biology. For example, by the time that the first mass newspaper appeared, photography was about to become a reality. People were being vaccinated routinely against at least some serious diseases, and the telegraph had been in existence for five years. The social sciences, by comparison, were still in the age of Plato.

It was not that there was a lack of ideas about the individual or the social order but more an embarrassment of riches. The wisdom of hundreds of philosophers was available. The problem was that they were all saying different things about human nature and society. There was no systematic and objective way to sort out valid conclusions from all the theories that could not be supported by facts. This was not so in the other sciences. Systematic observation, guided by reasoned theoretical perspectives and careful weighing of empirical evidence, had proved to be enormously successful in yielding reliable and valid generalizations. This procedure had brought Darwin to his historic conclusions about the origin of species; it was leading others to a host of discoveries in medicine, chemistry, astronomy, and physics. Was it not possible, and was it not wise, to try to adapt these strategies and procedures to study human beings in their individual and social activities?

Many scoffed at the idea or found it presumptuous. Some in well-established scientific fields dismissed such an effort as preposterous. Human behavior was too complex, they said, or too erratic and unpredictable. And how on earth could one quantify thoughts and emotions? Human activities did not follow immutable laws, they pointed out, as did the phenomena of the physical and biological world. Thus, the critics concluded, there were no regularities to be discovered by such a science even if the science might be possible. Others proclaimed that the whole idea was wicked. God had given human beings their destiny, and their behavior was the result of his divine plan. To presume that some sort of scientific approach could pry into such matters and see regular predictable patterns of action was little short of blasphemy!

## Quantitative Procedures

In spite of the opposition of skeptics and critics, social and psychological pioneers did break away from the undisciplined philosophies of the past. They began to make measurements of limited forms of behavior. By the 1840s Ernst Weber worked out a mathematically sophisticated system of "psychophysics" to describe patterns in people's perceptions of differences in the intensities of stimuli.[10] Toward the end of the century, the sociologist Durkheim assembled numerical data on deaths by suicide from various countries in Europe and developed an innovative theory concerning that ultimate act. It was not speculation; it was backed by impressive quantitative evidence.[11] Charles Booth used meticulous counting and classification to describe the way of life of London's poor in an early version of the survey.[12] Social psychologist Wilhelm Wundt in Leipzig developed the first laboratory for the precise measurement of human reaction times as early as 1879. He used a number of ingenious brass instruments and experiments.

As the new century began, these pioneering efforts led the way to the future. The social and behavioral sciences were about to become a reality. Still, it was clearly very difficult to use the experimental format or any other quantitative procedure for the study of anything but the most restricted forms of behavior. But new approaches were being developed by mathematicians and other scholars. These were the new techniques for examining the statistical parameters and distributions of numbers—their central tendencies, their scatter, and variability. Laws of probability had already been worked out, and these could be used to interpret the likelihood of any given pattern of differences between means. Pearson's procedure, called the "product-moment coefficient of correlation," was another major breakthrough. Its index, $r$, summarized the tendency of two arrays of numbers to rise and fall jointly.

The beauty of these new statistical techniques was that they were universal in their application to scientific problems. It did not matter whether the numbers used represented observations from agriculture, biology, communication, psychology, sociology, or zoology. These statistical procedures, and the many more that have come since those early times, opened the scientific method to the social and behavioral sciences. Communication research followed these traditions and depends on them in the same manner.

By the beginning of the 1920s, the teaching of statistical techniques began in earnest in the social and behavioral sciences. Yet this generated considerable debate. More conservative scholars in the older traditions rejected the radical new procedures, claiming that they were sterile and atheoretical. How could one understand the delicacy and richness of human life, they asked, by looking at a table of numbers or a statistical index? In the end, however, the quantitative procedures found increasing acceptance. With them came the standardized questionnaire as a means of generating numerical data, the random sample that could fit the underlying assumptions of the new statistical procedures, and the probability considerations for deciding whether a given generalization was merely a reflection of chance.

As the movement toward quantification became more sophisticated, additional procedures were devised for probing into areas previously not accessible to scientific approaches. The attitude scales, pioneered by sociologist Emory Bogardus and psychologist L. L. Thurstone, made it possible to reduce people's psychological orientations to numerical scale values. This touched off a tidal wave of attitude studies. The techniques of partial and multiple correlation, the analysis of variance, and nonparametric statistics were added to the tools available for research.

Calculation of large data sets remained a laborious procedure, and ways were invented to make this easier. Before there were computers there were mechanical calculators and electrical sorting with Holerith cards based on the same binary principle of the IBM card. It worked well enough. Calculation from large data sets was also facilitated by grouping the data into class intervals and working with their midvalues. The quantitative procedures of content analysis were developed from this base. These procedures became very important in communication research. The frequency with which specific words, phrases, or themes appeared in a given communication could be counted; statistical relationships between these data and other factors could then be studied. It was a useful procedure for showing trends in the treatment of issues over time or for comparing the treatment of a given type of content in various media.

It was not until these research tools began to be available that a scientific approach to the study of mass communication could get its start. But numbers alone are not enough: research cannot be done in a theoretical vacuum. The development of statistical procedures, measurement techniques, and research designs can only be effective in advancing a field if at the same time it develops hypotheses and theories that can be guides to what should be studied. For this reason, we need to understand how new frameworks emerged for understanding and explaining the influence of the media.

## RESEARCH BEGINS

By the later 1920s, as we have indicated, an understanding of the consequences of industrialization, urbanization, and modernization had led to a well-developed conception of mass society in which people were increasingly isolated from their fellow citizens and dependent on mass media. Given these two conditions, it seemed obvious to social scientists that mass communications had great power to influence and sway the individuals who made up their audiences.

There was also widespread concern among the public about the negative effects of mass communication. A host of moralists and critics had posted warnings about the effects of the popular press throughout the nineteenth century as newspapers and magazines became more widely read. In France, Gabriel Tarde had warned that newspapers were the cause of juvenile crime. Many conservative intellectuals warned that newspapers, with their great flow of stories about crime and vice transmitted to every town and village through the wire services were creating "newspaperism" among their readers. This unfortunate condition was said to afflict people who read numerous descriptions of scandals, crime, and other seamy situations in their daily papers. It was feared that such readers might be only too willing to imitate the immoral behavior described so vividly.

The Great War had also stirred the population and brought new and unsettling ideas, especially among the young. The question of what was happening to America's youth was posed clearly in a song that became popular just as the soldiers were returning from France. The lyrics asked "How you gonna keep 'em down on the farm after they've seen Paree?" The answer that seemed evident to many was that it was not going to be possible. The moral norms of the traditional American way of life seemed to be deteriorating, being replaced by looser and looser standards. As the 1920s began, dresses became skimpier, displaying bare arms and even knees; women were smoking in public, cutting their hair short, and wearing lipstick. Worse yet, young men and women were going out together unchaperoned in automobiles, and they were dancing to stimulating new jazz music in ways that would surely lead them astray. In short, America was thought by many to be in a state of moral decline, and it was considered essential that the causes of its downward path be discovered. To many the mass media seemed an obvious and visible cause, with the new moving pictures one of the most glaring candidates on which to place the blame.

Only after all these trends and beliefs came together did systematic research on the effects of mass communication begin. That is, people were concerned about the problem of media influences; research methods were available that could be used for objective studies; and social scientists believed they had a sophisticated understanding of the mass society to which the new media were delivering vast amounts of information. While scattered studies of existing media were conducted during the 1920s, it was a massive project, the Payne Fund studies of the relationship between movies and children, that effectively launched large-scale empirical research on the effects of mass communication. It was the first in a series of projects both large and small that were to replace speculation about the influence of the media with research evidence about their effects.

## NOTES AND REFERENCES

1. Harold D. Lasswell, "The Structure and Function of Communication in Society," In *The Communication of Ideas,* ed. Lyman Bryson (New York: Harper and Brothers, 1948), pp. 37–51.
2. Paul F. Lazarsfeld, Bernard Berelson, and Hazel Gaudet, *The People's Choice: How the Voter Makes Up His Mind in a Presidential Election* (New York: Columbia University Press, 1948).
3. Karl Marx, *Das Capital,* ed. Friedrich Engels (New York: International Publishers, 1967). This is a modern English translation of the original nineteenth-century work.
4. Ferdinand Tönnies, *Community and Society (Gemeinschaft und Gesellschaft),* trans. Charles P. Loomis (East Lansing: Michigan State University Press, 1957). This is an English translation of the original nineteenth-century work.

5. J. John Palen, *The Urban World* (New York: McGraw-Hill, 1975), p. 3.
6. Phillip Mauser and Leo Schnore, *The Study of Urbanization* (New York: John Wiley and Sons, 1965), p. 7.
7. Auguste Comte, *The Positive Philosophy,* trans. Harriet Martineau (London: George Bell and Sons, 1915), p. 293. This is an English translation of the original nineteenth-century work.
8. Tönnies, *Community and Society.*
9. Daniel Lerner, *The Passing of Traditional Society* (New York: Free Press, 1958).
10. E. G. Boring, *A History of Experimental Psychology* (New York: Appleton-Century-Crofts, 1929), p. 279.
11. Emile Durkheim, *Suicide, A Study in Sociology* (Englewood Cliffs, N.J.: Prentice-Hall, 1968). First published in French in 1897.
12. The social survey in its modern sense is usually thought of as beginning with the work of Frederic Le Play, in his *Ouvriers Européens* (1855), or with Charles Booth's 17-volume *Life and Labour of the People of London* (produced between 1891 and 1897). For discussions of both works, see Pitirim Sorokin, *Contemporary Sociological Theories* (New York: Harper and Brothers, 1928).

# chapter 2

# The Payne Fund Studies:
# The Effects of Movies on Children

**D**uring the 1920s, the motion picture industry suddenly thrust itself into the lives of virtually everyone in the United States. What was this new medium and what influence was it having on those who consumed its products? It was these questions that helped bring into existence one of the largest research projects ever undertaken in an effort to understand the relationship between a medium and a particular audience. Two additional trends taking place in the United States were to play important parts in establishing mass communication research as a field of scientific study. One was the increasing emphasis on the scientific method as a proper strategy for investigation in such fields as sociology, psychology, and education. The other was the extremely rapid rise in concern about the influence of the new motion picture industry. To understand why the first major scientific assessment of the effects of a mass medium was undertaken in the late 1920s, one needs to understand these two trends.

One important factor of the times was the maturation of the social sciences. Following World War I, the social sciences began to undergo an important transformation. Increasing attention was being given to the use of quantitative research techniques. The trend was given a boost when procedures were devised for the measurement of aspects of individual human behavior that had previously been thought ephemeral. For example, Emory S. Bogardus began the movement to assess racial and ethnic attitudes with his "social distance" scale that was first published in 1924.[1] This was soon followed by the more sophisticated work of Thurstone and Chave with their "equal appearing intervals" scale for measuring almost any kind of attitude.[2]

The 1920s brought statistics to social science research. Important new techniques based on probability had been invented by mathematicians. These were advocated in journals, books, and courses by leading psychologists and sociologists of the period, who showed the applications of sampling, measures of central tendency, correlation, and probability to behavioral research problems.[3] Similar transformations had been taking place in educational research in addition to other social sciences.

It was a controversial time, and many traditional social scientists resisted the trend. Critics charged that the move toward quantification was merely an attempt to "ape" the physical sciences in a shameless grab for a share in the prestige of those sciences. They pronounced that the emphasis on numbers would "dehumanize" the study of human behavior; it would create mind-boggling accumulations of meaningless facts; and it would destroy efforts to build insightful theories. But in spite of these gloomy predictions, the trend continued. By the end of the decade, the scientific perspective, much as we know it today, had taken a strong foothold in both psychology and sociology.

During the same period, American movies took over the world film market. The new medium got its start as the century changed. At first, movies were little more than amusing novelties—pictures that appeared to move. By the end of the first decade, nickelodeons were attracting millions of unsophisticated viewers with slapstick films of short duration. By the time of World War I, the movies had become a widely accepted form of family entertainment. It was in the 1920s, however, that motion pictures matured into a major mass medium that was a part of the life of almost every citizen. Hollywood—previously a rather drab village on the suburban fringes of Los Angeles—became the glamour capital of the world. Its film studios ground out a veritable tidal wave of films (hundreds a year) to satisfy the insatiable demands of the public for the new form of entertainment. Its stars represented fantasy success stories that fascinated shop girls and factory workers across the nation. Obscure people were "discovered" by the studios and propelled into instant fame and fortune. Millions were eager to learn of the smallest details of the stars' lives. They became gods and goddesses, adored by publics eager to pay to see their features projected silently on the screen in black-and-white. It was the American Dream in a new form, and it rivaled even the most fanciful rags-to-riches stories of earlier times. By the end of the decade, sound tracks were added, making the movies even more attractive. Theaters had grown larger and more opulent as ticket sales soared.

Going to the movies was a frequent event for most families—they were great fun. Also, there were very few alternatives for inexpensive recreation. Homes had neither radios nor television sets. Some had pianos and windup victrolas; a few even had books. But for the majority of families with limited means, taking in a motion picture was an enjoyable and affordable evening out. For those of dating and courting age, movies were made to order: couples in dark theaters could do more than just watch the films. For children, the Saturday matinee was the high point of existence. Many a youngster behaved reasonably well for days in a row on the promise that he or she could go to the show with the other kinds on Saturday afternoon.

All of these attractions had caused motion picture attendance to rise dramatically over a very short period of time. Data on movie attendance were not systematically gathered before 1922. During that year, some 40 million tickets were sold every week in the United States. By the end of the decade, the figure had more than doubled to 90 million! Among the movie-goers in 1929 were an estimated 40 million minors, and among these were approximately 17 million children under the age of fourteen.[4]

The content of the motion pictures produced in the 1920s was not much different from the content of movies today. There was less bare skin, sex, and blood, but the themes were very similar. Edgar Dale, a well-known educator, made an exhaustive study of the content of 1,500 films of the period.[5] As we will note later in greater detail, their content could be grouped into ten major thematic categories. However, a mere three of these categories—love, crime, and sex— accounted for nearly three-fourths of the total!

Adults during the period did not quite know what to make of it all. In a single decade, the startling new medium had burgeoned into a national preoccupation. In a society that had barely emerged from the Victorian era, the love, sex, and crime themes that dominated the films seemed to many to pose troublesome challenges to established moral standards. Above all, their great concern was what the movies were doing to the nation's children. A well-known educator of the time summarized the issues in the following terms:

> Motion pictures are not understood by the present generation of adults. They are new; they make an enormous appeal to children; and they present ideas and situations which parents may not like. Consequently when parents think of the welfare of their children who are exposed to these compelling situations, they wonder about the effects of the pictures upon the ideals and behavior of the children. Do the pictures really influence children in any direction? Are their conduct, ideals and attitudes affected by the movies? Are the scenes which are objectionable to adults understood by children, or at least by very young children? Do children eventually become sophisticated and grow superior to pictures? Are the emotions of children harmfully excited? In short, just what effect do motion pictures have upon children of different ages?[6]

Thus, the situation at the time was not unlike that faced by parents in the 1960s, when television had just emerged as a new national medium with a huge audience of children. The public was deeply concerned about effects, and it wanted answers.

By the mid-1920s, pressure began to mount on the motion picture industry. Numerous editorials, sermons, magazine articles, and other forms of public criticism raised questions and made charges that the movies were a negative influence on children. It became increasingly clear that research was needed. Social scientists were seeking opportunities to undertake assessments of the influence of movies on children. In 1928, William H. Short, executive director of the Motion Picture Research Council, invited a group of university psychologists, sociologists, and educators to design a series of studies assessing the influence of the movies on children; they responded enthusiastically. There was no government agency to which they could turn to obtain funds for such research, as there would be at a later time. However, a private philanthropic foundation (The Payne Fund) agreed to provide financial support. The end result was a series of 13 specific studies, done by well-known researchers, on various aspects of the influence of the movies on children. The investigations, known as the Payne Fund studies, were conducted over a three-year period from 1929 to 1932. They were published in the early 1930s in ten volumes. These classic works were reprinted in 1970 by the Arno Press and the *New York Times* (who generously provided a set of the reprints to the authors for purposes of the present book).

In retrospect, then, it was the coming together of two major social changes in the American society—the development of a more precise research capability in the social sciences and the deepening public concern over the mushrooming growth of the movies—that gave birth to the scientific study of mass communication. As we noted earlier, scholars had long been concerned with the influence of mass communication on individuals and society. However, this was largely in the context of "unmasking" the influence of propaganda rather than in terms of uncovering cause-effect relationships within the framework of science. The Payne Fund studies, therefore, represent the first major effort to bring such perspectives, strategies, and techniques to bear on the influence of a major medium on a specific category of people. In the section that follows, we present a brief summary of the individual studies.

## OVERVIEW OF THE PAYNE FUND STUDIES

The question of influences of the motion pictures on children was posed in a variety of terms by the researchers who worked on the Payne Fund studies. Over a dozen major investigations were undertaken simultaneously. Each was of relatively large scale; each had quite different goals. From the perspective of today, the majority of these studies are mainly of historical interest, in the sense that their findings would not be useful for understanding the influence of contemporary movies on modern youth. However, they all played a part in the development of mass communication research as a field of scientific investigation. Several of the studies remain important because they addressed problems that are still under active investigation today. It was these studies that provided a matrix of findings from which simple theoretical perspectives emerged, to be used in subsequent investigations for many years.

From the standpoint of their objectives, the Payne Fund studies fall into two rather broad categories. In one category, the goals are to assess the content of the films and determine the size and composition of their audiences. The second category attempts to assess the effects on those audiences of their exposures to the themes and messages of motion pictures. There were several kinds of major effects under study. Stated briefly, these were acquisition of information, change in attitudes, stimulation of emotions, harm to health, erosion of moral standards, and influence on conduct. In the paragraphs that follow, each of the specific investigations is described in very brief terms to give a more complete overview of the goals and scope of this pioneering research series.

## The Audience and Content of the Films

No actual records of movie attendance by age level were available during the period of the studies. To gain an understanding of the size and composition of the youthful audience, Edgar Dale used several different strategies and information sources to make estimates. Census data were, of course, available for every state and for the nation as a whole. The problem was to determine what proportion of the population at various age levels attended the movies and how often. Dale made studies of actual movie attendance in over 50 Ohio communities in order to estimate the size and composition of their youthful audiences. He then used these data as a basis of projection for the nation as a whole. He found that even children of five to eight years were going to the movies with some frequency. Children of school age attended much more often; in fact, they went more frequently than adults. Boys attended more often than girls. The main finding was that on the average, children in 1929 and 1930 went to the movies once a week.[7] In a society that did not yet understand motion pictures and their potential influence on children, these figures caused considerable concern.

What did these children see? Again, a study by Dale provided clear answers.[8] He reviewed, classified, and analyzed 1,500 films, 500 of which had been produced in 1920, another 500 in 1925, and the remaining 500 in 1930. He was able to classify their content into the following ten categories: crime, sex, love, mystery, war, children, history, travel, comedy, and social propaganda. He studied not only the general themes of the stories, but their locales or settings; the nature of their heroes or heroines; the actors' clothing styles; their portrayals of how people met, loved, and married; and how they engaged in crime, used vulgarity, consumed liquor and tobacco, and pursued goals identified as important in the films. In other words, it was a large-scale, systematic, and thorough content analysis of motion pictures produced and seen during a decade. The results were scarcely reassuring to critics of the movies. Over three-fourths of the films dealt with only three thematic categories—crime, sex, and love. More wholesome themes, such as travel, children's stories, and history, represented only an insignificant proportion of the total. The use of tobacco and liquor (in a period of prohibition) was openly portrayed.

## Acquiring Information

To study the retention of factual information presented in motion pictures, P. W. Holaday and George D. Stoddard conducted a study of over 3,000 children and adults.[9] It took them three years to complete their work. Seventeen full-length motion pictures were used as stimulus material. They tested audiences on details of the plots and on various kinds of information presented in the films. They found that even eight-year-old children acquired a substantial number of ideas from the movies (about 60 percent of the total learned by adults). In fact, retention of facts by all age groups was surprisingly high. Subjects were tested six weeks and three months after seeing the films. In some cases, retention was greater at the six-month period, suggesting a so-called sleeper effect that would be discovered again later.[10] The investigators concluded that movies provided a special learning format that led to unusually high retention of factual material, compared to the acquisition of facts in standard laboratory memory experiments.

## Changing Attitudes

One of the more sophisticated investigations of the series was that of Ruth C. Peterson and L. L. Thurstone,[11] whose purpose was to assess the construction of attitude measures. Generally, the attitudes under study were the orientations of children toward selected ethnic groups, racial categories, and social issues. Regular commercial motion pictures were used as stimulus material. Children's attitudes were measured before exposure to the film or films and then remeasured with a parallel instrument after seeing the picture material. In many cases, attitude change was found. The details of this study and its implications for the research trends that it stimulated will be discussed more fully in a later section of the present chapter.

## Stimulating Emotions

Studies of the capacity of films to arouse children's emotions were conducted by W. S. Dysinger and Christian A. Ruckmick,[12] who used both laboratory techniques and autobiographical case studies to assess the emotional impact of films. Several age categories of children were observed both in a lab setting and in actual theaters while viewing motion pictures. The 150 subjects used were selected to represent "average" intelligence levels. Some adults were also studied for comparison purposes. It was a dramatic form of research for the time. Electrodes and mechanical devices were attached to youthful viewers in order to record their galvanic skin responses and changes in their breathing patterns stimulated by the film content. These neurophysiological changes were used as indices of emotional arousal. Scenes of danger, conflict, or tragedy produced the greatest effects. Romantic and erotic scenes didn't seem to do much for very young children, but they blew the 16-year-olds off the graphs! Generally, males and females reacted similarly. By comparison, adults showed little emotional arousal to any of the scenes. The authors concluded that adults had learned to "discount" the films as fantasy, but children experienced substantial emotional arousal.

## Harming Health

To study movies as a potential danger to health, psychologists Samuel Renshaw, Vernon L. Miller, and Dorothy P. Marquis devised ingenious experiments on children's sleep.[13] A total of 170 boys and girls in an Ohio state institution for juveniles participated in studies of sleep "motility." Special beds and other apparatuses were used to measure how much they tossed and turned after seeing various categories of films. First, the researchers studied normal sleep patterns. Then they exposed their young subjects to motion pictures before bedtime. A variety of controls and conditions were used to explore different kinds of influences on sleep. Briefly, certain kinds of films did result in disturbed sleep. Such consequences, the authors claimed, could be detrimental to normal health and growth.

## Eroding Moral Standards

An elaborate study of the influence of motion pictures on standards of morality was conducted by Charles C. Peters.[14] His point of departure was the sociological theory of William Graham Sumner, whose analyses of folkways and mores were published at the beginning of the present century. Sumner's work on the nature and origins of such norms was so thorough that it has never been replicated and still stands as the definitive statement.[15] The goal of Peters's study was to determine whether specific kinds of actions or situations portrayed in the films paralleled or were in conflict with the standards of morality currently prevailing among several categories of subjects. He used written descriptions of movie scenes that included such actions as female aggressiveness in lovemaking (kissing and caressing in public), the portrayal of democratic practices and attitudes, and different forms of treatment of children by parents. Five categories of people responded to these descriptions in the preliminary standardization of the morality scale. These were college seniors, college faculty members and their wives, socially elite young women, factory working boys, and factory working girls. The result was a scale for "measuring the mores" of different kinds of people. The scale was then used to assess different patterns of approval and disapproval of samples of conduct taken from the films. Peters gathered such responses from 17 different categories of subjects whose backgrounds ranged from poorly educated workers to upper-status professionals. The general conclusion from this complex study was that many of the depictions presented in the movies, especially in the scenes of crime and sex (two of the most frequent themes) were contrary to the mores of the groups under study. Such findings were scarcely comforting to those who feared that the movies were providing unwanted influences on children.

## Influencing Conduct

As might be suspected, the issue of motion picture influences on conduct received more attention than any other specific topic. Three separate studies were devoted to the impact of films on various forms of behavior. Each of these deserves separate comment. Two of these investigations will be discussed in some detail following the overviews.

Frank R. Shuttleworth and Mark A. May contrasted children who attended movies frequently ("fans") with a comparison group who seldom or never attended.[16] The study attempted to assess general conduct, deportment in school, and reputation among peers. In all, some 1,400 children were studied. For the most part, it was a questionnaire study with a variety of paper-and-pencil questionnaires, rating scales, and other instruments used by both the children and their teachers. The investigators found that movie "fans" were usually rated lower in deportment by their teachers than those children who did not attend the movies frequently. The fans also had less positive reputations; they did worse in their academic work, and they were not as popular with their classmates as was the comparison group.

One of the most interesting of the conduct studies was an investigation by sociologist Herbert Blumer that probed the influences of motion pictures on general day-to-day behavior.[17] In this work, he depended primarily on the autobiographical method, in which subjects recalled earlier influences of the movies on their lives and on specific activities, such as play, modes of dress, hairstyles, and forms of communication. The autobiographical technique had been worked out to probe specific kinds of influences, including how the films had influenced the subjects' moods, emotions, interpretations of love and romance, ambitions, and temptations to behave in socially disapproved ways. Several hundred college students wrote such autobiographies, as did hundreds of high school youths, factory workers, and office personnel. Overall, the accounts seemed to indicate rather clearly that the content of the movies served as substantial influence on children. The subjects reported that they had imitated the movie characters openly in beautification, mannerisms, and attempts at lovemaking.

The movies had also stimulated a great deal of daydreaming and fantasy. In particular, the films had aroused strong emotions in their youthful audiences, including terror, fright, sorrow, and pathos. Although this type of research was called "exploratory" by the investigator, and even though it was based on relatively unsophisticated methods, it remains one of the more significant studies of the series. Certainly, its findings reinforced the alarms raised by critics of the movies.

A widely discussed study of conduct was that of Blumer and another sociologist, Phillip Hauser.[18] Their central focus was on ways in which motion picture content stimulated children to commit acts of delinquency and crime. It was a wide-ranging study that included case histories, questionnaires, essays, and life histories of delinquency-prone youngsters. Reports on movie experiences were gathered from reformatory inmates, ex-convicts on parole, female delinquents in a training school, grade school boys and girls in high-delinquency neighborhoods, and several other categories of children and adolescents. Material was also obtained from the heads of penal institutions and other authorities. The methods and strategies used in this study have come under wide criticism from criminologists and specialists in deviant behavior. Nevertheless, at the time, the findings caused considerable concern. According to the authors, motion pictures played a direct role in shaping the delinquent and criminal careers of substantial segments of those studied. Once again, the worst fears of the public were confirmed. Movies appeared to be driving at least some children to a life of crime!

As can be seen from this brief overview, each of the investigations in the Payne Fund studies was a work of substantial scope. Taken together, they constitute a research effort which would not be matched in size and diversity until 40 years later, when the federal government funded studies of the influence of televised violence on children. The Payne Fund studies therefore remain one of the largest scientific investigations of the influence of mass communication ever undertaken. In order to show in more detail the theoretical assumptions, the methodological strategies and techniques, and some of the major findings, the sections that follow present more detailed summaries of two of the Payne Fund investigations.

## STUDIES OF SOCIAL ATTITUDES, GENERAL CONDUCT, AND DELINQUENT BEHAVIOR

While the highlights of the research by Peterson and Thurstone and by Blumer have been summarized above, these particular studies offer significant lessons regarding the development of both research methods and theory concerning the effects of mass communication. For this reason, the separate investigations are reviewed more fully in the sections that follow.

### Motion Pictures and the Social Attitudes of Children

The purpose of the set of experiments by Peterson and Thurstone was to study the degree to which commercial motion pictures could change the attitudes of youthful subjects toward specific topics. Under investigation were attitudes toward people of different nationalities and races and attitudes toward socially significant topics such as crime, war, capital punishment, prohibition, and the treatment of criminals. The subjects were school children ranging from fourth-graders to college students.

The general strategy was straightforward. An initial measure was achieved by using a paired-comparisons scale developed around the particular attitude under study. The assessment was done in school classrooms in small communities near Chicago, with the cooperation of the authorities. The students participating were then given special tickets to the local movie theater. Since the experiments were done in communities with only one theater, the subjects naturally attended the right movie, using their free tickets. The film seen by the subjects was one that had been specially selected by the experimenters and was being shown by prior arrangement with the local exhibitor.

To obtain suitable films, the investigators had examined more than 600 candidate pictures. Sixteen were selected because they presented particularly favorable or unfavorable views toward one of the attitude topics under investigation. For example, *All Quiet on the Western Front* was an antiwar film. *Birth of a Nation* was (in many respects) antiblack. Others were pro-Chinese, pro-Jewish, and so on.

Approximately two weeks after the first attitude assessment and the next day after seeing the film, the attitudes of the subjects were again measured. No direct connection was made between the attitude assessments and the movie experience. Controls were used to ensure that only subjects who had actually seen the film were included in the final determination of attitude change. (It can be noted in passing that no attempt was made to use control groups.)

Within this general framework, two dozen experiments were completed. Some studied the effect of a *single* film on changing attitudes. Others studied the *cumulative* effect of two and even three pictures dealing with the same theme. Finally, a number of studies assess the *persistence* of attitude changes over long periods of time. These periods ranged from two to nineteen months.

**The Effect of Single Pictures.**   In a series of eleven separate experiments, the ability of a single exposure to a motion picture to modify attitudes was assessed. Under study were attitudes toward Germans, war, gambling, prohibition, the Chinese, capital punishment, treatment of criminals, and "the Negro" (the term would be "black" later). Each experiment followed the general strategy outlined earlier. The numbers of subjects ranged from 133 in a study of attitudes toward Germans to 522 in an investigation of attitudes toward the punishment of criminals. Because of the number of the experiments it is difficult to discuss the results in a simple way. However, in general, some of the experiments produced substantial attitude change. In others the subjects did not significantly change their orientations.

Two examples illustrate the nature of the results where significant change occurred. In Geneva, Illinois, 182 children in grades 9 through 12 saw a film entitled *Son of the Gods*. It was strongly pro-Chinese. The story concerned Sam Lee, a nice young Chinese-American who had been raised by an older Chinese man. The interpretation of Chinese life and culture was positive, and the characters presented were sympathetic. Figure 2.1 shows the results. The "before" mean was 6.72 and the "after" mean was 5.50. Statistically, a difference of 1.22 is 17.5 times its probable error. In short, there was a statistically significant attitude change in a favorable direction.

Another experiment showed even more striking results. The film *Birth of a Nation* (updated from its original form with the addition of a sound track) was shown to 434 high school children in Crystal Lake, Illinois. The film portrays blacks in negative terms and is considered an antiblack statement. As it turned out, few of the subjects in the experiment had known or even seen a black. Figure 2.2 shows that at the outset the subjects were relatively favorable, with a mean score of 7.46. The mean after the film had shifted to 5.93, a more negative position. A different of 1.48 is 25.5 times its probable error. Clearly, this particular movie had a substantial impact on the attitudes of its audience.

**Cumulative Effects.**   A series of experiments was conducted in which subjects viewed two or more pictures dealing with the same issue between their before and after measures. In these studies, 750 children in grades 6–12 were in the various experiments. They were all residents of Mooseheart, a community for

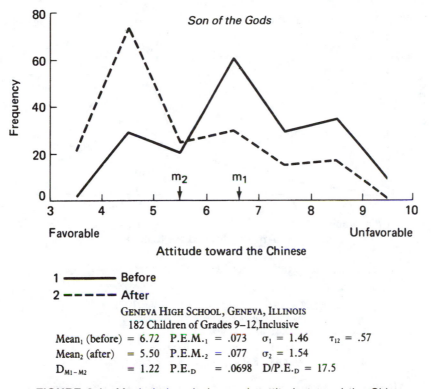

GENEVA HIGH SCHOOL, GENEVA, ILLINOIS
182 Children of Grades 9–12,Inclusive

Mean$_1$ (before) = 6.72    P.E.M.$_{.1}$ = .073    $\sigma_1$ = 1.46    $\tau_{12}$ = .57
Mean$_2$ (after)   = 5.50    P.E.M.$_{.2}$ = .077    $\sigma_2$ = 1.54
D$_{M1-M2}$       = 1.22    P.E.$_D$      = .0698   D/P.E.$_D$ = 17.5

**FIGURE 2.1**   Movie-induced change in attitude toward the Chinese

SOURCE: Ruth C. Peterson and L. Thurstone, *Motion Pictures and the Social Attitudes of Children* (New York: Macmillan, 1933), p. 19.

children of deceased members of a national organization. Two attitudes were under study. In one set of experiments, the subjects saw two antiwar films—*All Quiet on the Western Front* and *Journey's End*. In another set of experiments, subjects saw three films dealing with the punishment of criminals. These were *The Big House*, *Numbered Men*, and *The Criminal Code*. Each was a relatively sympathetic treatment of the plight of men in prison.

Overall, the results of the cumulative studies were clear. The films shown singly had minor or no effects in terms of attitude change. However, two or three films on the same topic produced significant attitude modification among the subjects under study toward the view expressed in the films.

***The Persistence of Attitude Changes.***   In 11 of the experiments selected from the studies of both single and multiple exposures, follow-ups were conducted at various intervals. In each case, parallel-form attitude scales measured the persistence of the changes achieved in the earlier experiment. The results of these studies can be seen in Table 2.1. The authors concluded that the effects of motion pictures on the social attitudes of children could persist for considerable periods of time. In one case, 60 percent of the original change was retained a year and a half later! In another case, the attitudes of the subjects had changed even more

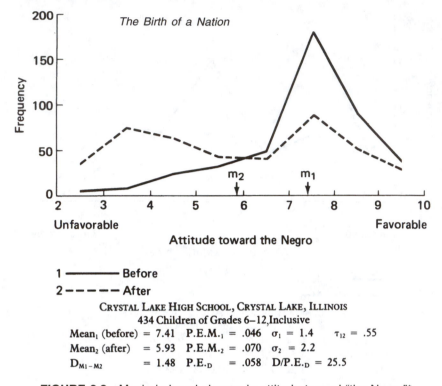

$\text{Mean}_1$ (before) = 7.41   P.E.M.$_1$ = .046   $\sigma_1$ = 1.4   $\tau_{12}$ = .55
$\text{Mean}_2$ (after)  = 5.93   P.E.M.$_2$ = .070   $\sigma_2$ = 2.2
$D_{M1-M2}$         = 1.48   P.E.$_D$   = .058   D/P.E.$_D$ = 25.5

**FIGURE 2.2**   Movie-induced change in attitude toward "the Negro"*

SOURCE: Ruth C. Peterson and L. L. Thurstone, *Motion Pictures and the Social Attitudes of Children* (New York: Macmillan, 1933), p. 37.

* Note the reversal of the positions of "Favorable" and "Unfavorable" from those of Figure 2.1. This was done in the original.

six months later than they had immediately following exposure to the film (a sleeper effect).

The general conclusions reached by Peterson and Thurstone were that the attitudes of children were definitely influenced by some films. These effects tended to be greater for younger children. Seeing two and three pictures treating the same topic in the same way achieved greater results than was the case with a single film. Finally, attitude changes resulting from exposure to motion pictures can persist for long periods of time.[19]

These attitude change studies were of lasting importance for several reasons. The study of quantitative attitude scales was in its infancy; however, the measurement procedures used by the investigators were based on relatively sophisticated theories derived from the Law of Comparative Judgement. This formulation still remains the underlying rationale for attitude measurement. Thus, the movie studies were a highly visible application of the new technology to a socially significant issue. In addition, the experimental format used in the studies followed the model of science that was being enthusiastically adopted by psychology and sociology.

**TABLE 2.1**  The persistence of attitude changes

| Place | Film | No. In Exp. Group | Interval | Percentage of Effect Remaining |
|---|---|---|---|---|
| Watseka, Illinois | The Criminal Code | 257 | 2$^1/_2$ months | 87% |
| Watseka, Illinois | The Criminal Code | 195 | 9 months | 78% |
| Geneva, Illinois | Son of the Gods | 117 | 5 months | 62% |
| Geneva, Illinois | Son of the Gods | 76 | 19 months | 60% |
| Crystal Lake, Illinois | The Birth of a Nation | 350 | 5 months | 62% |
| Genoa, Illinois | Four Sons | 87 | 6 months | 123% |
| Paxton, Illinois | All Quiet on the Western Front | 138 | 8 months | A change in the opposite direction |
| Mooseheart, Illinois | All Quiet on the Western Front and Journey's End | 572 | 2 months | 52% |
| Mooseheart, Illinois | All Quiet on the Western Front and Journey's End | 571 | 4 months | 22% |
| Mooseheart, Illinois | The Big House, Numbered Men, and The Criminal Code | 559 | 2 months | 100% |
| Mooseheart, Illinois | The Big House, Numbered Men, and The Criminal Code | 549 | 4 months | 111% |

SOURCE: Ruth C. Peterson and L. L. Thurstone, *Motion Pictures and the Social Attitudes of Children* (New York: Macmillan, 1993), p. 63.

For these reasons, and because the studies showed clear results, the Peterson and Thurstone research made a deep impact, on both the public and the scientific community.

## Movies and Conduct

In a very different type of research, Herbert Blumer collected autobiographical accounts from more than 1,800 young men and women, adolescents, and children. The general purpose of the study was to find out how motion pictures had influenced their childhood play, their attempts to imitate various elements of adult behavior, and their daydreams, emotional experiences, and general lifestyles. The goals of the research were sweeping. The methodology was *qualitative* rather than quantitative, and the findings can only be regarded as "exploratory" or "suggestive." Yet, in many ways, this is one of the most interesting of all of the Payne Fund studies because it shows in rich detail the way in which the 1,823 participants in the study thought that the movies had influenced their lives.

The researcher began his investigation with a preliminary study to help design a general format for the personal autobiographies. Students in university classes were "asked merely to write in as natural and truthful a manner, accounts of their prior experiences with movies, as best as these could be recalled."[20] These were extensive documents that required several weeks to prepare. From these accounts, Blumer constructed a set of guidelines for the preparation of auto-biographies by the main body of his subjects. These guidelines focused the subject on his or her interest in the movies during childhood. They asked the subject to recall influences on emotions or moods, patterns of imitation of the actors, the subject's remembered interest in love and romantic films, and ambitions and temptations that, in recollection, had been aroused by motion pictures.

These accounts were gathered from 634 university students, 481 college and junior college youths, 583 high school students, 67 office workers, and 58 factory workers. Considerable care was taken to preserve anonymity, ensure honesty, and encourage full disclosure. The statements were checked for internal consistency and what we would today call "face validity."

To these personal autobiographies, the investigator added information obtained in personal interviews with 135 of the subjects. In addition, information was derived from conversations among groups of students as they discussed the movies. Finally, data were obtained from structured questionnaires administered to 1,200 grade school children in the Chicago area.

This mass of material was not reduced to quantitative form. As the author explained it, the general plan of procedure followed in the report was to *let the facts speak for themselves*. This was accomplished by the liberal use of quotations from the autobiographies and general descriptions of the central themes that seemed to emerge from the materials.

***Influences on Childhood Play.***    Nearly all the subjects studied reported that the movies had been a rich source from which they drew ideas for play. They liberally impersonated screen characters in their games of "cowboys and Indians" and "cops and robbers." Depending upon what they had seen that week, they became Robin Hood, Joan of Arc, Rudulph Valentino, a royal knight, a princess in a far-off land, or an African big game hunter. At other times, they played at being a daring fighter pilot, Mata Hari, Dracula, Mary Queen of Scots, or the Phantom of the Opera.

> *Male. 19, Jewish, white, college sophomore:* In my childhood it was common for one to imitate consciously heroes of the screen. For in-stance, I would climb the lone tree that was in the yard of the Catholic school near us and hang by one hand or hammer my chest shouting "Tarzan" and the like. Jumping over fences on a run as did the heroes of the screen was usual in my young life. Fighting with one another, and after conquering him, placing one foot on his chest and raising our arms to the sky as Tarzan did was also common.[21]

Not only had the subjects impersonated actors and their screen roles, but they modeled their games on the plots seen in the pictures. Thus, one day some of the kids would attack a fort with wooden swords and "pretend" shields that were really the tops of wash boilers or garbage cans. The defenders would resist with lances made of sticks and helmets devised from old cooking pots. Auto races could be recreated among makeshift cars devised from apple crates; cavalry charges seen on the screen could be relived on the backs of trusty steeds that were really mops and brooms. Or, daring aviators could duel in the skies over Germany.

> *A boy of 11 years:* The picture I saw was *The Dawn Patrol.* After I came home, we played it. I pretended I was Richard Barthelmess. I pretended I was bombing the German ammunition dumps. Then I went over the airports and bombed the planes and killed the men. Then three German planes came after me. Von Richter, the best German aviator, came up too, and I shot him down and shot his pal also. But the other aviator came from the back and shot me.[22]

Girls of the period pretended to be the pampered darlings of rich parents, with dozens of suitors and fantastic wardrobes. The acted out the part of Juliet or that of beautiful captives of handsome sheikhs. Generally, costumes, weapons, and other artifacts seen in the films were improvised in addition to behavior patterns and social relationships. In short, the movies had a complex set of influences on children's play. The subjects, on the whole, recalled these influences with warmth and pleasure. Whether or not such effects were harmful in any way is not clear. In all likelihood, they were not.

***Imitation by Adolescents.***   Motion picture influences on childhood play were largely in the realm of fantasy and make-believe. Among adolescent moviegoers, however, a somewhat different type of influence was widespread. Forms of conduct such as beautification, personal mannerisms, and social techniques were imitated from movie portrayals and incorporated into the day-to-day behavior patterns of youthful audiences. The styles of dress and hair arrangements used by female stars in the films were a particular source of fascination for female adolescents. In searching for means to bring beauty into their own lives, they experimented enthusiastically with what they had seen on the screen.

> *Female, 19, Jewish, white, college sophomore:* I remember that I got my first striking illumination through the movies of the difference clothes may make in appearance. It was *Daddy Long-Legs* where Mary Pickford paraded for five scenes, bare-legged, in dark brown cast-offs, pig-tailed, and freckled-faced, good, sweet, but hardly beautiful; and then in the final scene, after a visit from Daddy and a bath in milk, with the curls down, the gangly knees covered, the ankles silk-shod, in pink satin, a pearl-studded dress, a reborn gorgeous queen, she emerged as striking as the caterpillar-butterfly transition. At home that night I tentatively hinted about putting my daily glass of milk to better use, wound my straight black, hair in tortuous curl papers, draped myself in red gauze, and compared effects. Since then I have carefully studied, attempted,

and compared the effects of these past mistresses of the art of dressing and make-up. They are always first with the latest, my most reliable guide to styles, colors, accessories, combinations, lines, and general effects.[23]

Another important area of influence was in those mannerisms that become identified as attractive or sophisticated in every age. Thus, the movies taught a generation of males how to light a cigarette in a "manly" manner; how to tip one's hat to a lady in a gallant way; or how to offer her one's arm properly. They taught girls how to purse their lips coyly; how to lower their eyelids enticingly; how to sit gracefully; or how to shed a dainty tear for maximum effect.

The films served also to bring some semblance of social polish to upwardly mobile youths who might not have had other role models in their daily lives.

*Male, 21, white, college senior:* As I got into high school and into my sixteenth and seventeenth year I began to use the movies as a school of etiquette. I began to observe the table manners of the actors in the eating scenes. I watched for the proper way in which to conduct oneself at a night club, because I began to have ideas that way. The fact that the leading man's coat was single-breasted or double-breasted, the number of buttons on it, and the cut of its lapel all influenced me in the choice of my own suits.[24]

The adoption of behavior patterns from adult models is a normal part of the socialization process during childhood and adolescence. The movie stars, however, appeared to be particularly attractive sources from which to obtain modeling influences.

*Female, 18, Negro, high-school senior:* Movies are the means by which a great many people obtain poise. This is especially true as far as girls are concerned. I am sure I haven't the poise of my movie idols, but I am trying to develop a more ladylike composure as I grow older. My father has caught me several times, as I stood before the mirror trying to tilt my head and hold my arms as the girls on the screen would do. He does not know that I am trying to create that sophisticated manner, which is essential for social success.[25]

Generally, then, the stars and their portrayals were imitated freely by millions of young Americans in the 1920s. In many cases, the forms of beautification, the mannerisms, or the techniques of social adaptation modeled from the movies were but brief experiments that were soon abandoned. In other cases, the people studied felt that these influences had been incorporated more permanently into their daily behavior patterns.

The preoccupation of the films of the period with themes of love and sex has already been noted. Lovemaking in the movies did not have much attraction for the younger children.

*Male, 20, white, college sophomore:* Love stories and pictures never held much attraction for me at this time (age 12). . . . Whenever we boys would go to see a love picture and the hero kissed the heroine we would always make a lot of noise and smack our lips very loudly.[26]

Among adolescents, however, the love and romance themes of the movies found an enthusiastic audience. In an era when there were only a limited number of sources from which young people could learn ways of relating to the opposite sex, and especially about techniques of kissing or the meaning of love and romance, the films provided fascinating lessons.

*Male, 21, white, college senior:* The technique of making love to a girl received considerable of my attention, and it was directly through the movies that I learned to kiss a girl on her ears, neck, and cheeks, as well as on the mouth.[27]

It was, of course, a more innocent time, and "making love" meant merely kissing and hugging. Nevertheless, the motion pictures were a training vehicle that provided not only models for intimate interpersonal behavior but media-constructed conceptions of passion, romance, courtship, flirting, and other forms of relationship between males and females.

***Daydreaming and Fantasy.*** The movies were a rich source for adolescent daydreams and fantasies. Two-third of the autobiographies studied discussed the films as a source of stimulation used during childhood to imagine playing fantastic adult roles: The boys rescued beautiful maidens, danced the tango in smart tuxedos, shot it out with desperados, and drove dog sleds across Alaska. The girls reveled in fabulous wardrobes, toyed with handsome admirers, bedecked themselves with jewels, and succumbed to tall, dark, Latin lovers.

The majority of the audience actually led rather dull lives. It was not unusual, therefore, that the vivid scenes of travel, adventure, glamour, wealth, luxury, success, romance, and heroism depicted in the films would be used in imagination as a basis for Walter Mitty–like constructions of deeply satisfying dreams. Contemporary students of the uses and gratifications provided by media content still pursue this line of inquiry.

***Emotional Possession.*** One of the more pronounced influences of film content of the 1920s on their youthful audiences was termed "emotional possession." The concept refers to a situation where an individual's emotions are aroused so strongly that he or she loses some measure of self-control. Seeing dramatic motion picture portrayals led young audience members to suffer in empathy, cower in horror, or feel overpowering affection. Such feelings were both strongly stimulated and made manifest in overt behavior (tears, screams, hiding, adulation, and so on) by some forms of communication content.

Powerful responses might be quite difficult to stimulate today among our more media-hardened youthful population. But during the 1920s, being frightened out of one's wits by a movie was a common phenomenon.

> *Female, 15, white, high-school sophomore:* The Phantom of the Opera, with Lon Chaney as the phantom, frightened me more than any other motion picture I have seen. He was made up as the most horrible creature with long teeth, glaring eyes, and a bald head. When he was unmasked by the heroine, I gasped and almost screamed. Although I tried to draw my eyes away from his terrible face, I couldn't; his ugliness was so fascinating. The entire picture was so weird and fantastic that the shivers ran up and down my back. For a long time after that, I dared not go near dark places, particularly the cellar. I did not let anyone else know I was frightened for fear they would call me silly.[28]

Another frequent response to films was to experience grief and sorrow over the plight of a movie character. Two-thirds of those who prepared autobiographies recalled such moving emotions vividly. Typical was the following report.

> *Female, 20, white, college junior:* The first picture that I ever cried at was *Uncle Tom's Cabin,* with Marguerite Clarke playing the part of little Eva. I didn't want to cry and tried my best to fight against my emotions, but it was of no use, the tears rolled down just the same. I read the story of *Wings* and in spite of myself I cried over it. When I saw the movie I tried to tell myself that I wouldn't cry as I had already read the book and could have myself steeled against any display of sorrow. It all went well until one of the last scenes and I found myself crying. Most any picture with a touch of pathos to it has me using my handkerchief a great deal.[29]

For some viewers, crying at the movies seemed to have a therapeutic effect. Many reported that they resisted such displays of emotion, but after crying profusely over the agonies portrayed in the plot, they often felt better.

***Other Emotional Influences.***    There were a number of other reported emotional reactions to film content that testified to the strong impact of films on children as they viewed them. Feelings of love and passion were clearly aroused for some. In many cases, these emotions were attached to the shadowy figures on the screen as boys and girls fell madly in love with their favorite star. In other cases, the portrayed actions of lovers in the films stimulated strong interpersonal feelings between couples in the audience.

> In the gloom of the Fox Theater, I sat with my gang, and I gasped in pleasurable anticipation as the tense moment approached. The hero placed his hands about the heroine's divinely small waist and pulled her

half-fiercely toward him. Her beautiful lips parted slightly; he looked into her heavenly eyes with infinite adoration and their kiss was perfect. My response was inevitable. My hand clutched Vera's; we thrilled in ecstasy.[30]

Although the autobiographies do not "contain graphic accounts of physical relationships," the movies clearly stimulated strong desires. Whether or not those pressures led to "the inevitable" is anybody's guess, but given the sexual norms of the time, they probably did not. The critics of the movies of the period were sorely concerned that the films were indeed inflaming the "baser passions." The author may have reinforced those concerns when he concluded that "emotional possession induced by passionate love pictures represents an attack on the mores of our contemporary life."[31]

Sheer thrills and generalized excitement were also a part of children's emotional response patterns to the movies. They shouted their relief when the hero escaped from danger; they groaned when things went badly. During the Saturday matinee, with audiences composed almost exclusively of children, whistles, screaming, laughter, cheers, shouts, and big sighs of relief were a normal part of the viewing experience. Nails were bitten, seats were clutched, eyes were covered, and caps were wrung into shreds.

Perhaps the most significant aspect of "emotional possession" in all its forms (according to Blumer) was that it often provided frameworks for perception and behavior choice long after the film had been seen. A familiar example is the reluctance of many children to enter dark rooms or to pass by graveyards at night, after seeing horror films and spook shows. Another familiar example was the young female who derived definitions of romance and courtship mainly from the films. Carrying these conceptualizations into real-life relationships with suitors sometimes led to disappointments. It was this type of long-term and indirect influence that was of concern to the researcher—although it could clearly not be established in an experimental design.

***Long-Term Influences.***   In the final sections of his report, Blumer tried to pull together in a general way the long-term and overall influences on children provided by their motion picture viewing. In so doing, he anticipated two theories of mass communication influence that have become more systematically developed in recent years. One is the "meaning" theory of media portrayals advanced by DeFleur and Dennis.[32] The other is the modeling theory of Albert Bandura.[33]

Blumer did not have these formulations available at the time. However, in commenting on the role of media portrayals in providing socially constructed meanings for various aspects of reality, he anticipated the central thesis of meaning theory.

One would expect that movies would be effective in shaping the images which people form of their world and in giving form to the schemes of conduct which they come to develop. Motion pictures depict types of life which are unfamiliar to many people and consequently shape their conceptions of such a life.[34]

In terms of modeling, the author noted that the films "show situations and various forms of conduct in very attractive ways." Because of that attractive quality, social relationships, patterns of behavior, or attitudes and values depicted in the movies provide clear lessons for children to copy—models for imitation and incorporation into one's own lifestyle.

Blumer found evidence in his autobiographies that motion pictures had indeed shaped modes of thinking and interpretation of many aspects of his subjects' worlds. These modes included stereotypes of ethnic and racial groups, of villains and heroes, of rich and poor, of wrongdoers and the righteous, and many other social categories. The movies provided conceptions of war, family life, work, sexual mores, romantic behavior, religious beliefs, the roles of men and women, parent-child relationships, college life, and hundreds of other social activities and arrangements. These depictions served not only as bases for belief and interpretation regarding activities removed from the lives of the subjects but as guidelines for daily conduct as subjects actually participated in real-life versions of what had been modeled on the screen.

Overall, then, Blumer's work *The Movies and Conduct* emerges as perhaps the most significant of all of the Payne Fund studies, in view of its early concern with two processes that have recently become the focus of both theory and research. Both meaning theory and modeling theory are now central to the analysis of the *long-term* influences of the media content on human behavior. We can also note that Blumer's work delved into other aspects of the effects of mass communication. For example, in the context of the motion pictures of the era, he made a very detailed analysis of the uses and gratifications provided by movie content for his youthful subjects. Movies were used in play, as a source of daydreams, and as guides to etiquette, dress, mannerisms, and beautification.

The limitations of the research are many by the standards of experimentation and quantification that came to dominate media research in the decades that followed. Yet those strategies—with their emphasis on stimulus-response conceptions, short-term effects, and point-by-point correspondence between components of a message and specific forms of response—are themselves being seriously questioned today. There is a real possibility that the detailed, subjective, and analytical procedures used by Blumer in his "exploratory study" revealed a greater richness and insight into the effects of the films than the "scientific" studies done at the same time.

## CONCLUSIONS AND IMPLICATIONS

What can we learn from this fascinating series of studies done when the movies were young? First, we can gain a profound respect for the imagination and diligence of the researchers who designed, conducted, and reported on the individual investigations. These were truly massive research efforts, involving (in total) tens of thousands of subjects. The investigators made use of the best research procedures, strategies, and techniques available at the time. Those strategies ranged from laboratory-type efforts (e.g., those of Dysinger and Ruckmick), with elaborate controls and apparatuses, to content analyses, surveys, field experiments, and the autobiographical approach of Blumer.

Interpreting the findings of this massive effort presents a very difficult picture. At that time they seemed relatively clear! The movies did seem to bring new ideas to children, influence their attitudes, stimulate their emotions, present moral standards different from those of many adults, disturb sleep, and influence interpretations of the world and day-to-day conduct.

These conclusions may well have been quite correct at the time. America was not a media society except in a limited sense during the 1920s. The only mature medium was the newspaper. Radio was only a toy. The movies came with a rush—almost overnight—to delight, frighten, thrill, and fascinate an audience of millions of children who had never seen anything like them. The idea that this new medium, suddenly thrust upon a society just emerging from the Victorian era, could have profound and visible effects upon such an audience does not seem far-fetched.

This does not mean that the findings of the Payne Fund studies provide useful guides for understanding media influences on children today. Contemporary society bears only a faint resemblance, in terms of media presence, to the simpler times of the 1920s. Today's children and adolescents are surrounded by media content to a degree unimaginable 70 years ago.

The importance of the Payne Fund studies lies elsewhere. Clearly, they were the great pioneering effort that established media research as a serious scientific field. They brought together in one extraordinary group of studies a major problem of public concern and the perspectives of young sciences. The fact that various disciplines participated in the research was a harbinger of things to come; the fact that a broad range of topics was studied with many different techniques was also an indicator of future directions.

When the findings of the Payne Fund studies were published, they confirmed the worst fears of the critics of the medium and the movie industry. W. W. Charters, who wrote a volume summarizing the main findings, concluded that "the commercial movies are an unsavory mess" and that "the producers ought to have heart" over their bad influences on children.[35]

Such conclusions played a part in reinforcing the *legacy of fear* that had been kept alive by strident denunciations of the evils of propaganda during the same decade and by the widely held beliefs about the horrors of newspaper influence current during the late nineteenth century. This legacy of fear was the key factor in bringing public pressure to bear on the movies to "clean up their act." By the early 1930s, the motion picture industry strengthened its Production Code and began enforcing it more rigidly through its Hays Office. After establishing such self-censorship, in which all the major producers cooperated, the movies of the mid- and late 1930s altered greatly the degree to which they portrayed socially controversial scenes. The Payne Fund studies were part of the effort by which this change was achieved.

In summary, the Payne Fund studies undoubtedly presented a reasonably valid picture of the influences of the movies of the 1920s on the youth of that period. The films were an influence on attitudes; they provided models for behavior; they shaped interpretations of life. They probably had as many prosocial influences (or at least harmless influences) as those that disturbed adults of the time. The Payne Fund studies were clearly the pioneer efforts that established the field of media research within the perspectives of science. They anticipated contemporary interest in meaning theory and the influence of models and focused the new field on such topics as attitude change, the sleeper effect, uses and gratifications, content analysis, modeling influences, and the social construction of reality. They placed an emphasis on quantitative, experimental, and survey methodologies, but they still made use of more qualitative approaches. Above all, the studies shifted the long-standing pattern of concern on the part of communication scholars with propaganda criticism that represented an earlier rhetorical form of analysis. In these senses, the Payne Fund studies will remain one of the most significant milestones in the development of mass communication as a scientific field of study.

## NOTES AND REFERENCES

1. For a full description of the history of this concept and its measurement, see Emory S. Bogardus, *Social Distance* (Yellow Springs, Ohio: Antioch Press, 1959).
2. L. L. Thurstone and E. J. Chave, *The Measurement of Attitude* (Chicago: University of Chicago Press, 1929).
3. Basing their ideas on the work of such pioneers as G. Udny Yule and R. A. Fisher, sociologists and psychologists were transforming their fields by advocating quantitative approaches to the study of human behavior. See F. Stuart Chapin, *Field Work and Social Statistics* (New York: Century Company, 1920); Robert R. Burgess, *Introduction to the Mathematics of Statistics* (Boston: Houghton Mifflin, 1927); Louis L. Thurstone, *The Fundamentals of Statistics* (New York: Macmillan, 1925).
4. Edgar Dale, *Children's Attendance at Motion Pictures* (New York: Macmillan, 1935), pp. 71-72.
5. Edgar Dale. *The Content of Motion Pictures* (New York: Macmillan, 1935), p. 8.
6. W. W. Charters, *Motion Pictures and Youth: A Summary* (New York: Macmillan, 1933), p. v.
7. Dale, *Attendance at Motion Pictures,* pp. 30-73. See also Henry James Forman, *Our Movie Made Children* (New York: Macmillan, 1935), pp. 12-27.
8. Dale, *Content of Motion Pictures.* Note especially Table 2, p. 17.
9. P. W. Holaday and George D. Stoddard, *Getting Ideas from the Movies* (New York: Macmillan, 1933), pp. 65-66.
10. Ibid., pp. 118, 145.
11. Ruth C. Peterson and L. L. Thurstone, *Motion Pictures and the Social Attitudes of Children* (New York: Macmillan, 1933).
12. W. S. Dysinger and Christian A. Ruckmick, *The Emotional Responses of Children to the Motion Picture Situation* (New York: Macmillan, 1933), pp. 110-119.
13. Samuel Renshaw, Vernon L. Miller, and Dorothy P. Marquis, *Children's Sleep* (New York: Macmillan, 1939), pp. 153-155 and 183-186.

14. Charles C. Peters, *Motion Pictures and Standards of Morality* (New York: Macmillan, 1933).
15. William Graham Sumner, *Folkways* (London: Ginn and Company, 1906).
16. Frank K. Shuttleworth and Mark A. May, *The Social Conduct and Attitudes of Movie Fans* (New York: Macmillan, 1933).
17. Herbert Blumer, *The Movies and Conduct* (New York: Macmillan, 1933).
18. Herbert Blumer and Philip M. Hauser, *Movies, Delinquency, and Crime* (New York: Macmillan, 1933).
19. Peterson and Thurstone, *Motion Pictures and Social Attitudes,* pp. 64-66.
20. Blumer, *Movies and Conduct,* pp. 3-12.
21. Ibid., p. 22.
22. Ibid., p. 23.
23. Ibid., p. 31.
24. Ibid., pp. 38-39.
25. Ibid., p. 40.
26. Ibid., p. 45.
27. Ibid., p. 47.
28. Ibid., p. 88.
29. Ibid., p. 96.
30. Ibid., p. 105.
31. Ibid., p. 116.
32. See: Melvin L. DeFleur and Everette E. Dennis, *Understanding Mass Communication* (Boston: Houghton Mifflin, 1981), pp. 26-27.
33. Albert Bandura, *Social Learning Theory* (Englewood Cliffs, N.J.: Prentice-Hall, 1977), p. 25.
34. Ibid., 141.
35. Charters, *Motion Pictures and Youth,* p. 54.

chapter 3

# The Invasion from Mars:
# Radio Panics America

On October 30, 1938, the United States was at war—invaded by monstrous creatures from Mars. At least that was the firm belief of a large segment of the 6 million people who were listening that night to CBS's "Mercury Theatre on the Air." What they heard was, of course, a radio drama—a chilling adaptation of H. G. Wells's science fiction masterpiece, *War of the Worlds*. Because the dramatization was presented in a clever newscast style, many listeners believed that the Martians were actually taking over. Others were driven to panic because the invasion seemed a direct threat to their lives. Many thought their world was ending; terrified people cried, hid, prayed, or fled into the countryside. The panic was, of course, an accident; there was no intent to frighten anyone. Nevertheless, what occurred that October night was one of the most remarkable media events of all time. If nothing else was proved that night, it was demonstrated to many people that radio could have a powerful impact on its audience. The broadcast also provided a unique opportunity for social scientists to study panic behavior triggered by a mass communication event. Before we begin a discussion of that research, it is important to take note of two features of the times that probably had a significant impact on the effect of the broadcast: (1) the popularity of radio and (2) the contemporary world situation (i.e., the historical setting).

Much to the dismay of newspapermen, radio had become the primary mode of mass communication and entertainment in the late 1930s, and the popularity of newspapers had begun to fade. It was estimated that of the 32 million families in the United States in 1938, 27 million had radios. Thus, a greater proportion of the population at that time had radios than had telephones, automobiles, plumbing, electricity, newspapers, or magazines.[1] The ownership of radios had been increasing dramatically; the number of radio sets owned by Americans had doubled almost every five years.[2]

Overall, radio had a deeply established role in the lives of Americans. It provided entertainment and brought the news of the world to the public almost as it happened. British Prime Minister Chamberlain explained the Munich concessions; President Roosevelt instilled confidence in the American population with his "fireside chats," in which he seemed to be speaking to each American personally. Radio made Edgar Bergen and Charlie McCarthy stars, popularized the music of the big bands and stars like Benny Goodman, and introduced millions of Americans to performers and performances of classical music. Thus, radio brought drama, soap operas, sports broadcasts, and music into the American home, but it also brought rapid and dramatic coverage of news events in a very tense and troubled time—the last was perhaps its most significant service.

The misery of the worst years of the Depression in the early 1930s was still vivid in people's minds in 1938. Many Americans had experienced the loss of their jobs or their farms or businesses. Many had seen their families hungry and even homeless; banks had foreclosed mortgages on a vast scale. For many, the solid rock upon which our social structure had been built turned out to be shifting sand. Although conditions had begun to improve by 1938, many people still wondered whether or not they would ever regain any sense of economic security. The complexity of modern finance and government, and the disagreements in the economic and political proposals of the various "experts," created an environment that the average American was unable to interpret.

The ominous and growing shadow of war added to these economic anxieties. On October 30, 1938, the Munich Crisis was still fresh in the memories of most Americans. The rise of Hitler and his transformation of Germany created anxiety for many. And if the threat of fascism were not enough, there was also communism. Both of these rising philosophies of government and politics were alien to the beliefs of most Americans. Indeed, at the time of the *War of the Worlds* broadcast, the American people had been hanging on the words of the radio broadcasts for weeks. They eagerly sought the most current international news. To facilitate the dissemination of this news, the broadcast industry had developed a new technique—"on the spot" reporting. Radio played a crucial role in keeping a nervous and news-hungry populace informed. Thus, it is no mere coincidence that the Halloween eve panic was created by a radio broadcast.

## THE MERCURY THEATRE AND
## *THE WAR OF THE WORLDS*

"Mercury Theatre on the Air," sponsored by CBS, had been broadcasting since June 1938. (The program lacked a commercial sponsor until the week following the *War of the Worlds* broadcast, when it obtained a lucrative contract with Campbell Soups.) The program was aired on Sunday evenings between 8 and 9 P.M. Eastern Standard Time. The dramatic programs were built around the name and talents of Orson Welles, cofounder, with John Houseman, of Mercury Theatre. Welles and Houseman selected the shows; Howard Koch wrote the dramatic scripts.

Interestingly, the panic broadcast almost did not come off. On the Tuesday preceding the broadcast, Howard Koch had not yet finished the show. He was having problems adapting Wells's novel into a dramatic format. A particularly troublesome problem was the novel's setting (England); in addition, it was written in narrative style. Koch recalled:

> I realized that I could use practically nothing but the author's idea of a Martian invasion and his description of their appearance and their machines. In short, I was being asked to do an almost original hour-length play in six days.[3]

At the time, Koch felt that under no circumstances could the story be made "interesting or in any way credible to modern American ears."[4] Koch pleaded with Houseman to have his assignment changed to another play. This might had been done if an interesting alternative project had been available. Houseman recalled that the "only possible alternative for that week was a dreary one—*Lorna Doone.*"[5] At the first rehearsal of the show, on Thursday, all involved agreed that the show was extremely dull. They thought that the only chance of success for the show would be to emphasize its newscast style—its simultaneous, eyewitness quality. Koch went back to work on the script, spicing up the newscast style with circumstantial allusions and authentic detail.

The revised script was rehearsed Saturday afternoon with sound effects but without its star. Welles did telephone later to find out how things were going. During that call, a CBS employee told him that it was "frankly not one of our better shows." Confidentially, according to this man, "it just didn't come off."[6] Twenty-seven hours later, many CBS executives would have been a good deal happier had that evaluation turned out to be accurate.

## The Broadcast

The Mercury Theatre always began with its theme. As 8 P.M. approached, Welles finished drinking his pineapple juice in the studio and poised himself, amid the debris of the frenzied preparation, to throw the cue to begin the theme. He signaled, and Tchaikovsky's Piano Concerto no. 1 in B-flat Minor began; when the music faded, routine introductions were made. Then an announcer indicated that a dramatization of H. G. Wells's *War of the Worlds* would be performed. About one minute into the hour—intoning as only he could—Welles began his narration:

> We know now that in the early years of the twentieth century, this world was being watched closely by intelligences greater than man's and yet as mortal as his own. We know now that as human beings busied themselves about their various concerns they were scrutinized and studied, perhaps almost as narrowly as a man with a microscope might scrutinize the transient creatures that swarm and multiply in a drop of water. With infinite complacence people went to and fro over the earth about

their little affairs, serene in the assurance of their dominion over this small spinning fragment of solar driftwood which by chance or design man has inherited out of the dark mystery of Time and Space. Yet across an immense ethereal gulf minds that are to our minds as ours are to the beasts in the jungle, intellects vast, cool, and unsympathetic regarded this earth with envious eyes and slowly and surely drew their plans against us. In the thirty-ninth year of the twentieth century came the great disillusionment.

It was near the end of October. Business was better. The war scare was over. More men were back at work. Sales were picking up. On this particular evening, October 30, the Crossley service estimated that 32 million people were listening to their radios.[7]

Then, very smoothly, without perceptible transition, an anonymous announcer followed him on the air, delivering a very routine bulletin:

> . . . for the next twenty-four hours not much change in temperature. A slight atmospheric disturbance of undetermined origin is reported over Nova Scotia, causing a low pressure area to move down rather rapidly over the northeastern states, bringing a forecast of rain, accompanied by winds of light gale force. Maximum temperature 66; minimum 48. This weather report comes to you from the Government Weather Bureau. . . . We now take you to the Meridian Room in the Hotel Park Plaza in downtown New York, where you will be entertained by the music of Ramon Raquello and his orchestra.

The audience then heard a CBS house orchestra playing the tango, *La Cumparsita.*

It is evident that the first few minutes of the broadcast were strictly realistic in regard to time frame and were perfectly credible, although somewhat boring. The adapted script of *War of the Worlds* started very slowly and continued to move at a snail's pace. There were some meteorological and astronomical bulletins, alternating with musical interludes and a rather dull scientific interview. These first few minutes were *intended* to bore or lull the listener into a false sense of security and furnish a solid base of real time from which to accelerate later into dramatic time. Some 12 minutes into the show, there was a news flash that "a huge, flaming object, believed to be a meteorite, fell on a farm in the neighborhood of Grover's Mill, New Jersey, 22 miles from Trenton."[8]

Musical interludes were then alternated with interviews with people on the scene. A few minutes later, the Martians reared their ugly heads and the scene was set. The dramatic action picked up speed after the audience had been significantly conditioned to additional scientific observation interspersed with a program of dance music. The program suddenly shifted from real time to the condensed and telescoped time required of dramatic presentations. The transition to dramatic time was outstanding, executed with such technical and dramatic skill that it was all but imperceptible.

Perhaps the skill of the transition helps to explain why much of the audience accepted a large number of events contained in a single broadcast as real, events that would have taken days, weeks, or longer to have occurred in fact. Within a span of 45 minutes, the Martians had blasted off their planet, set up their destructive machines, defeated our armies, disrupted our communications, demoralized the population, and occupied whole sections of the country! In addition, the United States had mobilized large bodies of troops; reporters had traveled great distances; government cabinet meetings were held; and savage battles were fought on land and in the air. Yet, it is estimated that approximately 1 million people believed all this to have taken place!

Because the actions of the Martians and the defenders of the country were compressed in time, it seemed unlikely that most people would mistake the broadcast for an actual occurrence—especially if they had heard the program introduction, which clearly stated that a dramatization of the Wells novel would follow. The entire "hoax" could easily have been recognized in these early minutes—except that few people were listening. Instead, they were being entertained by Charlie McCarthy and Edgar Bergen, then at the height of their popularity, on another network. The Crossley survey of listeners taken the week before the broadcast gave 34.7 percent of the listening audience to "The Edgar Bergen Show" and only 3.6 percent to the "Mercury Theatre on the Air." The critical factor here was the American listener's habit of *dial twisting*. That particular evening, Edgar Bergen had an unpopular guest who went on at approximately 8:12 P.M.; listeners began changing stations. By that time, the mysterious meteorite had already fallen on Grover's Mill, New Jersey; shortly thereafter, the Martians had shown their foul, leathery heads, and the New Jersey police authorities had rushed to the scene.

What made things more credible to the newly tuned listeners was the genuine-sounding appeal by the Secretary of the Interior around 8:31, at the height of the crisis:

> Citizens of the nation: I shall not try to conceal the gravity of the situation that confronts the country, nor the concern of your Government in protecting the lives and property of its people. However, I wish to impress upon you—private citizens and public officials, all of you—the urgent need of calm and resourceful action. Fortunately, this formidable enemy is still confined to a comparatively small area, and we may place our faith in the military forces to keep them there. In the meantime placing our trust in God, we must continue the performance of our duties, each and every one of us, so that we may confront this destructive adversary with a nation united, courageous, and consecrated to the preservation of human supremacy on this earth. I thank you.

Davidson Taylor, CBS's supervisor of the broadcast, was summoned from the control room near the end of the secretary's appeal. A few minutes later, when he returned, he appeared shaken. By now the Martians had swept all opposition aside as they advanced upon New York. Those participating in the broadcast thought it was going well. Taylor, however, had just learned how well. The CBS switchboards were uselessly swamped; a madness was sweeping the country because of the broadcast. Rumors had reached the network of panic injuries, deaths, and suicides. Taylor had been requested to interrupt the show imme-diately—to issue an announcement by the station about the broadcast.

The broadcast was less than a minute from the station break. The Martians were blanketing New York with poison gas. The music swirled, the "last announcer," Ray Collins, died heroically on the roof of the Broadcasting Building, and the boats in the harbor whistled until all who manned them were dead. As all these sounds died away, an amateur radio operator was heard, reaching weakly into the dark night to an empty world.

> 2X2L calling CQ
> 2X2L calling CQ
> 2X2L calling CQ
> Isn't there anyone on the air?
> Isn't there anyone?

There followed complete silence. Five seconds later, the network announcer broke the spell, shattering the "reality" of the end of the world:

> You are listening to the CBS presentation of Orson Welles and the Mercury Theatre on the Air in an original dramatization of *The War of the Worlds,* by H. G. Wells. The performance will continue after a brief intermission.

According to Houseman, the remainder of the show was well written and sensitively played.

In the last part of the broadcast, the play was clearly identified as a fantasy. The problem was that almost no one heard it. It described the adventures of a lone survivor and his observations on human society. The Martians finally died, but not by man's action. All his defenses had failed. What finally destroyed them was bacteria. The microorganisms of the earth overpowered the conquerors. Finally came the hope of rebuilding a new world.

The broadcast ended with an informal speech by Welles:

> This is Orson Welles, ladies and gentlemen, out of character to assure you that the *War of the Worlds* has no further significance than as the holiday offering it was intended to be. The Mercury Theatre's own radio version of dressing up in a sheet and jumping out of a bush and saying BOO! Starting now, we couldn't soap all your windows and steal all your garden gates, by tomorrow night . . . so we did the next best thing. We annihilated the world before your very ears, and utterly destroyed the Columbia Broadcasting System. You will be relieved, I

hope, to learn that we didn't mean it, and that both institutions are still open for business. So good-bye everybody and remember, please, for the next day or so, the terrible lesson you learned tonight. That grinning, glowing globular invader of your living room is an inhabitant of the pumpkin patch, and if your doorbell rings and nobody's there, that was NO Martian . . . it's Halloween.

Also identifying the presentation as fantasy were additional announcements made by CBS immediately following the broadcast. For example, one such announcement was aired right away:

For those listeners who tuned in to Orson Welles's Mercury Theatre on the air broadcast from 8 to 9 P.M. Eastern Standard Time tonight and did not realize that the program was merely a modernized adaptation of H. G. Wells' famous novel *War of the Worlds,* we are repeating the fact which was made clear four times on the program, that, while the names of some American cities were used, as in all novels and dramatizations, the entire story and all of its incidents were fictitious.

The four announcements CBS referred to occurred (1) at the beginning of the broadcast (when most people were not listening), (2) before the station break, about 8:35 (by this time, most of those who panicked were no longer listening, but fleeing), (3) right after the station break, and (4) at the end of the broadcast. Moreover, the most terrifying part of the broadcast, it should be remembered, came *before* the station break. Those listeners who failed to hear the original announcement therefore had ample opportunity to become frightened.

***The Panic.*** The panic began well before the broadcast had ended. Terrified people all over America prayed and tried frantically, in one way or another, to escape death from the Martians. The reaction was strongest in the New Jersey area (in a single block, more than 20 families rushed out of their houses with wet handkerchiefs and towels over their faces), but people were affected in all sections of the country. Some examples:[9]

*New York*—Hundreds of people fled their homes. Bus terminals were crowded. One woman telephoned Dixie Bus Terminal for information and spoke impatiently, "hurry please, the world is coming to an end and I have a lot to do."

*Rhode Island*—Hysterical people swamped the switchboard of the *Providence Journal* for details of the Martian invasion. Officials of the electric company reported that they received many calls urging them to turn off all lights so that the city would be safe from the enemy.

*Boston*—The *Boston Globe* was swamped with calls from frightened individuals. One woman said she could see the smoke and the fire brought about by the Martian invasion.

*Pittsburgh*—A man came home in the middle of the broadcast and found his wife in the bathroom with a bottle of poison in her hand and screaming, "I'd rather die this way than that."

*Birmingham, Alabama*—Many people gathered in churches and prayed. On the campus of a southeastern college—"The girls in the sorority houses and dormitories huddled around their radios trembling and weeping in each other's arms. They separated themselves from their friends only to take their turn at the telephone to make long-distance calls to their parents, saying goodbye for what they thought might be the last time."

*Kansas City, Missouri*—One telephone informant said that he had loaded all his children into his car, filled it with gasoline, and was going somewhere. "Where is it safe?" he wanted the know. The Kansas City Bureau of the Associated Press received queries on the "meteors" from Los Angeles, Salt Lake City, Beaumont, Texas, and St. Joseph, Missouri.

*Concrete, Washington*—The town experienced a power failure at the very moment the Martians were supposed to have been interrupting communications across the nation and disrupting the nation's power sources. This created mass hysteria because it appeared to confirm the broadcast.

Newspapers carried stories relating the shock and terror of many citizens for weeks after the broadcast. Around the world, newspaper accounts tried to recreate the atmosphere of terror that spread throughout America that October night.

As we shall show in a later section, several million people heard the broadcast. It has been estimated that about 1 million of these were frightened. Many of them engaged in panic behavior, a reaction that brought wide criticism to the producers of the show. Welles bore the brunt of most of the initial criticism. Reporters hounded him; outraged citizens threatened him. But the focus eventually shifted to CBS and Mercury Theatre. Legal actions were filed against both, seeking compensation for injuries and damages totaling millions of dollars. None of these suits ever went to trial, however; there was no legal precedent for such claims. CBS did choose to settle one claim. A man living in Massachusetts wrote:

I thought the best thing to do was to go away. So I took three dollars twenty-five cents out of my savings and bought a ticket. After I had gone sixty miles I knew it was a play. Now I don't have money left for the shoes I was saving up for. Will you please have someone send me a pair of black shoes size 9B?[10]

Against the advice of its lawyers, CBS sent the shoes.

The casualties turned out to be neither as numerous nor as serious as first thought. One young woman had broken her arm when she fell while running down stairs. The Federal Communications Commission held hearings on the broadcast and adopted a resolution prohibiting the use of "on the spot" news stories in dramatic broadcasts. CBS issued a public apology and promised no more Halloween scares. The incident was then officially closed.

## THE RESEARCH

The Office of Radio Research of Princeton University hastily organized a research study following the panic. The group had been formed a year earlier when the Rockefeller Foundation provided the university with funds to assess the influence of radio on listeners in the United States. The occurrence of the great panic suddenly presented it with a rare opportunity. Social scientists could study, for the first time, panic behavior triggered by a mass communication event. Funds for the special investigation were provided through a special grant from the General Education Board.

Although the scope of the investigation was limited in many ways, and the research had a number of methodological problems, the study became one of the classics of mass communication research. The results were reported in *The Invasion from Mars* by Hadley Cantril, written with the assistance of Hazel Gaudet and Herta Herzog. The purpose of the study was to discover the psychological conditions and the situational circumstances that led people to believe that the broadcast drama was real. The result was a sensitive study of the feelings and reactions of people who were badly frightened by the believed arrival of the Martians.[11]

The researchers were trying to answer three basic questions: (1) What was the extent of the panic (i.e., how many listened and how many panicked); (2) Why did this broadcast frighten some people when other fantastic broadcasts did not; and (3) Why did this broadcast frighten some people but not others?

## Methods

Because the research questions were so complex, several approaches were employed to seek out the answers. The results obtained by one method could thus be compared with those obtained by another. Such a pluralistic approach to the research was desirable because the phenomena under investigation were of so transient a nature. The following techniques were used: personal interviews, scientific surveys, analyses of newspaper accounts, and an examination of volume of mail. We shall discuss each of these in turn, in the order of their importance for the study.

*Personal Interviews.*   Much of the information contained in Cantril's book was derived from in-depth personal interviews with persons who listened to the broadcast. These interviews began one week after the broadcast and were completed by the time four weeks had elapsed. A total of 135 individuals were interviewed. Of these, 107 were selected because the broadcast had badly frightened them; an additional 28 listeners who had not been frightened by the broadcast were interviewed to provide a basis for comparison.

The interviews were limited to the New Jersey vicinity (Princeton's locale) for two reasons: (1) funds were limited and (2) the researchers wanted to ensure that there was proper supervision of this aspect of the research program. According to Cantril:

> Every attempt was made to keep the group representative of the population at large. However, no pretense is made that the group is a proper example of the total population.[12]

In addition, the respondents who had been frightened were identified almost entirely through the personal initiative and inquiry *of the interviewers.* Many more persons were identified than could possibly have been interviewed, given the funding limitations.

***Surveys.***   The results of several different surveys were included in this study. The most significant were (1) a special survey conducted by CBS the week after the broadcast in which the interviews were taken throughout the country from 920 persons who had listened to the broadcast and (2) a nationwide survey of several thousand adults conducted by the American Institute of Public Opinion (AIPO) about six weeks after the broadcast. Although the delay was unfortunate, it was also unavoidable. It took that long to obtain sufficient funding to conduct it. The results obtained, however, are extremely valuable because the institute reached many small communities and homes without telephones that were not regularly sampled by the radio research organizations.

***Newspaper Accounts and Mail.***   The study analyzed 12,500 clippings that appeared in papers throughout the country for three weeks following the broadcast. Analyses indicated continued interest in the broadcast, although the number of articles diminished somewhat at the end of the three weeks.

In addition, analyses of the volume of mail to CBS stations, the Mercury Theatre itself, and the Federal Communications Commission (FCC) were also undertaken. It was not surprising that huge increases in the volume of mail were reported. Interestingly, most of the letters to the Mercury Theatre in particular and to CBS stations in general were favorable, even congratulatory. However, letters to the FCC, the "watchdog of broadcasting," were generally unfavorable. It seemed that those who wanted their protests taken seriously did not hesitate to communicate with the proper authorities, whereas those who appreciated good drama gave praise where praise was due.

It is clear that even with the study's multifaceted approach, it had many methodological problems. For example, there was almost a haphazard aspect to the selection of subjects for personal interviews. This aspect of the research program was almost totally lacking in rigor. Moreover, the delays of up to four weeks in obtaining the interviews were unfortunate. One of the major scientific surveys also shared this shortcoming.

There was also a validity problem. Many people may have been reluctant to confess their gullibility in an interview after having read newspaper accounts, such as one by Dorothy Thompson, in which she claimed that nothing about the broadcast was in the least credible. Nevertheless, the authors freely admitted the shortcomings of their data-gathering procedures and qualified many of their findings. On the other hand, we must remember that no one anticipated that a panic would occur, and the delays in the research were therefore unavoidable. Although the findings many have limitations, they give us insight into and understanding of the reasons why a radio broadcast caused more than a million people to panic.

## The Findings

The findings have several dimensions. As we noted earlier, the study sought to determine the size of the audience (including how many were frightened), the unique aspects of the broadcast as a trigger for panic behavior, and why some listeners were frightened while others were not.

*The Size of the Audience.* The best evidence regarding "who listened" came from the American Institute of Public Opinion poll. It was estimated from their sample that 9 million adults heard the broadcast. If children were included, the number would increase to 12 million. The AIPO estimate was, however, much *higher* than that yielded by any other known audience measure. This may be due to the fact that its sample, unlike those of other surveys, included small communities and homes without telephones. Because of the wide discrepancy, Cantril pooled the results of the AIPO poll with the findings of C. E. Hooper, Inc., a commercial research organization that made continuous checks on program popularity. The Hooper figures indicated a listening audience of about 4 million for the Mercury Theatre broadcast on October 30, 1938. The pooled results yielded a final estimate of 6 million listeners—admittedly conservative.

*How Many Were Frightened.* The AIPO survey asked, "At the time you were listening, did you think the broadcast was a play or a real news report?" Twenty-eight percent of the respondents thought that it was news, and 70 percent of those who thought it was a news report were frightened or disturbed. Thus, AIPO estimated that 1.7 million listeners thought the broadcast was a news bulletin and 1.2 million were excited by the news. Even more conservative estimates place the number of people frightened at 1 million or more. Had the program enjoyed greater popularity, the panic might have been even more widespread, depending on whether or not they had heard the introductory announcements.

*Unique Aspects of the Broadcast.* What was there about this broadcast that caused it to frighten some people when other fantastic broadcasts did not? Cantril's research indicated that the following five factors were important in distinguishing *War of the Worlds* from other "frightening" programs.

1. The sheer dramatic excellence of the program was an important factor, Dorothy Thompson's remark about its credibility notwithstanding. No one reading the script can deny that the broadcast was so realistic for the first few minutes that it was almost credible, even to relatively sophisticated and well-informed listeners.

2. Radio was an accepted vehicle for important announcements. A large proportion of listeners, particularly those in the lower income and educational groups, had learned to rely more on radio for the news than on newspapers. Almost all of the listeners who had been frightened and were interviewed mentioned somewhere during the course of the interview the great confidence they had in radio. They expected that it would be used for such an important announcement. Listeners had learned to expect that dramas, musical programs, and the like would be interrupted or even cut off in an emergency in order to inform the public. A few examples of the respondents' comments indicate their attitudes toward and reliance on radio.

We have so much *faith in broadcasting.* In a crisis it has to reach all people. That's what radio is here for.

I always feel that the *commentators bring the best possible news.* Even after this I still will believe what I hear on the radio.

It didn't sound like a play the *way it interrupted the music when it started.*

3. The use of the "expert" in the broadcast gave it credibility. In many situations where events and/or ideas are too complicated, or too far removed from one's immediate experience, then only the expert is expected to understand them. The rest of the people must rely on the expert's interpretations. The logical "expert" in the panic broadcast was the astronomer, "Professor Richard Pierson," the chief character in the drama (played by Orson Welles). Other fictitious astronomers were also mentioned: "Professor Farrell of the Mount Jennings Observatory of Chicago," "Professor Morse of MacMillan University in Toronto," and "Professor Indellkoffer of the California Astronomical Society."

When the dramatic situation changed, other experts were introduced. "Gen. Montgomery Smith of the State Militia" provided expertise for organized defense. "Mr. Harry McDonald" of the Red Cross, "Capt. Lansing" of the Signal Corps, and the "Secretary of the Interior" all described the terrible conditions and gave orders to evacuate or attack. This technique appeared to have a powerful effect on the listeners.

I believed the broadcast as soon *as I heard the professor from Princeton* and the officials in Washington.

I knew it was an awfully dangerous situation *when all those military men were there and the Secretary of State spoke.*

If so many of these astronomers saw the explosions they must have been real. *They ought to know.*

4. The *use of real places* added a familiar frame of reference to the broadcast. The use of actual towns, city streets and highways, and so on in the broadcast were crucial cues for many people. For example, mention of places well known to them was particularly frightening to listeners in New Jersey and Manhattan. The towns of Grover's Mill, Princeton, and Trenton, New Jersey, were all mentioned early in the broadcast. Other familiar places such as Watchung Mountains, Bayonne, the Hutchinson River Parkway, Newark, the Palisades, Times Square, the Pulaski Skyway, and the Holland Tunnel were all familiar to residents of the New York/New Jersey area. Even listeners in other areas of the country recognized many of the names as real.

When he said, "Ladies and Gentlemen, do not use *route number 23,"* that made me sure.

I was most inclined to believe the broadcast *when they mentioned places like South Street and the Pulaski Highway.*

If they had mentioned any other places but streets right around here, I would not have been so ready to believe.

5. Tuning in late was a major factor in leading people to believe that the broadcast was real. It seems highly unlikely that a listener would take the broadcast seriously if the opening announcements had been heard. Indeed, data from two separate surveys (CBS, AIPO) indicated that the time a person tuned in was a major factor in determining whether or not the person was frightened by the broadcast. For example, among the questions asked as part of the CBS study were "At what part of the program did you tune in?" and "Did you realize it was a play or did you think it was a real news broadcast?" Forty-two percent indicated that they had tuned in late. As Table 3.1 shows, there was a very pronounced tendency for those who tuned in late to accept the broadcast as news, and for those who tuned in at the beginning to take it as a play. Only 20 percent of the persons interviewed who listened from the beginning thought they were hearing a news report.

Why did such a large percentage of the listeners tune in late? We mentioned earlier that Mercury Theatre was competing with the most popular program hosts on the air, Edgar Bergen and Charlie McCarthy. Most listeners heard their first routine and changed the station when an unpopular singer came on the show. Another reason people tuned in late was the contagion that the excitement of the show created. Many who were frightened called friends and relatives who

**TABLE 3.1**  Time of tuning in and interpretation (CBS survey)

| | Tuned in | | |
| Interpretation | From the Beginning (percent) | After the Beginning (percent) | Total Number |
| --- | --- | --- | --- |
| News | 20 | 63 | 175 |
| Play | 80 | 37 | 285 |
| Total percent | 100 | 100 | |
| Total number of cases | 269 | 191 | 460 |

SOURCE: Hadley Cantril, *The Invasion from Mars* (Princeton: Princeton University Press, 1940), p. 78.

then tuned in. In the AIPO survey, the respondents who tuned in late were asked, "Did someone suggest that you tune in after the program had begun?" Twenty-one percent responded that someone had. In the CBS survey, the figure was 19 percent.

Still, there *were* those who tuned in from the beginning yet believed the clearly introduced play to be a news broadcast. Analysis of the data revealed two main reasons such a misinterpretation came about. First, many people who had tuned in to hear the Mercury Theatre play thought that it had been interrupted for special news bulletins. They were familiar with this kind of interruption and had experience with it in the war crisis earlier that October. It was easier to accept the news interruption as irrelevant to the expected play than to infer that it was a part of the play. In the CBS survey, 20 percent listened from the beginning and thought it was a newscast. Of these, nearly two-thirds (61 percent) thought the interruption was authentic. Their comments make this apparent.

> I have heard other programs interrupted in the same way for news broadcasts.
>
> I believed Welles' statement that he was interrupting the program for a news flash.

The second major reason for the misunderstanding was that many people simply did not pay attention to the opening announcements. Some people kept their radios turned on and paid attention to them only when something of interest caught their attention. Since the beginning announcements frequently contained station identifications and commercials, many people were probably inattentive. For example, 10 percent of those people who heard it from the beginning said that they had not paid any attention to the announcements.

> My radio had been tuned to the station several hours. I heard loud talking and excitement and became interested.
>
> My radio was tuned to the station but I wasn't paying attention to it.

> We had company at home and were playing cards while the radio was turned on. I heard a news commentator interrupt the program but as first did not pay much attention to him.
>
> I started to listen only when the farmer began giving a description of the landing of the tube.

Tuning in late, however, was a much more important factor in determining whether the listener would follow the program as a play or as a news report than was ignoring or misunderstanding the beginning of the show.

**Why Some Were Frightened and Some Were Not.** In spite of the fact that many persons tuned in to the *War of the Worlds* broadcast late, certainly not all of them believed the show to be news. Even among those who believed the invasion to be real, the patterns of behavior differed significantly. To understand better the varying behavior demonstrated, Cantril and his associates placed the listeners into four categories, identifying why some were frightened while others were not (assuming that all persons at first thought the broadcast was a news report):

1. *Those who checked the internal evidence of the broadcast. (They made successful internal checks.)* The persons in this category did *not* remain frightened throughout the entire broadcast because they were able to discern that the program was fictitious. Some realized that the reports must be false because they sounded so much like science fiction literature.

   > At first I was very interested in the fall of the meteor. It isn't often they find a big one just when it falls. But when it started to unscrew and monsters came out, I said to myself, "They've taken one of those amazing stories and are acting it out. It just couldn't be real. It was just like some of the stories I read in *Amazing Stories* but it was even more exciting."

   Other persons in this category initially believed the broadcast to be news but could not believe the subsequent description of events.

   > It all sounded perfectly real until people began hopping around too fast. . . . When people moved 20 miles in a couple of minutes I put my tongue in my cheek and figured it was just about the smartest play I'd ever heard.
   >
   > I kept translating the unbelievable parts into something I could believe until finally I reached the breaking point—I mean my mind just couldn't twist things any more, and somehow I knew it couldn't be true literally, so I just stopped believing and knew it must be a play.

2. *Those who checked the broadcast against other information and learned that it was a play. (They made a successful external check.)* Like the listeners in the first category, these were suspicious of the "news" they were getting. Some thought the reports too incredible to believe; others realized things were moving too quickly. Some listeners checked simply because they thought it was a reasonable thing to do. Mostly, they compared the news on the program with some other information. Many checked to see if other stations were reporting the invasion. Some even looked up the program in the paper.

> I tuned in and heard that a meteor had fallen. Then when they talked about monsters, I thought something was the matter. So I looked in the newspaper to see what program was supposed to be on and discovered it was only a play.

3. *Those who tried to check the program against other information but who, for various reasons, continued to believe the broadcast was an authentic news report. (They made unsuccessful external checks.)* These people differed from those in category 2 (those who made successful external checks) in two ways. First, it was difficult to determine why they even wanted to check; they were not seeking evidence to test the authenticity of the reports. They appeared to be frightened individuals who wanted to find out if they were yet in any personal danger. Second, they used ineffective and unreliable checks. For example, the most frequent method of checking was to look out the window or go outdoors. Some telephoned their friends or ran to consult with their neighbors. Whatever "new" information they obtained tended to be used to verify their existing beliefs.

> I looked out of the window and everything looked the same as usual so I thought it hadn't reached our section yet.
>
> We looked out of the window and Wyoming Avenue was black with cars. People are rushing away, I figured.
>
> No cars came down my street. "Traffic is jammed on account of the roads being destroyed," I thought.
>
> My husband tried to calm me and said, "If this were really so, it would be on all stations" and he turned to one of the other stations and there was music. I retorted, "Nero fiddled while Rome burned."
>
> We tuned in to another station and heard some church music. I was sure a lot of people were worshipping God while waiting for their death.

4. *Those who made no attempt to check the broadcast or the event.* Many of these people were so frightened they stopped listening, became frenzied, or paralyzed with fear. Cantril subdivided them according to the apparent reasons for their actions.

**a.** Persons so frightened they never thought of checking.

> We were so intent upon listening that we didn't have enough sense to try other hook-ups—we were just so frightened.

**b.** Persons who adopted an attitude of complete resignation. To them, any attempt to check the broadcast appeared senseless.

> I didn't do anything. I just kept listening. I thought if this is the real thing you only die once—why get excited?
>
> The lady from the next floor rushed downstairs, yelling to turn on the radio. I heard the explosion, people from Mars, end of the world. I was very scared and everybody in the room was scared stiff too. There was nothing else to do for everything would be destroyed very soon. If I had had a little bottle of whiskey, I would have had a drink and said, "let it go."

**c.** Persons who felt that, in light of the crisis situation, immediate action was required.

> I couldn't stand it so I turned it off. I don't remember when, but everything was coming closer. My husband wanted to put it back on but I told him we'd better do something instead of just listen, so we started to pack.

**d.** Listeners who interpreted the situation in such a way that they were not interested in making a check.

In some cases the individuals tuned in so late that they missed the most incredible parts of the broadcast and were only aware that some type of conflict was in progress.

> I was in my drugstore and my brother phoned and said, "Turn the radio on, a meteor has just fallen." We did and heard gas was coming up South Street. There were a few customers and we all began wondering where it could come from. I was worried about the gas, it was spreading so rapidly but I was puzzled as to what was actually happening, when I heard aeroplanes I thought another country was attacking us.
>
> I knew it was some Germans trying to gas all of us. When the announcer kept calling them people from Mars I just thought he was ignorant and didn't know yet that Hitler had sent them all.

For other listeners, the events described did not appear to involve *immediate* personal danger.

> I was at a party, somebody was fooling around with the radio, and we heard a voice, the Secretary of Interior was talking. We thought it was a normal bulletin because of the conditions abroad. Then the local militia was called so we decided to listen. It sounded real but not like

anything to get panicky about. This riot or whatever it was was still a couple of miles away.

Both the personal interviews and the CBS survey indicated that those individuals who were able to make successful checks (either by internal or external tests) remained fairly calm. Those who checked unsuccessfully or not at all tended to become either excited or paralyzed. Thus, there was a very strong relationship between feelings, beliefs, and subsequent behavior.

The researchers found that those people who were frightened by the broadcast were *highly suggestible;* they believed what they heard without making sufficient checks to see if the information was accurate. But some people did not jump to conclusions but instead scrutinized what they heard and then rejected it as news. These people were said to possess *critical ability.* Cantril defined it in the following manner:

> By this we mean that they had a capacity to evaluate the stimulus in such a way that they were able to understand its inherent characteristics so they could judge and act appropriately.[13]

Thus, individuals possessing critical ability were able to assess the credibility of the events in the radio play against their knowledge of the world. And there were just too many events in the play that did not conform to their conception of reality.

Unfortunately, although the concept of critical ability was the single most promising "psychological tool" for examining the data, there was no way to measure it directly. However, the researchers hypothesized that it was related to the amount of formal education a person possessed. Education "instills readiness to examine interpretations before accepting them," they argued.[14] Indeed, such a relationship between education and orientation toward the broadcast was found, as shown in Table 3.2. While college graduates were not immune to panic behavior, the response to the broadcast varied in proportion to the amount of education an individual possessed.

**TABLE 3.2**  Education and interpretation as news (CBS survey)

| Education | Percentage Who Thought Program Was News Report | Total Number of Cases |
|---|---|---|
| College | 28 | 69 |
| High school | 36 | 257 |
| Grammar school | 46 | 132 |

SOURCE: Hadley Cantril, *The Invasion from Mars* (Princeton: Princeton University Press, 1940) p. 112.

***Religious Beliefs and Personality Factors.*** Religiosity was also an important variable in determining how an individual would react to the broadcast. Those with strong religious beliefs were likely to think that the invasion was actually an act of God and that the end of the world was near.

> We just sat and listened. You see we're good Christians and a Providence will take care of us. We're not afraid to die because we're prepared for it.
>
> At first I didn't think it was the end of the world because I read in the Bible, in Revelations, that the end of the world was coming by fire and I didn't think this was a fire. I thought buildings were being struck and falling down. But then I realized that eventually they might catch on fire so I thought the end was coming.
>
> The Bible says that the first time the end of the world was by flood and next time it will be by fire and that went through my mind.

Other individuals were found to be particularly susceptible to the broadcast because of personality factors such as (1) emotional insecurity, (2) phobic personality, (3) lack of self-confidence, and (4) fatalism. A person who believes that his life is in the control of somewhat mysterious powers is obviously capable of rationalizing *any* experience as preordained.

> I believe what is to be will be. I didn't pray during the broadcast.
>
> I just kept listening. I thought if this is the real thing you only die once—why get excited. When the time comes you go and there is no way getting away from it.

Finally, it was discovered in addition that the characteristics of the listening situation could also influence an individual's susceptibility to the broadcast. For example, a person who was told to tune in by a frightened friend would listen under different conditions from those of someone who tuned in for other reasons. If the person who called or informed the listener was someone in whom he or she had confidence, the listener would be particularly susceptible to accepting that person's opinion.

> I had just gone to the store to get some last-minute things for my daughter's party. When I came in my son said, "Mother, something has come down from Mars and the world is coming to an end." I said, "Don't be silly." Then my husband said, "It is true." So I started to listen. And really, I heard forty people were killed and there was gas and everybody was choking.

Moreover, the sight and sound of other people (even strangers) who were frightened might increase the emotional tension of an otherwise calm individual and thus reduce that person's critical ability.

I don't think we would have gotten so excited if those couples hadn't come rushing in the way they did. We were both very calm people, especially my husband, and if we had tuned in ourselves I am sure we would have checked up on the program but they led me to believe it was any station.

When I came out of the telephone booth, the store was filled with people in a rather high state of hysteria. . . . This hysterical group convinced me that something was wrong.

In short, the researchers found that "critical ability" was the most important factor in distinguishing those who panicked from those who did not. However, other factors such as religiosity and personality factors were also important. In fact, critical ability alone, as measured by the amount of formal education, was not a sure preventive of panic behavior. The authors concluded that critical ability may be overpowered by either an individual's own susceptible personality or by emotions generated in a person by an unusual listening situation.

***Causal Factors in Extreme Behavior.***    Recognizing that some people believed the broadcast to be true, one might then ask, Why did they become so hysterical? Why did they pray, telephone relatives, drive at dangerous speeds, cry, awaken sleeping children, and flee? Of all the possible modes of reaction they may have followed, why did these particular patterns emerge? The obvious answer is that this was a serious affair. As in all other panics, the well-being of individuals, their safety, or their lives were at stake. The situation was perceived as a real threat.

Social scientists generally agree that a panic occurs when commonly accepted values are threatened and when no possible elimination of that threat is in sight. The invasion by the Martians was a direct threat to life, one's own as well as that of loved ones. Indeed, it was a a threat to all other cherished values. Frustration resulted when no directed behavior seemed possible. One could either resign oneself to complete annihilation or attempt to escape. One could flee, call upon a higher authority for protection, or seek out someone stronger to destroy the enemy.

If listeners assumed the destruction was inevitable, their choices were limited. They could accept their fate in a number of ways: crying, prayer, gathering the family together. Or they could run. If they believed something could still be done to stop the enemy, they could appeal to stronger powers (e.g., God). But none of these alternatives attacked the problem directly. Nothing was done to remove the cause of the crisis. Panic behavior is characteristically undirected; it is, in terms of the situation, nonfunctional.

In short, the extreme behavior evoked by the broadcast was due to the threat to values that the situation created and the complete inability of the individual to alleviate or control the consequences of the invasion. People could not choose one value over another and thus preserve some; all stood to be lost. All their loved ones, their country, and indeed their world, would be ruined physically, financially, and socially. Believing total ruin imminent, panic was inescapable.

## CONCLUSIONS AND IMPLICATIONS

Overall, what were the principal findings and the major conclusions of the Cantril study? What was their importance from the point of view of developing mass communication theory and methodology? Finally, how did this broadcast, its aftermath, and the research project influence the public's perceptions of radio as a medium?

### Summary of the Findings

First, at least 6 million people listened to the program and, of those, at least 1 million were severely frightened or panicked. Second, there were several important reasons why this particular broadcast frightened many listeners whereas other such "fantastic" broadcasts did not. Among these reasons are:

1. The confidence that the American public had developed in radio. It had become their primary source of news, and the public expected that radio would be used to present important announcements.
2. The historical timing. The broadcast came at a time when Americans had endured years of economic insecurity and were facing the imminent threat of another war.
3. The sheer technical brilliance of the show—especially the innovative use of the "on-the-spot reporting" technique and the interviewing of "experts."
4. Tuning in late. Missing the announcement that the broadcast was a dramatic adaptation of the *War of the Worlds* was an important factor.

A third conclusion was that there were many reasons why some individuals panicked while others did not.

1. Those who possessed critical ability were most likely to discover that the broadcast was a play rather than news.
2. Those with strong religious beliefs were likely to believe that the invasion was real.
3. Personality factors such as emotional insecurity, phobic personality, lack of self-confidence, and fatalism were also important. Those manifesting such traits were more likely to believe that an invasion was taking place.
4. An individual's susceptibility to the broadcast could also be influenced by an unusual listening situation. For example, someone encouraged to tune in by frightened friends would listen under different conditions (expectations) from those of someone who tuned in the broadcast for other reasons.

Subsequent events made it evident that the social and psychological factors that contributed to the panic were not confined to the United States. A few years later, similar broadcasts of the *War of the Worlds* in Spanish induced panics in two Latin American countries—Chile and Peru. The idea for the Chilean program came from William Steele, a former writer for Mutual Broadcasting's "The Shadow" series, who was then writing for a station in Santiago. Steele set the scene for his adaptation in Puente Alto, 15 miles south of Santiago. Like Koch, he depicted horrible Martians overrunning the country. "News flashes" reported the Civic Center in Santiago destroyed, the armed forces defeated, and the roads flooded with fleeing refugees. Thousands of people all over Chile were panic-stricken.

At least one death was verified (an electric company employee, Jose Villarroel, died from a heart attack believed to have been brought on by his terrified state of mind). Ample warning had been given the public for this *War of the Worlds* broadcast during the week preceding it, by both radio and the press. It was said to be "all in fun." Announcements were repeated twice during the broadcast, warning that it was only a play. Again, as in the United States, many people failed to notice the message. In the aftermath of the broadcast, the indignant Chilean people pressured the station to close, and they sought to have Steele suspended. However, no official action was taken.[15]

In Lima, Peru, another similar broadcast also created a panic, although on a much smaller scale because there were fewer radios within the station's broadcast range. However, the aftermath was even more devastating. When the Peruvians discovered they had been tricked and the world was not coming to an end, they decided to put an end to the offending station. They burned it to the ground. Since that time, because broadcasts of *War of the Worlds* have demonstrated such power, there has been a conscious effort to keep the "Martian genie" from escaping its bottle. A broadcaster opens it at his own peril.[16]

## The Significance of the Study

The Cantril study has remained important in the history of mass communication for a number of reasons. It was the first study of panic behavior triggered by a mass medium. However, it has theoretical significance beyond that particular focus. The researchers were not trying to develop a theory about the effects of mass communication; they were more narrowly interested in the psychological and sociological factors associated with panic behavior. In retrospect, however, their framework for research in addition to their findings played a part in the evolution of contemporary media theory.

Looking back, it is clear that Cantril shaped his study around what we have called the selective influence perspective based upon individual differences. This perspective is obvious in one of Cantril's major research objectives—determining why some people were frightened or panicked while others were not. The answers to that question were found in the differences in critical ability, which led to selective forms of response to the broadcast. Certain personality factors also played a role (emotional insecurity, phobic personality, lack of self-confidence, and fatalism). Social categories were found to be important. Factors such as religion and education influenced the probability of perceiving the broadcast as news or as a play. Finally, in retrospect, a review of the findings reveals that social relationships were significant influences on the patterns of behavior people selected to cope with the invasion. The activities and perceptions of family, friends, and even strangers contributed to the meaning that the subjects attributed to the broadcast. Thus, although it was by no means clear at the time, the panic study was one of the first challenges to the magic bullet theory. It opened the way to theories stressing selective influences.

Methodologically, no innovative techniques were used in the study. In fact, the techniques that were used were not particularly impressive; indeed, more rigor should have been applied. Yet, given the unexpected nature of the event, and the constraints of time and money, it is remarkable that the research was performed at all with any degree of precision. The logistics of planning and obtaining funding for such a study require enormous investments of time. As a matter of fact, the bureaucracy of research that has developed in the intervening years would probably preclude such an "instant" research effort should another similar event occur.

Perhaps the real significance of the study was the way in which it confirmed public thinking about the effects of the mass media. In short, it reinforced the legacy of fear. October 30, 1938, continues to be remembered as the night American panicked. For many people, the powerful influence of radio had been proven in a most unorthodox manner. Contrary to the unnamed CBS employee's prebroadcast evaluation, the show did "come off." Of that, there can be no doubt.

## NOTES AND REFERENCES

1. Hadley Cantril, *The Invasion from Mars: A Study in the Psychology of Panic* (Princeton, N.J.: Princeton University Press, 1940, p. x.
2. Melvin L. DeFleur and Sandra Ball-Rokeach, *Theories of Mass Communication,* 3rd ed. (New York: Longman Inc., 1975), p. 93.
3. Howard Koch, *The Panic Broadcast: Portrait of an Event* (Boston: Little, Brown, and Company, 1970), p. 13.
4. John Houseman, "The Men From Mars," *Harper's,* 168:76, 1948.
5. Ibid., p. 76.
6. Ibid.
7. This quotation and those that follow (from the original radio script) are presented in full in Cantril, *Invasion from Mars,* pp. 4–43.
8. Ibid., pp. 10–11.
9. Houseman, "Men from Mars," pp. 10–11.
10. Ibid., p. 82.
11. Cantril, *Invasion from Mars.*
12. Ibid., p. xi.
13. Ibid., pp. 111–112.
14. Ibid., p. 112.
15. "The Men From Mars," *Newsweek,* November 27, 1944, p. 89.
16. Koch, *Panic Broadcast.*

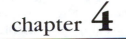

chapter **4**

# The People's Choice: The Media in a Political Campaign

The year 1940 was a fateful one for the United States. It represented the end of one era and the beginning of another. It was the last year during which the principal concerns of Americans were the issues associated with the Great Depression of the 1930s, and also the last peacetime year before the United States was plunged into war. The selection of a national leader in 1940, then, was a matter of far graver concern than any of the voters could imagine as the spring approached and the media campaign for the presidency slowly began to gear up. The incumbent was Franklin Roosevelt; the challenger, Wendell Willkie, an almost unknown candidate without prior political experience.

Franklin Delano Roosevelt was a very popular president. First elected in 1932, he inherited a country nearly paralyzed by the worst financial crisis in its history. The stock market had crashed late in 1929, and by 1932 banks were on the thin edge of failure all over the country. Unemployment soared as factories closed because people had no money to buy things. Farmers couldn't even give their crops away. People were going hungry, but food was rotting in the fields. It was a democratic depression; the previously well-to-do suffered along with ordinary people who worked with their hands in mines, mills, and farms. Bread lines were long in the cities, and rural people were driven from their farms when their mortgages were foreclosed.

Into this situation came the calm and cultured voice of Franklin Roosevelt, soothing people via the radio, telling them that "all we have to fear is fear itself." He was elected in a landslide, and in his first weeks in office he surrounded himself with a "brain trust' of liberal university professors who helped him design and set into motion a set of sweeping changes and social programs that were labeled the "New Deal" for the American people. These included the Social Security Act of 1935 and our basic welfare legislation, which provided a number of welfare measures, funded on a national basis for the first time in the history of the nation. Many other economic policies, governmental controls, and social programs were added. The country shifted jarringly away from the earlier reliance on unfettered free enterprise and a limited role for government to a profusion of social programs and policies funded by a progressive income tax and policed by a large bureaucracy in Washington.

These changes received great approval from the common people, from whom Roosevelt drew his political strength. The business community deplored them to the point where many people would not even use Roosevelt's name, but simply referred to him disgustedly as "that man in the White House." Nevertheless, he was reelected in 1936 in another landslide. He overwhelmed the hapless Republican candidate, Governor Alfred M. Landon of Kansas, and solidly swept 46 of the (then) 48 states.

But as Roosevelt entered his second term, he began to have serious political difficulties. For one thing, he tried to gain control of the U.S. Supreme Court (which had blocked some of his New Deal measures) by enlarging it considerably with appointees loyal to his administration. It didn't work. In fact, it backfired, and his "court-packing" attempt was a total humiliation. Undaunted, he pressed on with his enlargement of the role of the federal government in regulating and controlling the economy. He succeeded in "ramming through" legislation that provided for public housing, agricultural support programs, and an expansion of the power of organized labor. These were important additions to the earlier New Deal measures.

One major problem of the New Deal changes as a means of restoring prosperity to the country was that they didn't work very well. By 1938, it became clear that the country was sliding back into a recession. Roosevelt responded by initiating what he called "pump priming." He persuaded Congress to spend huge sums for make-work and welfare programs and public projects that would put the unemployed on the payroll. These measures put federal dollars into the pockets of working people, and some recovery resulted, even though the measures were very costly to the taxpayers. The country borrowed to pay its bills—a trend that continues even today.

In consequence, the Republicans began to realize what the limitations to Roosevelt's economic programs were. They began to smell just a hint of the possibility of defeating the Democrats in the next election in 1940. After all, they reasoned, Roosevelt had already been elected twice, and they would face a new Democratic candidate. Little did they know that shortly before the Democratic Convention in the summer of 1940, Roosevelt would decide to run for an unprecedented third term! Not suspecting this, the Republicans began to seek a candidate with just the right characteristics that would be needed to rout the Democrats or at least give them a run for their money.

A new area of intense debate emerged during that time, one that would have great significance for the future. It concerned the role of the United States with respect to the war that had broken out in 1939 in Europe. One large bloc of Americans—mainly conservative Republicans—were "isolationists." They demanded that the country remain completely neutral. In fact, in 1937 they succeeded in getting passed a National Neutrality Act. Roosevelt had signed the measure with misgivings. Later, as the European war intensified and Britain was threatened, he tried various ways to get around this act, with lend-lease programs and other efforts aimed at helping the British while avoiding formal hostilities with Germany. Those who sympathized with the idea of gearing up America's defenses because the country might be drawn into the war were advocates of "preparedness." The division between these two points of view was substantial and to a considerable degree paralleled party lines.

In 1940, the Republicans started with a number of contenders but eventually narrowed their field to three serious candidates for the nomination. One was Thomas Dewey, a young and aggressive district attorney from New York. He had gained the national spotlight because of his "racket-busting" activities and was acknowledged as an excellent speaker and a shrewd politician. His major shortcomings as a presidential nominee were his lack of experience in an important national office and his youth. At 37, he was so young as a possible president that Harold Ickes, the sharp-tongued Secretary of the Interior, ridiculed his candidacy by declaring that Dewey had "thrown his diaper into the ring."[1]

A formidable candidate was Ohio Senator Robert A. Taft, the son of former President William Howard Taft. He was a bitter opponent of the New Deal and an ardent isolationist. Taft's problem was his somewhat narrow political constituency. He represented the "Old Guard" among Republicans and was an outspoken advocate of a return to the "good old days" of a very limited role for government and a free-enterprise economy unbounded by the measures of the Roosevelt administration.

The "dark horse" was Wendell L. Willkie, a former Indiana farm boy who had risen in the world of business to head a giant public utilities corporation. Curiously, he had never been elected to public office or been appointed to high political position. Yet it was clear that he was an extraordinarily capable administrator and a man of considerable intelligence and personal charm. To try to gain the nomination, he had mounted a very well-financed and energetic campaign among his fellow Republicans. Willkie captured the nomination largely because the Republicans could not agree on anyone else. What finally convinced the delegates was that he had a background that would make him attractive to a broad spectrum of voters. He was not a moss-backed conservative, and he did not take a strong isolationist position. In fact, he was actually a former Democrat and something of a liberal! This caused a great deal of concern among Old Guard Republicans. In fact, it led conservative Senator Jim Watson to tell Willkie as he pushed for the nomination as the Republican presidential candidate, "Well, Wendell, you know that back home in Indiana it's alright if the town whore joins the church, but they don't let her lead the choir the first night."[2] Nevertheless, Willkie finally captured the nomination in the convention on the sixth ballot and went on to confront the mighty Roosevelt.

In many ways it was a David and Goliath battle. Roosevelt had won his party's nomination overwhelmingly on the first ballot, and he had no serious opposition.

Roosevelt was deeply entrenched; his name was known and respected throughout the nation; he was a skilled orator who made effective use of radio as a new medium of national politics; and he was a consummate politician who had crushed every previous opponent.

Willkie, on the other hand, was a brilliant and engaging man with a rather tousled and rumpled "down-home" look. He often wrote his own speeches and delivered them somewhat awkwardly at times. But he was a tireless campaigner who hammered skillfully at the significant issues where Roosevelt was weakest. In a short time, he developed a considerable national following, considering the nature of his opponent.

In the end, of course, Roosevelt won decisively. He gained 449 electoral votes to Willkie's 82. The popular vote gave Roosevelt a large margin of nearly 5 million. Willkie conceded defeat graciously and made a national plea for an end to the internal differences in the nation that had arisen during the campaign. Roosevelt admired him greatly and gave him significant roles and missions that Willkie performed in the national interest. Roosevelt even explored with him the prospects of a joint ticket in 1944. All in all, it was a great election.

## THE RESEARCH PROCEDURES

The small book in which the research project on this election was reported is titled *The People's Choice,* by Lazarsfeld, Berelson, and Gaudet. Its subtitle, *How the Voter Makes Up His Mind in a Presidential Election,* rather succinctly summarizes the main focus of the investigation. More generally, the authors state their objectives in the following terms:

> We are interested here in all those conditions which determine the political behavior of people. Briefly, our problem is this: to discover how and why people decided to vote as they did.[3]

The investigators chose the survey method to find answers to their research question. In fact, the study represents one of the most imaginative uses of survey designs and techniques in the history of social science.

The methodology and techniques of survey research have proven to be one of the most significant contributions of the social sciences to the study of human behavior in the twentieth century. The use of this research tool began with the primitive surveys among mining families in France during the last century and early in the new century with Charles Booth's exhaustive studies of London's poor. However, it was during the 1920s that the basic techniques of modern survey research were finally put together. Sampling theory and applied procedures had been developed by statisticians and had come into use by scientists in many fields. The idea of sampling was combined with systematic interviewing procedures and adapted for use in many kinds of sociological studies. This new approach to social research was so effective that it was quickly adopted by public opinion pollsters, market researchers, and many other professionals interested in assessing the characteristics, behavior, or ideas of large aggregates of people. Combined with procedures for statistical analysis and control, it came to rival the experiment as a major tool of social and behavioral science.

By the time of the election of 1940, the survey method had been highly refined and was little different from what it is today. Its major pitfalls and limitations had become increasingly understood, along with its numerous advantages. As we noted, the study of mass communication and political behavior that was conducted during the presidential election by Paul F. Lazarsfeld and his associates, using the survey method, represents a remarkable appreciation of this research strategy. Their sophisticated study still stands as a monument to good survey research and represents a high point of innovation and precision in the study of the effects of mass communication during a presidential political campaign. The investigators were able to probe deeply into the influence of political propaganda presented by the media as voters pondered their choice of a candidate.

The study was funded by the Rockefeller Foundation, Columbia University's Office of Radio Research, *Life* magazine, and Elmo Roper, the public opinion analyst. The investigation was on a large scale. It made use of a professional field staff and 15 locally hired but carefully trained interviewers. Some 3,000 households were initially contacted to gain data that would be used in designing the study. Later, repeated interviews would be held with samples of these people, In an era before computers were available, organizing, processing, and interpreting the mass of statistical data assembled from thousands of detailed interviews was a formidable task. The first version of the results was not available in published form for four years.

## Erie County, Ohio

The researchers had to select a site for their investigation. They reviewed many possibilities and finally settled on a small county in Ohio. In 1940, Erie County had a culturally homogeneous population of about 43,000. Its population size had been stable for about 40 years; its inhabitants were almost all white and almost evenly divided between farming people and those involved in the industrial labor force.

Erie County is located in the northern part of the state on the lake of the same name. It is about halfway between Cleveland and Toledo. The main city, Sandusky, with its population at that time of 25,000, was both the county seat and principal industrial center. There were three newspapers in Sandusky, but many people read the *Cleveland Plain Dealer.* Radio stations from Cleveland and Toledo were received clearly, and all major networks were represented.

Erie County had one additional characteristic that intrigued the investigators considerably. *In every presidential election in the twentieth century, the county had deviated very little from the national voting patterns.* The authors of *The People's Choice* disclaimed this as one of their main reasons for selecting Erie

County as the site of their research. However, the county's representative voting patterns were certainly a plus in using the results of the study to interpret the relationship between the media and political behavior on a wider basis. The researchers maintained that Erie County was finally chosen because it was small enough to permit effective supervision of interviewers; free from sectional peculiarities; not dominated by a large urban center; and diverse enough in terms of its rural-urban split to make meaningful comparisons possible.

## The Panel Design

In May 1940, every fourth house in Erie County was visited by an interviewer. The results of these initial contacts permitted the investigators to select some 3,000 persons in such a way that they were representative of the county as a whole. The key variables in this determination were age, sex, rural-urban residence, education, nativity, telephone ownership, and automobile ownership.

From these 3,000 individuals, four separate stratified samples of 600 persons were drawn. Each of these samples was matched in such a way that all four were like each other and representative of the county as a whole. The four samples were called "panels" because they were used to construct an innovative *panel design.* The purpose of this special research design was to provide effective controls to assess the effects of repeated interviewing. It must be kept in mind that the purpose of the research was to study the formation of voting decisions *over time.* In more specific terms, this meant observing respondents repeatedly between May, at the start of the campaign, through early November, the time of the actual election.

The procedure used to make such repeated observations was a monthly survey, in which the same individuals were interviewed as the campaign progressed. It was an excellent idea, because each subject could be interviewed before making a decision for whom to vote, again at the time of that decision, and after the decision had been made. The role of the mass-communicated political propaganda could be related to political behavior at each of these stages. The only problem with repeated observations is that they might be an influence on the very process under study. Perhaps, it was hypothesized, the voter who was interviewed repeatedly over a seven-month span would reach different decisions and see the issues differently than one who was not interviewed, or interviewed only once.

The panel design was an ingenious method for discovering whether, and to what extent, such repeated interviews did influence decisions about the election. The general idea was to use one sample of 600 subjects as the "main panel" to be interviewed every month, from May to November. However, another panel of 600 (Control A) was to be interviewed during the third month (July). The results of a number of key variables could then be compared to see if the main panel differed, and to what degree, from the main control panel.

As shown in Figure 4.1, the same thing was done during the fourth month (August) using Control B. Finally, in October, Control C was interviewed along

|  | May | June | July | August | September | October | November |
|---|---|---|---|---|---|---|---|
| Timetable |  | REP. CONVEN. | DEM. CONVEN. |  |  | ELECTION |  |
| Interview Number | 1 | 2 | 3 | 4 | 5 | 6 | 7 |
| Group | Total | Main Panel 600 | Main Panel 600 | Main Panel 600 | Main Panel 600 | Main Panel 600 | Main Panel 600 |
| Interviewed | Poll (3,000) |  | Control A 600 | Control B 600 |  | Control C 600 |  |

**FIGURE 4.1** Outline of the panel design and schedule of interviews

SOURCE: Paul F. Lazarsfeld, Bernard Berelson, and Hazel Gaudet, *The People's Choice: How the Voter Makes Up His Mind in a Presidential Election* (New York: Columbia University Press, 1948), p. 4.

with the main panel. Overall, then, 600 people were under repeated monthly observation with seven interviews between May and November. Three other panels of 600 each were interviewed as controls in July, August, and October, respectively. The final interview with the main panel was just after the election in November.

As it turned out, the interviews with the matched control panels showed few differences from the results obtained with the main panels. In other words, the repeated interviews did not seem to have any notable influence on the behavior of the voters who were studied month after month.[4] This finding laid to rest any suspicions that the interviewing itself changed the decisions or the behavior of the main panel. Although it was an expensive procedure, the additional interviewing with the controls did provide larger numbers of cases on which to base conclusions on many of the issues under study.

The most significant aspect of the panel technique was that a given individual could be followed longitudinally over the time period of the election as he or she became interested in the election, began to pay attention to the media campaign, was influenced by others, reached a decision, possibly wavered or changed sides, and finally voted. The usual one-shot survey cannot provide such data over time. The same is true of an experiment that is particularly difficult to repeat with the same subjects. As the authors put it, the panel design was an effective method for studying a whole list of questions:

What is the effect of social status upon vote? How are people influenced by the party conventions and the nominations? What role does formal propaganda play? How about the press and radio? What of the influence of family and friends? Where do issues come in, and how? Why do some people settle their vote early and some late? In short, how do votes develop? Why do people vote as they do?[5]

Neither the research report of the investigators nor the summary of their work in the present chapter provides full and complete answers to all these questions. Nevertheless, a number of important insights into many of the issues can be summarized.

## THE RESULTS

Generally, the findings obtained in this large-scale study can be divided into two broad categories: those that help us in understanding the voters themselves and the forces that influenced their political ideas and behavior, and the role of the mass media political propaganda in helping to shape their voting decisions. The sections that follow present the highlights of what the results revealed.

### Assessing Participation in the Election

Political life in the United States was more predictable before World War II than it has been since. Generally, the country had been dominated by the Republican Party until Roosevelt won in 1932. After Woodrow Wilson left the White House, a series of Republican presidents—Harding, Coolidge, and Hoover—were all more or less firmly committed to the idea that "the business of America is business." In other words, the route to national prosperity and a more abundant society was held to be through fostering private enterprise, limiting the role of government, and avoiding participation in the troubles of foreign nations. It was a conservative philosophy, but for decades it had seemed to work. Until the crash of 1929, the country had experienced rather steady growth.

When the Great Depression shattered the economy, Franklin Roosevelt put together a broad coalition of organized labor, northern blacks, liberal Jews, and a huge base of poor people who had not previously been politically active. With the country reeling from hard times, it had not been difficult to pin the blame on Hoover and the Republicans and to formulate and implement Roosevelt's New Deal. He sharply elevated the role of government in regulating business, gave increasing power to organized labor, brought considerable change to the federal income tax structure, and developed a national welfare system. These moves polarized the two parties. Later, his strong sentiments and policies concerning national defense preparedness and sympathy toward aiding Britain further split the two groups. These clear differences in the ideologies and composition of the two parties led the researchers to look for social characteristics of voters that would predispose them to lean toward one candidate or the other.

***Social Categories and Voting Predispositions.***    Following the lead that the social composition of the two parties differed, the hypothesis was formulated that those who intended to vote as Republicans or Democrats would differ in *socioeconomic status,* and that such SES differences would predispose them to vote in one way or the other regardless of who the candidates were. *Religion* provided another such variable. Republicans and those inclined toward their views were more likely to be Protestant, while Catholics were more likely to favor the Democrats. Other variables that would predispose voters in this way were thought to be *rural-urban residence* (with farmers more likely to vote Republican), *occupation* (with blue-collar laborers more likely to be sympathetic toward the Democratic candidate), and *age* (with older people more conservative generally and more likely to lean toward the Republican candidate). Each of these possibilities was examined with care to see how it correlated with claimed party affiliation and an intended vote for the Democratic or Republican candidate.

Generally, the variables were interrelated in a number of complex ways, but the following summary provides an overview of the general picture:

1. Those high in socioeconomic level (SES) were more likely to intend to vote Republican than Democratic.
2. Fewer laborers than white-collar workers intended to vote Republican. (However, if SES level was held constant, occupation seemed to make little difference).
3. Self-identification made a difference. Persons who felt that they belonged to "the business class" generally intended to vote Republican. If self-identification was with "the laboring class," the intention was more likely to be Democratic (regardless of the actual occupation of the person).
4. Religious category was a strong influence on voting intention. At all levels of SES and among all occupations, Catholics leaned toward a Democratic vote and Protestants toward the Republicans.
5. Age was very significant as a predictor of intended voting patterns. Among both Protestants and Catholics, younger people leaned toward the Democrats and the older toward the Republicans.

These complex relationships were painstakingly sorted out and illustrated with bar charts based on simple percentage comparisons. Armed with today's linear models for multivariate analysis, and a computer to do the "slave labor" of computation, a far more efficient analysis would be possible. Nevertheless, the overall finding that emerged was expressed elegantly enough: "Different social characteristics, different votes."[6]

***An Index of Political Predisposition.***   The predisposing factors noted above made it possible to develop for each subject an index of the likelihood of a Democratic or a Republican vote. This was done before knowing how the person actually voted in November, basing the predictions on the hypothesis that the variables would be predictive. Later, three of the factors were found to have provided the greatest predictive value. These were SES, religion, and rural-urban residence. For each person, the researchers constructed an index of political predisposition (IPP) and used this in studying the way in which the subjects reached their voting decisions. The index classified the voters into six categories:

(1) strongly Republican, (2) moderately Republican, (3) slightly Republican, (4) slightly Democratic, (5) moderately Democratic, and (6) strongly Democratic. For example, a person was classified in category (1) if he or she was a rich Protestant farmer. At the other end, a person was in category (6) if he or she was a Catholic laborer living in Sandusky. (Category 7 was combined with 6.) Others were in the intermediate categories, depending on their SES level and their mix of the other critical factors.

This IPP proved to be remarkably well correlated with vote intention. Figure 4.2 shows the relationship. Clearly, the social composition of the public made a considerable difference. Later, the way in which these predispositions led people to attend and respond to media propaganda in different patterns will be brought out.

The concept of political predisposition based on social categories was to prove valuable in understanding the process by which people initially formed and then solidified their vote intention, even if they themselves did not know what they were going to do initially. The simple fact is that most eventually went in the direction predicted by their IPP category. Their social categories led them to be selective in their exposure to media propaganda and selective in influences from other people. This was clearest for people toward the ends of the scale, but considerably less clear for those subjected to conflicting forces if they were somewhere in the middle categories.

**FIGURE 4.2**  Political predisposition and voting pattern

SOURCE: Paul F. Lazarsfeld, Bernard Berelson, and Hazel Gaudet, *The People's Choice: How the Voter Makes Up His Mind in a Presidential Election* (New York: Columbia University Press, 1948), p. 26.

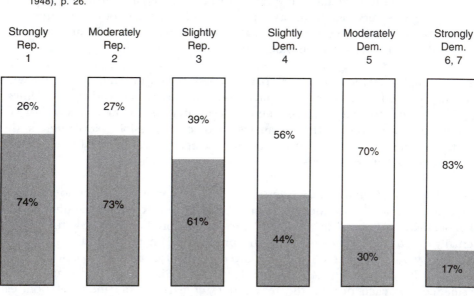

***Democratic and Republican Ideas about Public Affairs.***    Not all voters are aware of the critical issues confronting their nation, even during a presidential election when the issues are receiving heavy attention in the campaign. However, thinking about the issues does make a difference in voting intentions and behavior. Those leaning toward the Republicans or the Democrats had different ideas about social and economic matters in 1940, and the researchers tried carefully to probe these differences in awareness and thinking to see how they influenced vote intention. For example, on such issues as "unemployment," "relief" (welfare), and the WPA (a make-work program using federal funds to reduce unemployment), members of both parties conceded a Roosevelt victory to the poor, who after all were the recipients of such measures. However, the Republicans did not feel that these were the kinds of people who should be helped by federal expenditures. Republicans wanted a more favorable climate for business rather than increased expenditures on social benefits for the needy. On the other hand, more than half of the Democrats felt that a Willkie victory would benefit only business groups and the relatively well-to-do. Republicans tended to deny this and maintain that stimulating business would provide more jobs and consequently a more prosperous nation. In short, both groups tended to see Willkie as a pro business candidate and Roosevelt as a working family candidate. Thus, the rich man versus poor man theme was salient during the entire campaign.

The war in Europe also provided ample grounds for political differences. We noted earlier that one large segment of the society was "isolationist" and wanted to stay completely clear of the "mess in Europe." Another part of the population felt that Hitler's and Mussolini's totalitarianism was threatening to overwhelm democracy in Europe and that it was only a matter of time until America would have to become involved. With these isolationist versus interventionist views in the background, Republicans generally opposed the recently passed conscription (draft) bill, and were against increases in military aid to Britain. Democrats, on the other hand, were behind various measures related to "national preparedness" and efforts to aid Britain. Military participation in the war, however, was not thought by either party to be likely in the near future.

In addition to the domestic economy and national defense, there was a host of other issues on which Democrats and Republicans found themselves on different sides. Roosevelt's third term was one. Farm issues and policies toward labor were others. The strikingly different personalities of the candidates appealed to different types of voters. Willkie's lack of experience in foreign affairs troubled some; his strong business background attracted others. Roosevelt's boldness in reshaping American government put some people off; his imaginative leadership made a great deal of sense to others.

These were the kinds of issues around which the media campaign was organized. Each of these topics provided the basis for newspaper editorials, radio commentaries, magazine articles, movie newsreels, political speeches, and arguments between friends. They were debated in every setting from dingy barrooms to lofty mansions. And it was these issues that provided the grounds upon which people formed their opinions, reached a decision concerning their vote, decided to remain aloof, shifted from one candidate to another, or remained firm in their resolve.

Before the media campaign could interact with predispositions of the voters, however, their interest in the election had to be stimulated sufficiently so that they would attend. Not everyone was equally interested at the outset. In fact, interest in the election was a function of a number of variables.

*Variables Related to Interest in the Election.*    The social composition of the parties and their opinions about the issues are not the only significant factors that shape a presidential election. The level of interest in the election and the campaign is also critical. Throughout the interviewing, program data were collected to try to assess what variables—what categories of people or their personal characteristics—would provide the best index of their interest in the election. As it turned out, the best predictor was the simplest of all: the respondent's self-rating of his or her level of interest. During the interviews, the respondents were asked to classify themselves according to their level of interest. In other words, people were asked to indicate whether they had (1) great, (2) moderate, (3) mild, or (4) no interest in the election. These four were later reduced to three by combining moderate and mild. This provided only a crude ordinal measure of level of interest, but the researchers justified the procedure by their findings. Those who claimed the highest level of interest were more familiar with the issues and had clearer opinions that those who claimed less interest. The most interested also participated more in election events and were more likely to attend to political communications and discuss them with others.

Interest was also related to some of the social categories discussed earlier. For example, both a higher SES and educational level were positively correlated with interest. The least interested respondents tended to be the poor and the relatively uneducated. Urban versus rural residence was not a predictor of level of interest, but age certainly was. Regardless of educational level and nearly everything else, it was the older respondents who had the highest level of interest in the election. Finally, men were more interested than women.

Level of interest was a good predictor of actual participation in the voting. As might be suspected, the greatest proportion of nonvoters was found at the lowest level of interest. Figure 4.3 shows the dramatic impact of this variable. It can be added that nonvoting tended to be deliberate rather than accidental or unwitting. In two out of every three cases of nonvoting, the respondents had indicated their intention not to vote early in the campaign. There were, in 1940, factors operating to produce alienation among at least some citizens.

## Factors Influencing Voters at the Time of Final Decision

A respondent's level of interest in the campaign was a good indicator of how *early* or *late* he or she reached a final decision concerning which candidate to vote for. Another strong factor at the time of final decision was the degree to

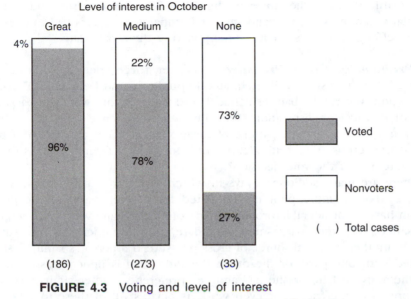

**FIGURE 4.3**   Voting and level of interest

SOURCE: Paul F. Lazarsfeld, Bernard Berelson, and Hazel Gaudet, *The People's Choice: How the Voter Makes Up His Mind in a Presidential Election* (New York: Columbia University Press, 1948), p. 46.

which the person was caught in *cross pressures,* or, in other words, conflicts and inconsistencies among the variables that influence vote decision.

***Early versus Late Decisions.***   The more interested people were in the election, the earlier they reached a decision as to how they would vote. This held true regardless of party affiliation or other factors. Nearly two-thirds of the respondents with a "great deal" of interest in the election had already made up their minds by May when the interviewing began (even though the nominees had not yet been selected in their respective conventions). Only one-eighth of such respondents waited until late in the campaign to make their choice. As we will note later, this closing of the mind early in the campaign was an important condition, because it had a strong influence on their mass communication behavior with respect to selecting political propaganda from the media.

On the other side of the coin, those with less interest decided on their candidates much later. This posed some interesting problems for those in charge of the media campaigns. How could these people whose minds remained open be attracted to a particular candidate? One difficulty was that even though they were uncommitted, they were also uninterested. This meant that they paid little attention to political propaganda. At the same time, in a close election their votes could spell the difference between victory and defeat.

Toward the end of the campaign, the pool of such uninterested and undecided potential voters grew smaller and smaller. Campaign managers had to exert their greatest efforts to interest people in supporting their candidate.

***The Problem of Cross Pressures.***     Earlier, three specific variables were discussed that most sharply differentiated Republicans and Democrats. These were SES, religion, and rural-urban residence. These three factors were the basis of the index of political predisposition (IPP). But what happened when an individual was caught in a conflicting pattern of these variables? For example, if a person is both prosperous and a Catholic, or both poor and a farmer, what is the most likely outcome of the vote decision?

There are many additional ways in which a person can be caught in cross pressures. For example, people who voted for a given party in the previous election have a considerable probability of voting the same way again. Yet, if they are disaffected by their party's new candidate, they are under cross pressure. The family is another potential source of cross pressure. If a person's family is strongly affiliated with one party or the other, the individual is under pressure to vote with them, even if he or she has another preference. Other similar sources of cross pressures are friends or even work associates. All of these together make up a considerable web of potential cross pressures, some stemming from social categories and some from social relationships.

But whatever the source of such cross pressures, one effect was clear. Cross pressures *delayed* the voter's final decision. Among the various sources of cross pressures, the most influential in causing delays was the family. The reluctance of many voters to commit themselves to a particular candidate was often traceable to exactly this kind of difference with family members.

Cross pressures and their associated delays have implications for the media campaign of political propaganda. Voters under cross pressures delay their vote hoping that some event will occur to resolve their indecision. This indecision makes these voters fair game for political managers, who hope to get into their propaganda just the right message to break the indecision and attract the person to their candidate. Toward the end of the campaign, efforts are intensified to attract undecided voters, and these efforts can pay off. Thus, both the potential voter with low interest in the campaign and those under cross pressure become targets of special efforts as the media campaign begins to come to an end.

The overall effects of low interest and cross pressures were very different for different kinds of voters. In other words, the process of delay did not work in the same way for all people. Some remained undecided until the last moment. Others moved tentatively to one candidate but then shifted later to the other. Still others reached a decision, fell back into doubt, went over to the other side, and eventually shifted back to the earlier choice. For the most part, there were three main patterns of changes that described such voters. Some 28 percent were *crystallizers*. They simply delayed reaching a decision until the last minute. These were evenly divided between the parties. Another 15 percent were *waverers*. They started out in May with a clear vote intention. Later in the campaign they slid back into indecision, but later returned to their original choice. Finally, a smaller proportion (8 percent) were *party changers*. They started out with a clear vote intention but eventually deserted to the other candidate. The simplest generalization that emerged from all of these data was that individuals who leave their party and fall into indecision usually return to their first choice. Those who change from one party to another, however, seldom return.

## Major Effects of the Media Campaign

One of the main results of the study was to identify three clear patterns of influence of the mass-mediated campaign of political propaganda. These patterns describe the way in which mass-mediated information can play key roles in leading voters to form voting decisions, given their existing pattern of political predispositions. In other words, there is a considerable amount of interaction between the predisposing social characteristics of voters, what they select and use from the political propaganda presented by the media, and their ultimate voting choice. These complex relationships can best be understood by examining three concepts that identify the patterns of influence of the mediated propaganda. These are *activation, reinforcement,* and *conversion.*

*Activation.*    Political communications activate latent predispositions. They do so by presenting effective arguments to people who selectively attend to them because they are consistent with their predisposing orientations. This is true both for formal propaganda presented by mass-mediated campaigns and more personal persuasion presented by family members or friends.

Activation refers to the process of making something manifest or observable. In the case of a voter, it refers to bringing the individual to a conscious decision that is consistent with the kinds of predisposing variables identified earlier as making up the IPP. Since about half of the voters had already made up their minds in May, and some never did reach a decision, activation took place only among a limited number of voters. The best estimate places it at about 14 percent among the people studied.

The activation of political predispositions is a process that takes place in stages or steps. These steps identify the relationship between the voter's latent predispositions and political persuasion presented as either media propaganda or personal influences:

1. *Propaganda arouses interest.* We showed earlier that interest was a key variable in reaching a decision to vote. Thus, a rising level of propaganda gets attention and begins to increase interest.
2. *Increased interest brings increased exposure.* This is a circular effect. The more people pay attention, the more interesting the campaign becomes, and this increases their interest even more.
3. *Increased attention causes the voter to select information.* As interest and attention increase, the more likely it is that the voter will select

information consistent with his or her underlying predispositions. Thus, selective attention reinforces predispositions, which in turn increases selectivity.

4. *Votes crystallize.* The latent becomes manifest. The voter is now aware of the candidate and the candidate's position on the issues. This awareness is highly selective, but it leads to the forming of a decision based on a body of information.

The process of activation is somewhat inconsistent with the concept of the "rational" voter, supposedly the ideal in a democratic society. Such ideal voters would review carefully the issues and the candidates and make a decision on the basis of enlightened self-interest only after learning and assessing all of the facts. Activation, on the other hand, takes place because voters already are strongly predisposed to one party or the other and they crystallize their vote to support that party's candidate. It is hardly a rational model, because the opposition is given little systematic consideration. Nevertheless, activation is one of the principal effects that results from the flow of information during a political campaign.

*Reinforcement.*   More than half of the voters had already consciously selected their candidate before the interviewing began in May. They were not certain who their party would select in the convention, but they intended to vote for him in any case. For those people the propaganda campaign served quite another purpose. Campaign managers have to supply such already-decided voters with a continuing flow of arguments and justifications for remaining right where they are. This is a very important function of the media campaign. We noted that about half of the people interviewed already knew in May for whom they would vote. If such partisans are not kept in line, they could become waverers, or even worse, party changers. As the researchers put it:

> Party propaganda—from his own party—provides an arsenal of political arguments which serve to allay the partisan's doubts and to refute the opposition arguments which he encounters in exposure to media and friends—in short, to secure and stabilize and solidify his vote intention and translate it into an actual vote. A continuing flow of partisan arguments enables him to reinterpret otherwise unsettling events and counterarguments so that they do not leave him in an uncomfortable state of mental indecision or inconsistency.[7]

Generally, then, reinforcement is far less dramatic than the process of persuading voters to desert their party for the other camp. However, because such a large proportion of the voters are involved, it is far more important. A failure to understand the reinforcement effects of political propaganda could easily cost a candidate the election.

*Conversion.*   When ordinary people think of the influence of political propaganda, they usually have conversion in mind. Through the clever use of words, emotional appeals, or even rational arguments, it is assumed, individuals can be persuaded to desert their candidate and switch sides. But does it really happen? The answer is a highly qualified "yes," but only in a few cases and in particular circumstances. In Erie County, there were people who were converted, but they were few indeed. Only about 8 percent of the voters made a switch.

There are a number of reasons why it is unrealistic to look for large numbers of conversions. For one thing, fully half of the voters never wavered from their early decisions, making them unavailable for conversion attempts. Clear-cut political predispositions anchor another large proportion of voters in their party, even though they remain undecided and undergo the process of activation and eventually reach a decision that is entirely consistent with those predispositions: These voters are not open to conversion. Only those who remained less interested and who were under strong cross pressures were the prospects for conversion when they did reach a tentative decision. In such decisions, their commitments were weak, unsupported by strong interest, ties to a party, or a consistent network of social pressures. The numbers of such people grew smaller and smaller as activation and reinforcement took place, as interest grew stronger, and as cross pressures were resolved. In the final stages, only a handful could be persuaded to switch from an earlier tentative vote decision. For the most part, the authors concluded, the completely open-minded voter who remains undecided until the end, or who switches from one candidate to another because of compelling logic in the discussion of issues, exists only in textbooks on civics.

*Overall Effects.*   The speeches, newspaper editorials, magazine articles, radio talks, and all the rest making up the presidential campaign had three principal effects. They activated the indifferent voter who was predisposed, reinforced the partisans, and converted a few of the doubtful. For Erie County as a whole, the Republicans made gains over their pattern of support in the election that had been held four years earlier. The 1936 election had been a considerable victory for Roosevelt in the county. Basically, his modifications of the American economic and governmental institutions made during his first term were well received by the electorate. But events since 1936 had, to a degree, dimmed that enthusiasm. The issues of the third term, the slow recovery from the Depression, the war clouds in Europe, and the unknowns of the new welfare state troubled many people in Erie County. For these reasons they had returned in the direction of their basically conservative orientations of the past. Nationwide, of course, the election went overwhelmingly to Roosevelt. However, the conservatives of Erie County decided that their day would come at a later time.

## Patterns of Attention to Campaign Propaganda

Those who design and manage presidential campaigns devise detailed, compre-hensive, and sophisticated strategies in their efforts to attract the votes of the electorate to their candidate. This was as true in 1940 as it is now. At that time, of course, television was only an experimental device being studied in laboratories and test sites. The media of the campaign were radio, newspapers, and magazines. And, in the case of magazines, the country was still in the era of the general, huge-circulation periodical, such as the *Saturday Evening Post.* Some specialty magazines, such as the *Farm Journal,* also played a role.

Whatever the medium, the purpose of political propaganda is to capture the attention, whet the interest, and shape the decisions of voters. As the authors of *The People's Choice* put it, political messages are designed

> . . . to corral the timid, lead the willing, and convince the reluctant. Partisan leaders of opinion—the newspaper editor, the columnist, the free-lance writer, the syndicated cartoonist, the radio commentator, and the local sage—all edge into the campaign by placing the weight of their authority behind the cause of their favorite candidate. Propaganda is let loose upon the land to control or inform, to constrain or tease poten-tial voters into the appropriate decision.[8]

In other words, an enormous amount of political information is transmitted by the media at election time. However, the big question is not how much was printed, broadcast, or said, but how many in the audience attended and under-stood that information. The big question also includes another issue. Was the media exposure more or less evenly spread through the population, or was it concentrated more among some kinds of people?

This last issue is one with considerable theoretical relevance. Early thinking about propaganda was that, like magic bullets, it struck all members of the mass audience equally and created uniform effects among them in a very direct way. This idea was, as we have seen, under considerable question by the time the present research was undertaken. However, the research strategy of *The People's Choice*—in particular, the repeated interviewing—permitted the researchers to address fairly directly the question of who attended to a particular medium and with what outcome. It was an opportunity, in other words, to test the major propositions of the magic bullet theory. To be historically accurate, *The People's Choice* researchers did not actually pose their investigation of patterns of media attention in those terms. They simply wanted to know whether every voter received a more or less equal exposure to the media, or whether attention to the campaign was concentrated among a few. And, if the latter were the case, who were they, and what did the exposure do to them? Yet, in retrospect, their study *did* test the magic bullet theory, even if the authors did not specifically set out to do so at the time.

An associated issue under investigation in 1940 was the question of the relative importance of the three major media. Did people attend to radio, the newspapers, or magazines in an equal manner, or was one a dominant source of political information for certain kinds of people? Answers to these several questions were provided as the analysis examined the formation of decisions about choosing a candidate in relation to patterns of attention to mediated propaganda.

***The Concentration of Exposure.***    Who listened and who read? Those were critical questions concerning the outpouring of political information during the election. The answer was that close attention was given to the media propaganda by some but certainly not all. The pattern was dependent upon what medium, what candidate, what issues, and what voters were under consideration. Patterns of attention, in other words, were very *selective.* They were by no means spread evenly among the electorate. For example, during the last 12 days of the campaign, 54 percent of the respondents had attended to at least one political talk on radio; another 51 percent had read at least one front page campaign story in a news-paper; and 26 percent had read a campaign-related article in a magazine. Earlier in the campaign, such material had been ignored by one-half to three-fourths of the population interviewed. But even in the last days of the campaign, only part of the voters attended to any of the material, and a very large proportion ignored the media campaign altogether. In other words, as the campaign moved into its last days, a flood of political material was directed at the voters. But, as the researchers put it, "far from drowning any of these people, it did not even get their feet wet."[9]

Who were the people who did attend to the messages? Actually, with remarkable consistency, political propaganda presented by the various media reached the *same* segment of the population. In other words, those who listened to material about the campaign on the radio also tended to read about the same issues in the newspapers and follow the treatments of the topics in magazine stories. Thus, there was a segment of the population that was heavily exposed to the campaign propaganda whereas the remainder gave the same material only little, if any, attention.

Who were these people who received multiple exposure? The answers to that question have already been suggested in previous analyses of the process by which people arrive at their voting decision. Those who attended most to the media were the *highly interested* voters, those who had *already decided,* and those of *higher SES.* In particular among those categories, it was the more affluent, well-educated, and older males who lived in urban areas.

There are a number of possible explanations for this pattern of concentration of attention among particular kinds of voters. The researchers suggested that such people probably believe that they have an especially large stake in the outcome of the election. Certainly, they tend to be more politically aware, and they have a deeper understanding of the issues. But whatever the explanation of this particular pattern of concentration, it was clear that the propositions of the magic bullet theory concerning uniform patterns of attention and influence from the media were not consistent with the findings. So much for the magic bullet theory!

***Radio versus Print.***   The study of the presidential election provided one of the first large-scale investigations of what was, in 1940, still a relatively new medium of mass communication. Radio was compared with newspapers (and magazines) in terms of their comparative roles in the campaign. No one really understood radio as an instrument of politics. Ten years earlier, only about 40 percent of American homes had radio ownership. By 1940, that figure had risen so rapidly that virtually everyone had a receiver. In fact, the figure in that year was 1.4 sets per household, on the average, in the United States. In a decade, radio had become a giant and had saturated the American population.

But how did this new medium compare with the venerable newspaper? After all, the mass newspaper had been around for a century. Its role in politics was virtually undisputed. In 1940, newspapers were still close to their all-time peak of popularity in American society. Only a decade earlier, Americans had subscribed to daily newspapers at near-record levels of 1.32 per household. In the highest year, 1910, the figure had been 1.36 subscriptions per household; in 1940, the figure was still high, at 1.18. This compares to a mere 0.62 subscriptions per household in 1994.

Some had begun to claim that radio was the medium of the future in politics, and that even in 1940 it was more meaningful than print in the campaign because the audiences could hear the speeches of the candidates and get a feeling for their personal qualities far more than reading about them. Others felt that the printed word still retained its authority and that a mere gadget like radio could never replace the newspaper as a medium for the serious presentation and exchange of political ideas.

The researchers decided to sort out this question—to try to find out to what media people had attended and how much they had been influenced by these media. They proceeded by getting people to identify in very specific terms exactly what newspaper editorials, news stories, or speeches they had read, and how this exposure had influenced their thinking about the issues. They probed into what magazine stories the voters had read, what kinds of information they had learned from such sources, and how this had helped shape their political views. They also had their respondents indicate what particular programs they had listened to on the radio—what speeches they had heard, what commentaries, and so forth. By such detailed assessment of the exposure patterns for each medium among various categories of voters, the relative role and comparative significance of newspapers, magazines, and radio could be determined.

As it turned out, radio had played a larger role in the campaign than anyone had suspected. When respondents were asked which media were "helpful" as they were making their decisions, about two-thirds mentioned both radio and newspapers about equally. However, when the voters were asked to indicate which of the media was the "most important" source for political information that played a part in their decisions, radio clearly led (by roughly a 50 percent margin).

Radio was also more heavily used by the Democrats. In both 1936 and 1940, the majority of the nation's newspapers openly supported the Republicans. Presumably, this was because of the close ties newspapers had to the business community. Meanwhile, Democrats had turned to radio as an alternative. Roosevelt, in particular, used the medium masterly as a political tool. He often went on the air to explain his programs to the nation. He held periodic "fireside chats" via radio, in which he spoke informally concerning the issues of the day. Because of these "fireside chats," his voice was well known to almost everyone. Willkie, on the other hand, was not an effective radio personality, and this hurt him in the election.

In the final analysis, radio emerged as a medium favored by the Democrats, and newspapers were favored by the Republicans. But in spite of the overwhelming support given by newspapers to the Republican candidate, he lost badly. Radio emerged as a politically potent medium with considerably greater significance than the printed page. It was the beginning of an era in which the personal qualities of the candidates could come under the close scrutiny of the electorate via a medium of telecommunication, bringing the personality of the presidential hopeful to a level of significance not known in earlier times.

It can be added that magazines played a minor role in the election. Some 15 to 25 percent of the respondents obtained political information from magazines. For those individuals, magazines did play a part in shaping their political views and decisions, along with exposure to political propaganda from the other media. In other words, few voters, if any, relied solely on magazines for their information. They used them to supplement information obtained from newspapers and radio.

## Personal Influence and the Two-Step Flow

As the interviewing progressed month after month in Erie County, it became increasingly apparent that there were sources of influence on people's political decisions that had not been given sufficient attention when planning the study. The interviewers were discovering that people received a great deal of their information and influence directly from other people! Whenever the respondents were asked to report on their recent exposure to political communications, they mentioned discussions about politics with friends, relatives, or acquaintances much more frequently than exposure to radio or print. Face-to-face discussions were a more important source of political influence than the researchers had anticipated.

The significance of personal influence was not realized until the study was well under way. It was a serendipitous finding that simply emerged as the research was in progress. For that reason, no formal hypotheses had been built into the study to assess this phenomenon. However, once the investigators realized that people were talking to each other extensively about the election, and that these interpersonal exchanges played a key role in leading the voters to their decisions, they quickly revised what they were doing and gathered as much data concerning this interpersonal flow of information and influence as they could.

The hypothesis the investigators developed would have a significant impact on the direction of mass communication research for many years. They called it the "two-step flow of communication." After examining their data they concluded that some individuals among the people they had studied were serving as "opinion leaders." These were people who were heavily exposed to the political campaign to whom others, who had lower levels of exposure, knowledge, and interest, would turn for information and advice. The opinion leaders would pass on to these others information that they had received from firsthand exposure to the media, along with their own special interpretations of what it all meant. Thus, the heavy involvement of people in political discussions led the researchers to suggest that "ideas often flow *from* radio and print *to* the opinion leaders and *from* them to the less active sections of the population."[10] This was their formal statement of the two-step flow hypothesis.

There were a number of reasons, the researchers pointed out, why personal influence would be particularly effective in helping shape people's decisions—in many cases, much more effective than persuasive information presented in more formal media. For example, personal influence from opinion leaders was more likely to reach the undecided and the uninterested voter, both of whom were all but impervious to the political campaign presented via the media. The opinion leaders were also likely to be trusted as nonpurposive sources of information and interpretation. Political propaganda presented by radio and print, on the other hand, is clearly designed to persuade and is therefore not trustworthy. There is also the factor of flexibility. In a casual discussion setting, the person giving another his or her views can be very flexible and counter resistance that might occur—a fact well known by all effective sales people. The factor of reward can be added. When one agrees with or accepts the views or interpretations of another who is trying to "set us straight," a considerable amount of social approval is likely to be forthcoming. It is rewarding to accept personal influence; yet this factor is absent in more formal media presentations. Finally, one seldom mistrusts an intimate source. This may be largely because those who exercise personal influence do it unwittingly. And those whose views are modified may not even realize that this is happening to them. Generally, then, as information moves from the media to the opinion leaders and from them to the less active, the idea that they are engaging in political persuasion or are accepting political influence may never cross their minds.

## CONCLUSIONS AND IMPLICATIONS

*The People's Choice* was one of the most important studies in the history of mass communication research for several reasons. First, it showed how an innovative survey design could be used in longitudinal research. Many important forms of social behavior are processes that take place over time. Typically, researchers study subjects with an experiment or a survey at only one point in that time. Sometimes, to try and get around that limitation, they will study different samples of people representing cohorts at different stages in the process, but this has many pitfalls. The panel design used in *The People's Choice* got around those limitations and pitfalls by following the same subjects through the entire process. The design effectively answered the question of which influences were introduced by the repeated assessments. The answer in this case was none. Although there is no guarantee that repeated interviewing will never influence subjects, the panel design continues to be a major procedure used in longitudinal research.

A second major contribution of the research was its insights into the role of political propaganda presented by the media during the campaign. The findings showed clearly that such propaganda activated those with latent predispositions based on social category membership; reinforced those whose decisions were already firmly anchored by the constraints of those category memberships; and even swayed a few to move from one side to the other. The conversion process, however, was shown to be very limited. It occurred mainly among voters who had made a tentative earlier choice to which they were only weakly tied. Such individuals were not much interested in the campaign, and they were under confusing cross pressures from their social category memberships.

These findings on selective influences based on social categories were to prove to be theoretically significant in ways that the researchers of the time could not appreciate. Activation and reinforcement—the principal media effects according to the study—are really quite limited by comparison with the kinds of effects of the media envisioned by the critics of World War I propaganda. The legacy of fear had people believing that clever politicians could use newspapers—or even the new medium of radio—to sway and control the political behavior of the masses at will. The specter that alarmed critics the most was that of clever manipulators controlling the mass society in such a way that democratic nations could be converted to fascism, or even worse, to communism. *The People's Choice,* however, showed that conversion on this scale was extremely unlikely. The effects were not all-powerful, swaying helpless audiences uniformly and directly. They were limited effects linked to the demographic characteristics of the audiences in highly selective ways. Opinion leaders, a small category, were selectively influenced by the media. However, the majority of the people remained little touched by the propaganda from the media. As it turned out, interpersonal channels brought them more influence than the media.

Above all, it was the issue of the "two-step flow" that caught the imagination of a new generation of researchers. The edition of *The People's Choice* that became widely available to the scientific community did not appear until 1948. Following that, research on the interpersonal processes linked to mass communication burgeoned. The two-step flow hypothesis, in other words, opened up a new theoretical vista. Social relationships between people had definitely *not* been thought to be significant in the process of mass communication. Mass society theory, and its mass communication derivative, the magic bullet conceptualization, had stressed a *lack* of social ties between people. Yet here were research findings from a large-scale study showing that ties between people were one of the most important parts of the mass communication process.

The two-step flow hypothesis emerged serendipitously from the research. But in many ways the hypothesis seems, in retrospect, the study's most important contribution. It certainly called into question most of the assumptions of the magic bullet theory, and it did little to vindicate continued belief in the legacy of fear. But in spite of this, both ideas remained in force among the beliefs of the public regarding the influence of mass communication on people.

Overall, *The People's Choice* remains one of the most sophisticated survey research studies in the history of social science. Its place in the development of mass communication theory is undisputed. It forced communication theorists to reconsider the concept of mass society, the idea of powerful influences, the role of social category membership, and the significance of interpersonal ties. Few studies in the history of mass communication research have had such an impact.

## NOTES AND REFERENCES

1. Arthur M. Schlesinger, Jr., Fred L. Israel, and William P. Hanson, eds., *History of American Presidential Elections, Vol. 4* (New York: Chelsea House Publishers, 1971). See chap. 1 by Robert E. Burke, "Election of 1940," p. 2923.
2. Ibid., p. 2925.
3. Paul F. Lazarsfeld, Bernard Berelson, and Hazel Gaudet, *The People's Choice: How the Voter Makes Up His Mind in a Presidential Election* (New York: Columbia University Press, 1948).
4. Ibid., p. 159 (n. 2).
5. Ibid., p. 6-7.
6. Ibid., p. 21.
7. Ibid., p. 88.
8. Ibid., p. 120.
9. Ibid., p. 121.
10. Ibid., p. 151.

chapter 5

# Audiences for Daytime Radio Serials: Uses and Gratifications

**B**y the late 1930s, the United States had already become a "media society." The country was served by nearly 2,000 daily newspapers, several dozen national magazines with huge circulations, and thousands of other periodicals. It also had an enormously popular film industry and a very successful system of hundreds of radio stations linked through nationwide networks. Each of these industries had a solid economic base and a large labor force of professional communicators. Above all, each had an immense and enthusiastic audience. Thus, as the depression years of the 1930s came to an end, reading, going to the movies, and listening to the radio absorbed ever-increasing amounts of time in the daily schedules of most Americans.

The change to a media society had come suddenly. While print had been around for centuries, more contemporary media had literally just arrived. The movies became a major medium about the time of World War I. During the 1920s, almost overnight, radio had become a home medium—transformed from its early functions as a wireless telegraph. The arrival of these new media was so recent at the end of the 1930s that the implications of the massive flow of popular culture, news, and sports that they delivered to the society were not yet clear.

At the end of the 1930s, relatively little was known about media audiences in the sense of how and why they attended to various kinds of content. How did they select the content from the daily tidal wave of media messages, the specific information to which they gave their attention? That is, what did they read, listen to, and watch? Were audiences merely passive, accepting whatever came their way via the airwaves, movie theaters, or print media? Or were they far more active, deliberately seeking some kinds of content and rejecting others? Furthermore, what functions did these messages serve for those who received them?

These were important questions. If audiences were active rather than passive, explanations of their behavior would clearly have to go beyond the older magic bullet assumptions that members of media audiences were merely passive receivers waiting to attend and uniformly respond to whatever messages were transmitted. Such questions implied that the uses of media content by audiences and the gratifications they experienced as a result of attending were an important topic for research.

Until about 1940, only a limited amount of research on mass communication had been systematically undertaken. The social scientists involved in the Payne Fund studies (see chapter 2) had focused on the movies and their influences on children. However, the functions and influences of radio were yet to be systematically assessed. Cantril's research on the dramatic Orson Welles broadcast in 1938 was insightful. However, that was a one-time study of an unusual event. It did not reveal much about radio's broader roles in the society or its influences on the daily lives of its audience.

In short, before World War II there simply was no community of academic research scholars specializing in the scientific investigation of the process and effects of mass communication. There certainly was no academic field devoted to teaching and research on media influences. A few degree programs designed to train print journalists had been established in institutions of higher education, and there was a scattering of courses on radio or film offered here and there. However, the idea that such efforts could be extended to the development of mass communication as a serious research-based academic discipline with its own schools and curricula would never have occurred to most members of the established academy. Indeed, if it had, most would have dismissed such a notion as irresponsible and pretentious.

## THE BEGINNINGS OF A DISCIPLINE

In spite of this paucity of efforts, a small number of farsighted pioneers saw clearly the growing importance of the mass media in American society and its implications for both higher education and research. It seemed to them that, since literally millions of people read newspapers and magazines every day, went to the movies regularly, and listened to the radio during a significant part of their waking hours, such widespread behavior could not be ignored. Even though it was outside the usual subjects of study in universities, it seemed obvious that the process and effects of mass communication warranted serious scientific study and even the development of a new discipline. Toward that goal, Paul F. Lazarsfeld, then a professor at Columbia University, and Frank N. Stanton, president of the Columbia Broadcasting System, collaborated on the number of research projects aimed at providing a better understanding of the role and influence of the media. In particular, they were concerned with radio.

In the early 1940s, these two pioneers made a prediction that in retrospect seems remarkably prescient:

As time goes by, it becomes increasingly evident that the field of radio research will ultimately merge with the study of magazines, newspapers, films and television into one broader discipline of communications research.[1]

As it turned out, that is precisely what happened a few decades later. Lazarsfeld and his associates played a central role in establishing that discipline. His studies of the influence of the media in a presidential election (*The People's Choice*, summarized in chapter 4) was a major contribution to that effort.[2] Today, most universities in the United States and many colleges have a school, department, or program in communication in which studies of the media play an important part. While many offer professional or preprofessional training for work in media industries, teaching and research on the process and effects of mass communication are also central to their activities. In addition, professional organizations, technical journals, and doctoral programs focusing on mass communication teaching and research have come into existence. Thus, Lazarsfeld and Stanton's "broader discipline of communications research" has become a reality.

## THE OFFICE OF RADIO RESEARCH

In 1937, a significant step was taken to provide for a more systematic program of research on the influences of radio. Through a generous grant from the Rockefeller Foundation, an Office of Radio Research was established at Columbia University. Directed by Paul Lazarsfeld, the mission of the group was "to study what radio means in the lives of listeners."[3] Within that framework, Lazarsfeld and his associates not only designed and conducted their own studies but also set out to collect work done in the industry, and by scholars in other universities, to include in a series of publications. By this means they began to develop techniques needed for a methodology of mass communication research and a growing body of data about the influence of radio on audiences.

From this setting came a series of studies that provided a new perspective on the behavior of audiences for mass communications, and radio in particular. The new perspective challenged the older magic bullet idea, that people passively attended to whatever the media presented and responded to such messages immediately and uniformly. Indeed, one of the major projects of the radio research group showed clearly that people actively sought out certain forms of preferred content, made use of what they obtained from the medium in various ways, and experienced a number of different kinds of satisfactions and rewards from their experience. The project included several studies that focused on radio's *daytime serials*—the ubiquitous and very popular "soap operas" that began on radio and which have survived on television up to the present time. In the late 1930s and early 1940s, these colorful dramas were avidly followed by millions of listeners every day, just as their televised counterparts are today.

At the time, the idea of studying audiences for the daily soap operas raised many eyebrows in traditional academic circles. Such entertainment was obviously little more than *kitsch*—popular culture of an especially trivial variety. It seemed to follow, therefore, that those who gave such a subject matter serious attention were engaging in a less than serious pursuit. Academics studied serious cultural products—symphonies, dance, the theater, poetry, and painting. Conducting research on popular culture—how and why ordinary people attended to daytime radio serials to learn what satisfactions they derived from such material—seemed intellectually thin at best.

In spite of the lack of acceptance and enthusiasm by many colleagues, a number of researchers felt that it was important to find out how millions of people selected certain forms of radio content every day, why they were absorbed by what they heard, and what satisfactions exposure to such materials provided. After all, a new society was unfolding in which mass communications were playing an increasingly important part. Radio was a major medium, and it was time to try to find out what it was doing to the people who regularly consumed its products.

One of the first major programs of research sponsored by the Office of Radio Research, then, focused on the nature and influences of the daytime radio serials. It was from this milestone in mass communication research that the term *uses and gratifications* came into use as a perspective for mass communication research. This term came to identify a broad conceptualization of the process and effects of mass communication that strongly challenged the older magic bullet theory.

## COMPARING LISTENERS AND NONLISTENERS

Under the direction of Herta Herzog, a former student of Lazarsfeld, a massive amount of information on the characteristics of daytime serial listeners and why they attended was brought together into a single report.[4] The main sources of evidence were four separate studies. One was a nationwide investigation that had been conducted among 4,991 nonfarm women. Another was a study of a cross section of the Iowa population, which included 5,325 women. A third was a study of 1,500 women in Erie County, Ohio (as part of the research on the role of the media in the presidential election of 1940, which was reported in *The People's Choice*[5]). The radio component of that study had also yielded information on daytime serial listening. Finally, a fourth study, based on interviews with women in three American communities—Syracuse (New York), Memphis (Tennessee), and Minneapolis (Minnesota)—had been undertaken by CBS.[6] It yielded supplementary information.

### The Size and Enthusiasm of the Audience

One of the first tasks of the Herzog report was to provide information on the size and dedication of the audience. There is little doubt that daytime serials broadcast on radio in the early 1940s had large numbers of enthusiastic followers. Indeed, for some of their listeners, the soap operas were one of the most important parts of their lives. To illustrate, Herzog quotes an article that appeared in the *New York Post* on August 6, 1942. The story was about a young woman, Toni Jo Henry, who had been convicted of murder and was on death row awaiting execution. One of her greatest concerns was about her favorite soap opera, to which she listened every day. To her dismay the serial was being discontinued for the summer and it would not start again until September—after her execution. When the producers of the serial learned of her distress, they prepared and sent to Ms. Henry a short synopsis of the story that would be broadcast in installments for September until the following June. It is not clear whether that made her ultimate fate seem less ominous.

To give a numerical perspective, the 5,325 women in the Iowa study were classified according to their radio listening habits. Some 23.5 percent indicated that they listened regularly and that serials were among their five favorite programs. Another 24.4 percent listened regularly, even though serials were not among their favorites. A small number listed serials as among their favorite programs but did not listen on a regular basis. Overall, the figures indicate that nearly half of the people studied (47.9 percent) could be classified clearly as *regular listeners* to the daily dramas, and an additional 5.1 percent spent at least some time attending to them. In contrast, 47 percent could be classified as *nonlisteners* in that they neither attended regularly nor listed serials as among their favorite radio programs. All in all, then, there was at the time of the study a massive audience for daytime radio dramas. Nearly half of American women seemed to be listening regularly to one or more of the 20 or so soap operas that were regularly on the air.

## Questions That Guided the Research

Generally, the research was designed to probe two broad questions concerning the relationship between the daytime serials and the audiences that attended to them. First was the question of the *characteristics* of the women who sought out and attended to the daytime serials. The second was what *uses* they made of the information derived from listening and what *gratifications* the serials provided.

These questions were approached within a psychological perspective. For example, Herzog posed the "gratifications" question around the satisfactions the audience obtained by listening.

> What satisfactions do listeners say they derive from daytime serials? As psychologists, what is our judgment on these assertions? Do their remarks, interpreted in terms of general psychological knowledge, enable us to explain their devotion to the serials?[7]

Another perspective was that, in trying to interpret the results, it was anticipated that the effects of the serials on their audiences would be of a long-term and additive nature. In this the researcher was anticipating what DeFleur and Dennis would later call *accumulation theory*.[8] That is, whatever the influences of the serials were on those who watched regularly, Herzog anticipated that they would accumulate over a period of time. Accumulation theory defines this process as an "adding up" of minimal effects. As Herzog put it:

> From the standpoint of social research, we should like to know the effects of these serials upon women who have for years listened to them regularly. And yet, we should not expect a single conclusive result. Unlike a single concerted campaign, with effects that can be measured by modern devices of social research, the putative influences of the serial have developed through slow accretions. Consequently, they are diffi-cult to determine.[9]

Within these psychological and long-term perspectives, Herzog began by posing more focused questions as guides to her analysis. These were based on assumptions about the relationship between hypothesized "likely differences between listeners and nonlisteners to daytime serials."[10] Specifically, there were five psychological characteristics that the researcher felt would distinguish those who listened regularly from those who did not. That is, she speculated that

1. *Regular listeners would be characterized by a greater degree of social isolation* (than nonlisteners). That is, women who spent more time listening to the serials would have more difficulty in establishing and maintaining relationships with others and would be involved somewhat less in social activities compared to nonlisteners. (This hypothesis is consistent with "mass society" theory.)
2. *Regular listeners would have fewer intellectual interests.* It was anticipated that this would be revealed in several ways. It was felt that those who regularly followed the daytime serials would have lower levels of educational attainment and that they would read less and prefer reading material at a lower level of sophistication.
3. *Regular listeners would be less concerned with public affairs.* That is, women who listened frequently would be less likely to follow the news closely, to vote, and generally to be concerned with public affairs and current events than nonlisteners.
4. *Regular listeners would differ on such personality characteristics as self-assurance and would be beset with greater worries.* That is, women who attended to the serials regularly were expected to be less personally secure than nonlisteners and to see themselves as worrying more as compared to other women.
5. *Regular listeners would have a marked preference for radio listening.* That is, women who listened regularly to the serials would do so in large part because they liked listening to radio entertainment generally, and this preference would be greater among listeners than among those who did not follow the daytime dramas.

To address each of these issues, different types of data were assembled from one or more of the four studies noted above (nationwide nonfarm women; Iowa cross section; Erie County, Ohio, group; and CBS survey subjects).

## Social Participation

To assess the question of social isolation versus participation, data from the Iowa study of 5,325 women were used. The women were divided into regular listeners and nonlisteners and compared on three factors: (1) attending church and participating in church affairs, (2) attending other meetings and social gatherings, and (3) going to the movies. The results are shown in Table 5.1 below:

**TABLE 5.1**  Social participation of listeners versus nonlisteners (median number of attendances)

|  | Listeners | Nonlisteners |
| --- | --- | --- |
| Attended church or church affairs (last 2 weeks) | 1.54 | 1.62 |
| Attended other social gatherings (last 2 weeks) | 0.58 | 0.74 |
| Went to the movies (last 4 weeks) | 0.58 | 0.51 |
| Total number interviewed | 2,545 | 2,780 |

None of the differences in the table were statistically significant. Therefore, it is clear that the researcher's anticipation that listeners and nonlisteners would differ on the factor of social isolation was not justified. In retrospect, it is not easy to understand why movie attendance was included. One can, after all, go to the movies alone, which would not appear to be evidence of social participation in the same sense as going to church or attending social gatherings. In any case, the data indicate rather convincingly that those who followed the daytime serials closely were not social isolates.

## Range of Intellectual Interests

To determine if the frequent listeners had more narrowly focused intellectual interests than nonlisteners, Herzog compared the two groups on two indices: amount of formal education, and amount and type of reading. A third comparison with respect to area of residence (in terms of living on farms, in small cities, or in larger urban areas) had been planned. However, as it turned out, the data needed from the Iowa and the nationwide studies did not provide for adequate representation of the categories needed, and this effort was not successful.

First, in the comparisons based on educational attainment, Herzog hypothesized that those who attain a higher level would have a greater range of intellectual interests than those with less schooling. Data on this issue were obtained from both the nationwide survey of nonfarm women and the Iowa cross-sectional study. One of the problems of such comparisons is that educational level is associated with several other factors, one of which is income. This made it necessary to sort out the statistical influence of education in order to separate it from the influences of the other two variables. As it turned out, with suitable cross tabulations, these multiple relationships could be observed in relatively simple tables. Table 5.2 illustrates the approach.

Moving from left to right across each row, the data in Table 5.2 clearly imply that as education increased, the proportion that listened regularly to the daytime serials declined. The most avid listeners for each income level appear to be those who had not continued beyond grade school. College-educated respondents were much less likely to be among the fans. There was one minor problem in the table. Herzog noted that the 50.0 percent figure for grade school respondents with high incomes may be a statistical artifact due to the small number of the category ($N = 84$). While there appears to be a negative relationship between income and listening, Herzog believed that the relevant independent variable was actually educational attainment. That is, those higher in income were generally better educated and therefore less likely to be regular listeners.

The same relationships between listening, education, and income were studied with the use of data from the Iowa cross section. Table 5.3 shows that the results were very similar.

Again, moving from left to right across each row, the data in Table 5.3 strongly suggest that the higher the educational attainment, the lower the percentage who were regular listeners. The same pattern appeared with income as in Table 5.2. As in the earlier table, education appears to be the relevant independent variable. Those with lower levels of education were generally less affluent, and this was the factor leading to a higher level of listening to the daily serials.

**TABLE 5.2**  Percent of nonfarm women in the nationwide survey who listened regularly to daytime serials, by income and educational level

| Income Level | Grade School (%) | High School (%) | College (%) |
| --- | --- | --- | --- |
| Low | 45.5 | 41.0 | 29.9 |
| Medium | 38.9 | 37.8 | 27.2 |
| High | 50.0 | 36.8 | 22.0 |
| Total number interviewed | 1,538 | 2,687 | 685 |

**TABLE 5.3**  Percent of women in the Iowa cross-sectional survey who listened regularly to daytime serials, by income and educational level

| Income Level | Grade School (%) | High School (%) | College (%) |
| --- | --- | --- | --- |
| Low | 51.6 | 50.6 | 34.5 |
| Medium | 50.5 | 49.5 | 42.0 |
| High | 46.1 | 43.9 | 33.4 |
| Total number interviewed | 1,774 | 2,757 | 541 |

It is worth noting that there is feature of the measurement of income in Table 5.3 that would probably be regarded as flawed by today's standards. Herzog noted in a footnote in the original research report that "income expresses interviewer's rating of the economic status of each respondent."[11] It is doubtful that this mode of measuring income would be regarded as valid by today's researchers.

Similar tables from the two studies were constructed with several age levels in place of income categories. However, the results did not show a clear pattern. At some levels of educational attainment, younger women listened more; in others, the older women. Furthermore, the differences between them were not striking. In other words, age was not an independent variable associated with listening.

In spite of their flaws, these data on the influence of education on listening reveal a fairly clear pattern. Generally, they appear to support the guiding hypothesis that regular listeners would be characterized by a more limited range of intellectual interests (insofar as this is indicated by lower educational attainment). The two separate studies confirm each other, and they are based on large numbers of respondents.

The second way in which Herzog pursued the guiding hypothesis regarding intellectual interests was by comparing the amount and type of reading that was characteristic of listeners and nonlisteners. Here, the data showed an interesting pattern. While the listeners and nonlisteners did not differ in the *amount* that they read, they clearly did so in terms of *type* of reading material that they selected.

Herzog began by gathering data from three of the studies that contained information on the amount of reading by respondents. The data showed that the two categories were essentially similar. As Herzog explained:

> . . . listeners and nonlisteners do not differ materially in the amount of their reading. Three of our studies which included questions on the number of books, magazines and newspapers read are in complete agreement on that score. Moreover, a specific inquiry in the Ohio county study revealed that listeners and non-listeners utilized the public library to the same extent.[12]

The second way of assessing reading characteristics (as an index of range of intellectual interests) was to look at the type of material selected by listeners versus that of nonlisteners. Data for this comparison were available from the 48 percent of the 5,325 women interviewed in the Iowa cross section who identified various magazines that they regularly read. The focus of this contrast was on reading at different intellectual levels in order to determine if those who listened to the serials were more likely to read magazines representing a narrower range of intellectual interests. It was a clever way to assess this factor, because the magazines studied did differ considerably in their level of sophistication.

To illustrate the ways in which the magazines differed, those at each end of an intellectual continuum can be briefly compared: At the low end was *True Confessions,* a magazine of the time that made limited intellectual demands on its readers. This magazine contained supposedly true accounts of troubled individuals who had presumably told their stories, often of tragic human relationships, to the writers of the articles. Actually, many of the stories were written by reporters trying to earn a few extra dollars. They obtained their "true" stories by rummaging through old police files to find cases that suggested heartrending experiences of people who had suffered tragic circumstances. The "confessions" were written in a simple style, loosely suggesting that they were derived from personal accounts. Generally, they were lurid tales of human relationships gone awry.

At the opposite end of the intellectual continuum was the *New Yorker.* At the time it was comparable to what it is today, a periodical of sophisticated content providing interpretation of political issues, views of the arts, and insights into urban life. Clearly, it was designed with a relatively sophisticated reader in mind. Between these two were a number of widely circulated general magazines, some of which are still published. Table 5.4 shows how listeners and nonlisteners compared on this index of intellectual sophistication and interests.

Table 5.4 shows the percentage of the readers of each of the nine magazines who were regular listeners to the daily radio serials. Moving from top to bottom of the column of Listeners, a clear pattern is revealed. As the level of sophistication of the magazine increased, smaller and smaller percentages of its readers were women who listened regularly to the daily soap operas. These data tend to confirm the hypothesis that regular listeners have a more limited set of intellectual interests as compared to nonlisteners.

Herzog drew several conclusions from these data. First, if a magazine is preferred by those who listen regularly to the daily serials, it is one of two types. Either it has content that resembles the stories presented in the serials or it focuses on home life. Nonlisteners have much less interest in such magazines and are more likely to prefer those toward the bottom of the table. She cautions, however, that none of the magazines on the list were actually read by large proportions of the women in the Iowa sample, so these interpretations must be tempered with caution against overgeneralizing.

**TABLE 5.4**  Percentage of readers of different magazines in the Iowa cross-sectional survey who were regular listeners

| Magazine | Listeners (%) |
| --- | --- |
| *True Confessions* | 67 |
| *True Story* | 66 |
| *Household* | 57 |
| *Parent's* | 55 |
| *Time* | 33 |
| *Vogue* | 31 |
| *Harper's* | 29 |
| *Mademoiselle* | 28 |
| *New Yorker* | 25 |

Generally, the data on intellectual range and interests of the women who were studied suggest strongly that those drawn on a daily basis to the daytime serials were more limited on this factor than nonlisteners. They clearly had a lower level of educational attainment, and their preferences in magazine reading were at a less challenging level than those of nonlisteners.

## Concern with Current Events and Public Affairs

A third research question guiding Herzog's examination of listeners and non-listeners was whether they differed in their interest in, and concern with, events in the news and public affairs, such as elections. The assumption was that those with broader intellectual interests would be higher on both these indicators. This assessment of intellectual interests was approached in two ways: One was to compare the two categories in terms of their preference for radio news programs. The other was to compare them on the basis of participation in the political process—specifically, their patterns of voting or nonvoting and their expressed levels of interest in the 1940 presidential election.

In comparing the categories on the basis of preference for news over other kinds of radio programs, it must be remembered that radio provided much greater coverage of the news than is now generally the case. People today who regularly view network TV news programs on a daily basis would have turned to their radio counterparts during the early 1940s. In other words, it was an important medium by which people kept abreast of public affairs and current events.

Three of the major studies provided information on preferences in radio programs by which to compare soap opera listeners and nonlisteners. Table 5.5 shows the source of the data, the numbers of respondents involved, and the percentages of each group who indicated that news was among their favorite kinds of radio programs.

The data show that the two groups did not differ in any consistent or dramatic way. Therefore, using interest in radio news programs as an index of concern with current events did not sharply separate listeners from nonlisteners.

For the second part of the inquiry—the general concern with public affairs centered on voting—data were collected during the study of the 1940 presidential election in Erie County, Ohio. In this investigation, most of the women were reinterviewed at least once between May and election day in November—some

**TABLE 5.5** Percents of listeners and nonlisteners who mentioned news as among their favorite radio programs

| Source of Data | Total Number Interviewed | Listeners (%) | Nonlisteners (%) |
|---|---|---|---|
| Nationwide nonfarm group | 4,991 | 31.7 | 36.4 |
| Ohio county cross section | 1,500 | 56.1 | 54.0 |
| Iowa state cross section | 5,325 | 79.1 | 81.0 |

of them several times. This made it possible to match samples of 300 very carefully. In Table 5.6, all five samples were interviewed in May; two of these five, in October; and one on election day.

Comparing the last two columns, it is clear that there were more nonvoters among the regular listeners to the daytime serials. Because the differences are all statistically significant, Herzog concluded that serial listeners participated less in public affairs, as indicated by voting in the election.

An additional assessment of interest in public affairs was made by comparing women from the Ohio study in terms of their expressed "interest" in the presidential election. Here, the results seem to contradict those obtained from the comparison of nonvoters. Table 5.7 shows the proportion of women in each category who expressed "a great deal of interest" in the process. The sample interviewed on election day was excluded in this comparison, presumably on the grounds of heavy news coverage that would inflate interest levels.

Obviously, these data show a pattern that is the reverse of that displayed in Table 5.6. It was the listeners who indicated a higher level of interest in the election. Herzog interpreted this as meaning that the listeners may have *said* that they were interested in the election, but they did not actively *pursue* that interest to the point of voting. At the same time, the reversal of these patterns clouds the entire issue and a clear conclusion cannot therefore be reached.

Generally, then, there is at least some evidence that the range of intellectual interests of the listeners is less than those who were not regular fans of the soap operas. It was clear that listeners had less educational attainment. While they appeared to read as much as their nonlistening counterparts, there were significant differences in what they read. Those magazines whose content was like the stories in the serials were more likely to be read by listeners; the more

**TABLE 5.6**  Percentages of listeners and nonlisteners who were nonvoters

| Date of the Interview | Total Number Interviewed | Listeners (%) | Nonlisteners (%) |
| --- | --- | --- | --- |
| May 1940 | 1,500 | 20.5 | 18.6 |
| October 1940 | 600 | 25.6 | 20.1 |
| Election Day | 300 | 31.7 | 18.2 |

**TABLE 5.7**  Percentages of listeners and nonlisteners who expressed a "great deal of interest" in the election

| Date of the Interview | Total Number Interviewed | Listeners (%) | Nonlisteners (%) |
| --- | --- | --- | --- |
| May 1940 | 1,500 | 25.5 | 20.1 |
| October 1940 | 600 | 34.2 | 29.2 |

intellectual and sophisticated magazines were not. Finally, while the differences between the two were clear on voting, their respective claimed levels of interest in the election were in the opposite direction. Perhaps the best generalization that can be formed on this issue of concern with public affairs and current events is that there appear to be some grounds for accepting a hypothesis that listeners are lower on this factor than nonlisteners. However, no final answer was provided by the data examined in these studies.

## Personality Characteristics

A fourth research question Herzog addressed was to see if listeners differed from nonlisteners in terms of selected personality characteristics. Herzog approached this task in two ways: one was to determine if the two categories differed in terms of self-assurance, the other was to compare them on the basis of "worrying," as compared to other women.

As Herzog pointed out, the assessment of personality characteristics through the use questionnaires and interviews in survey research was in its infancy at the time of the study. For the lack of a better procedure, the classification of the respondents as to their level of self-assurance was done by the interviewers on the basis of their observations of subjects. While this might seem chancy, it will be recalled that in the Ohio county study, many respondents were interviewed repeatedly, which provided a better basis for such an assessment than a single contact. As it turned out, there were only minor differences between the two groups on this factor. Nonlisteners were by a slight margin higher on the scale of self-assurance. However, no clear generalization would be drawn that the two groups differed in terms of self-assurance.

Much the same result was apparent from a comparison of listeners and nonlisteners in the Iowa survey on another personality dimension. Each was asked, "Do you think that you worry more, less, or the same as compared with other women?" Again, only minor differences were found between the two groups, and they were not statistically different. Furthermore, data from the three-city study yielded much the same results.

The best overall conclusion that can be drawn regarding these comparisons of personality characteristics was that not much was revealed. The listeners were not less self-assured than nonlisteners, nor were they beset with higher levels of worries. It can be added that the methodological sophistication of this part of the study was not high by today's standards.

## Preferences for Radio Listening

A fifth comparison between listeners and nonlisteners contrasted their uses of radio versus other sources of information. Specifically, two questions are involved: First, were there different patterns of radio listening (aside from the daytime serials) between the comparison categories? That is, did the soap opera fans prefer listening to the radio in general more than the nonlisteners, or were the two groups about the same? Second, did listeners use their radios as a source from which to get information about politics to a greater degree than nonlisteners?

One of the sharpest contrasts between listeners and nonlisteners turned out to be in their uses of radio in both of the above ways. Obviously, the listeners attended more to the serials during the day, but they also extended their listening into the evening. The serial fans devoted an average of 2.43 hours in the evening listening to the radio. Nonlisteners to the serials spent only 2.15 hours with their sets during the evening. Furthermore, the soap opera listeners indicated that they continued to listen to radio programs until 10 P.M. four nights a week on average. In contrast, nonlisteners reported only half as many hours of late-night listening.

Another way Herzog looked at radio preferences was to compare the sources from which listeners and nonlisteners obtained their information about the presidential election. Table 5.8 lists the answers provided by just over 600 respondents interviewed in October 1940 to the question, Where do you think you will get most of your information about issues and candidates in the coming presidential election?

Two conclusions stand out clearly from Table 5.8. One is that radio is a more likely medium of information for the serial listener than for the nonlistener. The second is that the nonlistener places relatively greater reliance on print media than does the listener. These are statistically significant differences. It is clear, then, that those who listened regularly to the daily serials were generally more reliant on the medium. They spent a greater number of their evening hours listening than did respondents who were not soap opera fans, and they relied on radio more for information about the presidential election.

In summary of the five categories of differences that Herzog researchers looked for between listeners and nonlisteners to the daytime serials, a rather mixed picture emerged. Soap opera fans did not resemble the individual portrayed in the magic bullet theory as socially isolated. However, there was evidence that their range of intellectual interests was lower than those who had less enthusiasm for the daytime serials. Soap opera enthusiasts also differed somewhat in their concern with public affairs. No clear conclusions could be reached in terms of personality differences between the categories. Finally, daytime serial fans made greater use of radio in general than did nonlisteners.

**TABLE 5.8**  Sources of political information identified by listeners and nonlisteners

| Source of Information | Listeners (%) | Nonlisteners (%) |
|---|---|---|
| Radio | 40.2 | 33.3 |
| Newspapers and magazines | 32.4 | 41.7 |
| Friends and relatives | 25.4 | 22.0 |
| Public speakers and newsreels | 2.0 | 3.0 |
| Total percent | 100.0 | 100.0 |
| Total number interviewed | 299 | 363 |

## USES AND GRATIFICATIONS
## PROVIDED BY LISTENING

The attempt to develop a psychological profile of the daytime serial listener was only partially successful. The data used were obtained from prior studies and in some cases bore only rather indirectly on the hypotheses under assessment. To expand understanding of the gratifications that those who paid close attention to the serials were receiving, and to probe how they were using the information presented in the plays, Herzog undertook additional analyses.

In this phase of the report, no effort was made to contrast listeners and nonlisteners. It was a probe into the nature of the satisfactions that the listeners obtained from their experience and how they made use of information presented in the plays. This objective was pursued through the use of three sources of data. One was a relatively small qualitative investigation based on case study interviews. This project was completed as a preliminary to the larger Iowa cross-sectional study. The second used data drawn from the quantitative Iowa survey, which had included questions on how respondents used information from the serials. The third was a second, small, qualitative study based on interviews with listeners in two urban settings, New York and Pittsburgh. From these sources, three major forms of uses and gratifications were identified: *emotional release, wishful thinking,* and *valuable advice* for handling their own lives.

In the first, relatively small, qualitative study, Herzog conducted intensive interviews with 100 listeners to the daytime serials. As noted, this was actually a kind of pilot study for the larger Iowa survey. However, it revealed a considerable number of details as to why the respondents liked the serials so much. In particular, it showed what uses they made of the information presented in the dramas and the kinds of satisfactions that they derived from listening. From this small study, Herzog was able to identify all three forms of uses and gratifications listed above. Once identified, the factor of advice was followed up more extensively in the other two projects.

### Emotional Release

Some of the listeners interviewed in the initial in-depth case study seemed to enjoy the plays because they could listen to the troubles of other people. It made them feel better to hear about the difficulties experienced by the characters in the stories. Hearing about their problems provided some compensation for the distress the listeners experienced in their own lives.

Herzog provided psychological interpretations of specific cases that came up in the interviews. For example, one woman whose husband had died was having a hard time bringing up her two children. She enjoyed the difficulties of a soap opera heroine who was trying to decide whether or not to marry. The listener did not want the heroine to marry at all and preferred that she sacrifice herself by staying single and continuing her work at the orphanage. Herzog explained that this was a form of compensation for the listener's own resented fate by projecting a worse one on the character in the story.

Some listeners found enjoyment in identifying their own problems with those of the long-suffering characters in the plays. Mostly, the listeners' own problems were of a more minor nature, and they often magnified their own difficulties to a level where they were equated with those of the soap opera heroes and heroines. This allowed the listener to feel superior to others who had not had such intense emotional experiences.

Whether or not these psychological interpretations would have been developed in exactly the same way by other researchers, it seemed clear that many listeners were very gratified by the chance to cry over the plight of the characters in the serials, to enjoy the happy situations portrayed, and to obtain satisfaction from the feelings of aggressiveness that the dramas aroused. Emotional release and vicarious emotional experience, in other words, were important forms of gratification derived from the listening experience.

## Wishful Thinking

Another form of gratification revealed by the in-depth interviews of the case study was wishful thinking. Listening to the daily dramas provided more than entertainment. Some of the characters engaged in behavior or led lives that listeners wanted to enjoy themselves. To illustrate, one woman's husband was chronically ill. Although she was happy with her marriage, she listened regularly to a particular serial for the "funny episodes." She pretended that they had happened to her and her husband, and thereby gained vicarious satisfactions from her listening experience.

Another woman listed two serials as among her favorites because of the way they portrayed family life. Her own life was bleak by comparison. Her daughter had run away from home and had married. Her husband stayed out of the house "five nights a week." The serials she followed portrayed a much more favorable picture of a successful wife and mother and generally happy family relationships. She enjoyed pretending that her own circumstances were like that.

## Valuable Advice

A third kind of gratification that was apparent from the interviews conducted in the case study was that the serials provided many of their listeners with explanations as to how to handle problems that they themselves might experience. A typical comment was "If you listen to these programs and something turns up in your own life, you would know what to do about it."[13] This kind of response came so frequently that a special item on the matter was included on the questionnaire used in the Iowa study. Essentially, it asked whether listening to the daytime serials helped the respondent deal better with problems in her own everyday life. Of the 2,500 respondents identified as listeners in the Iowa data, 41 percent gave a positive answer.

Herzog made an analysis of those women who claimed that they had been helped by listening to the radio serials. Table 5.9 shows the numerical results.

Reading across the rows, these figures show a declining pattern at both levels of worry as education increases. In fact, the pattern is the same for both groups. Thus, two conclusions emerge from these data: First, the lower the educational attainment of the respondent, the more likely she was to claim that the programs had been helpful. Second, those respondents indicating that they worried more than others more often claimed to have found relief by listening to the serials.

Herzog also looked at how many serials the listener followed each day. The more stories heard, the more the individual felt that she had been helped. To illustrate, among those who heard only one story daily, 32 percent claimed to have been helped by advice obtained from the serial. In contrast, among those who regularly followed six or more, 50 percent claimed to have been helped.

Further efforts were made to understand just what respondents meant by being "helped"; that is, what kinds of problems were alleviated by advice derived from the serials? As it turned out, there were a great many. Common among them were interpersonal relations, such as how to get along with a husband or boyfriend. One women had a husband who typically came home tired and grumpy. She usually responded to him in kind. However, after hearing a favorite character in a serial handle that kind of problem by being nice, she adopted a cheerful manner instead of being nasty. Those with children often found ways to handle behavioral problems in a different way. A listener who felt that women normally slapped their children when they misbehaved heard a soap opera heroine using a different technique. The character in the play deprived the child of something. The respondent liked that better and adopted the technique. Some felt that they learned how to express themselves better in difficult situations. For example, when a friend's wife died, she phrased her condolences in the same terms that she had heard used in a similar situation in one of the serials. Another woman was able to cope with her advancing age better after listening to an older woman handling the problem in a serial. Still another was able to cope better when her son had to go to war after hearing a similar episode in a serial.

Herzog pointed out that many problems remained in trying to sort out the influences of these daily dramas on their audiences. For one thing, much of the "advice" presented by the stories of the serials had little to do with the lives of their listeners. For example, one woman felt that she had learned a great deal from one of the serials about what to do when one suddenly came into a great deal of money. Although the listener realized that such a situation was very

**TABLE 5.9** Level of worry and educational attainment of listeners who claimed that they were being helped by advice from the serials (%)

| Level of Worry Compared to Other Women | Grammar School | High School | College |
|---|---|---|---|
| More | 52 | 50 | 42 |
| Less | 44 | 37 | 34 |

unlikely to happen to her, she felt good that she would know what to do. Another listener reported that she had learned what to do if she were to meet a "crippled man." She was able to sort out the conditions under which she would marry him. The fact that she was already married did not prevent her from feeling good that she had derived a plan if this event should occur. It was not at all clear whether the listeners understood the solutions they had derived or whether following them would actually help or make things worse.

Finally, Herzog raised the question as to whether those who wrote the scripts for the stories understood the social responsibility entailed in influencing millions of women trying to cope with their personal difficulties. The data examined indicated that the large numbers of women who closely followed the daytime serials were not as well educated or as intellectually resourceful as those who were not avid listeners. Many were using the plots and characters in the plays as guides to their own daily actions. It was a situation that disturbed many thoughtful people in the society, and it certainly seemed to warrant further study.

## CONCLUSIONS AND IMPLICATIONS

In summary, this relatively massive summary of data shows that, at the time, audiences for the daytime serials were both large and enthusiastic. Contrary to the conceptions of mass society, those who listened most avidly were not different in terms of social isolation from those who did not. They did, however, have a lower level of educational attainment and preferred less sophisticated reading material (suggesting a lower level of intellectual interest). Regular listeners claimed to be as interested in public affairs (in the form of a presidential election) as nonlisteners, but they did not carry their interests into action by voting to the same degree. An attempt to show that listeners had a different personality profile than nonlisteners was not particularly successful. Limitations on methodologies of personality assessment may have been a factor. Clearly, however, those who listened to the daytime serials spent more time with radio, even during the evening hours, than those who were not soap opera fans.

The uses and gratifications provided for their listeners by the daily serials included emotional release, wishful thinking, and advice regarding their own lives. The issue of advice was pursued by analyzing data from three sources: a case study project involving in-depth personal interviews, a large-scale survey that was part of the Iowa cross-sectional survey, and detailed interviews of subjects in two urban areas. Among the listeners, women who worried more felt that they received good advice from the serials. They also listened to a larger number of serials than other listeners. Generally, the advice they derived from their listening focused on how to deal with interpersonal relations, such as grumpy husbands or children who misbehaved, or interpersonal problems, such as what to say in difficult circumstances. Many of the listeners felt good that they gained advice on how to handle unrealistic problems that actually were quite removed from their own lives.

The daytime serial study had a number of implications. It stimulated considerable interest in the issue of how audiences select content from the media,
how they use that information, and the gratifications derived from the experience.
The focus on the psychological characteristics of the individual in an audience,
and how they play a part in leading the person to choose particular messages
from the great flow of media content, remains an important perspective today
in the study of the process and effects of mass communication.

The "uses and gratifications" approach to studying audience attributes and
behavior was adopted by other early researchers, as interest in understanding the
nature and influences of mass communication continued to develop. Shortly after
the publication of the research on daytime serial listeners, other studies of uses
and gratifications of audiences for other media soon followed. In one well-known
example, sociologist Bernard Berelson studied a strike by eight major newspapers
in New York City.[14] It began on June 30, 1945, and New Yorkers were deprived
of their newspapers for a period of two weeks. The study focused on the question
of "what missing the newspaper means." As it turned out, it meant a great deal.
Different people achieved different kinds of gratifications from different features
of the paper. In addition, they used many kinds of information for practical
purposes. In short, newspapers served both rational and nonrational functions
for people and fulfilled many different kinds of needs. When they could not obtain
the paper, they turned to other sources—magazines, radio, and out-of-town
newspapers—to try to fill the void, but it wasn't the same.

Later researchers continued to probe the psychological implications of media
uses and gratifications. As will be seen in chapter 11, this perspective was used
as a guide to the first large-scale study of how children related to television at a
time when that medium first came into widespread use.

At the time of the daytime radio serial project, the large numbers in the radio
audience who listened regularly to the soap operas raised a number of both hopes
and concerns on the part of Herzog and her associates. After all, those audiences
represented a cross section of almost *half* of all American women at the time.
As the results have shown, that audience was enthusiastic about the serials and
often inclined to learn the incidental lessons that they presented. Because of this,
Herzog was hopeful that the daytime serials—and indeed, radio in general—would
become an agent of positive social change. In particular, through the plots and
characters presented in the dramas, some of the problems faced by the nation
might be addressed. She was particularly concerned with race relations in an era
before the civil rights movement began and when serials failed to portray people
in working class occupations. In addition, she hoped that listeners would become
more realistic and less inclined to engage in wishful thinking. As she later put it:

[In the years ahead] We shall have to combat prejudice and wishful
thinking by information and the analysis of complex situations. The
future in which colored nations will play a much greater role can be
anticipated by realistic handling of race problems. A world in which
some form of central planning is likely to remain can be reflected in

plots where the role of the individual in the community is constructively treated. The increasing importance of labor can be shown by the introduction of characteristic types. These are the needs and obligations. Can they be carried through?[15]

Needless to say, the problems of the nation—whether those defined by Herzog or by somebody else—have not to this date been noticeably ameliorated by daytime serials.[16] They remain today, repositioned on television, much the same in content as they were in 1940. While they sometimes portray human frailties and social problems, they are a form of relatively unsophisticated popular culture and are not designed primarily to promote social improvement, ameliorate problems, or increase appreciation of the arts on the part of their audience. They serve those who finance their broadcasts as vehicles within which to present advertising messages that will generate commercial profit. Viewed from that perspective, there is considerable doubt that they will *ever* become a major force that will change the nation for the better. However, in spite of what many contemporary critics would regard as their shortcomings, daytime serials remain immensely popular, just as their radio counterparts were more than a half century ago.

## NOTES AND REFERENCES

1. Paul F. Lazarsfeld and Frank N. Stanton, *Radio Research 1942-1943* (New York: Duel, Sloan, and Pearce, 1944), p. vii.
2. Paul F. Lazarsfeld, Bernard Berelson, and Hazel Gaudet, *The People's Choice: How the Voter Makes Up His Mind in a Presidential Election* (New York: Columbia University Press, 1948).
3. Lazarsfield and Stanton, *Radio Research 1942-1943*, p. vii.
4. Herta Herzog, "What Do We Really Know about Daytime Serial Listeners?" in Paul F. Lazarsfeld and Frank N. Stanton, *Radio Research 1942-1943*, p. 3-33.
5. Lazarsfeld, Berelson, and Gaudet, *The People's Choice*.
6. This was a nationwide study of listeners to 20 daytime serials being broadcast on CBS and NBC at the time. CBS studied these programs for three weeks and then continued certain portions "for several weeks" to follow up on several questions. They noted that the numbers of listeners studied ranged from 687 for the most popular serial to 154 for the least popular. More specific data are not available. See Paul F. Lazarsfeld and Frank N. Stanton, *Radio Research 1942-1943*, pp. 3-33.
7. Herzog, "What Do We Really Know?" p. 4.
8. For a discussion of accumulation theory, see Melvin L. DeFleur and Everette E. Dennis, *Understanding Mass Communication,* 5th ed. (Boston: Houghton Mifflin, 1994), pp. 572-579.
9. Herzog, "What Do We Really Know?"p. 3.
10. Ibid., p. 5.
11. Ibid. See footnote to Base Table 6A, Appendix, p. 556.
12. Ibid., p. 9.
13. Ibid., p. 25.

14. Bernard Berelson, "What Missing the Newspaper Means," in Paul F. Lazarsfeld and Frank N. Stanton, *Communication Research 1948-1949* (New York: Harper Brothers, 1949), pp. 111-129; see also Penn Kimball, "People without Papers," *Public Opinion Quarterly* 23 (fall 1959): 389-398.
15. Herzog, "What Do We Really Know?" p. 32.
16. The portrayals of social problems on the TV versions of the daytime serials are not always designed in ways that would be helpful to their audiences. See Shearon A. Lowery, "Soap and Booze in the Afternoon: An Analysis of the Portrayals of Alcohol Use in the Daytime Serial," *Journal of Studies on Alcohol* 41 (September 1980): 829-838.

# chapter 6

# The Iowa Study of Hybrid Seed Corn:
# The Adoption of Innovation

Before the Industrial Revolution, changes in society and in the ways in which human beings related to each other took place only slowly. A few people did invent things or bring them from other societies, and some were widely adopted. Occasionally, an innovation spread rapidly, as was the case with both gunpowder and the printing press. But for the most part, the limited number of inventions or new culture traits from other societies that were eventually adopted took many decades or even centuries to come into wide use. Consequently, preindustrial, traditional societies changed at a snail's pace, and their social structures, institutions, and cultures remained relatively stable over long periods of time.

One reason for the slow pace was not only that the rate of innovation was low but also that processes of communication were essentially limited to word of mouth. There were few cities; the overwhelming majority of people lived and worked on farms. Few traveled very far from where they were born, and only a small number had contact with written materials. Even after the printing press became available, literacy tended to be limited to an affluent and urbane elite who could afford to buy the limited number of books, the early versions of newspapers, and the few primitive magazines that became available. Overall, these were not conditions that led to the rapid and widespread adoption of new things or ideas.

The Industrial Revolution changed all of that. It began near the end of the eighteenth century and accelerated during the nineteenth and twentieth centuries. Throughout this period, the rate of invention increased. In the early 1800s, the speed and efficiency of travel increased sharply, as steam-driven machines took over from wind, animals, and feet.

As industrialization increased, literacy become more common. In the United States, the proportion of the population that learned how to read rose sharply,

**115**

particularly during the last half of the nineteenth century as statewide systems of free (tax-supported) and compulsory education were increasingly adopted. Increased literacy made possible a rising tide of mass communications. In the 1830s the penny press became the first mass medium serving truly large numbers of readers on a daily basis. The newspaper was supplemented by nationally circulated magazines, especially during the last half of the 1800s. Instantaneous communication via the telegraph began in the 1840s, just before the Civil War, and via the telephone just afterward (1870s). Broadcasting and film were added early in the 1900s. With these media in place, what had been a trickle of information flowing through the society by word of mouth became a torrent via various media. News as to the availability and the characteristics of a multitude of new products, perspectives, technologies, and ideas was transmitted easily and quickly by these media to a huge population of potential adopters. All of these changes provided circumstances favorable to both the development and spread of innovations.

Throughout this period, significant social and cultural changes took place, not only in the use of new technologies but also in basic lifestyles. Fundamentally altered were ways in which goods were produced, distributed, and consumed. A great advertising industry developed to sell the goods and services of the Industrial Revolution. Cheap amusements based on popular culture became an urgent necessity when armies of industrial workers with at least some leisure time crowded into urban centers. The demand for entertainment and news fired the growth of wide-reaching media empires. Print, film, and broadcasting in all their various forms expanded to meet those needs.

The Industrial Revolution not only brought mass media and popular culture but also altered the very organization of society. The factory system and related economic growth greatly expanded the social class structure. Differentiated social levels of income, status, and power were created by people's positions in complex commercial enterprises, industrial production systems, and governmental bureaucracies. Populations were mixed through migrations as people sought economic opportunity. They moved between countries, from farms to cities, and from one region of the country to another. The result was many kinds of unlike people living together in urban environments. This diversity reduced the free flow of information through informal channels based on friendship, traditional community ties, and kinship. The old order of the traditional society was disappearing. People were less guided by tradition, less tied to their neighbors, and less bound to their extended families. More specifically, people became increasingly dependent on mass media as a means by which they could become aware of new products, ideas, and other innovations.[1]

## INNOVATIONS AS A BASIS OF SOCIAL CHANGE

By the beginning of the twentieth century, a veritable tidal wave of inventions had been produced in industrializing societies such as the United States. New machines, ideas, procedures, devices, and a host of other cultural traits were constantly being invented or borrowed from other societies. This flow of innovations had the capacity to alter almost every conceivable aspect of life. Some, like ragtime music, became instant successes and were immediately adopted by large numbers in the population. Others, like Esperanto, a universal language proposed to unite all people on earth, were ignored by all but a few enthusiasts.

A question of obvious significance in such an age of change was, Why is one new thing, practice, or idea well received and widely adopted, while another is all but ignored? That question was seen as critical to understanding the dynamics of social and cultural change based on the adoption of innovations. As Gabriel Tarde, the French sociologist posed the issue in 1890:

> Our problem is to learn why, given one hundred different innovations conceived of at the same time—innovations in the forms of words, in mythological ideas, in industrial processes, etc.—ten will spread abroad, while ninety will be forgotten.[2]

Tarde's answer was to search for universal "laws of imitation," relating the characteristics of "things" to human "desires" through a process of "suggestion." He wanted, in other words, to identify the human *decision-making process* that led people to adopt or reject a given innovation when it came to their attention. However, while Tarde posed the issue succinctly, his laws of imitation were based on psychological concepts that quickly became outmoded. They did not survive the test of time. Moreover, while he was concerned with the effects of the newspapers on crime, he did not see the connection between the adoption of innovation and the creation of public awareness of a particular invention through the use of mass communications.

Scholarly concern with social and cultural change continued into the 1900s. Early on, social scientists began to see similarities between the cumulative *pattern* of growth over time in the adoption of an innovation by a population and certain cumulative frequency curves of increase that had been developed by students of biology. For example, biologists reported that the growth of a population of fruit flies in a restricted container followed an S-shaped curve. At first, their number was small and the fly population increased only slowly. Then, assuming an abundant food supply, the rate of growth in their numbers accelerated ever more swiftly. After reaching a maximum rate per period of time, however, the curve of population growth began to slow. Eventually, it leveled off and the size of the population stabilized.

Similar S-shaped patterns had been identified in human populations. For example, by the 1920s, curves of this kind describing cumulative growth patterns over time had been noted by economists in studies of consumer demand and other economic data.[3] Formulas that were capable of describing such patterns included those for the Pearl-Reed logistic, the Gompertz, and the normal frequency ogive. (These are all essentially bell-shaped curves, but when plotted in a cumulative manner, they form what is often called an S shape.)[4]

These similarities between growth patterns in biology and economics and in the adoption of certain social and cultural phenomena fired the imagination of social scientists during the 1920s. In some ways they promised fulfillment of Tarde's search for "laws" of imitation—or at least universal regularities in patterns of adoption of new traits by human populations. For example, sociologist F. Stuart Chapin studied growth patterns in social institutions over varying spans of years and decades, finding cumulative S-shaped curves describing the adoption of such phenomena as the commission form of city government. He had high hopes that some sort of universal pattern would eventually be revealed:

> If independent verification of our results comes from such future stud-
> ies, then the trends and laws of growth suggested by this study may be
> found to be universal principles. Even with our limited data, it is inter-
> esting to note that the phenomena of growth of political structure is
> quite similar to the growth of (organic) cellular structure.[5]

By the mid-1930s, there seemed little doubt that the spread of a particular cultural trait did follow a specific regular pattern as a society adopted it. That is, the spread of a trait through a society could be described by some type of S-shaped curve.

The logical next question was, *Which S-shaped curve described the pattern best?* That is, was there a particular identifiable formula that described the universal curve of adoption? That specific question was addressed by sociologist H. Earl Pemberton in a classic study of three very different cultural phenomena that historically had spread through a number of different societies and states. The cultural traits whose spread he chose to study were (1) the adoption of postage stamps by 37 countries between 1836 and 1880, (2) the number of states (in the United States) that adopted constitutional limits on taxation by local government between 1835 and 1885, and (3) the enactment of compulsory education laws by both northern and southern states over periods of four decades. He gathered data on the dates of adoption of these cultural items by these political entities and plotted the resulting curves over time. He concluded that in each case, a particular curve of adoption had been found:

> The population units adopting a culture trait in successive time periods
> tend to be distributed around a mean time according to a normal fre-
> quency distribution. The curve of diffusion is simply the cumulative
> expression of this symmetrical binomial distribution. This form of dis-
> tribution according to time of trait adoption results from the fact that
> the conditions of culture interaction producing successive adoptions of
> the trait are identical to the conditions known experimentally to result
> in a normal frequency distribution.[6]

Thus, Pemberton made a strong case that there was a specific universal pattern—the normal ogive—governing the diffusion process for those culture traits that had spread through their relevant populations. However, he did not really face the problem that had been posed so concisely by Tarde in 1890, namely, Why is it that some traits become widely adopted while many others are not taken up at all? To try to answer that question, Tarde had tried to focus on the psychological *process* by which individuals became aware of, considered, and then made a decision to accept or reject a given culture trait for adoption. This is a very different objective from the one pursued by Chapin and Pemberton, who sought the collectively determined *pattern* by which those innovations that do achieve widespread acceptance move into a society over time.

Actually, Pemberton *did* propose an explanation of the process, although he did not elaborate on the idea. He maintained that the rate of adoption at any given time (from the quote above) "results from the fact that the conditions of culture interaction producing successive adoptions of the trait are identical to the conditions known experimentally to result in a normal frequency distribution." But exactly what does that mean? What are those conditions "known experimentally" that "result in a normal frequency distribution"? Readers who are familiar with the theory of the normal curve will recognize them as *randomly generated events.* In fact, the normal distribution was originally described by Abraham De Moive in his 1730 book *The Doctrine of Chances* as one describing a population of purely random probabilities.[7] Thus, instead of trying to account for the acceptance of a new cultural trait in terms of some sort of psychological laws of imitation, as did Tarde, Pemberton essentially proposed that the adoption of innovation is based on chancelike encounters between people in some form of "cultural interaction."

By the 1940s, then, it seemed clear that those innovations that did spread through a population were likely to follow an S-shaped curve of adoption, and the one that seemed to fit best was a cumulative normal ogive. It appeared that a universal law was within reach. However, what was unclear was just what took place *among individuals* when a new invention or some other innovative cultural trait became available in their society. That is, it was not yet understood how the innovation came to their attention and how they decided whether or not to adopt it. Neither Tarde's explanation in terms of the imitation factors he proposed nor that of Pemberton in terms of random encounters between people provided effective insights into why some innovations were widely adopted while others were largely ignored. What was vitally needed was a more adequate understanding of the *process* that took place as people found out about, pondered, perhaps tried out, and then accepted or rejected some innovation, whether it was a new form of technology, a new idea, or a new cultural trait of any other kind.

As it turned out, those insights would be provided by a study that at the time did not seem even remotely related to issues in mass communication. It was a study by rural sociologists of how an agricultural innovation was adopted by a number of Iowa farmers who raised corn. However, over a number of decades this study, which was relatively obscure at the time, has come to be regarded as a milestone in mass communication research. It was the first in a long series that has revealed a more complete understanding of how adoption takes place and the role of communication in the process, including the part played by mass media in bringing an innovation to the attention of a relevant population.

## THE CONTRIBUTION OF RURAL SOCIOLOGY

In order to understand why and how the seminal study of the adoption of innovation came to be conducted by rural sociologists, one must first understand the background of that field. That background includes the nature of rural sociology and why its practitioners turned their attention to the adoption of new practices among farmers.

The story begins with the Morrill Act, which President Lincoln signed in 1862. That federal legislation was to have truly significant consequences for both American agriculture, higher education in the United States, and our under-standing of the adoption of innovation. Essentially, the act set aside and deeded to each of the states "an amount of public land, to be apportioned to each State a quantity equal to thirty thousand acres for each senator and representative in Congress."[8] The purpose was to help the states establish educational institutions that would be of special benefit to rural youth. The act required that "the leading object shall be . . . to teach such branches of learning as are related to agriculture and the mechanical arts. . . ."[9] As a consequence, the states established what have since become the so-called "land-grant" universities. Many of these institutions still retain the word *state* as part of their name (e.g., Ohio State, Pennsylvania State, Michigan State, and so on).

Later, in an effort to stimulate the growth and quality of the nation's agricultural industry, federal funds and other financial supports were provided to each of these institutions for an agricultural experiment station. The mission of these stations was to conduct research on ways to improve crops, land management, animal husbandry, and related agricultural matters. They also offered instruction to help train farmers in the use of these procedures and technologies. In addition, they employed "extension agents" who were specialists in various fields related to agriculture. These agents served as field advisers to farmers to help them solve specific problems pertaining to crops, animals, or related matters.

As the land-grant institutions grew during the present century, they took on additional missions. Many became academic institutions that closely resembled their more traditional counterparts. Early in the century, most of the land grant institutions were called "state colleges" (as in Washington State College), and the "of Agriculture" or "of Agriculture and the Mechanical Arts" portion of the title had been dropped. Still later, during the decades following World War II, these titles were changed even further, and most of the land-grant institutions became "universities." As these changes took place, the institutions organized their various academic departments internally into traditional "colleges" and "schools," such as a college of arts and sciences, a school of education, or a college of agriculture (in which departments and other groups continued the basic agricultural mission). By the 1930s, most of these changes and consolidations had already been accomplished.

Among those academic units typically included in a school of agriculture was a department of rural sociology. As is still the case, rural sociologists focused their research attention on human problems among farmers, agricultural workers, and other rural residents. As Thomas Valente and Everett Rogers have noted, before

World War II, sociologists working on human problems among rural populations were often regarded with some suspicion by their deans and other administrators in schools of agriculture.[10] The reason was that such colleges received the lion's share of their budgets from the U.S. Department of Agriculture, which was financially at the mercy of Congress. Few bureaucrats or college administrators welcomed any kind of controversy with that body. But, during the 1930s, just such unwelcome controversies had arisen over the research of certain rural sociologists. Reports had been published on human problems on corporation farms in California and on dissatisfying race relations in Mississippi. This offended certain members of Congress and led them to criticize rural sociology. Thus, both bureaucrats in the Department of Agriculture and college administrators at the time often perceived the studies of rural sociologists as of dubious value and possibly, politically dangerous.

After World War II came to a close, an additional set of background conditions became important. American agricultural technology began to move forward rapidly. For example, new pesticides had been developed, and innovations came rapidly in the use of antibiotics to control animal diseases. Farm machines were greatly improved; new chemicals came into use to control weeds; and hormone supplements were developed to add to feeds so as to increase animal growth. As a result of these remarkable innovations, American farmers began to increase their productivity per acre and per worker at an unprecedented rate. Indeed, the production of food and other agricultural products became so efficient that great surpluses began to develop. Eventually, programs had to be devised that paid farmers *not* to grow crops. New federal programs severely limited the amount of acreage that they could place in production and still receive price supports.

One of the main factors in these developments that became evident was that farmers did not all instantly adopt the innovative marvels that resulted from the research. For example, even though a new way of plowing, a new kind of weed spray, or a new type of animal feed could be shown to improve productivity, farmers sometimes ignored, or at least resisted, adopting these new technologies. A few farmers seemed to take up such improvements rather rapidly. Eventually, many others would follow. However, adoption was seldom universal. This frustrated the agricultural scientists who conducted research that resulted in improved farm technology and practices. Resisting their contributions, they felt, was not rational, and reasons for such resistance needed study.

It was against this background that the problem of resistance versus adoption of innovation, which had so interested Tarde, Pemberton, Chapin, and other students of social change, was to become an important area of study among rural sociologists. Several early investigations of the effectiveness of a communication medium—agricultural bulletins issued by the Federal Extension Service—in promoting new farm technologies were undertaken by rural sociologists. Though most of the resulting research reports were known only within limited circles, they suggested the importance of this line of inquiry. These relatively obscure studies indicated that the *process* by which farmers adopted new agricultural technology included communication in one way or another.

Rural sociologists soon came to realize that the human problem of the adoption of innovations was an important area of research that fit well with the goals and objectives of the schools of agriculture. As this line of inquiry by rural sociologists progressed, it gained approval and support from their administrators. Instead of suspicion and rejection, rural sociologists began to find ready acceptance for their studies. One of the studies that was undertaken as a result took place at Iowa State University, one of the major land-grant institutions. It looked at human factors in the adoption of an important agricultural innovation.

## THE DIFFUSION OF HYBRID SEED CORN
## IN TWO IOWA COMMUNITIES

One of the most important innovations in agricultural technology during the years preceding World War II was the development of hybrid seed corn. The term *hybrid* refers to the offspring of any genetically mixed parentage. With respect to a plant, it means the crossing of varieties of unlike genetic constitution by controlled pollination. If the parent plants are appropriately selected, such hybrids can have a vigor and resistance to such factors as drought and disease that are not found in the contributing strains. Just such qualities were present in the hybrid seed corn that was developed in the late 1920s at Iowa State University and at other land-grant institutions. The innovation was then produced and sold to farmers by hybrid seed companies during the depression years of the 1930s.

While such seeds undoubtedly have many advantages, there is one negative feature that must be considered. Hybrid seed does not reproduce. Thus, farmers who had for generations reserved seed from their current crop so as to plant another year could not do so with the hybrid varieties. They had to purchase new seeds for every planting. That, of course, represented a considerable expense—especially during the 1930s, which had been so difficult for farmers. Offsetting this economic disadvantage, however, was the fact that the use of hybrid seed led to much larger crops of better overall quality and with somewhat less risk to the perils of drought. Still, there were these trade-offs, and they came to be important factors as individual farmers considered adoption. Nevertheless, the benefits seemed so clear for the nation's food supply that during the 1930s the U.S. Department of Agriculture (through extension services, experiment stations, and land-grant institutions) increasingly advocated the use of hybrid seed by midwestern corn farmers.

By virtually any measure, hybrid seed corn was a great success as an agricultural technology. As Bryce Ryan and Neal Gross reported in 1943:

> The introduction of hybrid seed corn has been the most striking technical advance in midwestern agriculture during the past decade. Although a few experimenters had been acquainted with this new and sturdier seed for many years, only since 1937 has it become a nationally

important production factor. It has been estimated that between 1933 and 1939 acreage in hybrid corn increased from 40,000 to 24 million acres (about one-fourth of the nation's corn acreage.)[11]

In spite of the fact that the use of this agricultural innovation had spread rapidly among corn growers in many parts of the country, relatively little was known about the process of adoption on an individual basis. By 1939, for example, 75 percent of the farmers in Iowa were planting hybrid seed. Yet no studies had been made *why* such farmers had altered their traditional practice of saving seed from year to year. What information did they receive, through what channels, and how did this influence their decision making?

A study of the adoption of innovation that is now regarded as a classic is that of Ryan and Gross. Published in 1943, the study was designed by Ryan as a means of focusing on hybrid seed corn and its adoption among two groups of farmers in Iowa. At the time, Ryan had been on the faculty of the Iowa State University in the department of rural sociology since 1938 and was interested in processes of social change, and especially in nonrational aspects of economic decision making. Gross, who became Ryan's graduate assistant in 1941, played a key role in gathering the data through interviews with farmers. The data from the study were used in his master's thesis.[12]

## Purpose of the Study

The overall goal of the study was stated by Ryan and Gross in the following terms:

> Analysis of this diffusion has a special significance in that it represents a farm trait which can almost unqualifiedly be termed a "good (economic) farm practice." The study of its spread may offer some factual knowledge of conditions attendant to the eminently successful diffusion of a rational technique.[13]

In more specific terms, a number of significant questions were explored. First, what background factors, such as the general condition of the economy, played a part in the decisions of farmers to take up this new kind of seed? That is, were farmers inhibited by the cost of purchasing the seed or were their decisions accelerated by the prospect or larger profits? Second, exactly how did this innovation come to their attention? In other words, what were the channels of information by which adopters first learned of the innovation? For example, what were the roles of radio, print media, personal contacts with change agents (such as salesmen), information and advice received from friends, or communications from other sources? Moreover, what was the relative importance of each of these channels in the individual's ultimate decision to adopt? Third, how long did it take between awareness and action? Specifically, once the farmer knew of the new seed, did he begin using it right away, or did it take some time? If so, how much time lapsed before adoption? And finally, what was the *pattern* by which the innovation spread over time? That is, did it follow a cumulative normal ogive, as had been the case with those innovations studied by Pemberton, or what?

## Method

To provide answers to these questions, Ryan designed a study based on personal interviews with farmers who were raising corn. He selected two small communities about 40 to 50 miles from Ames, the site of Iowa State University. Each of the 259 farmers finally included in the study lived near either Jefferson or Grand Junction, quite typical of small towns in the Iowa Corn Belt. Each farmer studied (all of which were males) had more than 20 acres in production and was included in the sample only if he had begun planting corn before hybrid seed became available. Thus, each respondent in the sample had been able to adopt the new seed as an innovation.

Gross interviewed each of these respondents. Data were gathered as to when they had begun their first use of hybrid seed corn (if they indeed were using it). They were asked to identify their earliest source of information about the new kind of seed and when that information had come to their attention. The respondents were also asked to evaluate the importance of these sources. That is, how important were they in leading them to take up the practice?

## Findings

One thing that Ryan and Gross found was that adoption tended to be on a gradual and almost experimental basis. Few farmers had switched their entire acreage from the older, freely pollinated seed to the new hybrid in a single planting. Most had tried it out on a smaller plot before making the change. The general economic state of the nation may have been an important background factor here. The 1930s were, after all, the years of the Great Depression. Farmers had suffered grievous losses early in the decade, when many could not sell their crops and simply had to let them remain in the fields to rot. Then, as the Roosevelt administration developed federal programs to support agriculture, things got better. However, laying out a substantial amount of money for a new kind of seed, even with the promise of a more bountiful harvest, was still a gamble. Thus, the essential conservatism of midwestern farmers, plus the economic difficulties of the time, held back wholesale and immediate adoption.

How did the innovation come to their attention? A number of different channels were involved. Nearly half cited salesmen from the seed companies as their earliest source of information. About 10 percent learned of its existence from advertisements on the radio. Articles in farm journals accounted for an additional 10.7 percent. Only 14.6 percent named neighbors as their initial source. A few learned from the university's extension service, another small number from relatives and so on.

Not all of these sources were equally important. For example, even though neighbors were not named with great frequency as the origins of their earliest information, they were identified as the *most influential* source. In the opposite direction, while salesmen were identified as the most frequent source of initial information, they were not as significant as neighbors in their ultimate decision to adopt. Table 6.1 shows the percentages of these various categories as initial sources and as influences in their decisions to adopt.

The time factor between first learning and decision to adopt turned out to be a complex one. Generally, there was a gap of several years between the time when a farmer first heard of hybrid seed corn and the point at which he actually began to plant it. In fact, there was a modal time lag of between five and six years between first hearing of the innovation and actually adopting it (see Figure 6.1). Thus, a lot of farmers knew about hybrid seed corn before they took action to plant it.

There was a also a complex relationship between time and the degree to which various interpersonal and media sources were active as channels of information and influential in the adoption decision. As Figure 6.2 shows, salesmen were clearly the most active sources of information for those who adopted in the early period when farmers were learning of the existence of the new seed (1928 to 1935). And, as Figure 6.3 shows, they were also quite influential among those who adopted early during the first half of those years during which most adoptions were actually made (1935 to 1940). That influence declined sharply during the period, however, and for those who adopted late (after about 1936), salesmen were much less significant in the decision to adopt.

Of the interpersonal channels, neighbors were important in two ways. They played an increasingly significant role in bringing the seed to the attention of adopters during the early 1930s, and they became increasingly influential throughout the years when the new seed was actually being adopted. Indeed, they were far more influential than salesmen during the last half of the 1930s. Mass media, such as farm journals and radio advertising, were clearly not as

**TABLE 6.1** Operators citing specific original sources of knowledge of hybrid seed and most influential sources

| Source | Original Knowledge (%) | Most Influential (%) |
|---|---|---|
| Neighbors | 14.6 | 45.5 |
| Salesmen | 49.0 | 32.0 |
| Farm journal | 10.7 | 2.3 |
| Radio advertising | 10.3 | |
| Extension service* | 2.8 | 2.4 |
| Relatives | 3.5 | 4.2 |
| Personal experimentation | | 6.6 |
| All others** | 9.1 | 7.0 |
| Total | 100.0 | 100.0 |

\* Including county agent, bulletins, etc.
\*\* Including unknown.
SOURCE: Bryce Ryan and Neal C. Gross, "The Diffusion of Hybrid Seed Corn in Two Iowa Communities," *Rural Sociology*, 8 (March 1943).

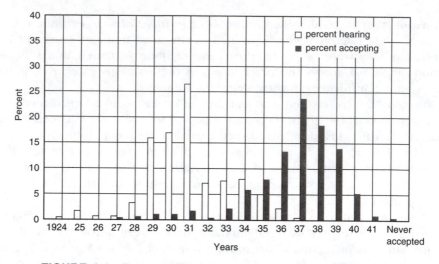

**FIGURE 6.1** Farm operators first hearing of hybrid seed corn and first accepting it, by years

SOURCE: Bryce Ryan and Neal C. Gross, "The Diffusion of Hybrid Seed Corn in Two Iowa Communities," *Rural Sociology,* 8 (March 1943).

**FIGURE 6.2** Percents of farm operators first hearing of hybrid seed corn through various channels, by year first heard

SOURCE: Bryce Ryan and Neal C. Gross, "The Diffusion of Hybrid Seed Corn in Two Iowa Communities," *Rural Sociology,* 8 (March 1943).

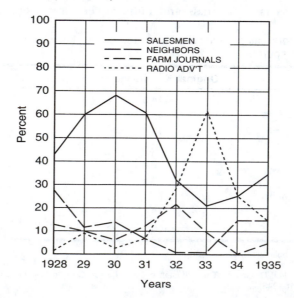

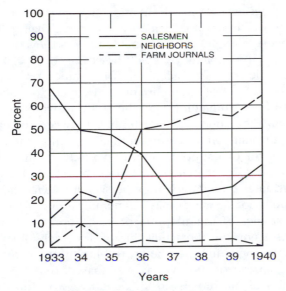

**FIGURE 6.3**  Percents of farm operators accepting hybrid seed corn in different years assigning major influence to various sources

SOURCE: Bryce Ryan and Neal C. Gross, "The Diffusion of Hybrid Seed Corn in Two Iowa Communities," *Rural Sociology*, 8 (March 1943).

important in the adoption of this particular innovation as interpersonal contacts. However, both played some part in bringing the innovation to the attention of the respondents, particularly before 1935.

## IMPLICATIONS

Clearly, the processes of interaction identified by Ryan and Gross as underlying the acquisition of this agricultural technology did not fit the assumptions of random activity suggested by Pemberton. That is, the idea that salesmen, county extension agents, relatives, mass communicators, or other parties mentioned in Table 6.1 were in some form of chancelike interpersonal contact with the farmers under study does not make sense. Indeed, what they described was a web of relatively orderly social and media contacts, in which established patterns of social interaction with neighbors and salesmen, plus attention to mass communications, played the central roles in creating awareness of the innovation and defining it as important on the part of those who would adopt it.

It was that finding, that the adoption of innovation depends on some combination of well-established interpersonal ties and habitual exposure to mass communications, that made the Ryan and Gross study important. It became a milestone not because it revealed how a particular kind of corn seed came to be used by farmers in Iowa but in part because it moved attention from *pattern* to *process* in the study of the adoption of innovation as a basis for social change. Tarde had tried to identify that process in 1890 but was not able to do so, given the undeveloped state of sociology and psychology. By 1943, however, the social sciences were ready to incorporate the process of adoption of innovation on an individual basis into the general body of concepts important to the study of social change.

For students of mass communication, the study provided a foundation and conceptual framework for understanding the link between *awareness* of something new—often through information supplied by mass media—and *action* resulting in some form of adoption. Adoption might mean purchases of an advertised product, changes of beliefs advocated by an information campaign, modifications of attitudes brought about by persistent public relations efforts, or other changes in behavior in which mass communications played a role.

As additional studies of the adoption of innovation were undertaken, the boundaries between studies of the acquisition of new technology and the study of influences of mass communication began to blur. By the early 1960s, interest in research on the spread of innovations had soared. In 1962, Everett Rogers reviewed 506 studies of the process in his definitive work on the process and effects of the diffusion of innovations.[14] The innovations under study by that time included medical practices, agricultural technology, educational changes, birth control methods, consumer products, manufacturing techniques, and a variety of other inventions and changes.

As the focus of scholarship broadened from pattern to process, efforts were increasingly made to understand the nature and sequences involved when individuals made decisions to acquire and use something new. One result was conceptual clarity. For example, Rogers defined an innovation in a straightforward manner as "an idea, practice or object that is perceived as new by an individual or other unit of adoption."[15] This definition has significant advantages. For one thing, it makes the perception of the individual the key to what constitutes an innovation. That is, it does not matter whether or not something is in fact "new." It can be regarded as an innovation if it *appears* to be new to the adopter. Furthermore, his definition is consistent with the earliest studies of the process in that it applies equally to individual persons (such as farmers) or to other kinds of adopters (such as nations, cities, organizations, and other kinds of groups).

Rogers clarified the work of Ryan and Gross by identifying five major stages in the adoption process. These were *awareness, interest, evaluation, trial,* and finally, *adoption.* In the first stage, the potential adopter learns of the existence of the innovation. It is at this point that the mass media, as well as interpersonal contacts, bring the relevant information to the attention of the potential user. This part of the process was well mapped by Ryan and Gross in their classic study of hybrid seed corn.

Rogers also addressed the question of whether awareness of an innovation is created on a random basis (suggesting the interpretation advanced by Pemberton). The answer is that this seems most unlikely. For example, becoming aware of hybrid seed corn would have meant little to the average city dweller, even if he or she might have encountered the information by chance. However, it was significant information for a corn farmer in Iowa. Thus, Rogers concludes that awareness is undoubtedly related to some type of *need* that could potentially be satisfied by the new product or technology.[16]

Once the individual is aware of the innovation, his or her interest may be aroused. If not, the process ends with this second stage. But if interest has been aroused, mass communications as well as interpersonal contacts may play a critical role. That is, interest can lead the individual to search actively in a purposive way for more information about the innovation. As Rogers points out, all of the variables that lead to selective use of media and other information sources become important at this point.[17]

Once the nature of the innovation is understood, the third stage becomes important. The individual has to evaluate whether or not it will indeed meet the need that was a necessary condition in the previous stage. Rogers calls this a sort of "mental trial" stage, during which the person decides whether the problem-solving advantages of adopting the innovation outweigh its disadvantages (costs, risks, effort, etc.).[18]

In the fourth, or trial, stage the innovation is actually used. If possible, this is done on a small scale. This was clearly the case among the Iowa farmers, who often planted a small part of their acreage in the new corn so as to compare it with what they had been doing. But for many innovations, small-scale trials may not be possible. In some cases, the new item can be used temporarily before a final decision is made. Taking a test drive in a new car before a final purchase decision is made would be one example. If small scale or temporary use is possible, many potential adopters pass through this trial stage.

The final stage is actual adoption. The individual has made a decision and the new item is acquired. Presumably, it continues to be used on a more or less permanent basis. The individual becomes a part of the population who has adopted, and he or she is added to the S-shaped curve.

An additional line of inquiry opened by the Ryan and Gross study was a concern with the differences between *types of people* who adopted the innovation at various points along the accumulating curve. Distinctions were discussed between what they called "early acceptors" (true innovators who were the very first to try out the new seed), "early adopters" (a slightly larger number who began using after seeing it demonstrated by the early acceptors), the "majority" (who adopted in large numbers between 1940 and 1941), and "later acceptors" (who did not take up the innovation until most of their neighbors were already using it). Thus, in addition to the shift from *pattern* to *process* as a major emphasis, as discussed earlier, the hybrid seed corn study also identified types of *people* as a focus of concern.

In later years, differences between types of people in terms of categories of adopters came to be exhaustively studied.[19] For example, Rogers brought together the pattern, the process, and the types of people into a synthesis of adopter categories on the basis of a personality trait of "innovativeness." Figure 6.4 shows how each type of individual relates to the adoption curve.

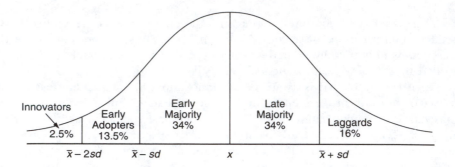

**FIGURE 6.4**  Relationship between types of adopters classified by innovativeness and their location on the adoption curve

SOURCE: Everett M. Rogers, *Diffusion of Innovations,* 3rd ed. (New York: Free Press, 1963), p. 247.

**FIGURE 6.5**  Shapes of curves of diffusion for innovations that spread over various periods of time

SOURCE: Everett M. Rogers, *Diffusion of Innovations,* 3rd ed. (New York: Free Press, 1963), p. 11.

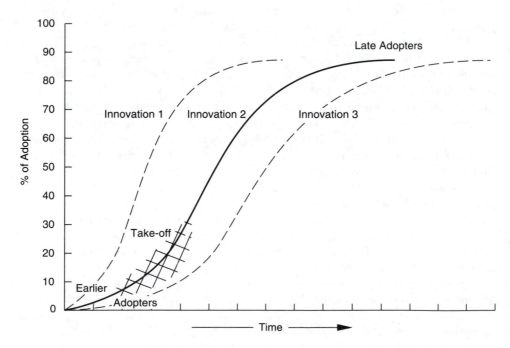

Rogers also defined *diffusion* in a way that identified the major related concepts. Essentially, he maintained, it is the process by which an *innovation* is *communicated* through certain *channels* over *time* among the members of a *social system.*[20] As the hybrid seed corn study (and earlier research) indicated, as this process takes place, some sort of S-shaped adoption curve describes the proportion of a relevant population of potential adopting units who have taken up the time at various points in time. However, as research accumulated, it became clear that different types of innovations diffuse at different rates. This creates a *family* of different-appearing curves. For example, some innovations may sweep through a set of adopters rather swiftly (such as home TV receivers between 1950 and 1960). Under these conditions, they will form a curve such as that described by Innovation 1 in Figure 6.5. Others (such as daily newspapers between about 1840 and 1910) may take many decades to become widely adopted, and their diffusion pattern will form a curve such as that of Innovation 3.[21] Thus, the pattern of adoption (swift or slow) that will be followed by any particular innovation will depend on the particular trait and the characteristics of the social system, as well as the types of people who become aware of its existence and potential value for their purposes.


## CONCLUSIONS

The Ryan and Gross study became a milestone because it focused attention on the major factors involved in the adoption of innovation: (1) a specific innovation, (2) processes of interpersonal and mass communication that created awareness of the item, (3) a specific kind of social system, and (4) different types of individuals who made decisions at various stages as use of the item diffused. Furthermore, it provided a pivotal point at which scholarly interest began to shift from an almost exclusive concern with the pattern formed by adoption in a population over time to the behavior involved in the process of adoption.

For the study of mass communication, an important point concerning the hybrid seed corn study concerns the relative role played by media versus that of interpersonal channels in creating awareness. Actually, the Ryan and Gross study emphasized diffusion as a sociological phenomenon. That is, the research did *not* show that mass communications were particularly important, either in informing the relevant population about the innovation or in persuading them to adopt it. For many other kinds of innovations today, that would not be the case; the media would be far more significant. The reason that mass communications played a relatively minor part in the diffusion of the adoption of the hybrid seed corn in Iowa at the time is that the setting was a rural environment closely resembling a traditional society where word-of-mouth communication channels were more important. Moreover, it was not the kind of innovation that would normally be advertised via the common mass media that were operative at the time. Thus, among the farmers studied, interpersonal channels (salesmen and neighbors) were far more important in bringing the innovation to the attention of potential adopters than were radio, movies, magazines, or newspapers.

In pointing to the role of interpersonal communications, the Ryan and Gross study parallels what was independently found by Lazarsfeld and his associates in the discovery of the two-step flow process in the very different setting of *The People's Choice* (chapter 4), and by Katz and Lazarsfeld later in their research on personal influence in still another setting (chapter 9).

In a more urban setting, then or now, where one's neighbors may be total strangers, one would seldom expect to receive a great deal of information about an innovation by word-of-mouth channels. For some, family and friends may play a part; neighbors may not be so important. People may live in the same building, but contacts between them tend to be far less frequent than between families living on adjacent farms. Indeed, in cities there may be no contact with neighbors at all. Moreover, salespeople do not have the same access to residents in urban environments as they have with rural populations.

Overall, for city dwellers the mass media are undoubtedly far more significant as sources of first learning of almost any new idea, product, or service. People hear of a new soft drink or laxative from ads on television; they find out about a new model of a fishing rod or kind of computer software from magazines devoted to their interests; they learn of a new hairstyle or slang expression in a movie. Even an innovation related to their occupation or business will usually come to their attention via a newsletter or specialty magazine rather than from neighbors or from family and friends. Thus, the ratio between interpersonal and mass media channels is likely to be drastically reversed for most innovations adopted in more urban settings.

Nevertheless, the study of hybrid seed corn set the stage for a flood of research that greatly expanded our understanding of the process of the adoption of innovations of all kinds, regardless of whether those who consider the new trait first learned by interpersonal channels or via the mass media. The important points revealed by the Ryan and Gross study were the ideas of stages in the adoption process, the different categories of adopters, and the channels by which they receive different influences from various sources. These contributions remain as an important conceptualization of the way in which new traits spread through a relevant population of adopting units.

Finally, Rogers estimated that by September 1993, more than 5,000 studies of the diffusion process and their patterns over time had been published.[22] Studies of the adoption of innovations have been widely pursued in such fields as national development, public health, geography, marketing, the adoption of media technologies, changes in manufacturing processes, educational innovations, new government policies, and dozens of others.[23] Clearly, the modest study of the ways in which farmers in two communities in Iowa had adopted a new kind of hybrid seed corn has had a profound intellectual impact in understanding the role of mass communication in this kind of social and cultural change.

## NOTES AND REFERENCES

1. For a discussion of dependency theory, which describes this type of change in channels of communication, see Melvin L. DeFleur and Everette E. Dennis, *Understanding Mass Communication,* 5th ed. (Boston: Houghton Mifflin, 1994), pp. 18-19.
2. Gabriel Tarde, *The Laws of Imitation,* trans. Elsie C. Parsons (New York: Henry Holt, 1903), p. 140. First published in Paris in 1890.
3. See Simon S. Kuznets, *Secular Movements in Production and Prices* (Boston: Houghton Mifflin, 1930).
4. For a pioneering discussion of such curves applied to biological phenomena, see Raymond S. Pearl, *The Biology of Population Growth* (New York: Alfred A. Knopf, 1925).
5. F. Stuart Chapin, *Cultural Change* (New York: Century Company, 1928), p. 376.
6. H. Earl Pemberton, "The Curve of Cultural Diffusion Rate," *American Sociological Review* 1 (August 1936): 547.
7. See James W. Tankard, Jr., *The Statistical Pioneers* (Cambridge, Mass.: Schenkman Publishing, 1984), pp. 21-38.
8. Morrill Act, ch. 130, §1, 12 Stat. 503 (1862).
9. Ibid.
10. The authors are grateful to Thomas W. Valente and Everett M. Rogers, for providing them with their paper "The Rise and Fall of Rural Sociological Research on the Diffusion of Innovations: The Ryan and Gross Paradigm." This paper was presented at the Midwest Sociological Society, Chicago, April 1993. A number of the sections of the present chapter concerning the state of agricultural research and rural sociology are based on this report.
11. Bryce Ryan and Neal C. Gross, "The Diffusion of Hybrid Seed Corn in Two Iowa Communities," *Rural Sociology* 8 (March 1943): 15.
12. The authors are grateful to Bryce Ryan (with whom one of the authors became acquainted after Ryan retired as chairman of the Department of Sociology at the University of Miami in Coral Gables, Florida) for sharing some of his recollections of the Iowa State project.
13. Ryan and Gross, "The Diffusion of Hybrid Seed Corn," p. 16.
14. Everett M. Rogers, *Diffusion of Innovations,* 3rd ed. (New York: Free Press, 1963), p. 5.
15. Ibid., p. 11.
16. Ibid., pp. 81-82.
17. Ibid., pp. 82-83.
18. Ibid., p. 85.
19. See, for example, "Adopter Categories as Ideal Types," in ibid., pp. 247-270.
20. Ibid., p. 11.
21. For an extended discussion of the spread of these media through American society, see DeFleur and Dennis, *Understanding Mass Communication,* 5th ed.
22. Personal correspondence with the authors.
23. Rogers, *Diffusion of Innovations,* pp. 38-86.

# chapter 7

# Experiments with Film: Persuading the American Soldier in World War II

On Sunday, December 7, 1941, Americans, in near disbelief, heard from their radios that Japanese aircraft had without warning attacked U.S. naval and other military forces at Pearl Harbor. The heavy loss of life and disastrous destruction of ships, aircraft, and Army bases left the nation reeling. Nearly a quarter of a century of peacetime had come to a sudden end.

How could it be? Who were these strange people who came from nowhere to commit such a dastardly deed? The Japanese, in the minds of most Americans—if they thought of them at all—were a rather pathetic little nation of slant-eyed people who made cheap imitations of products developed by more advanced countries. It simply did not seem possible that such people could dare to assault the might of the United States of America! Nevertheless, the forces of the Empire of Japan had blasted most of the U.S. Pacific Fleet to ruined hulks and had humiliated the armed forces of what Americans regarded as the finest nation on earth.

The next day, President Franklin D. Roosevelt in a special joint session of Congress addressed the country by radio to declare that a state of war existed between the United States and the Empire of Japan. The President called December 7 "a date which will live in infamy." The state of war was extended to include all of the Axis powers who were allied with Japan.

In the days that followed, Japan's victories at Pearl Harbor were to be repeated in other areas of vital significance to the United States. The Philippines were quickly overrun, and their American defenders were subjected to a terrible "death march" on the Bataan peninsula. The Japanese overran virtually the whole Southwest Pacific, threatening Australia and New Zealand. They even landed on remote parts of Alaska. For the first time, the United States was called upon to fight for its very existence against the hostile forces of a foreign enemy.

## THE NATION AT WAR

World War II was a conflict with a clear-cut moral purpose. The Axis powers (Germany, Japan, and Italy) vowed to subdue the world with military might and to dominate it with their various brands of dictatorship and fascism. The Allied forces, made up of the United States, what was left of the British Empire, and the remnants of various armed forces from countries that had been overrun by the early victories of the enemy, vowed to fight back to an eventual "unconditional surrender" of the Axis nations.

From the point of view of the United States, it was a war with the highest possible justification—a very different situation from more recent conflicts. The Japanese had "stabbed America in the back." In the minds of most citizens, the Japanese were sneaky, cruel, and virtually subhuman. The Germans had overrun helpless people in Europe and violated every treaty that had been forged at the end of World War I. They were widely held to be ruthless, cunning, and brutal. The Italians, on the other hand, were regarded with low esteem—a joke as soldiers, but a bother nevertheless.

All of these attitudes and beliefs were quickly taken up and reinforced by the mass media, by thousands of political speeches, cartoons, posters, and barroom exchanges. Hollywood epics and newspaper editorials portrayed the Germans as "pretty tough," but the Japanese as monkeylike people who should not be taken seriously. Some people maintained that the enemy would be easily defeated and the war brought to an end within a year. But as many a soldier, sailor, and marine found out later in combat, crude stereotypes obscured the fact that the enemy was tough, determined, and thoroughly courageous.

### Turning Citizens into Soldiers

For a few weeks after Pearl Harbor, volunteers lined up at the recruiting offices and even scuffled with each other to be among the earliest to enlist. But the rush to get into the fight soon waned, and the less enthusiastic had to be brought in by the Selective Service System—the draft. Actually there was little resistance; to be a "draft dodger" during World War II was considered a disgrace. Even those classified as 4-F (not suitable for military service because of health or occupation essential to the war effort) were all but accused of being cowards. By the war's end, some 15 million Americans, mostly males but also many dedicated females, had donned uniforms.

The sheer logistics of locating, sorting, classifying, training, and assigning 15 million people to military duties staggers the imagination. Nevertheless, it was done. Young men and women from every walk of civilian life were transformed from their roles and statuses as bank clerks, secretaries, truck drivers, farmers, and so on, into riflemen, artillerymen, bosuns, sergeants, cooks, signalmen, pilots, navigators, and all of the other specialists that were required by the military services. What is more, it was done in a very short time.

Camps were set up in all parts of the nation, and recruits were quickly brought in for training. The men's hair was cut short, and they exchanged their civilian clothes for uniforms. Awkward at first, they soon settled into the routines of training—close order drill, the correct use of weapons, the intricacies of military life, and the inevitable specialized training required in the complex division of labor of a modern army or navy.

Teaching a recruit such matters as wearing a uniform and how to salute, march, and use weapons is the less difficult part of military training. Beyond that lies the more complex task of shaping his motivation and morale. He has to be taught to hate the enemy and love his country, to be intensely dedicated to his military unit, and to place its survival and welfare above his own. In other words, in developing an effective fighting force, it is essential to instill attitudes and loyalties that can provide critical psychological and social supports that sustain the combat soldier when the going gets tough. As a matter of fact, the vast majority of those so trained never saw combat. Nevertheless, they had to be taught to place military goals above their personal convenience and comfort even when the job was boring, seemingly endless, and obviously insignificant. For those who would see combat, indoctrination was needed to prepare them psychologically to confront and defeat a very determined and dangerous enemy. There was simply no other choice.

Turning millions of young civilians into effective teams of military personnel was no easy task. The training was made more difficult by the sheer diversity of American society. Draftees were called into service from every corner of the country. They came from ethnic communities in urban centers, small towns in the Midwest, farms in the rural South, and cattle ranches in the Far West. Not only were they diverse in regional origin, but they varied greatly in every other respect. They differed in education, income, occupation, religion, political affiliation, and so on. This diversity in social origins meant that the recruits also represented a broad range of individual differences in intelligence, aptitudes, values, skills, and other psychological factors. It was not easy to assess their differences and to assign these human resources to military tasks that they were capable of performing. To do so, the Army (and other services) made use of psychologists, sociologists, and other social scientists who developed tests to measure intelligence and other attributes so that the proverbial "square pegs" among the recruits would not wind up in the "round holes" among the tasks that needed to be performed.

## The Lessons to Be Learned:
## The *Why We Fight* Films

Another serious problem was the sheer ignorance of the majority of the draftees concerning public affairs. Few of the recruits had any real grasp of the complex international events that had led up to the entry of the United States into the war. They knew well enough that "the Japs were the dirty guys" because they had bombed Pearl Harbor in a sneaky way. They also knew that "the Germans were mean guys" because they had overrun some of the countries of Europe and wanted to take over the world. That was about it! Beyond these simple ideas, the majority had very little knowledge of the political history of the period between the two world wars, the existence or substance of the negotiations between the United States and Japan before Pearl Harbor, the sequence of events that led to the rise of totalitarian governments in Europe, or the strategies of those governments for world conquest.

Why were they so ignorant of international events? In large part, the United States was isolated from world problems, by both its physical location in the new world and its preoccupation with its own internal affairs. Since the end of World War I, Americans had been focusing their attention on such domestic matters as Prohibition, the Great Depression, the dust bowl, and the New Deal. The troubles in Europe and Asia were beyond the interest and comprehension of all but a few of the draftees. Yet it was essential that the recruits have a good understanding of these events.

The U.S. Army was painfully aware of the need to inform its recruits, but how it could be done was another matter. Army leaders saw immediately that they needed a rapid and effective means of teaching soldiers about the nature of the enemy, their allies, and why it was necessary to be there training for war. The use of *a series of training films* to do the task quickly and for large numbers of trainees seemed a sensible way to get the job done. However, there were no such films, and they would have to be prepared very quickly.

Early in 1942, General George C. Marshall, newly appointed chief of staff of the Army, turned to Hollywood to assist in the preparation of the necessary orientation films. Specifically, he sought the aid of Frank Capra, a well-known director. His proposal was simple:

> Now Capra, I want to nail down with you a plan to make a series of documentary, factual information films—the first in our history—that will explain to our boys why we are fighting and the principles for which we are fighting.[1]

Capra wanted to help, but he wasn't certain that he was the right person to do the job. He explained to General Marshall that he lacked the right kind of experience. He had never made documentary films before. General Marshall had a simple answer:

> Capra, I have never been Chief of Staff before. Thousands of young Americans have never had their legs shot off before. Boys are commanding ships today who a year ago had never seen the ocean.[2]

Capra was convinced and began work immediately. In a very short time, he had produced seven 50-minute documentary films, and the army started making them a part of the training program for its recruits.

The style of the films was for the most part objective and documentary, with direct quotations, reference to official sources, animated diagrams, cuts from domestic newsreels, and cuts from foreign newsreels and propaganda films. The visual presentation was drawn together by a running narration which told the story of the war and explained the scenes. While the general tenor of the films was "let the facts speak for themselves," they were not dryly factual. Foreign speech was frequently translated into English with a "foreign accent," "production" shots using actors were employed to tie the documentary material together, the films were scored throughout with background music, and montages and trick photography were used in trying to achieve vivid and dramatic presentation.[3]

Generally, these seven films traced the history of World War II from the rise of fascism in Italy and Germany, and the Japanese attack on Manchuria in 1931, through America's mobilization for war and participation in the conflict following Pearl Harbor.[4] The title of the series was *Why We Fight,* and the films were seen by hundreds of thousands of Americans as they trained for war. However, only four of these films were used in the research described in the present chapter. The content of these four films can be summarized briefly.

*Prelude to War.* This first film in the series described the rise of Mussolini and fascism in Italy, the rise of Hitler and Nazism in Germany, and the manner in which a military clique gained control in Japan. It showed the Japanese attack on Manchuria in 1931 and the Italian conquest of Ethiopia in 1935. In contrast, the film showed how the United States had followed a noninterventionist policy and had not prepared for global war. It made clear how the Axis countries had emphasized the growth of aggressive militarism and the massing of armed might. The major theme of the film was that the three Axis countries had joined in a plan to conquer the world and to divide it up to suit themselves. There was no way for the United States to ignore the war, and it had to defend itself; this defense was all the more difficult because of the lack of preparedness.

*The Nazis Strike.* This film presented a summary of the past military conquests of Germany under Bismarck and Kaiser Wilhelm, indicating that Hitler's aggressions were repeat performances of such behavior. The way in which Hitler had built up his war forces was described, and his first acquisitions of territory were shown (the Austrian *Anschluss* and other actions in which Britain tried to appease Hitler by agreeing to his activities). The straw that broke the camel's back was Hitler's attack on Poland, which brought a declaration of war by Britain and France. The Polish campaign was shown in great detail to illustrate the ruthlessness, brutality, and efficiency of the German forces. The major theme of the film was that Hitler could not be appeased and that the Allies had to stop him by declaring war.

*Divide and Conquer.* This was a sequel to *The Nazis Strike.* It continued to show the strategy of the Nazis. It explained how they overran Denmark and Norway to the north. They were aided in this activity by traitors among the local populations (called "quislings," after Vidkun Quisling, a Norwegian Nazi collaborator) and by the failure of Allied efforts to help the Norwegians. To the south, the Nazis invaded the Low Countries (Holland and Belgium) and broke through the Maginot Line—the French defensive fortresses—which permitted the Germans to move through France and catch Britain in a kind of pincers from both north and south. The theme of the film was that the early defensive strategies relied upon by the Allies were unsuccessful in the face of the strategy and tactics used by the Germans.

*The Battle of Britain.* This film dealt with Hitler's plan for world conquest, which had succeeded thus far as his forces defeated France and forced the British to evacuate their armies from the beaches at Dunkirk. The next step was to conquer Britain itself. If Hitler had taken over the British Isles and neutralized the British fleet, the United States would have found itself in a very dangerous situation. The film showed how Hitler failed to conquer England because of the tough resistance of the British, both in the air and on the ground. The Royal Air Force stopped the Luftwaffe cold, even after weeks of the latter's relentless bombing and fighter attacks; the British were bombed severely, but they continued their war effort in spite of the attacks. Thus, winning the "Battle of Britain" gave the United States precious time to prepare.

## Overview of the Research Mission

Generally, two basic assumptions were made by the War Department concerning the *Why We Fight* films. First, it was assumed that they would do an effective job teaching the recruits *factual knowledge* about the war, the enemy, and the Allies. Second, it was assumed that such factual knowledge would shape *interpretations* and *opinions* in ways needed to improve acceptance of military roles and the sacrifices necessary to achieve victory.

In more detail, the orientation program using these films had a number of specific objectives that were spelled out in a directive from the office of the chief of staff to the Information and Education Division, which was in charge of the orientation program. According to this directive, the films were intended to foster:

1. A firm belief in the right of the cause for which we fight.
2. A realization that we are up against a tough job.
3. A determined confidence in our own ability and the abilities of our comrades and leaders to do the job that has to be done.
4. A feeling of confidence, insofar as is possible under the circumstances, in the integrity and fighting ability of our Allies.
5. A resentment, based on knowledge of the facts, against our enemies who have made it necessary to fight.
6. A belief that through military victory, the political achievement of a better world order is possible.

Each of the films had been designed to achieve these objectives, although every one of the seven *Why We Fight* films told only a part of the story.

The big question, of course, is, Did the films work? The films seemed great, and common sense implied that showing them to the recruits as part of their training would not only teach them factual information but would raise their commitment and morale. Yet common sense is not always an adequate basis for reaching reliable conclusions. A systematic and objective evaluation was needed to see if these films were in fact reaching their goals. To accomplish this assessment, the task of designing and conducting evaluation studies of the orientation program was assigned to a special unit within the War Department's Information and Education Division.

Early in the war, the Army had taken the precaution of bringing a number of distinguished social and behavioral scientists into the service. These scientists, in consultation with civilian colleagues, assisted the armed services with a variety of problems involving psychological measurement, evaluation of programs, surveys of many kinds, and studies of "morale." Within the Information and Education Division, the Research Branch was composed of the Experimental Section and the Survey Section. These units often cooperated with the Military Training Division of the Army Service Forces. Indeed, the present research represents just such a cooperative venture between the Experimental Section and Training Division.

While there were a number of psychologists and social psychologists involved in the evaluation of the *Why We Fight* series, the main team that planned and conducted the studies for the Army consisted of Frances J. Anderson, John L. Finan, Carl I. Hovland, Irving L. Janis, Arthur A. Lumsdaine, Nathan Macoby, Fred D. Sheffield, and M. Brewster Smith. The report on which the present summary chapter is based was prepared as volume three in the "American Soldier" series, which was published several years after the war. The authors of the report were Carl I. Hovland, Arthur A. Lumsdaine, and Fred D. Sheffield. Like the others in the longer list above, each went on after the war to become an internationally known psychologist. The remaining sections of the present chapter are devoted to a presentation of the highlights of *Experiments on Mass Communication*, which brought together the results of the film evaluation studies and a number of additional experiments on communication issues. The work touched off a considerable interest, as we will note later, in the experimental study of the persuasion process.[5]

## THE FILM EVALUATION STUDIES

Several experiments were carried out, aimed at assessing the degree to which exposure to the films described above resulted in changes in their audiences. These changes were, broadly speaking the acquisition of *factual information* about various aspects of the war and modification in the recruits' interpretations and *opinions* concerning the six objectives listed earlier.

In designing this research, the experimenters had advantages that had seldom before existed regarding control over their subjects. They could choose where, when, and how many subjects would see a particular film. They did not have to rely on voluntary cooperation in the completion of the questionnaires. They were already in possession of a substantial amount of background information on each subject from Army records, to which they had complete access. The population they were studying had limited variation in terms of age, sex, race, and current residential circumstances. And finally, the costs of the research were not really a consideration. For contemporary scholars struggling with the realities of research today, such conditions would seem made in heaven.

## Assessment of *The Battle of Britain*

Somewhat parallel experiments were completed on each of the four films described earlier. The main difference between them was that the research on *The Battle of Britain* assessed the impact of a single film, whereas the remaining experiments studied the cumulative impact of two or more films or made use of alternative research designs.

*Objectives.*    *The Battle of Britain* presented a considerable amount of factual material, but in the list of the Army's six objectives to be achieved it emphasized number four (a feeling of confidence in our Allies). The overall purpose of the research itself was to measure both knowledge and opinion orientations among the subjects before they saw the film, to expose them to the film, and then to assess any *change* in knowledge and opinions that had been created by seeing the moving picture.

Various procedures and strategies were used to minimize the influence of other sources of information about topics covered in the movie so that whatever change took place could realistically be regarded as due to exposure to the film. The situation of the subjects, relatively isolated from civilian life, was an aid to the researchers in this respect.

*Experimental Procedures.*    The research was organized around (1) the use of an *experimental group* of subjects that actually saw the film and a *control* group of very similar subjects who did not see the film and (2) the administration of anonymous checklist questionnaires to both groups *before* and *after* the time when the experimental group viewed the film. While such procedures are now common in research, at the time this was a relatively new research strategy in communication studies. This way of conducting such an experiment is called a "before/after design with control group." However, an additional study was done with an "after-only" design, where no "before" measure was used and the control and experimental groups were simply compared after the film was shown to the experimental group.

The measuring instruments for the experiment were constructed with great care, and each item that finally became a part of the questionnaires was carefully pretested to make certain that it could be understood by the subjects and that it gathered the exact information that was needed by the researchers. Such pretesting, item by item, is a hallmark of careful research procedures today.

The items finally used in the checklist questionnaires were of two types. These were (1) *fact-quiz* questions, such as those found on a multiple choice test, where the subject selects the correct answer from a list of alternatives, and (2) *opinion* items, either in a multiple choice style, expressing varying opinion positions from which the subject could select that closest to his own, or agree/disagree statements that the subject could endorse or reject as consistent with his own opinions. Some of these opinion items were highly related to the factual information and were quite specific. Other items dealt with broader and more general issues less tied to the facts. The questionnaires also included several personal history items (education, age, and so on) that could be used, along with handwriting, to match the before and after questionnaires of each subject. Finally, there was a need to direct the attention of the subjects away from the idea that they were simply being tested to see what they had obtained from the film. The study was portrayed to the soldiers as a sort of "general opinion survey." For this reason, the questionnaire contained a number of "camouflage" items intended to distract the subjects from perceiving its actual purpose. (Ethical considerations today might raise questions about deception, but it was not a problem for the Army at the time.)

Two such questionnaires were prepared around the content of *The Battle of Britain.* They were intended to be parallel and to cover the same items in essentially the same way. This permitted a "before" and "after" measure to be made on each subject without using the same measuring instrument, which could have confused the results.

The time interval between seeing the film and responding to the "after" questionnaire was one week. (One segment of the group of subjects was measured nine weeks later to study long-term effects. This will be discussed later.) At one camp, 2,100 subjects (half of whom saw the film) were studied in the "before/after with control group" design. In another camp an additional 900 were studied in the same way. Finally, the "after-only with control group" design was used for the study of another 1,200 subjects. Overall, this added up to an impressive 4,200 subjects, all of whom responded to the questionnaire at least once and half of whom saw the experimental film.

The sampling was done in a practical way by selecting company units rather than individuals. However, considerable effort was made to equate or "match" the experimental groups and the controls. Various background variables on the soldiers were studied well beforehand, and those companies most alike in their distribution of such variables as age, region of birth, and scores on Army tests were paired.

As was mentioned, the questionnaires were presented to the men as a "general opinion survey" to find out "how soldiers felt about various subjects connected with the war." The subjects were assembled in platoon groups (of about 50 men) to fill out the questionnaires in their mess halls under the watchful eyes of trained personnel. Anonymity was assured, and no officers were present.

To distract the men from wondering why they had to respond to the questionnaire twice (in the before/after design) it was explained that "the questionnaire had been revised" on the basis of the earlier results, and it was being studied again. In fact, the second version had REVISED printed in large type at the top. A number of other precautions were taken to avoid suspicion that some other purpose was at stake.

**Results.**    The outcome of the evaluations of *The Battle of Britain* can best be understood by contrasting the responses of the control and experimental, or as we will call it, the "film" group. We noted that various objectives were built into the content of the film, and these were assessed by items in the questionnaire. Simple percentage comparisons show the influence of the film in reaching those objectives. A difference of 6 percent between the control and the film group constitutes a statistically significant result, ruling out chance and implying that the film did have an effect on those who saw it.

Generally, it is convenient to review the findings around four major issues, which define broadly the kinds of effects that the makers of the film hoped to achieve. These effects concern the following questions:

1. Was the film effective in improving *factual knowledge* about military events?
2. Did the content of the film alter the *opinions and interpretations* of viewers regarding several major themes presented in the film?
3. How much did the film improve the *general attitudes* of the soldiers toward their British Allies?
4. Was the film a significant factor in improving *overall motivation* among the recruits to fight a tough war?

Each of the above was a complex issue, and only the highlights of the results of the experiment can be presented. Nevertheless, the findings were relatively clear.

First, the film did have a major effect on the acquisition of factual knowledge. Differences between the control and the film groups were consistently large. For example, the questionnaire asked why the Germans "were not successful at bombing British planes on the ground." The answer given in the film was "because the British kept their planes scattered at the edges of the field." Only 21 percent of the control group checked this answer, whereas 78 percent of the film group got it right. Similarly, other factual items were consistently answered correctly by much larger proportions of the film group.

The effects of the film on opinions and interpretations were also in the direction desired by the designers of the film, but the differences between the control and film groups were not as great as with the factual material. There were four major content themes present in the film about which opinions or interpretations could be altered. Each can be discussed briefly.

One major content theme was that the actual battle of Britain was a major defeat for the Nazis. Many of the soldiers had not previously interpreted the German bombings of England early in the war in this light. The film increased the percentage of soldiers who concluded that the German raids were part of a preparation for invasion and that the Nazis suffered a defeat. For example, one questionnaire item stated that "the heavy bombing attacks on Britain were an attempt by the Nazis to . . ." The key answer provided by the content of the film was "to invade and conquer England." Only 43 percent of the control group checked this, whereas 58 percent of the film group selected this answer. Several similar items showed parallel patterns.

A second content theme in the film was that the British resisted heroically. Items in the questionnaire probed the degree to which the control and film groups differed in their opinions on this issue. A typical item asked, "What do you think is the real reason why the Nazis did not invade and conquer Britain after the fall of France?" Only 48 percent of the control group checked the answer provided by the film, "The Nazis tried and would have succeeded except for the determined resistance by the British." By contrast, this answer was selected by 70 percent of those who saw the film.

Two additional content themes in the film produced similar results. More of the film group agreed that the Royal Air Force did a magnificent job than did the control group. And finally, the belief that the British resistance provided other nations time to prepare (the fourth content theme) was held by more of the film group than the control group. Generally, then, the experience of seeing the film did alter the opinions and interpretations of its viewers regarding these four content themes.

The film had less effect on the general attitudes of the soldiers toward the British. In contrast to the clear influence on learning factual information about military events, and in changing opinions concerning the content themes of the film, the viewing experience did not improve general attitudes toward the British Allies. This was found in a variety of items where the differences between the control and film groups were consistently negligible. For example, the questionnaire posed the following item: "Do you feel that the British are doing all they can to help win the war?" The difference between the control and the film group in terms of those who answered positively was only 7 percent. A number of other items designed to measure general attitudes toward the British showed even smaller differences between the two groups. On several of these items, two and three percentage points of difference were found. In other words, it could not be concluded that the film had improved attitudes toward the British.

The film was also clearly ineffective in strengthening the overall motivation and morale of its viewers. Major objectives of the film were to increase willingness to serve, encourage attitudes toward demanding unconditional surrender, and deepen resentment of the enemy. To put it simply, the film had no effect at all on these issues. On such items as whether the trainees would prefer military duty in the United States or overseas, only 38 percent of the control group wanted to go fight. For the film group—supposedly fired up by the film—the comparable figure was 41 percent, not a statistically significant difference. Similarly, about the same percentage of the control group and the film group thought unconditional surrender was important (control group, 60 percent; film group, 62 percent). Finally, resentment of the enemy, measured by several items, showed differences that ranged from 1 to 4 percent between the two groups. It was not possible to conclude that the film improved motivation or morale. These were very important findings. Their significance to mass communication theory will be made clear.

There were many additional issues probed by analyzing data from the questionnaire. Mainly these issues pertained to checks on whether or not one set of ideas in the film might have adversely affected reactions to some other set of ideas to create a kind of "boomerang" effect. Generally, no significant effects of this kind were located.

The research design used with *The Battle of Britain* was also used with the other three orientation movies that were part of the overall film evaluation studies: *The Prelude to War, The Nazis Strike,* and *Divide and Conquer.* However, the last two films were shown to the men in combination to test for cumulative effects. Two days were allowed between these showings, and then the combined effects were measured by the questionnaire in the usual way.

The findings of these additional studies need not be presented in detail because they parallel on almost every point those obtained from the evaluation of *The Battle of Britain.* Instead, the implications of the findings from the research on all of these films can be discussed together because of their close similarity.

*Implications.*    The film evaluation studies made use of research procedures such as sampling, control groups, matching, pretesting, and measurement that were the equal of some of the best social science research conducted today. There are few grounds, if any at all, to reject the findings of these experiments as misleading because of methodological or procedural flaws.

The films themselves were produced by the best talent in the nation at the time, and no expense was spared in their production. Even by today's criteria, more than a half century later, these films offer a powerful message, in which totalitarian and militaristic forces make brutal war on neighboring nations that had done little to provoke such a conflict. The films portray, in short, a very convincing argument. There are few features of these films, other than color photography, that could be used to improve their technical, dramatic, or persuasive quality.

Given these qualities of the stimulus material and of the assessments of their impact, what can be said about the overall results? Clearly, these films did well in achieving some kinds of results but poorly at gaining other objectives. The authors of *Experiments on Mass Communication* summarized the findings of the film evaluation studies as follows:

1. The *Why We Fight* films had marked effects on the men's knowledge of factual material concerning the events leading up to the war. The fact that the upper limit of effects was so large—as, for example, in the cases where the correct answer was learned well enough to be

remembered a week later by the *majority* of the men—indicates that highly effective presentation methods are possible with this type of film.

2. The films also had some marked effects on opinions where the film specifically covered the factors involved in the particular interpretation, that is, where the opinion item was prepared on the basis of film-content analysis and anticipated opinion change from such analysis. Such opinion changes were, however, less frequent and in general less marked than changes in factual knowledge.

3. The films had only very few effects on opinion items of a more general nature that had been prepared independently of film content but that were considered the criteria for determining the effectiveness of the films in achieving their orientation objectives.

4. The films had no effects on the items prepared for the purpose of measuring effects on the men's motivation to serve as soldiers, which was considered the ultimate objective of the orientation program.[6]

An important issue is *why* these films were so ineffective in achieving their hoped-for objectives. As noted above, neither attitudes nor motivations were influenced. Hovland and his colleagues had a number of possible explanations that they explored as best they could. For example, they speculated that information from the civilian mass media about many of the topics and themes treated in the films had reached the recruits before they were drafted (after all, material was used in the films from earlier newsreels). This could have reduced the differences found between control and film groups because a substantial number in each case already had positive attitudes toward the British and at least some motivation to serve. By contrast, neither the control nor the film groups had the factual type of knowledge presented to any great degree, so larger effects could be predicted.

Moreover, motivation to serve and fight in the armed forces is a very complex phenomenon with many dimensions: pressures from one's family, general social norms, fear of death or injury, or prior feelings about the combatants. All could have been factors in the dynamics of change when trying to modify such motivation through the use of persuasive films. There are a number of additional issues about which one can speculate, the amount of time between film and measurement being one of those issues. For example, there may be a "sleeper" effect. That is, even though little change had taken place in the viewers by the time the measurements were made after seeing the film, perhaps much later the film's influences could have been found. Finally, there is the question of the entire configuration of a given subject's values, system of beliefs, and personality traits. These can interact in a dynamic way with new stimulus material to produce one kind of effect or another. However, in spite of rather sophisticated attempts to address some of these issues, no clear answers were obtained as to why these films achieved clear effects in the area of factual knowledge but failed to do so with respect to attitudes and motivations.

## Other Film Studies

In using a film to try to change knowledge, opinions, attitudes, or motivations, it is important to know how the audience itself evaluates the film. That is, do they like the film and find it interesting and objective, or do they dislike it, become bored by it, or believe it to be a biased presentation? Such perceptions on the part of the audience may be closely related to whether or not a given film can achieve the objectives for which it was designed.

The Army researchers made extensive studies of the reactions of the men to various aspects of the orientation films. They were concerned about their level of interest and whether the viewers saw it as "propaganda" designed to manipulate them. The researchers were also concerned as to whether the soldiers saw the movies as Hollywood products, staged with actors and props, or as films of actual events as they happened.

Another significant question about films as media for training or orientation is, How do they compare to the available alternatives? Films like the *Why We Fight* series are obviously very expensive to produce, and the process takes a long time. In contrast, a recorded radio-type program with a lecture, or even filmstrips (which are like projected slides), can be used with narration and are both inexpensive and rapid to produce. Finally, if a film *is* used for training or orientation, what are some ways by which retention of the material presented can be enhanced? For example, having the audience engage in discussion of the content in small groups is one way; having a speaker lead them in a simple review is another. All these questions and issues were under study, and the *Why We Fight* films provided convenient vehicles for trying to find answers. As we will note, however, other kinds of films were also used in these parts of the research program.

*Audience Evaluation of Films.*   Both questionnaires and group interviews were used to try to understand how the recruits themselves evaluated the *Why We Fight* films at the time they saw them. The questionnaires were aimed at three basic issues: Did the men *like* the films? What did they think was the *purpose* of the films? And did they believe that the films gave a *true picture* of the events depicted? For the most part, the men studied were those involved in the film evaluation studies who had seen the film. However, as we will indicate, some additional subjects were included.

In general, the men liked the *Why We Fight* films. They liked some more than others, but fewer than 10 percent gave a negative appraisal on any film (or could give no answer). Those who did not like the films tended to be less educated or to have foreign-born parents from Axis countries.

The *Battle of Britain* study provided more information about the perceived purpose of the film than some of the other films under study. The majority of the men questioned simply saw it as an effort to teach them the facts of the war in an interesting way. Few thought that they were being used as "guinea pigs" or manipulated in some way. A sizable number did connect the film with its real objective. For example, 27 percent on the questionnaire studies wrote in on the space provided for comments that its purpose was "to raise our morale," "to improve the fighting spirit," or even "to make us want to kill those sons of bitches." Even with this recognition of its manipulative intent, they still tended to like the film.

The majority of those involved in the study saw *The Battle of Britain* as a true picture of what had happened during those days when Britain stood alone. (Some 65 percent gave such an evaluation.) Another 33 percent believed that it gave essentially a true picture even though it was "one-sided" at times. Only a handful (2 percent) said that it did not give a true or honest picture. Similar assessment of the film *The Nazis Strike* yielded results with even larger numbers believing that the film was truthful (some 81 percent), a smaller number feeling that it was basically truthful, if one-sided (18 percent), and only 1 percent thinking that it was "mostly untrue or one-sided."

These audience evaluations are important in trying to sort out the overall effects of the films. The evaluations indicate that there were no glaring problems with the films themselves: By and large the soldiers liked them; they did not see them as untruthful propaganda, and they did not feel improperly manipulated. The reasons for the films' failure to achieve their objectives in the areas of attitudes and morale lie elsewhere.

Group interviews (what we would call "focus groups" today) were conducted with 150 men selected so as to be a representative cross section of the recruits under training. These men were not part of the film evaluation experiments discussed earlier but a completely different group. The interviews were conducted with small groups in an informal setting after the subjects had seen the film; each interview group discussed the film, and an effort was made to put together a picture of how the men evaluated the film.

About the only additional insights obtained from this approach were that some of the men thought the films had some poor features. For example, in the air combat footage, the same German plane was shown being shot down several times. Some of the men thought that shots of Hitler and his staff planning the assault on England were Hollywood actors. (They were not; the footage was genuine.) Generally, however, the findings from these group interviews supported those obtained from the questionnaire studies.

A second series of studies of audience evaluation of films did not focus on the *Why We Fight* series, but another separate and rather different series. These were short features, similar to newsreels, shown in conjunction with regular feature films at the base theater. Attendance at these regular entertainment movies was, of course, voluntary. However, those who went to the movies saw a different short feature each week, called *The War*, as part of the regular program. Each of these short features was made up of five episodes, with the content of each varied every week. However, the same titles for these episodes were used in each issue of *The War*. For example, issue 5 of *The War* had the following five episodes:

Episode a: *Finishing School.* This showed training of amphibious (Ranger) troops in invasion tactics such as embarking and disembarking and advancing under live ammunition.

Episode b: *Back Home*. This showed machine tools being produced by a small family shop in Connecticut which was awarded the Navy "E" for (an "excellent") contribution to war production.

Episode c: *I Was There*. This featured an Army nurse's eyewitness account of the bombing of Manila and the fall of Corregidor, with action shots to illustrate part of her commentary. The whole story was told in the nurse's voice and was introduced and concluded by shots of the nurse telling her story.

Episode d: *First Birthday*. This documentary reviewed the founding and first year's activities of the Women's Army Corps and depicted the training and duties of WACs.

Episode e: *Snafu*. This was an animated cartoon showing the adventures of a comic character called "Private Snafu," whose complaints about Army routine and duties led to his magically being put in charge of the camp, with disastrous consequences.[7] ["Snafu" was a military acronym for "situation normal, all fucked up."]

Two means of studying evaluations of this type of film were used. Questionnaires filled out by men who had seen the film were used, and a special recording device (called the "program analyzer") was used in the theater itself. This device consisted of a small box for every viewer with two clearly marked buttons. As the viewer watched the film, he pushed down the "like" button if he found the material interesting. If not, he pushed down the "dislike" button. There was no neutral button, but the viewer could refrain from pushing either the like or dislike buttons.

The results from these two approaches show similar patterns. Figure 7.1 summarizes the questionnaire data, and Figure 7.2 shows a typical pattern obtained from the use of the program analyzer. The findings are not definitive because of the limitations on sampling. But, along with supplemental information obtained from written comments on the questionnaires, and after pulling together findings from studying four separate issues of *The War*, the following generalizations seemed to apply:

1. Where the film simply showed someone talking, interest tended to be low.
2. Where real shots of military action were shown, interest was high.
3. Where shots of action were shown with voice-over narration, interest remained high.
4. Repetition of shots seen earlier in the film (as in seeing the same plane shot down) was not well received.
5. Highly realistic material, as opposed to Hollywood versions acted out with props, was much preferred.

Again, these were tentative conclusions pertaining only to the films studied that should not be regarded as guides to audience evaluations of all kinds of films.

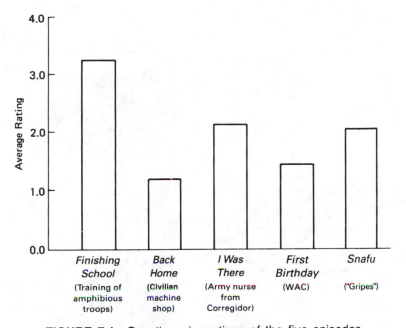

**FIGURE 7.1** Questionnaire ratings of the five episodes in Issue 5 of *The War.* The men were asked to rank the five episodes in the film as "best," "2nd best," and so forth. Ratings for each episode were then scored as follows: "best," 4 points; "2nd best," 3 points; "3rd best," 2 points; "4th best," 1 point; "worst," 0 points. The values plotted are the average scores for the men whose polygraph records are averaged in Figure 7.2.

SOURCE: Carl I. Hovland, Arthur A. Lumsdaine, and Fred D. Sheffield, *Experiments on Mass Communication* (Princeton, N.J.: Princeton University Press, 1949), p. 110.

Yet, they offer useful hypotheses for studying other types of training films for military personnel.

***Alternative Presentations.***   The relative effectiveness of various media for accomplishing a given objective still merits much research attention. The Army researchers made attempts to probe this issue. They were quite aware that this is a very difficult question to answer, as it is based on assumptions that the medium may have special properties that themselves can influence change in the audience.

Among the studies completed, three still appear to be important. One compared a motion picture to a filmstrip presentation of the same subject; a second compared two types of radio program styles (a "commentator" to a dramatized "documentary"); and the third compared the technique of having an introductory lecture to a film (before seeing it) to a review summary of its salient points (after seeing it). The purpose was to see whether the introduction or the review was the best means of enhancing learning from an instructional film.

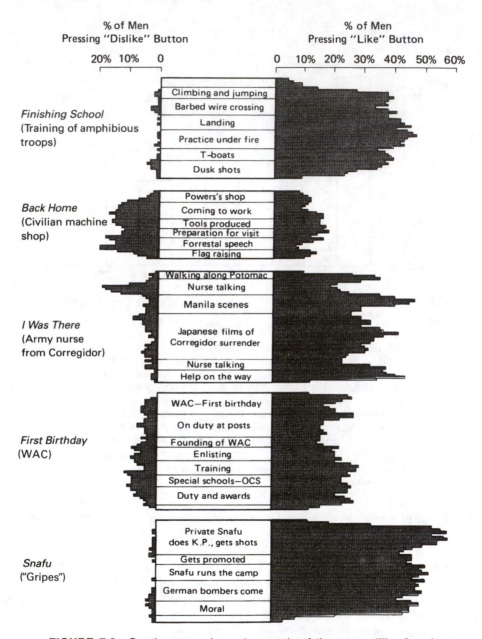

**FIGURE 7.2** Continuous polygraph records of the group "likes" and "dislikes" during showing of issue 5 of *The War*.

SOURCE: Carl I. Hovland, Arthur A. Lumsdaine, and Fred D. Sheffield, *Experiments on Mass Communication* (Princeton, N.J.: Princeton University Press, 1949), p. 111.

Although common sense tells us it that a motion picture with a sound track is obviously a better training device than a filmstrip supplemented with a verbal presentation, the findings did not support such a conclusion. Six companies were matched on the Army's General Classification Test (AGCT) and the educational level that they had achieved. Two were designated as the control group. Two others saw a 43-minute sound film designed to reach map reading. The remaining two companies saw a 50-minute filmstrip presentation on map reading with an accompanying lecture.

After viewing these presentations, the soldiers (plus the control group) responded to a 39-item multiple choice test on the topics covered in the film and the filmstrip. The comparative effectiveness of the two media is shown in Figure 7.3. As it turned out, the film with sound had no inherent advantage over the still pictures of the filmstrip (supplemented with the lecture). The experiment was by no means definitive, but it points to the need for empirical checks on untested assumptions that one medium (e.g., television) automatically has some "greater power" than a simple medium presented along with a lecture.

Of the remaining two studies in this series, the one of most contemporary interest is the comparison of the introductory versus the review lectures on the content of a film as a means of enhancing learning. Videos are still widely used in teaching settings, and this issue has not been fully tested in more recent times.

More specifically, the question addressed by the research was the following: In using a film for training purpose, is it better that an instructor provide a preliminary commentary on the major points that will be covered in the film, or that the film's salient points be reviewed after the audience has seen the film? Which approach will most increase learning from the film?

In the Army studies on this issue, four platoons of soldiers were shown the 43-minute film on map reading after receiving a 20-minute lecture on its main ideas. Another four platoons saw the film first and then had a 20-minute review of its salient points. Care was taken that the persons doing the reviews and preliminary lectures were not greatly different from each other in terms of style or ability. The trainees did not know that they were part of a research effort.

**FIGURE 7.3**  Average test scores received by men in each group (*N* = 253 in each group)

SOURCE: Carl I. Hovland, Arthur A. Lumsdaine, and Fred D. Sheffield, *Experiments on Mass Communication* (Princeton, N.J.: Princeton University Press, 1949), p. 126.

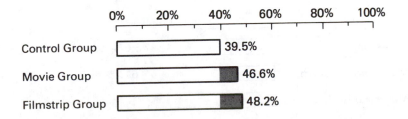

After these presentations, each soldier took a 15-item quiz about the major topics that had been covered in the film. The results of this testing are summarized in Figure 7.4. As can be seen, viewing the movie by itself (as did the control group) improved performance rather considerably. However, both the introductory lecture and the review increased learning even more. The former seemed to have a slight advantage, but the difference was not significant. Results such as these indicate that just "showing a movie" is not the most effective practice in using film (or video) as a teaching device. Supplementing the film with an oral presentation before or after the film enhances learning effects.

## Films and Intellectual Ability

A complex question concerning the film evaluation research described earlier (the *Why We Fight* series) concerns the degree to which different patterns of effects were observed among different categories of viewers. In the U.S. Army studies, the influence of such demographic variables as education, religious affiliation, marital status, intellectual level, and other social categories on the learning of factual material and opinion change was studied wherever possible. Among all these variables, the one most often related to differences in the results was the intellectual ability of the viewer. A brief summary of some of the main findings relating intellectual ability to learning factual material and to opinion change will demonstrate the major points.

*Measurement.* It was not possible to give the soldiers who saw the *Why We Fight* films, or who served in the control groups, an IQ test. This not only would have been difficult but also would have violated the assurances of anonymity involved in the research. Fortunately, it was not necessary to do this. Two indices of general intellectual ability were readily available. One was the individual's score on the AGCT. A considerable accumulation of research had established that these scores were highly correlated with intelligence test scores. An even simpler index was the level of educational attainment of the soldier. Research had also established

**FIGURE 7.4** Average test scores for each group (*N* = 253 in each group)

SOURCE: Carl I. Hovland, Arthur A. Lumsdaine, and Fred D. Sheffield, *Experiments on Mass Communication* (Princeton, N.J.: Princeton University Press, 1949), p. 143.

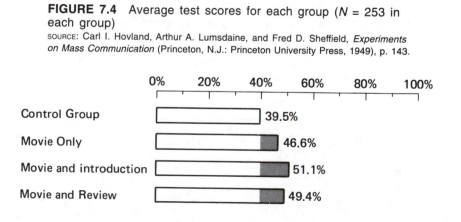

the high correlation between amount of schooling completed and IQ test scores. Educational attainment was also, logically enough, highly correlated with AGCT scores. For this reason, the researchers felt confident that they could categorize the men in terms of simple classifications of educational attainment (such as completion of grade school, high school, or college) and use this as a reliable index of intellectual ability. And, since all subjects in the film evaluation studies had been asked to give their level of educational attainment, the data were already a part of their questionnaire responses.

To determine if seeing a film such as *The Battle of Britain* had different effects on men in these three educational levels, the control and the film groups from the evaluation studies were contrasted. Simple comparison of the percentages in each group who had learned factual information, or whose opinions had been changed, were sufficient, and for the most part, the results showed clear patterns.

*Learning Factual Material.*    It was found, first of all, that even before seeing the films, the men with the most education already knew more factual information about the war than those whose educational achievements were lower. For example, on a brief fact quiz, the men in the control groups (who never saw the film) showed very different levels of factual knowledge, depending on their educational level. Only 21.1 percent of those who had only completed grade school could answer all of the items on the fact quiz correctly. The figure for high school men was 28.6 percent, and for college men it was 41.8 percent. These figures represent significant differences.

Similar findings were noted in studies of the map-reading film. Before seeing the material, those with higher levels of education *already* knew larger percentages of the answers to the multiple choice test on map reading than those in lower categories (grade school, 26.1 percent; high school, 28.9 percent; and college, 37.1 percent). In other words, intellectual ability, as measured, was a significant indicator of the initial level of factual knowledge commanded by the men, even before they saw any of the films.

But even though those with higher levels of intellectual ability already knew more, they also learned more from the film. A 29-item factual information test was prepared on the *Why We Fight* films. Comparisons were then made of the percentages of these items learned, on the average, by the men in each of the three intellectual levels. Substantial differences were found. For example, the grade school men averaged only 16.3 percent on this test after seeing the films. The high school men averaged 36.6 percent, and the college men had 54.2 percent correct. These differences in levels of performance were even more pronounced when only the items of greatest difficulty were taken into account. Clearly, intellectual ability was the key factor in accounting for how much an individual learned from the films.

*Opinion Changes.*    The relationship between educational attainment and opinion change presents a more complex picture. A trend was noted for the effects of the films on opinion change to increase with higher educational level.

However, in some opinion items, the opposite was found. But another situation was noted in the data that helped to explain what had happened. The more factual the material that had to be grasped, especially more difficult material, the more opinion change was seen only among the men of higher educational attainment. The authors considered such changes "informed opinion." On the other hand, the men of lower levels often changed their opinion position on the basis of a minimal number of facts or those easier to grasp. This was considered "uninformed opinion." To make matters even more interesting, the findings showed that men of lower levels were prone to change their opinion on the basis of facts that men of higher educational level did not regard as particularly valid.

*Implications.*   Increased educational attainment led to increased levels of initial knowledge. However, it also led to learning more factual material from the film. On opinion change, the more complex the issue and facts concerning it, the more likely that opinion change would be primarily among the more educated men. Those of lower levels tended to change their opinions on issues of lesser complexity, less well supported by the facts, and on issues that more educated men found difficult to accept. While, as Hovland and colleagues note, these are tentative conclusions based on this research only, it would appear that the less educated (and presumably less intelligent) are easier to sway with propaganda.

## ADDITIONAL STUDIES OF PERSUASION

The research findings on films summarized above were obtained for the most part from evaluation studies where the film had been prepared by persons other than the experimenters, and it was introduced in its entirety as the experimental treatment. In these studies, the dependent variable was one or more of the objectives set by the War Department for the film series. Extraneous variables were controlled by the variety of techniques, methodologies, and designs.

Another type of research on the effects of communication on opinion change employs variations in some specific aspect of the message, some characteristic of the audience, or some factor in the communication setting. Generally, such research seeks to find those conditions of the persuasive message, the communicator, the mode of presentation, and the like that will lead to a maximum degree of opinion change. The underlying assumption is that changes in opinion (or attitude, value, belief, and so on) are *keys to changing overt behavior.* After all, mere changes in opinion mean relatively little unless they are linked to changes in action.

The remainder of the present chapter summarizes briefly the results of two (from a set of three) experiments that sought such keys to opinion change. One experiment attempted to see whether opinion change after seeing a persuasive communication had short-term or stable long-term effects. The second experiment assessed a persuasive message that was structured in one of two ways. One structure was one-sided and presented only arguments in favor of an opinion change under study. The other was essentially the same persuasive message, but some points on the opposite side were also presented in an effort to make the message seem more objective. The goal, of course, was to see which provided a better key to changing opinions in the direction desired by the communicator.

## Short-Term versus Long-Term Effects

A significant question in the search for ways to change people's opinions through the use of persuasive communications is whether the effects achieved, if any, will disappear rapidly or persist over a long period. Studies of remembering and forgetting have been made by psychologists since the 1880s. Such research has established that there is a "curve of forgetting" of factual information learned by a subject. The greatest amount of forgetting takes place rather quickly, and then the curve levels off after a few days to decline more slowly. Since opinion changes are based on factual information, the Army researchers hypothesized that opinion changes would follow a somewhat similar pattern. That is, they expected changes of opinion achieved through persuasive communications to have a relatively short life, with the subject regressing over time to his earlier position.

The study of short-term versus long-term effects was carried out with one of the orientation films—*The Battle of Britain*—because the film was clearly capable of producing effects on both factual knowledge and opinion change. The sample used for this study had already been given their "before" measures as part of the film evaluation studies. In those studies, the subjects took their "after" measures a week after seeing the film. All that was needed was a group of subjects who had seen the film and whose opinions could be measured a relatively long time after seeing the film. It was also necessary, of course, to match the various groups so that any differences in effects could be assigned to the time variable rather than to differences of some other kind between the two sets of subjects.

The "before/after with control group" design was used for both the short-term subjects and the long-term group. The long-term group was treated in the same manner as the short-term subjects, expect that they received their "after" questionnaire *nine weeks* after seeing the film (rather than one week). Table 7.1 shows the general plan.

A clear pattern of forgetting factual material was found. On a ten-item fact quiz based on *The Battle of Britain,* there was a substantial decrement in recalling facts when comparing the short-term and the long-term experimental groups. Over the nine weeks, the long-term groups retained only about 50 percent as many of the fact items as had the short-term group at the end of the first week after seeing the film.

But the main question was the influence of time on opinions. To assess opinion shifts caused by the film, and to compare the long- and short-term subjects, a 15-item opinion measuring instrument was prepared and used. The results of the comparison revealed some unexpected findings. On approximately a third of the opinion issues, the long-term group showed less change than the

**TABLE 7.1**   General research design for comparing short-time and long-time effects of seeing an orientation film

| | Short-time Groups | | Long-time Groups | |
| --- | --- | --- | --- | --- |
| | Experimental (3 Companies) | Control (3 Companies) | Experimental (2 Companies) | Control (2 Companies) |
| First week | "Before" questionnaire | "Before" questionnaire | "Before" questionnaire | "Before" questionnaire |
| Second week | Film showing | — | — | — |
| Third week | "After" questionnaire | "After" questionnaire | — | — |
| Eleventh week | — | — | "After" questionnaire | "After" questionnaire |
| No. of subjects | 450 | 450 | 250 | 250 |

SOURCE: Carl I. Hovland, Arthur A. Lumsdaine, and Fred D. Sheffield, *Experiments on Mass Communication* (Princeton, N.J.: Princeton University Press, 1949), p. 183.

short-term group. This was the pattern to be expected from the "curve of forgetting." After all, the underlying factual material had shown a clear pattern of being forgotten. However, on more than half of the 15 opinion issues under study, the long-term group showed a *greater* change than the short-term group. This was not expected. The researchers referred to this kind of outcome as a sleeper effect. It was difficult to explain, but what had happened was that the subjects had forgotten some of the facts in the film on which their opinions had originally been changed to some degree. Then, freed from the factual basis, the opinions changed even more.

In an attempt to better understand this sleeper effect, a number of rather complex analyses of the data were made. The analyses were not particularly enlightening except in one case. There was a high probability of being influenced by the film on a long-term basis if one was *initially predisposed* toward a given opinion change (on a particular topic). Finally, the authors noted that changes in opinion of a general rather than specific nature may show increasing effects with lapse of time. Such general opinions are less firmly anchored to specific facts.

The sleeper effect raises many difficult psychological problems, and the investigators felt that they could not answer them within the context of the data of their studies. The effects of time on opinion change following persuasive communication remains a significant issue around which much research was organized in the years following the Army studies. The problem of initial position on an issue, however, was to prove a valuable key to understanding some of the effects in the next study to be discussed.

## Effects of Presenting One versus Both Sides of an Argument

When attempting to change opinions on a controversial topic, is it more effective to present only the materials and arguments supporting the position of the communicator ("one side")? Or is it better to introduce at least some of the opposing arguments ("both sides") to make the persuasive communication look like a balanced treatment of the issues? These were the main questions for a study of the influence of a persuasive message that was used in 1945, toward the end of the war. New draftees were still being trained even though the European war was clearly about to end. The grim facts were that the war in the Pacific was seen likely to continue for two years or more. Although American forces had defeated the Japanese in a number of bitterly fought assaults on island bases, the main body of the Japanese Army had remained at home, anticipating a major invasion attempt. It was estimated that if this were to take place, the Americans would probably suffer from half a million to a million casualties. In fact, the war could drag on for years. The Japanese had reserved supplies at home in spite of the heavy bombings of major cities. Each island was a fortress. Even children had been trained to fight invaders. And there was the vast Pacific to cross: the Americans would have to bring troops and supplies over thousands of miles of ocean. Even the high-level planners in the War Department did not know of the atom bomb that made the assault on Japan unnecessary. This closely guarded secret weapon was known only to a handful at Los Alamos, to the President and his staff, and to a few select people in the military. Thus, the War Department issued directives to begin preparing *all* troops to anticipate a long war. A factor complicating this need was that, with Italy out of the war and Germany clearly about to collapse, the majority of the soldiers felt that the war was about to end. This posed a potential morale problem of serious proportions. The troops *had* to be made to understand and believe that there were still several tough years ahead and that there was no choice but to carry on.

Under the new directives, the social scientists of the Experimental Section set about to study the most effective ways to persuade trainees that it would be a long and difficult war in the Pacific. The keys to such persuasion were badly needed. For this reason, the social scientists moved away from films made in Hollywood and prepared their own persuasive messages so that they could build in various message factors in a search for those keys. Fortunately for many hundreds of thousands of American young men, the atom bomb *was* used, and the war came to a speedy end. This aspect of the bomb's use tends to be overlooked today. In any case, if it had not been used, it is likely that this phase of the research program would have been greatly extended.

Included in the routines of the training camp was a weekly "orientation hour" that had been used for soldiers to see films, fill out questionnaires, participate in discussions, and so on. This tradition made it possible to use the same general approach for the new research program as had been used earlier with the *Why We Fight* film evaluations.

***Persuading with Radio.***   Since there was no time to prepare films, the more rapid and flexible medium of radio was used. The Armed Forces Radio Service prepared recorded materials according to the specifications of the researchers. The new research program began with a study organized around the issue posed at the beginning of the present section. Would a one-sided radio talk be more effective in changing the opinions of the soldiers concerning the probable length of the war in the Pacific, or would it be more effective to use a radio talk that presented at least some of the arguments on both sides (with the weight of arguments still on the side of a long war)?

Some careful preliminary work was done before designing the two radio programs. Interviews were held with 200 men to see how long they thought that the Pacific war would last and why they felt the way they did. What, in other words, were the counterarguments to the position that the war would be lengthy? This preliminary work paid off, because those counterarguments could be carefully rebutted by material included in the radio messages.

The two transcripts were prepared as a commentator's analysis of the Pacific war. The one-side presentation (about 15 minutes in length) marshaled all the factual information and arguments supporting the conclusion that the war would last at least two more years. The both-sides presentation had essentially the same material, but an additional four minutes of arguments on the other side were included early in the message. These were then carefully rebutted. Overall, the program as a whole supported the conclusion that the war would last at least two more years.

The "before/after with control group" design was used to assess the results. Considerable effort was made to obscure the idea that there was an experiment going on or that the men were being tested in some way. The before and after measurements took place in very different locations for very different announced purposes. Furthermore, in each case the central items were embedded in larger questionnaires addressed to different purposes. This camouflaging of the experiment within other important activities appears to have been entirely successful.

As in previous experiments, the subjects were selected in group units. A total of 24 platoons were used in all; 625 men were involved, with 214 in each of the two experimental groups and 197 in the control group. The after measures were made one week after the men in the experimental groups heard the radio programs. Once again, anonymity was assured, but it was possible to match the before and after questionnaires with the use of background data and handwriting.

***Results of the Radio Experiments.***   When the results were first reviewed, it appeared that the two forms of the persuasive message had not achieved different results. The opinions on the length of the war were compared for both experimental groups (one side versus both sides) by calculating the percentage of men from each treatment who thought that the war would last more than a year and a half. These differences could then be compared to those found for the two measures of the control group. The results are shown in Table 7.2. Thus, it appeared that both programs were capable of changing the opinions of the men concerning the length of the war.

A different pattern of results became evident when the initial opinions of the men were taken into account. For those who were initially *opposed* to the conclusion that it would be a lengthy war, the one-side program had some effect (36 percent extended their estimates). But for such men, the both-sides program had a much greater effect (48 percent extended their estimate). This is a difference of 12 percent. On the opposite side, the effects were even more

**TABLE 7.2** Overall effects of the two programs on distribution of estimated length of war

| | Percentage Estimating a War of More Than One-and-One-Half Years | | |
| | Experimental Groups | | |
| | Program I "One Side" | Program II "Both Sides" | Control Group |
| --- | --- | --- | --- |
| Before | 37% | 38% | 36% |
| After | 59 | 59 | 34 |
| Difference | 22% | 21% | –2% |
| Probability | <.01 | <.01 | |

SOURCE: Carl I. Hovland, Arthur A. Lumsdaine, and Fred D. Sheffield, *Experiments on Mass Communication* (Princeton, N.J.: Princeton University Press, 1949), p. 210.

striking. For those who initially *favored* the opinion that the war would be longer, 52 percent extended their estimates after hearing the one-side radio commentary. But when these initially favorable men heard the both-sides program, only 23 percent extended their estimate. This is a difference of 19 percent and in the opposite direction. Clearly, initial position on the issue seemed to be one of the keys concerning the effectiveness of a persuasive radio message.

Intellectual ability proved to be another important key to the results. A striking set of differences was found when comparing men of different educational attainment levels (used as an index of intellectual ability). Briefly summarized, the two-sides program was more effective with those of at least high school level (49 percent changed to a long war estimate). The one-side program produced a change of 35 percent in this category. Exactly the opposite was found for men with limited schooling. For those with only grade school or less, the one-side program persuaded 46 percent to extend their estimates. The two-sides program brought only 31 percent of this category to make such an opinion change.

When both initial position and intellectual level were considered, even greater differences were noted. For example, among those of lower education who initially favored a longer estimate, the one-side program brought an increased estimate of the war's length among 64 percent. This result can be compared to the effects of the both-sides program on the same type of men. Here, estimates of the length of the war actually *decreased*. It appears that the two-sides program confused these poorly educated men and created an effect in the opposite direction from that desired by the communicator. For other combinations of initial position and intellectual ability, the differences were not dramatic.

## CONCLUSIONS AND IMPLICATIONS

The various research programs described in *Experiments on Mass Communication* constitute a remarkable effort to bring the expertise of the social psychologist and other social scientists to the practical problems imposed by the urgencies of a national crisis. The researchers, drawn into the war effort from the academic world, were able to make a significant contribution to the practical problems of designing and testing orientation, teaching, and persuasive communication. But perhaps their most important contribution was that they uncovered significant features of the process of persuasion that would be explored by communication researchers in the decades that followed the war.

The film evaluation studies showed that this form of communication could teach factual material effectively to large numbers of people in a short time. The studies also showed that it was possible to alter opinions and interpretations of those facts and that at least some of these opinions would remain stable through time. Yet it was clear that the films did not create more general effects on broader attitudes and motivations. In other words, the persuasive effects of the films were *clearly limited.* Such communications were not the all-powerful shapers of the psyches of their audiences that had been assumed by the magic bullet theory of prior decades. The findings from *Experiments on Mass Communication* led clearly toward a "limited effects" hypothesis concerning the short-term influences of a single communication on its audiences, rather than a "powerful effects" interpretation.

From the standpoint of methods, the film evaluation studies and the other Army programs set new standards for communication research. The "before/after with control group" design was not new to social science, but it had not been used so effectively before in communication research. It became a standard. The meticulous care taken in studying the *Why We Fight* films posed other models for later researchers. The investigators carefully analyzed the content of each film and developed their questionnaires around their findings. They took numerous precautions to pretest and fine-tune their instruments. They carefully disguised what they were doing so that their subjects would not modify their behavior according to some conception of the demands of the experiment. They matched groups, used controls, and camouflaged their tests and assessments in larger survey instruments. Finally, they carefully sorted through every set of results so that they understood as fully as possible what they had found and why. Of course, their lack of concern over costs and their almost complete control over their subjects made this a unique situation that would be hard to duplicate in civilian life.

The results of their experiments supported the perspective that the effects of mass communication are strongly influenced by *individual differences* between the members of the audience. Individual differences led to selective perception, interpretation, and change. Such factors as the initial position of the subject were found to be very important in understanding the results. Similarly, there were differential influences that were related to the *social categories* (e.g., educational attainment) of the audience. Curiously, however, the researchers did not look into the *social relationships* that prevailed among their subjects as a source of influences on their results. Research on the role of the mass media in an election campaign was uncovering such influences, but the results of that work were not known to the Army researchers at the time.

Perhaps most of all, the Army research on how to persuade the American soldier represents a significant turning point in the study of mass communication.

It can be seen in retrospect as the end of an era when the assumptions of the magic bullet theory were still thought to be viable. In its place, and in many ways as a result of these experiments, a new search began—a search for the "magic keys" of persuasion. The basic assumptions of the magic keys theory of persuasive communication are closely related to what DeFleur has referred to as the "psychodynamic approach" to persuasion.[8] It is assumed that there is some set of characteristics that can be built into the message that will modify the structure of functioning of the cognitive/emotional processes within the individual. If all goes well, these in turn will lead to changes in decisions and subsequent patterns of overt action in the direction desired by the communicator. Thus, within this perspective, it is important to discover whether a one-side or a two-side form of communication will alter opinions more effectively. Supposedly, if opinion is altered, it can be assumed that some form of action will then be altered. The authors of *Experiments on Mass Communication* fully believed that there was a regular relationship between attitude and opinion states and forms of overt action—a set of assumptions that does not seem so attractive today.[9]

But at the time, when researchers were undisturbed by the thought that opinions and attitudes might *not* be directly correlated with overt behavior, the magic keys approach to communication research appeared to hold great promise. In fact, it became the dominant perspective on research on persuasive communication for many years to follow:

> Untold numbers of studies have tried to identify ways in which we can persuade people to view some perceptual object differently—and thereby cause them to act toward that object in modified ways. If only the right combination of words, message structure, emotional appeals, type of communicator, or mode of presentation can be found (so the vision goes) then people's subjective orientations can be reshaped and their patterns of overt behavior can be influenced.[10]

So, the search of the magic keys began in earnest. It was the ultimate idea of pragmatic application of social and behavioral science. Find the ways to persuade people to buy, vote, give, accept military training cheerfully, and so on, and the world will beat a pathway to the door of communication scholars and researchers. Unfortunately, as will be seen in later chapters, the search for the magic keys, like the search for the Philosopher's Stone, has had less than spectacular results.

## NOTES AND REFERENCES

1. Frank Capra, *The Name above the Title: An Autobiography* (New York: Macmillan, 1971), p. 327.
2. Ibid., p. 237.
3. Carl I. Hovland, Arthur A. Lumsdaine, and Fred D. Sheffield, *Experiments on Mass Communication* (Princeton, N.J.: Princeton University Press, 1949), p. 22.

4. For a detailed analysis of the films' techniques and content, see Paul Rotha, *The Film Till Now* (New York: Funk and Wagnalls, 1949), p. 462.
5. Hovland et al., *Experiments on Mass Communication.*
6. Ibid., pp. 64–65.
7. Ibid., p. 215.
8. Melvin L. DeFleur, *Theories of Mass Communication,* 3d ed. (New York: David McKay, 1970), p. 141; see also 4th ed. (1982), p. 218.
9. DeFleur, *Theories of Mass Communication,* 4th ed. pp. 247–248; see also H. Schuman and P. Johnson, "Attitudes and Behavior," in A. Inkeles, J. Coleman and N. Smelser, eds., *Annual Review of Sociology* (Palo Alto, Calif.: Annual Review, Inc., 1976).
10. Timothy G. Plax and Melvin L. DeFleur, "Communication, Attitudes, and Behavior: An Axiomatic Theory with Implications for Persuasion Research." Paper presented at the annual meeting of the Western Speech Communication Association, Portland, Oregon, 1980.

# chapter 8

# Communication and Persuasion: The Search for the Magic Keys

World War II was finally over. Through that brutal struggle, the world—and America—was changed forever. Before the war, the nation had remained somewhat isolated; its concerns had been mainly with its own affairs. However, by the end of the war it had been thrust into global responsibilities for which its people were ill-prepared. Yet they responded both ideologically and militarily; the nation rose to the challenge and prevailed against formidable odds. The United States had become the most powerful nation on the earth and the unquestioned leader of the "Free World."

The war years also had a profound impact on the American national consciousness. Americans had come to nurture an almost boundless faith in their ability to solve the world's problems. Beginning militarily as a marked underdog, they had marshaled their industrial and military might to crush the powerful forces of fascism. Once that was accomplished, and the war over, the United States set out to solve the problems of its former enemies. It helped them to rebuild their ravaged countries and economies, an act of generosity unprecedented in the world's history.

Perhaps the greatest victory of the war was America's conquest of the atom. It was an amazing feat; science had won the battle by splitting the atom. This accomplishment brought the role of science a new significance in modern life. Although atomic power had been developed for use as a weapon, many thoughtful people saw in it a bright vision for the future—unlimited power for peaceful purposes.

Thus, it was science that emerged from the war as the great hope of humankind. And science dedicated to basic research seemed the most important kind. Once new principles were uncovered, they could then be used by pragmatic, innovative Americans to make a better world for everyone. That postwar dream fired the imagination of all scientists—and social scientists were no exception.

There was much work to be done by social and behavioral scientists. The world was still filled with prejudice, discrimination, and bigotry. And now that nuclear weapons were a reality, the task of improving relationships between peoples seemed more urgent that ever. Badly needed, for example, was a better understanding of how people's beliefs, attitudes, and behavior could be modified in socially approved ways through carefully designed persuasive communication. If basic research into the "laws" of persuasion could be successful, then such knowledge could be used to achieve many prosocial goals. It seemed clear enough from earlier research on communication, such as that done by the Army researchers in training camps during the war, that there were underlying regularities waiting to be discovered by careful scientific research. Once those keys to the communication-persuasion relationship were available, they could be used to unlock the mysteries of how opinions and attitudes could be modified. Then it would be possible to change overt behavior patterns in socially desirable ways which would lead, in turn, to prosocial behavior. Thus, such keys were critical in order to improve the human condition.

This mission held great appeal to social psychologists such as Carl Hovland, who had been one of the principal researchers in the Army's investigations of the persuasive use of films. Prior to the war, Hovland had been a "rising star" in experimental psychology at Yale, but the demands of the war altered the direction of his career. While the Army research involved the investigation of "practical" problems, Hovland could see the implications of that research for building a *systematic theory of persuasion*. Thus, the seeds of a new program of scientific research were planted and took root in Hovland's wartime experience. During the war, he had worked with an outstanding group of social scientists, including Irving Janis, Arthur Lumsdaine, Fred Sheffield, Nathan Macoby, and M. Brewster Smith. When he returned to Yale at the end of the war, he took Janis, Lumsdaine, and Sheffield with him. Together they founded a broad-based research program drawing on scholars and theories from several disciplines.

## THE RESEARCH PROGRAM

Between 1946 and 1961, the Yale Program of Research on Communication and Attitude Change conducted more than 50 experiments that produced a considerable body of published results. Hovland remained the driving force behind the research during the entire period. The theoretical bases as well as the framework for the program's experiments were outlined in *Communication and Persuasion* (1953), the first major book to emerge from the research program.[1] *Communication and Persuasion* reports the results of a number of investigations of the ways in which opinions and beliefs are modified by persuasive communications. Funded by the Rockefeller Foundation, the work involved the efforts of some 30 social scientists—mainly psychologists, but including sociologists, anthropologists, and political scientists.

It should be noted that the Yale program did not actually study mass communication or actual media campaigns. It made use of experiments in a variety of settings. The research dealt with more intimate, interpersonal channels of communication, such as live speeches and illustrated lectures. A few of the studies did use recorded speeches and written passages, but they were not used to simulate mass communication situations. Nevertheless, many scholars of the time felt that the laws of persuasion would operate similarly in both the experimental and real-life situations and that uncovering the keys to the process in the laboratory would also lead to an understanding of their operation in mass communication persuasion.

The project focused on several areas thought to be important to the persuasion process. These areas were generated by the researchers' definition of communication. They defined communication in terms of "stimuli" that create changes in the responses of people. More specifically, they defined communication as "the process by which an individual (the communicator) transmits stimuli (usually verbal) to modify the behavior of other individuals (the audience)."[2] This stimulus-response definition was characteristic of the way in which psychologists viewed the process of communication at the time. Harold D. Lasswell had formulated a well-known statement that indicated that the proper study of the act of communication was to look at *who* said *what* to *whom* over what *channel* with what *effect*.[3] Thus, the main categories of analysis were (1) the communicator, (2) the content of the communication, (3) the audience, and (4) the actual responses made by the audience. Selected topics, such as communicator credibility and group conformity effects, were then studied in each of these categories.

There are several reasons why most of the research reported in *Communication and Persuasion* was conducted in controlled experimental settings. For one, most of the researchers had backgrounds in experimental psychology. They were therefore familiar with, and had confidence in, experimental methods. More importantly, the researchers were searching for causal regularities—the "laws" of persuasion. They believed that in this search it was necessary to use methods that they thought would allow for causal interpretations of their data.

The nature of the experimental situation was basically the same throughout the various studies. Messages were constructed for the project, then tested under specially defined circumstances where the effects of various factors influencing persuasion could be isolated. The communication was one-way. No verbal interaction was allowed between senders and the receiving audience. In addition, interaction was restricted between audience members during the experimental sessions. Moreover, the subjects were part of a "captive" audience (i.e., they were not allowed to leave the sessions once they had begun). The topics presented in the studies were carefully chosen: they were selected on the basis of their relative neutrality, in other words, "to arouse little motivation for either suppression or distortion."[4] Finally, standard methodological precautions were taken throughout

the studies. These precautions included careful attention to questionnaire construction; independent test administrators; assurances of anonymity; and so on.
In general, the research techniques used in the project were rigorous, and
attention to detail appeared complete.

## Assumptions About the Nature of Opinion and Attitude Change

Hovland and his associates measured persuasion in terms of the amount of
attitude and opinion change achieved. They viewed attitudes and opinions as
intimately related yet analytically distinct. The term *opinion* was used in a very
general sense by the authors. It referred to "interpretations, expectations, and
evaluations." For example, this term included beliefs about the intentions of
others, anticipations of future events, or appraisals of the consequences of
alternate courses of action. While *opinion* was used to refer to a broad class of
anticipations, *attitude* was more exclusive; it was reserved only for explicit
responses approaching or avoiding some object, person, group, or symbol. In
other words, attitudes possessed positive and negative "drive value."

Another factor that distinguished an attitude from an opinion was that
opinions could always be verbalized and attitudes need not be: An attitude might
be unconscious. However, the researchers' formulation includes a high degree
of interaction between attitudes and opinions. A change in general approach and
avoidance orientations (attitudes) might affect a person's expectations (opinions)
on a number of related issues. A more important aspect of this interaction for
the research reported in *Communication and Persuasion* was that change in a
person's general attitude might result from changes in opinion. Hovland, Janis,
and Kelley assumed that attitudes were mediated by verbal beliefs, expectations,
and judgments and that one of the primary ways in which communications could
change attitudes was to change those verbal responses (opinions).

Some important methodological problems arose out of this conceptualization
of opinions and attitudes. When the authors said that opinions could be verbalized
and were "implicit responses," they meant that they were the verbal answers a
person gives in inner speech. They were thus to be distinguished from overt
verbal responses, the answers to those questions as expressed to others. Typically,
the overt and covert answers are identical, but they need not be—especially if
external constraints (e.g., social pressure) hinder their free expression. Thus, the
methodological problem in the context of this research was, How do you observe
changes in the implicit responses? Hovland, Janis, and Kelley resolved this
problem by assuming that under certain conditions (which they tried to arrange)
the overt verbalizations approximated the implicit verbal responses. Thus, they
elicited verbal responses to questionnaire items, where the questions they used
were designed and administered to minimize distorted responses to the items.

Another methodological problem that confronted the authors was whether
they were measuring real opinion change rather than simply change in response
to the question items. They handled this problem by using a series of items that

approached the subject matter from a number of points of view. In addition, they used stimuli (e.g., language) similar to those found in everyday situations. The ultimate justification for the questionnaires, in their eyes, was their utility. The questionnaires allowed the investigators to observe consistent relationships between communicated stimuli and changes in verbal responses. The researchers checked the validity of these relationships by comparing them with observations from other studies. In addition, they also checked the relationships by examining behavioral data concerning changes in voting, buying products, and contributing to charities.

## The Theoretical Model

The researchers assumed that attitudes and opinions were *enduring*. That is, they assumed that a particular attitude or opinion would persist unless the individual underwent some new learning experience. And, in fact, the theoretical framework presented by Hovland, Janis, and Kelley was a learning model—in essence, a stimulus-response model.

In the learning of new attitudes, Hovland and his associates believed that three variables were important: attention, comprehension, and acceptance. The first of these factors, *attention,* recognizes the fact that not all message stimuli that a person encounters are noticed. Driving down a freeway littered with signs, for example, you may notice only a fraction of the persuasive messages that you pass. Lacking your attention, the attempted persuasion will not be successful. But even when an appeal is noticed, it might not be effective. The second factor posited by Hovland and his colleagues, *comprehension,* recognizes the fact that some messages may be too complex and too ambiguous for their intended audience to understand. Thus, a highly complex campaign speech on the budget deficit, for example, may be totally ineffective in persuading the economic novice to vote for or against a particular candidate. Finally, a person must decide to accept the communication before any real attitude change takes place. The degree of *acceptance* is largely related to the incentives that are offered. The message may provide arguments or reasons for accepting the advocated point of view, or it may engender expectations of rewards or other pleasant experiences. For example, a sign on the highway may tell you that a nationally known restaurant is only minutes off the freeway, thus promising you something better than you had planned at the next truck stop. Stimulus-response theories regard this assumption as basic—attitudes are changed only if the incentives for making a new response are greater than those for making the old response. In short, the theoretical model of Hovland and his associates suggests the following steps in the process of changing attitudes or opinions:

1. A recommended opinion (the stimulus) is presented.
2. Assuming that the subjects have paid attention to and understood the message, the audience responds or reacts. That is, they think about their initial opinions and also about the recommended opinion.

3. The subjects will change their attitudes if incentives (rewards) for making a new response are greater that those for making the old response.

Overall, the research discussed in *Communication and Persuasion* could be described in terms of three of its principal characteristics. First, it was primarily concerned with theoretical issues and basic research; its main purpose was to discover the "laws" of persuasion. Second, the principal theoretical approach used was a version of stimulus-response learning theory in which it was assumed that attitudes (and opinions) could be changed *only if* the incentives for change are greater than those for stability. Third, the methodological emphasis was on controlled experimental research.

## THE EXPERIMENTS AND THEIR FINDINGS

Both the experiments and their findings were numerous and complex, and were discussed in detail by the authors. There were far too many studies to review each separately. For the sake of simplicity, only the major ideas in each of the four categories (communicator, content, audience, response) will be discussed. A representative study in each category will also be presented.

### Characteristics of the Communicator

The first area discussed in *Communication and Persuasion* was that of the communicator's credibility. It was assumed by the researchers that the effectiveness of a communication depended to a considerable extent upon who delivered it. Government agencies, for example, take great pains to have their statements to Congress presented by the most acceptable advocate. Even backyard gossips liberally sprinkle the names of respectable sources throughout their rumors. How often, for example, have you heard "it came from a good source" attached to a rumor?

Hovland and his associates were particularly interested in how differences in the credibility of the communicator would affect (1) the way in which the presentation and the content of the presentation would be perceived and evaluated by members of the audience and (2) the degree to which the attitudes and opinions of the audience members would be modified. The researchers limited their investigation to the influence of the following two factors: (1) "expertness," or "the extent to which the communicator is perceived to be a source of valid assertions,"[5] and (2) "trustworthiness," or "the degree of confidence in the communicator's intent to communicate the assertions he considers most valid."[6] It would appear to be obvious that "expertness" of the sources is an important factor. For example, previous research had found that the credibility of an advertisement appears to be related to some extent to the reputation of the particular magazine in which it appeared. As an example of this, consider your own reaction when you read a sensational news story. Does it make any difference to you whether the story appeared in the *New York Times* or a tabloid like *The National Enquirer?*

Trustworthiness also appeared to be an important factor from previous research. For example, in chapter 7, it was indicated that men who viewed the film *The Battle of Britain* and thought it was "propaganda" showed less opinion change in the direction advocated by the film than did those who viewed the film and thought it simply "information." Again, in everyday life we often wonder about people's "ulterior motives." If we perceive a person as having a definite *intention* to persuade us, the likelihood is increased that this source will be perceived as an individual with something to gain by our persuasion; therefore, that person is less worthy of trust.

To test the effects of variations in expertness and trustworthiness, Hovland and Weiss designed an experiment in the series that consisted of presenting an identical communication to two groups. Four different topics were used. Table 8.1

**TABLE 8.1**   The topics of four persuasive communications and the sources to whom they were attributed

| | High-Credibility Source | Low-Credibility Source |
|---|---|---|
| A. *Antihistamine Drugs:* Should the anti-histamine drugs continue to be sold without a doctor's prescription? | *New England Journal of Biology and Medicine* | Magazine A (A mass circulation monthly pictorial magazine) |
| B. *Atomic Submarines:* Can a practicable atomic-powered submarine be built at the present time? | J. Robert Oppenheimer | *Pravda* |
| C. *The Steel Shortage:* Is the steel industry to blame for the current shortage of steel? | *Bulletin of National Resources Planning Board* | Writer A (An antilabor, "rightist" newspaper columnist) |
| D. *The Future of Movie Theaters:* As a result of television, will there be a decrease in the number of movie theaters in operation by 1955? | *Fortune* magazine | Writer B (A woman movie-gossip columnist) |

SOURCE: Carl I. Hovland, Irving L. Janis, and Harold H. Kelley, *Communication and Persuasion* (New Haven: Yale University Press, 1953), p. 28.

lists the topics of the articles and the sources to whom they were attributed. In one group, the articles were attributed to *high-credibility* sources, and in the other they were attributed to *low-credibility* sources.[7]

Both affirmative and negative versions of each topic were employed. Opinion questionnaires were administered before, immediately after, and a month after the communication. In the questionnaire given before the communication, college students were asked to judge the trustworthiness of a long list of sources, including those used in the study. Analysis of these judgments showed that the sources that the researchers felt had high credibility did, in fact, have high credibility; that is, they were judged so by the subjects. The same was true for the low-credibility sources: They were judged by the students to be low in trustworthiness. The subjects were then given the articles to read. Each student received a booklet containing one article on each of the four topics; the name of the source was given at the end of each article. Then, another questionnaire was administered immediately following this reading, asking for their opinions and evaluations of the article.

The results of the experiment showed that differences in initial attitude toward the source influenced evaluation of the presentations. Even though the communications judged were identical in content, the presentations were considered to be "less fair" and the conclusions "less justified" when the source was of low credibility. (See Table 8.2).

**TABLE 8.2** The effects of high- and low-credibility sources on evaluations of fairness and justifiability of identical communications

| Topic | A. Percentage considering author "fair" in his presentation | | | |
|---|---|---|---|---|
| | High-Credibility Source (N*) | (%) | Low-Credibility Source (N) | (%) |
| Antihistamines | 31 | 64.5 | 27 | 59.3 |
| Atomic submarines | 25 | 96.0 | 36 | 69.4 |
| Steel shortage | 37 | 24.3 | 26 | 19.2 |
| Future of movies | 29 | 93.1 | 33 | 63.7 |
| Mean | | 65.6 | | 54.9 |

| Topic | B. Percentage considering author's conclusion "justified" by the facts | | | |
|---|---|---|---|---|
| | High-Credibility Source (N) | (%) | Low-Credibility Source (N) | (%) |
| Antihistamines | 31 | 67.7 | 27 | 51.8 |
| Atomic submarines | 25 | 80.0 | 36 | 44.4 |
| Steel shortage | 37 | 32.4 | 26 | 26.9 |
| Future of movies | 29 | 58.6 | 33 | 42.4 |
| Mean | | 58.2 | | 41.8 |

*N = number of cases used.
SOURCE: Carl I. Hovland, Irving L. Janis, and Harold H. Kelley, *Communication and Persuasion* (New Haven: Yale University Press, 1953), p. 29.

Table 8.3 displays the effects of source credibility on opinion change in these subjects, taken immediately after the exposure. Opinion change in the direction advocated by the communication occurred significantly more often when the communication originated from a high-credibility source that when it originated from a low-credibility source. More specifically, the expected difference was obtained on three of the four topics, the exception being the one that discussed the future of movies.

However, the researchers obtained additional data on these opinion changes four weeks later, and the differences between the effectiveness of the high-credibility and low-credibility sources had disappeared. This resulted from both (1) a decreased acceptance of the point of view advocated by the high-credibility source, and (2) an increased acceptance of the position advocated by the low-credibility sources. Of course, the first could be attributed to forgetting the content. However, the second suggested that the negative effects of the untrustworthy source wore off and permitted the arguments presented in the communication to produce a delayed positive effect, known as a "sleeper effect" (discussed in chapters 2 and 7). Thus, the researchers concluded that the effect of the source is maximal at the time of communication but decreases with the passage of time more rapidly than the effects of the content.

Based upon this evidence and the results derived from follow-up studies, the researchers concluded:

1. When a communication was attributed to a low-credibility source, it was considered to be more biased and unfair in its presentation than when it was attributed to a high-credibility source.
2. High-credibility sources had a considerably greater immediate effect on audience opinion than did low-credibility sources. However, after a few weeks, the positive effects of high-credibility sources and the negative

**TABLE 8.3** Net changes of opinion in direction of communication for sources classified by experimenters as high or low credibility*

| | Net Percentage of Cases in Which Subjects Changed Opinion in Direction of Communication | | | |
| --- | --- | --- | --- | --- |
| | High-Credibility Source | | Low-Credibility Source | |
| Topic | (N) | (%) | (N) | (%) |
| Antihistamines | 31 | 22.6 | 30 | 13.3 |
| Atomic submarines | 25 | 36.0 | 36 | 0.0 |
| Steel shortage | 35 | 22.9 | 26 | −3.8 |
| Future of movies | 31 | 12.9 | 30 | 16.7 |
| Mean | | 23.0 | | 6.6 |
| Difference | | 16.4 | | |
| $p$ | | <.01 | | |

*Net Changes = positive changes *minus* negative changes.
SOURCE: Carl I. Hovland, Irving L. Janis, and Harold H. Kelley, *Communication and Persuasion* (New Haven: Yale University Press, 1953), p. 30.

effects of low-credibility sources tended to disappear. There were no differences between the two sources in either subject evaluations of the presentation or in their acceptance of the conclusions that each source advocated.

3. The immediate effects on opinion were not the result of differences in either the amount of attention the audience paid to the communicator or of the audience's comprehension of the presentation. Tests taken of the amount of information retained by the audience revealed that the audience learned what was said equally well, no matter what the perceived credibility of the communication. Variations in source credibility thus influence primarily the motivation of the audience to accept the conclusions that were advocated.

## The Content and Structure of the Message

The study of the effects of the content in a communication on persuasion was broken down into two areas: (1) motivating appeals and (2) the organization of persuasive arguments. Motivating appeals were defined as "stimuli which operate as appeals that arouse motives to accept recommended opinions."[8] Hovland, Janis, and Kelley discuss three major classes of such incentives: (1) substantiating arguments, (2) positive appeals, and (3) negative appeals. Substantiating arguments tend to lead the audience to believe that the conclusion advocated in the presentation is true or correct. Positive appeals emphasize the rewards of accepting those conclusions, whereas negative appeals (including fear-arousing content) depict the unpleasant consequences of not accepting that conclusion. The researchers present evidence involving only negative, fear-arousing appeals.

*Fear Appeals.*   Research into fear-arousing appeals was designed to investigate factors that determine the degree to which threat appeals are effective or ineffective in producing opinion change. Research in this area focused on two problems: (1) identifying content stimuli that were effective in arousing fear or threat and then (2) determining how they facilitated or interfered with the overall effectiveness of the communication.

The researchers assumed that any intensely disturbing emotion, such as fear, guilt, anger, and so on, has the functional properties of a drive. In other words, these emotions provide motivation for some kind of behavior. A successful fear appeal arouses, then relieves, emotional tension. The tension is removed through the presentation of new opinions for acceptance that provide solutions to the problem. Specifically, the actual persuasion process using fear appeal involves the following steps:

1. The individual is first exposed to relatively neutral content, which defines the topic of communication.
2. Threat statements follow, which are interpreted as referring to a genuine danger and which evoke anticipations such as "This might happen to me."

3. As these anticipations are mentally rehearsed, the individual experiences a marked increase in emotional tension.

4. While in a state of high emotional tension, the individual is exposed to other statements in the communication that make assertions about ways of averting the threat. That is, the threat can or should be avoided by performing the recommended action or by adopting the recommended attitude.

5. As the reassuring recommendation is mentally rehearsed, emotional tension subsides.

6. The reduction of emotional tension operates as a reinforcement of the reassuring recommendation, and thus this new response will tend to occur on subsequent occasions, when similar stimuli are present.

As part of the research program, Janis and Feshbach tested the above model of fear-arousing communication.[9] Using the entire senior class of a large Connecticut high school as subjects, they presented a 15-minute lecture to four randomly assigned groups. Three of those groups saw lectures concerning dental hygiene; each of the lectures contained essentially the same information about the causes and prevention of tooth decay. However, each group was given a separate form of lecture containing a different amount or threat of fear-arousing material. Form 1 contained a "strong" appeal, emphasizing the painful consequences of tooth decay and gum disease. Cancer and blindness were even mentioned as possible consequences of such dental neglect. Form 2 presented a "moderate" appeal in which dangers were described in a milder, more factual manner. This appeal, at its worst, emphasized mouth infections, sore swollen gums, and tooth decay. Form 3, on the other hand, presented a "minimal" appeal that contained few references to the consequences of tooth neglect, although "cavities" were mentioned several times, as were "decayed teeth." The fourth group, the control group, was given a nonthreatening lecture on the human eye. Measures were taken before and after the lectures. These included (1) a measure of each subject's feelings about the possibilities of tooth decay, taken before and after the lecture; (2) a measure of emotional arousal taken immediately after the lecture; and (3) a measure of each subject's conformity with prescribed dental practices, taken one week before and one week after the lecture.

Overall, the lectures did elicit the anxiety that was predicted. As Table 8.4 indicates, all three forms of the presentation produced different amounts of emotional arousal, with the amount of arousal positively correlated with the amount of threat presented. Specifically, the strong appeal produced greater emotional tension than did the moderate appeal, which, in turn, produced greater tension than did the minimal appeal. Additionally, there was a marked increase in worrying about the possibility of tooth decay after the lecture, which again correlated positively with the amount of threat. This led Janis and Feshbach to conclude that content factors that increase the meaningfulness of a threat (i.e., elaborating on the consequences and relating them to the audience) tend to increase the level of emotional arousal.

**TABLE 8.4**   Subjects reporting feelings of worry or concern evoked during the dental hygiene communication (%)

| | Experimental Groups | | |
| --- | --- | --- | --- |
| Questionnaire Responses | Exposed to Strong Appeal (N = 50) | Exposed to Moderate Appeal (N = 50) | Exposed to Minimal Appeal (N = 50) |
| 1. Felt worried—a "few times" or "many times"—about own mouth condition | 74 | 60 | 48 |
| 2. Felt "somewhat" or "very" worried about improper care of own teeth | 66 | 36 | 3 |
| 3. Thought about condition of own teeth "most of the time" | 42 | 34 | 22 |

SOURCE: Carl I. Hovland, Irving L. Janis, and Harold H. Kelley, *Communication and Persuasion* (New Haven: Yale University Press, 1953), p. 70.

Furthermore, it was found that fear appeals did increase conformity with recommended practices. However, the results were surprising, to say the least. It was the minimal appeal (not the strongest appeal) that produced the greatest changes in conformity with the communicator's recommendations! (See Table 8.5.) In fact, the group exposed to the strong threat failed to differ significantly from the control group. Overall, Hovland, Janis, and Kelley concluded that a minimal amount of fear appeal is the most effective in terms of persuasion. Moderate and strong appeals may be effective in arousing interest and a high degree of emotional tension, but they decrease the overall effectiveness of the presentation by evoking some form of interference. For example, when a communication arouses intense feelings of anxiety, individuals will sometimes fail to pay attention to what is being said and miss the intended message. Other individuals, when exposed to anxiety-producing communications, may react to the unpleasant experience by becoming aggressive toward the communicator and rejecting his or her statements. In short, high levels of anxiety can interfere with the person's attending to, comprehending, or accepting the communication.

*Message Organization.*   Whether or not a persuasive communication is effective depends not only on the nature of the motivating appeals used but also upon the organization of the arguments used in support of the position advocated. Typical problems discussed under this topic include (1) whether or not a conclusion should be explicitly stated, (2) whether or not both sides of an argument should be presented, and (3) if both sides are to be presented, which one should be presented first.

Overall, the results of the studies on these topics were rather predictable and in line with the findings of earlier research. For example, Hovland and

**TABLE 8.5** Effect of the illustrated talk on conformity to dental hygiene recommendations

| | Group | | | |
| --- | --- | --- | --- | --- |
| Type of Change | Strong (N = 50) | Moderate (N = 50) | Minimal (N = 50) | Control (N = 50) |
| Increased conformity | 28% | 44% | 50% | 22% |
| Decreased conformity | 20 | 22 | 14 | 22 |
| No change | 52 | 34 | 36 | 56 |
| Total | 100 | 100 | 100 | 100 |
| Net change in conformity | +8% | +22% | +36% | 0% |

| Reliability of Differences | Critical Ratio | Probability Value |
| --- | --- | --- |
| Control vs. minimal | 2.54 | <.01 |
| Control vs. moderate | 1.50 | .07 |
| Control vs. strong | 0.59 | .28 |
| Strong vs. moderate | 0.95 | .17 |
| Strong vs. minimal | 1.96 | .03 |
| Moderate vs. minimal | 0.93 | .18 |

SOURCE: Carl I. Hovland, Irving L. Janis, and Harold H. Kelley, *Communication and Persuasion* (New Haven: Yale University Press, 1953), p. 80.

Mandell performed a study to test the relative effectiveness of either explicitly drawing a conclusion or leaving it implicit.[10] The topic used was "Devaluation of Currency." The communication was tape-recorded and presented as a transcription from a radio program called "Education for Americans." All subjects (college students) heard the identical communication, but for half of them the part containing the explicit conclusion drawn was omitted. It was found that much more opinion change occurred when the conclusion was explicitly drawn by the communicator. However, the researchers cautioned that the intelligence and the degree of sophistication of the members of the audience, in terms of the issue being presented, are important factors in the relative effectiveness of other methods of presentation. Thus, with a sophisticated audience, it might be more effective to leave the conclusion implicit.

Another issue that relates to the organization of persuasive messages is the question of one-sided communications versus two-sided communications. For example, if you are arguing in favor of reduced TV time for children, should you present only arguments that are favorable to your position, or should you acknowledge and attempt to refute an opposing viewpoint? The issue, of course, had been dealt with in the film research discussed in chapter 7. In that work, Hovland, Arthur A. Lumsdaine, and Fred D. Sheffield argued that, on the whole, there was no difference between a one-sided and a two-sided presentation in terms of opinion change. However, few answers are "all or none," and Hovland et al. did find some differences when special conditions were considered (see chapter 7).

One study in this particular research program that provided some interesting results was one conducted by Lumsdaine and Janis. They considered the effectiveness of a one-sided message versus a two-sided message. Their special interest, however, was which of these two types of messages would be most likely to prepare an audience to resist influences of subsequent counterpropaganda. Their subjects were high school students with whom they used two different versions of a recorded radio program. In both versions, the commentator presented the view that the Soviet Union would not be able to produce A-bombs in quantity for at least five years. One group, however, received a one-sided version and were presented only arguments that supported the speaker's position. (They were told, for example, that Soviet scientists had not yet discovered all the crucial secrets, and that even after acquiring all the know-how, the Soviet Union still did not have sufficient industrial potential to produce the bombs in quantity.)

The second group received a two-sided version that contained all of the arguments in the first group's presentation, reached the same conclusion, but also discussed the main arguments on the other side of the question. (For example, they were given the additional information that the Soviet Union had many first-rate atomic scientists and that Soviet industries had made a tremendous recovery since the war.) A week later, half of the subjects in each group were given a second communication in which another speaker advocated a position opposite the one presented in the original communication. That is, he argued that the Soviet Union had probably already developed the A-bomb and would be producing it in large quantities within two years. The main question used to measure the effects of the communication was, "About how long from now do you think it will be before the Russians are really producing *large numbers* of atomic bombs?"[11] Questionnaires were filled out several weeks before the presentations and after the presentations. The results showed that when there was no subsequent exposure to counterpropaganda, the two versions were equally effective in changing opinion. However, when there *was* subsequent exposure to counter-propaganda, the two-sided version was more effective in producing sustained opinion change. The researchers concluded that when the two-sided presentation was used, the listeners were led to accept the recommended opinion; they had already taken into account the opposing arguments and thus had a basis for either ignoring or discounting contradictory arguments. This process of inducing resistance to later persuasive attempts was labeled "inoculation." (This became an important concept in the study of attitude change.)

The last major issue considered in message organization was the old "primacy versus recency" debate. In other words, when there are occasions in which it is most effective to present both sides of an argument, which side should be presented first for maximum impact? Will the side presented first or the side presented last be the more persuasive? After reviewing the existing research, Hovland et al. concluded: "It is doubtful it will ever be meaning[ful] to postulate a Law of Primacy in social psychology."[12] This issue, in other words, was one that Hovland thought best laid to rest. In short, then, the most effective message is one in which a conclusion is explicitly drawn and both sides of the argument presented; the order of presentation does not really make a difference.

## The Audience

The audience was first studied in two ways. The researchers examined the effects of group membership and group conformity on the acceptance of persuasive communications. In addition, personality factors and their effects upon persuadability were examined.

***Effects of Group Membership.***   Hovland et al. argued that individuals' conforming tendencies stem from membership in groups. The tendencies are based upon knowledge of what behavior is expected of them by other members and upon the individual's motivation to live up to those expectations. Thus, group norms often interfere with the effectiveness of persuasive communications because they tend to make the individual resist change. The researchers were therefore particularly interested in "counternorm communications," that is, in messages that argue in direct opposition to group norms.

Previous research had shown that the more highly a person valued his membership in a group, the more closely his attitudes and opinion conformed to the consensus within that group. From this, Kelley and Volkhart hypothesized that individuals who highly value their membership in a group will be less influenced by communications contrary to the group's norm than will those who do not value membership as much. That is, opinion change will be inversely related to the degree to which the person values group membership.[13]

In testing this hypothesis, they experimented with 12 troops of Boy Scouts from a large New England industrial community. The boys filled out a questionnaire in which they were asked how highly they valued their membership in the troop and what their attitudes toward woodcraft were. These attitudes were compared with attitudes about other, more urban activities. A week later, the boys were presented with a speech in which a non-Scout adult criticized woodcraft activities and suggested that the Scouts would be better off learning about the city. Finally, each group was divided in half, and everyone filled out the questionnaire again. Half of each group was told that their answers would be kept secret (private condition), while the other half was told that their responses would probably be made known to the rest of the group (public condition).

The results of this experiment at least partially confirmed Kelley and Volkhart's hypothesis; that is, when the opinions were expressed privately, the boys who most valued their scout membership were the least influenced by the communication. However, in the public condition, the results were inconsistent and no definite pattern could be identified. Overall, however, the authors argued that the findings did support the general hypothesis that persons who were strongly motivated to remain members of the group would be the most resistant to communications that presented recommendations contrary to the standards of the group.

***Personality Factors in Persuadability.***    The authors argued that the effects of a communication are partly dependent upon the characteristics of individual members of the audience. Thus, taking account of personality characteristics should improve predictions concerning the way in which a given type of audience (or a given individual within the audience) will respond. Therefore, the researchers believed that investigations of personality factors were necessary if they were to discover the elusive "laws" and thus be able to predict the degree to which a persuasive communication will succeed in changing beliefs and attitudes.

Hovland and his associates discussed two general types of personality factors: intellectual abilities and "motive factors." Intellectual abilities are significant because they determine the way an individual attends to, interprets, and assimilates the many communications to which he or she is constantly exposed. However, Hovland and his associates believed that for those individuals who possess "at least a certain minimum of essential intellectual abilities," "motive factors" are probably more important determinants of individual differences in persuadability. Motive factors are said to involve "predominant personality needs, emotional disturbances, defense mechanisms, frustration tolerance, thresholds of excitability, etc., which may facilitate or interfere with a person's responsiveness to many different types of persuasive communications."

The authors concluded, in regard to the relation between intellectual ability and the persuadability, that it was a complex matter. On the one hand, it is *easier* to persuade individuals with high intelligence than those low in intellectual ability. This is because the former have more ability to draw valid inferences when exposed to persuasive communications that rely primarily on impressive logical arguments. At the same time, those with high intellectual ability are also more likely to be critical of the arguments presented. They will therefore be *less likely* to be influenced than those with low intellectual ability when they are exposed to persuasive communications that rely primarily on unsupported generalities or false, illogical, irrelevant argumentation. The researchers hypothesized that there would be an interplay between intellectual factors and motive factors. Mental ability alone would be insufficient data when predicting the influence of individual differences on persuadability. Some individuals, the researchers hypothesized, had personality needs that inclined them to be highly gullible. What motive factors, then, make for indiscriminate acceptance of persuasive communications? Janis attempted to link personality characteristics to susceptibility of persuasion. The experiment measured opinion change in 78 male college students. Each student was exposed to the same set of three persuasive communications. In addition, the researchers obtained information about the personality characteristics of the subjects. Thus, it was possible to examine the relationship between opinion changes and personality factors.

The students were given a series of written communications similar to magazine articles or news commentaries or editorials. These materials provided a series of factual statements in an attempt to convince the audience that a particular belief or expectation was the correct one. Because the communications were in simple language, it is probable that all of the student subjects had the minimal skills necessary for absorbing the message.

Each subject was exposed to the communications in a standard way. The subject had to read all three communications; in addition, he had to present one of them orally, then listen to oral presentations of the other two. The subjects' initial opinions on these issues were obtained through an opinion questionnaire administered approximately four weeks earlier. They key items in the questionnaire for this study focused directly on the issues dealt with in the communications: (1) the number of movie theaters in business in three years, (2) the amount of meat available to the population of the United States in two years, and (3) the length of time before a cure for the common cold is discovered. No one in this original survey gave estimates that were anywhere as low as the ones advocated by the communication. After exposure to the communications, questionnaires containing these three items were administered to each subject again. Approximately two-thirds of the subjects lowered their estimates; they changed in the direction advocated by the communication to which they had been exposed.

Janis then divided the subjects into categories on the basis of the degree of change they exhibited: high, moderate, and low persuadability. The "high" category contained 32 cases; all these individuals had been influenced by all three communications. Another 21 cases were classified as "moderate"; they were influenced by two of the communications. The "low" category was composed by of the 25 cases in which the individuals were influenced by one or none of the persuasive communications. The three groups were then compared with respect to personality characteristics.

Personality data were obtained from two independent sources. Janis obtained detailed clinical reports for 16 of the subjects who had received psychiatric counseling. In addition, he administered a personality inventory to all 78 subjects at the time they completed the precommunication questionnaire. Both sets of data indicated that there were marked differences between the men who were highly influenced and those who were relatively uninfluenced by the persuasive communications. Those who were highly influenced possessed low levels of self-esteem. They expressed feelings of social inadequacy; for example, they showed concern about feelings of shyness, lack of confidence in their conversational abilities, high concern about the possibility that friends may have a low opinion of them, and uneasiness at social gatherings. Moreover, this group was also described as "aggressively inhibited." In other words, they rarely criticized others, rarely felt angry toward anyone, rarely felt like resisting the demands of others, and felt a lack of resentment when deceived by others. In addition, the group was also highly characterized by depression. They often reported feeling "blue," "unhappy," and "discouraged." In short, then, the study found that high persuadability was associated with feelings of social inadequacy, inhibition of aggression, and depression, in addition to general levels of low self-esteem.

Up to this point, we have been discussing personality factors associated with persons who are relatively easy to persuade. The researchers did, however, discover three distinct personality traits associated with those who are difficult to persuade. These traits were persistent aggressiveness toward others, social withdrawal tendencies, and acute psychoneurotic complaints. Persons who openly expressed hostility and displayed overt aggression toward others in everyday life were found to be relatively unaffected by persuasive communications. Moreover, socially withdrawn persons, those extremely indifferent toward others, were typically resistant to change. This was also true of persons displaying acute psychoneurotic symptoms—notably, obsessional ideas, hypochondriacal complaints, insomnia, and work inhibitions. The author hypothesized that these symptoms interfere with the person's attention, comprehension, and acceptance, thereby explaining why such individuals are difficult to influence.

While in this chapter we have categorized the research presented in *Communication and Persuasion* as focusing on the communicator, the communication, and the audience, all the studies in Hovland et al.'s book examined the *effects* of communications. Thus, all of the studies were implicitly concerned with the responses of the audience. Some, however, examined special aspects of the audience's response to communications.

## Audience Response Patterns

The two issues that the Yale program focused upon in its analysis of response factors were (1) active versus passive participation by the subject and (2) the duration of the effects of the communication. More specifically, does active participation by individuals have any effect on attitude or opinion acquisition or change? Is attitude or opinion change brought about by persuasive communications typically long-term or short-term change?

*Active versus Passive Participation.*   In everyday life, most people occupy several roles, such as mother, wife, lawyer, and community member. When fulfilling some of the behavior required by these roles, some individuals may find themselves expected to express ideas that are not necessarily in accord with their private beliefs. What happens to an individual's private opinion when this person is induced to assert what had been said in a communication as though it represented his or her own opinion? This is a question that the researchers sought to answer. Janis and King compared the opinion change of two groups: "active participants" and "passive controls."[14] In one group, subjects were induced to play a role that required them to deliver a persuasive communication to others; in the other group, the subjects were required only to read and listen to the same communication. The experiment was conducted in a series of small group meetings involving male college students. Each student was given an "oral speaking test." In the process, they were exposed to three different communications. The purpose of the study was supposed to be to assess their ability to speak effectively in a group conference. At the end of the session, ratings were obtained from each subject on each speaker's performance. In addition, the subjects answered a series of questions concerning their interest in, and their opinions on, the various topics covered. The subjects were told that this information was necessary in order to study agreement among different judges. The researchers compared each subject's postcommunication answers with those he had given in a general opinion survey approximately four weeks earlier. They were thus able to detect opinion changes produced by the communications.

Subjects were asked to give an informal talk in each of the experimental sessions. The talk was based upon a prepared outline provided by the researchers. Each active participant was instructed to play the role of a sincere advocate of the point of view he was presenting. The others listened to this talk and read the outline as he spoke. Each subject delivered a talk in turn, while the other two were passively exposed to the communication. None of the subjects knew which topic he would speak on in advance, in order to prevent selective attention effects.

In each communication, the speaker talked about a controversial issue involving future events. In all cases, the communication took an extreme position. While the arguments were highly relevant, they were also highly biased; they emphasized evidence that supported only one side of the issue. Communication A predicted that two out of three movie theaters would be forced out of business in the next three years because of the intense competition of television and other recent events. The essence of communication B was that within the next two years the availability of meat to the civilian population of the United States would decline to 50 percent of its present level. Communication C argued that a completely effective cure for the common cold was very close to development; it would probably be available in the next year or so.

The results indicated that active participation (in the experimental role-playing) was a much more effective way of changing opinions than passive participation (merely listening to and reading the outline). Additional studies of this topic in the research program yielded similar results. All confirmed the importance of active participation in bringing about opinion change.

***Duration of Opinion Change.*** While all the studies in the Yale program focused to some degree on the duration of opinion change, many issues relevant to this topic have already been discussed. The researchers raised two questions when they addressed this topic: (1) What are the factors dealing with learning and remembering the content of a communication, and (2) What are the factors dealing with the persistence or acceptance of the communicator's conclusions?

Research on the learning and retention of content delineated several important factors. In general, it was found that the meaningfulness of the content will influence retention. That is, the more vivid and the more emotional the material, the better the retention. Also, the more completely the material is initially learned, the longer it will be remembered. Moreover, the type of retention required was found to be an important factor. Specifically, the rate of forgetting depended upon the criteria used to evaluate retention; for example, simple recognition was easier than total recall. Finally, it was found that the motivation of the audience will influence both the quality and quantity of retention. That is, "unpleasant" material tended to be forgotten more rapidly than "pleasant" material.

In terms of the retention of opinion change, or acceptance of the communicator's conclusions, the researchers reviewed a previous study that provided insight. Hovland and Weiss, in a study described earlier, found that a "high-credibility" source was initially more successful in producing opinion change than was a "low-credibility" source. However, after four weeks, differences between the sources' respective success ratios had disappeared. This was due to increased acceptance of the low-credibility source and decreased acceptance of the high-credibility source (the sleeper effect). While forgetting could account for the decreased acceptance of the high-credibility source, it could not explain the delayed opinion change in positive direction. The researchers hypothesized that a dissociation between the communication and the communicator might be producing the sleeper effect. In other words, arguments and conclusions were being recalled without associating them with the source.

Hovland and his associates therefore conducted a study to find out what would happen if the subjects were reminded of the source at a later testing. They used a total of 330 high school seniors as subjects during regular class periods. The subjects were asked to listen to a recording of an educational radio program and judge its educational value. During the program, a guest speaker gave a talk favoring extreme leniency in the treatment of juvenile delinquents. Three different versions of the introduction to the speaker were used in the experiment. In the positive version, he was identified as a juvenile court judge—well trained and well informed. In a neutral version, he was identified as a member of the studio audience, chosen at random. No additional information was given concerning him. In the negative version, he was again presented as coming from the studio audience, but it was also divulged that he had been delinquent in his youth and that he was presently free on bail after an arrest for peddling dope.

After hearing the speech, each group completed an opinion questionnaire concerning juvenile delinquency. Three weeks later, all three groups completed the same questionnaire, except that *half* of each group heard the same introduction again (a "reinstatement of the source"). Initially, the positive communicator had the greatest effect, and the negative communicator the smallest effect. When the source was not reinstated, there was a decline in agreement with the positive speaker and an increase in agreement with the negative speaker, just as in the Hovland and Weiss study. When the source was reinstated, however, the extent of agreement with the positive communicator increased and agreement with the negative source decreased. The effects produced by the reinstated sources were approximately equal to those that were produced by the original communication. The researchers concluded that overall, with the passage of time, the content of a statement is less likely to be associated spontaneously with the source. That is, people often remember *what* was said without recalling *who* said it.

In general, the two most common results concerning retention effects were (1) an individual may be exposed to a communication and accept the communicator's point of view (at the time), but after a period of time revert to his or her previously held attitude; and (2) an individual may at first reject the communicator's point of view but after a time "come around" to the communicator's position. Of the two, the first was the more common.

## CONCLUSIONS AND IMPLICATIONS

Overall, what were the principal findings and the major conclusions of the *Communication and Persuasion* studies? Moreover, what was their importance from the point of view of developing the theory and the methodology of mass communication? Finally, what did the researchers find regarding the "magic keys" to persuasion? Do we know, from their work, the right combination of words, message structure, emotional appeals, type of communicator, and so on, to change people's attitudes and opinions? These questions need careful review.

In summary, the many separate but related studies of the Yale Communication Research Program can be categorized as focusing on the communicator, the message, the audience, and the audience's responses to persuasive communications. In terms of the communicator, the program found that *source credibility* was an important factor in obtaining immediate opinion change. Low-credibility sources were seen as more biased and more unfair that high-credibility sources. The researchers also found that the effects of the communicator's credibility diminish over time, because members of the audience tend to dissociate the message from the communicator. However, these credibility effects can be reinstated simply by reminding the audience who said what. Overall, however, most of the opinion change obtained was short-term rather than long-term. Thus, while it is not difficult to change opinion immediately after a persuasive communication, when the change is measured a month later, the audience often has "reverted" to its original opinion.

The *content* and *structure* of the message were also found to have important effects. Threatening or fear-arousing materials were shown to arouse emotional tension and to produce opinion change, if used in the proper amounts. It was necessary to be careful not to evoke so much fear that high levels of anxiety resulted, since such intense feelings of anxiety can interfere with the individual's acceptance of the communication. In terms of structure, communications should generally state their conclusions explicitly, unless the audience is intelligent and sophisticated. Moreover, both sides of an issue should be included if it is likely that the audience will be exposed to subsequent counterpropaganda.

The studies of the audience provided some interesting, if not always conclusive, results. For example, the studies found that people who value their *membership in groups* highly will be least affected by communications that advocate positions counter to the norms of the group. *Personality factors* were also examined, and it was discovered that persons who have low self-esteem are easily influenced. In addition, people who are aggressive toward others and who have psychoneurotic tendencies are very difficult to influence.

Finally, the research into response factors indicated that *active participation* in the communication, such as having to deliver a speech and argue one side of a question, changes opinions in the direction argued more effectively than does passive participation, such as reading the speech or listening to it.

There are several reasons why *Communication and Persuasion* is an important study in the history of communication research. Even though the research did not focus directly on mass media, it led to a greater understanding of the process of persuasion—a truly significant issue in mass communication. Its studies led to a better understanding of the many facets of persuasion, such as the nature of credibility, "inoculation" against propaganda, the nature of fear appeals, group allegiance, the sleeper effect, and audience participation. And this new understanding was just a beginning; media researchers have followed these leads ever since. It does not matter that the findings reported in *Communication and Persuasion* did not always hold up in subsequent studies. These studies were the seeds from which sprouted a veritable garden of research, sinking its roots in the firm soil prepared by Hovland and his associates. Sometimes the results obtained were found to be wrong. The (inverse relationship) results obtained with the fear appeals, for example, were not confirmed in later studies. Indeed, it has been found that the greater the fear, the greater the opinion change.[15] That is, there is often greater attitude/opinion change following high-intensity fear appeals.

The Yale program studies were innovative methodologically. They introduced many refinements in the use of the methods of experimental psychology applied to the study of the effects of communications. The project provided for experiments with "strategic variations" to test for and isolate the effects of relevant variables. Some researchers, however, have questioned the use of experimental methodology by itself to study persuasion. They have raised the often-repeated objection, Can research conducted under artificial conditions be generalized to more natural conditions? The researchers in the Yale program obviously felt that this could be done. As mentioned earlier, they felt that experimental research was essential to the formulation of a theory in which basic "laws" could be postulated. These "laws" would then allow social scientists to make valid predictions about future events. This, they thought, was the real goal of any kind of research. Thus, they argued that not only was the experimental method a valid one in this context, but that it was also basic to understanding. It is important for us to remember, however, that the results obtained in any experiment are *not,* in and of themselves, conclusive. They should not be taken as "the answer." Their potential validity lies in replication and in the integration of the findings with data from other sources (e.g., survey generalizations, field observations, etc.). Even Carl Hovland, in later years, came to recognize the importance of survey data:

> I should like to stress . . . the mutual importance of the two approaches to the problem of communication effectiveness. Neither is a royal road to wisdom, but each represents an important emphasis. The challenge of future work is one of fruitfully combining their virtues so that we may develop a social psychology of communication with the conceptual

breadth provided by correlational study of process and with the rigorous but more delimited methodology of the experiment.[16]

However, in spite of its drawbacks, the use of the experimental design has had profound and lasting influence on the conduct of communication research. That influence continues today.

The theoretical model used in this study was a version of learning theory that assumed that attitudes and opinions could be changed by persuasive communications only if the incentives for change were greater that those for stability. However, before an individual can be influenced by a persuasive communication, he or she must first attend to it and accept it. The researchers were looking for the "keys" to this process. What kind of communicator was most effective? What was the best way to design and structure a message? And what role did personality factors and group allegiances play? Obviously, the general theoretical approach was that of *selective influence,* based upon individual differences. Other theories of selective influence, such as those based upon social categories and social relationships, were not pertinent to this research program. The subjects, for the most part, fell into one major social category: students. Most were college students, but some were high school students. In addition, the researchers did no look into the *social* relationships that prevailed among their subjects as a source of influence.

The researchers began with the hope of discovering basic "laws" of persuasion. The idea was that once those keys to the communication-persuasion process were available, they could unlock the mysteries behind many social doors. With the possession of these magic keys, we would be able to modify opinions, attitudes, and, theoretically, behavior; we could then reduce prejudice and discrimination, and improve relationships between human beings. In light of the advancement of the "hard" sciences, obtaining this knowledge seemed urgent.

But did these researchers find the magic keys? Not really. Certainly, new findings resulted from the experiments. We remain uncertain whether experiments portray the "real world," but we gained information about the characteristics of an effective communicator; we learned how to "inoculate" subjects from later propaganda; we learned that active participation is more effective than passive. Overall, we learned a great deal concerning immediate, or *short-term,* opinion change. But we did not learn how to modify opinions and attitudes permanently, or even for as long as three or four weeks. How could we accomplish some of our real world goals—such as reduction of prejudice—when opinions and attitudes apparently tend to revert to the status quo ante? Certainly, the new information seemed useful to some people, such as advertising consultants. Armed with it, they may have persuaded more of us to buy products that we ordinarily would not have purchased and didn't know we needed. But this information did not dramatically improve our social world—not as the Yale group had hoped. However, Hovland and the other researchers at the Yale communication program did not give up on the search for the magic keys. *Communication and Persuasion* was only a start. For years to come, the search would continue. Carl Hovland led the way; a host of others followed.

## NOTES AND REFERENCES

1. Carl Hovland, Irving Janis, and Harold H. Kelley, *Communication and Persuasion* (New Haven: Yale University Press, 1953). Two other books, *The Order of Presentation in Persuasion* (1957) and *Personality and Persuadability* (1959), refined and extended some of the findings presented in *Communication and Persuasion*.
2. Hovland et al., *Communication and Persuasion*, p. 12.
3. Harold D. Lasswell, "The Structure and Function of Communication in Society," in *The Communication of Ideas*, ed. Lyman Bryson (New York: Harper and Brothers, 1948), pp. 37–51.
4. Hovland et al., *Communication and Persuasion*, p. 9.
5. Ibid., p. 21.
6. Ibid.
7. Carl I. Hovland and Walter A. Weiss, "The Influence of Source Credibility on Communication Effectiveness," *Public Opinion Quarterly*, 15 (1951): 635–650.
8. Hovland et al., *Communication and Persuasion*, p. 56.
9. Irving L. Janis and Seymour Feshbach, "Effects of Fear-Arousing Communications," *Journal of Abnormal and Social Psychology*, 48 (1953): 78–92.
10. Carl L. Hovland and W. Mandell, "An Experimental Comparison of Conclusion-Drawing by the Communicator and by the Audience," *Journal of Abnormal and Social Psychology*, 47 (1952): 581–588.
11. Janis and Feshback, "Effects of Fear-Arousing Communications," *Journal of Abnormal and Social Psychology*, 47 (1952): 581–588.
12. Hovland et. al., *Communication and Persuasion*, p. 9.
13. Harold H. Kelley and Edmund H. Volkhart, "The Resistance to Change of Group-Anchored Attitudes," *American Sociological Review*, 17 (1952): 453–465.
14. Irving L. Janis and B. T. King, "The Influence of Role-Playing on Opinion-Change," *Journal of Abnormal and Social Psychology*, 48 (1958): 487–492.
15. See, for example, K. L. Higbee, "Fifteen Years of Fear Arousal: Research on Threat Appeals, 1953–1968," *Psychological Bulletin*, 72 (1969): 426–444. See also H. Leventhal, "Findings and Theory in the Study of Fear Communications," in L. Berkowitz, ed., *Advances in Experimental Social Psychology*, vol. 5 (New York: Academic Press, 1970), pp. 119–186.
16. Carl Hovland, Address to the American Psychological Association, 1965.

# chapter 9

# Personal Influence: The Two-Step Flow of Communication

The decade following World War II (1945-1955) was an extraordinarily active period for research on the effects of mass communication. Carl Hovland and his associates followed up the Army studies by conducting experiments on communication issues. The Erie County study of the presidential campaign had uncovered the possible significance of social ties between members of the audience in the second stage of the "two-step" flow. Other researchers were turning their attention to other media (to be discussed in chapters to follow). All of these studies were pressing forward vigorously the task of discovering the principles, processes, and influences of mass communication. This enthusiastic curiosity was aided by a growth in sophistication of the research methods available to social scientists. Although the computer was not yet at hand for academic researchers, statistical procedures were highly developed, and the electric calculating machines of the day permitted the analysis of relatively large data sets.

Controversies raged in both academic and political circles regarding the implications of our society's expanding ability to communicate on a mass scale with its citizens. For some, the escalating technology of the media seemed to hold high promise for improving both society and the human condition. Mass communication could save democracy, some said, because the media had the capacity to create informed public opinion. The media could become a kind of mass society version of the "town meeting," where citizens would have increasing access to accurate and complete accounts of the events, issues, and problems that required their attention and decisions. The growing power of the mass media to enlighten people, in other words, would make possible that expansion of the human consciousness forecast by Charles Horton Cooley at the beginning of the century.[1] Although newspapers were the only mass medium of his time, he felt that the huge increase in access to information that they provided for ordinary people had brought humankind to the dawn of a new era of enlightenment.

For others, the media continued to loom as menacing agents that threatened the destruction of democracy. The expansion of the media from print, to film, to broadcasting, seemed only to make it easier to shape and control the ideas of people who were becoming increasingly defenseless against media suggestions. In a society thought to be characterized by increasing urbanization, industrialization, and modernization, the original magic bullet theory, linked with the related conception of mass societal organization (chapter 1), seemed to provide a clear basis for concern about the effects of the media. The legacy of fear of mass communications, in other words, appeared to many citizens to be increasingly justified as the media continued to expand.

As research intensified, however, communication scholars were forced to reassess their thinking. The problem was that the powerful effects that had been attributed to the media—both good and bad—simply did not seem to be there. The earliest large-scale research, such as the Payne Fund studies (chapter 2) and the investigation of the *War of the Worlds* broadcast (chapter 3) had seemed to support the conclusion that the media had immediate, powerful, and direct influences on their audiences. But subsequent studies, with more careful research designs, controls, and measurements, showed far less dramatic effects. The idea that the media controlled people's beliefs, attitudes, and behavior was not being supported by the accumulating evidence. This was not only true of the large-scale studies reviewed thus far in the present book, but of the hundreds of smaller efforts that were increasingly appearing in the research journals.

In his well-known book summarizing the findings in the entire field of mass communication studies that had accumulated up until about 1958, Joseph Klapper maintained that the main conclusions were approximately the following:[2]

1. The media appear to have *less* power than the average citizen has assumed (then or now). No case can be made for simple cause-effect relationships between a person's paying attention to some message conveyed by the mass media and his or her beliefs, attitudes, or behavior.
2. Many studies have found that the messages conveyed by the media do have effects on their audiences, but these effects are relatively *minor*.
3. The conditions under which these messages have effects on their audiences are far *more complex* than had been suspected by social scientists who first studied the media.

Replacing the hypothesis of powerful and immediate effects was not an easy matter, or one that took place overnight. For one thing, the public was deeply committed to the kind of thinking represented by the magic bullet theory. Thus, by the early 1950s the study of mass communication was proceeding with vigor, but for social scientists the findings seemed to demand new approaches to further investigation of the mass communication process.

Increasingly, research came to be designed not to uncover assumed awesome power of mass communication but to trace more subtle and complex patterns of its influence. The research community, if not the public, clearly believed that a hypothesis of *minimal effects* was closer to reality. To some communication scientists, this was a source of disappointment and frustration. One prominent researcher even decided that studying the media was no longer worthwhile and declared the field to be dead.[3] Many others, however, remained excited by media research and designed numerous innovative studies of the more subtle and indirect influences of mass communication.

One important large-scale study of indirect influences of the mass media was actually a follow-up of the research reported in chapter 4, on the impact of a mass-communicated presidential campaign. The new effort probed into the nature of opinion leaders and the kinds of influences they had on their followers. It focused on, in other words, those who were involved in the second stage of the two-step flow of communication. The research was actually planned in 1944, and its field work was started in 1945. However, its data analyses and final report were not completed for a decade. Its findings were finally published in 1955 by Elihu Katz and Paul F. Lazarsfeld in their book *Personal Influence: The Part Played by People in the Flow of Mass Communication.*[4] It was with this research that the present chapter is principally concerned. The book was much more than simply a research report; it was an effort to interpret the authors' research within a framework of conceptual schemes, theoretical issues, and research findings drawn broadly from the scientific study of small groups. By that time, small-groups research had developed rapidly.

## THE PART PLAYED BY PEOPLE:
## THE NEED FOR A NEW APPROACH

With the recognition that the process of mass communication was far more complex than anyone had previously thought, researchers from several disciplines sought to find the many factors that played a part in shaping what happened between media and mass. The Hovland team of social psychologists was convinced that the keys were in such factors as message structure, which could interact with individual differences in personality factors, including attitudes, emotions, credibility or other variables that influenced perception, remembering, or motivation to respond. The sociologists who had uncovered the two-step flow process felt that a more promising focus of research would be on the close personal groups that Cooley, at the beginning of the century, had labeled *primary groups.*[5] Katz and Lazarsfeld reviewed this concept in some detail.

Actually, the idea that primary groups might play an important role in the process of mass communication was an almost radical departure from earlier thinking about the media. We showed in chapter 1 that the first rather simplistic stimulus-response theories dealing with the influences of mass communication in modern life were premised on assumptions about "mass" society, with its emphasis on individuality, loss of meaningful interpersonal ties, and a reduction of informal social controls. Yet, at the heart of the two-step flow idea is the assumption that very opposite kinds of variables might be important. The two-step flow concept presumed a movement of information through interpersonal networks, from the media to people and from there to other people, rather than directly from media to mass.

It seemed to follow, then, that a member of the audience of mass communication was not an impersonal individual without effective social ties to others. More likely, the audience member was in some way *influenced* by his or her ties with others in the interpretation of mass media messages and in making decisions whether to act one way or another on the basis of such messages.

Preliminary evidence from Lazarsfeld et al.'s *The People's Choice* (see chapter 4) clearly suggested that it was one's family and peers that were the most important in the secondary stage of the two-step flow. In other words, the primary group was an obvious and logical focus for research aimed at better understanding the movement of messages from media to audiences via the two-step flow.

## The "Rediscovery" of the Primary Group

As soon as it became apparent that close social ties played a part in the flow of information from media to mass, it seemed in retrospect that communication researchers should have started with such a model in the first place! The problem was that the theory of mass society led inevitably to assumptions that people in modern social life were isolated and individualistic. But as research on contemporary populations and social systems progressed, it had become increasingly apparent that the theory of mass society was not a very accurate model. Over and over, the important role of close personal ties in modern life was being uncovered in major research studies on social behavior.

The primary group, in other words, was *rediscovered* in modern urban society. The term *rediscovery* is appropriate because the concept became important shortly after the turn of the century with the work of social psychologists who were concerned with the process of socialization. The primary group was seen as a very important source from which people derived their "human nature." This was at a time when the famous *nature* versus *nurture* debates sought to settle whether personality was mainly a product of inherited factors or was heavily influenced by learning in social settings. The result of those debates was that older theories of human nature based on such biological factors as "instinct" became increasingly obsolete to many social scientists. The influence of learning from social and cultural sources became correspondingly more predominant in theories of human socialization.

But while earlier students of socialization had given primary group interaction a central place in their thinking, this idea did not carry over into the accounts of those who were examining other kinds of social processes. Mass society thinking, in other words, continued to dominate the conceptual formulations of most social scientists. Then, starting in the early 1930s, a series of studies, one after the other, began to find that primary social relationships were a significant factor in the way people behaved. A very brief summary of several of these "rediscoveries" of the primary group will place the issue in perspective. Such a perspective is important in understanding the new direction in mass communication research represented by the *Personal Influence* project.

The classic rediscovery of the primary group as a set of influences that helps us understand life in modern society emerged as a central theme in the work of Fritz J. Rothlisberger and William J. Dixon.[6] Theirs was a study of worker productivity in a factory that made parts for the Western Electric Company. Called the Hawthorne studies (after the name of the plant), the research showed that the so-called piece rate system for motivating greater worker productivity was often ineffective because workers had strong personal ties to each other. They did not act in an individualistic manner to maximize their own rewards but regulated their output in conjunction with the norms and expectations of their fellow workers with whom they had close personal ties.

In the late 1930s, social scientists studying the patterning of social relationships in American communities found that clique structures (e.g., primary groups) played a key role in placing people socially in one level or another.[7] In fact, in determining patterns of social stratification, cliques turned out to be second only to the family in importance.

Finally, during World War II, research on American soldiers and their willingness to fight revealed that combat motivation was associated with attachment to a close personal group.[8] Primary groups, in other words, emerged within the framework of a large, formally organized social structure (the army) and determined to a considerable degree the willingness of individuals to carry out their roles in an effective manner. Soldiers would fight tenaciously if it meant protecting the lives of their buddies. Such factors as hatred of the enemy or broad ideological values counted for relatively little on the actual field of battle.

## The Contribution of Small-Groups Research

What did all of this mean for the investigation being summarized in the present chapter? One implication was that the development of theories about the nature of mass communication needed to rest upon the assumption that small intimate groups have a profound influence on nearly every aspect of social life—including the activities engaged in by people involved in the flow of information from media to mass. Once this assumption was made, it opened much broader vistas for conceptualizing the *process* of mass communication. It meant that the accumulated findings of social and behavioral science research concerning the nature and functioning of small groups became a fertile source for insights into how people could be expected to act in a mass communication setting. The research findings provided concepts and generalizations about how people could be expected to act and interact as they perceived messages from the media, told those messages to others, received influences from others whom they trusted, and eventually made some form of response to media content.

By the time the Katz and Lazarsfeld study of opinion leaders and their influences was first begun, small-groups research was off to a good start. By the time the research report was written a decade later, the accumulated findings of the social sciences regarding the nature and functioning of small groups was impressive indeed. In *Personal Influence,* the authors presented a detailed summary of the relationship between their study of opinion leaders and a host of factors to which their research objectives were related. For the most part, this work was an ex post facto analysis. Such an "after the fact" strategy is often criticized because the research is conducted first without the organizing framework of a strong conceptual basis, which comes later when the theoretical implications are sorted out against the findings of previous studies or inter-pretations. Nevertheless, the author's analyses did illustrate the broader base of evidence, regarding the primary group and the functioning of close interpersonal ties, that needs to be taken into account in the study of the two-step flow of communication. The authors discussed how opinions and attitudes within such groups tend to be shared. Dozens of studies were summarized to show that people tend to conform to the norms and expectations of such groups and that numerous benefits result from such conformity.

***Small Groups and Meaning Theory.***   As an illustration of the significance of the study of small groups in general to the development of theory in mass communications, the authors pointed to the functions of such groups in providing *meanings* for their members regarding ambiguous situations for which individuals do not have an adequate or standard interpretive framework. During the 1940s, Kurt Lewin, a well-known social psychologist, and his followers studied the process by which a "social reality" is created in small group settings:

> Experiments dealing with memory and group pressure on the individual show that what exists as "reality" for the individual is to a high degree determined by what is socially accepted as reality. This holds even in the field of physical fact: to the South Sea Islanders the world may be flat; to the European it is round. "Reality," therefore, is not an absolute. It differs with the group to which the individual belongs.[9]

It is through social processes that we develop meanings for the words and labels that make up our language. Few people can have, or even want to have, personal and direct experience with every aspect of reality for which we have a label (e.g., "death in the electric chair"). Nevertheless, we collectively construct a socially derived reality that we share and use to provide meaning to such labels.

Although these authors did not extend their ideas to the mass media, it has become clear today that the mass media, as well as small groups, are an important part of the social processes of communication by which we collectively develop social constructions of reality. This idea is at the heart of what DeFleur has called the *meaning theory* of the effects of the mass media."[10]

The significance of the social reality function of small groups for Katz's and Lazarsfeld's research on personal influence was explained by them: In a presidential election the media provide confusing and often contradictory facts about the issues and candidates, yet the individual must choose between one or the other, even in this ambiguous situation. He or she can turn to members of the primary group for interpretations, which then become "reality."

***Values and the Reference Function.*** The values shared in small groups are another source that draws people to the groups as sources of influence and interpretation. Research had shown that people with similar values tended to be drawn toward each other and to form close-knit groups. When people are in a system of close and interdependent interaction with one another, they tend to demand of each other a high degree of conformity. Thus, the primary group becomes a "reference group" to whom its members turn for interpretations, advice, and influences as they shape their responses to the external world. An important part of that external world is what they encounter, or think that they encounter, in mass communication.

Many other aspects and functions of small groups in daily life are discussed in *Personal Influence.* Indeed, the first half of the work is a rich source of ideas of how mass communication behavior is linked to other important social processes and activities:

> The whole moral of these chapters is that knowledge of an individual's interpersonal environment is basic to an understanding of his exposure and reactions to the mass media. Thus, planning for future research on the short-run influencing effects of the mass media must build, first, on the systematic investigation of the everyday processes which influence people and, secondly, on the study of the points of contact between those everyday influences and the mass media.[11]

To this, most researchers even today would say amen. Unfortunately, too few have chosen to follow the path pointed out by Katz and Lazarsfeld in the mid-1950s.

## THE DECATUR STUDY OF OPINION LEADERS

Leadership comes in many forms. Most visible are official leaders that head formally organized groups—corporations, labor unions, schools, government, clubs, banks, and so on. The leaders are easily identified in any community by their official positions of power and authority. The decisions of these leaders can clearly have an impact on the ebb and flow of the vital social and economic political processes of community life.

But another kind of leadership is far less visible. It is informal and often unwitting. It takes place when people turn to others at their same social level whom they know and trust. They do this because they need advice or inter-pretations to try to make sense out of some complex situation confronting them. They need to understand the dimensions of the reality before them so that they can make sensible decisions and act in their own best interests. The others they select as leaders in this process are people like themselves whom they feel command some special expertise, or possess some special wisdom, regarding the topic about which a decision must be made. When ordinary people make decisions on such matters as to what to believe, purchase, join, avoid, support, like, or dislike, they turn to *opinion leaders* for advice. Often, the opinion leader's personal influence is both given and received without either party consciously recognizing it as such.

It is this type of informal personal influence that was under investigation in what has come to be called the Decatur study (after the community in which it was done). As we noted earlier, the research was designed to follow up more systematically the idea of the two-step flow of communication, first noted in the study of the presidential election in Erie County, Ohio (see chapter 4). The research was conducted under the auspices of the Bureau of Applied Social Research of Columbia University. Financial support for the project was supplied by Mcfadden Publications, Inc. (presumably because of its potential implications for advertisers) and the Roper polling organizations (presumably because of its implications for understanding the process of opinion formation).

The study focused on the role of opinion leaders as they influenced others in four areas of decision making in day-to-day life. These were (1) *marketing* (where choices must be made regarding foods, household products, and small consumer items); (2) the world of *fashion* (where choices must be made concerning clothing, hair styles, and cosmetics); (3) *public affairs* (a potentially confusing arena of political and social issues in the news, civic activities, and national and local events); and (4) the selection of *movies* to see (again, a multiplicity of choices). In other words, the problem was to determine who influenced whom in these areas where decisions often have to be made, but where there are many potential choices and few clear definitions of objective reality.

## The Research Procedures

To locate instances of personal influence regarding these four topics, the research procedures included selecting a suitable community to study, drawing a sample of people to interview (on two separate occasions, once in June and once in August), identifying leaders and followers, and studying the characteristics of each. A fairly unique feature of the research plan was the intention to trace out who had, in a face-to-face manner, influenced whom. In other words the researchers wanted to study opinion leaders who were in actual contact with recipients of their influence on a day-to-day basis. It was not their intention to study persons who might be influential by virtue of their prominent position in the social, political, or business life of the city.

***Selecting the Research Site.*** The financial resources available for the investigation played a key role in dictating the size of the community to be studied. The plan was to maintain a ratio of no fewer than one interview to every 20 homes in the city. Since 800 interviews were anticipated, this indicated a community with a population of approximately 60,000. The Midwest was chosen as a region within which to locate such a community, on the grounds that this part of the country was generally less characterized by sectional peculiarities. The problem, therefore, was to locate the most "typical" communities in the Midwest that were of the required population size.

First, all cities in the range 50,000 to 80,000 located in Ohio, Michigan, Indiana, Illinois, Wisconsin, Iowa, and Kansas were listed for detailed demographic, social, and economic analysis. This search yielded 28 cities. From these, all that were suburban communities dominated by a large city were eliminated. This left 18 potential sites. For each of these, data were assembled on 36 indices relevant to the problem under study. These indices provided key information on population composition, economic status, commercial activities, mass communication usage patterns, and the general quality of community life.

With all of this information at hand, it was possible to reduce the list to three cities that deviated the least from the central tendencies (Decatur, Illinois; Terre Haute, Indiana; and Springfield, Indiana). Of the three, Decatur was judged to be the most consistently typical in the clusters of variables thought to be potentially significant to the research goals. As such, it was chosen as the site for the research.[12]

***The Sample.***    The authors of *Personal Influence* provide relatively little information about the actual procedures used to develop their original sample. In fact, they provide only the following paragraph:

> Within Decatur, the sample to be interviewed was drawn according to usual probability methods and nothing special need be said about it. Within each household, women residents (not domestic help) age 16 and over were interviewed alternating on successive interviews between older and younger women whenever more than two women occupied the same household.[13]

Elsewhere[14] they indicate that a sample size of 800 was dictated by their financial resources. It is not clear, however, whether this sample size was actually achieved in their first round of interviews (in June). However, it should be kept in mind that the final assembly of data was not simply a compilation of results from a single social survey. As will be made clear, the researchers sought to apply *sociometric* methods to their research by tracing out who claimed to have influenced whom concerning the four topics discussed above.

## The Problem of Defining and Locating Personal Influence

This was a pioneering study into a largely unknown territory. Very little was known at the time about what kinds of people influenced others on an informal basis. Therefore, no clear guidelines were available a priori concerning the best means to identify informal influentials or to gather quantitative information on instances of opinion leadership. Consequently, several approaches were tried.

***Alternative Approaches.***    Four different strategies were tried to locate opinion leaders and instances of personal influence. One technique was an attempt to identify "generally influential" people who gave advice or interpretations to others on a range of topics. The question was whether opinion leadership was *specific* to a particular topic, or whether people turned to the same individuals more generally. There was some limited evidence that there were general influentials. For example, in the initial interviews, respondents were asked if they regularly turned to a particular person for advice concerning public affairs (a rather general topic). Specifically, the question was asked: "Do you know anyone around here who keeps up with the news and whom you can trust to let you know what is really going on?" About half of the women studied could identify such a person. This varied considerably with age and education. Older, better educated women were more able to identify such a generally influential person. Younger women with less education often could not. Even so, the "generally influential" individuals were for the most part the *husbands* for the married women, *male parents* for the unmarried, and *male friends* for the once married. In fact, women of all categories tended strongly to nominate males rather than females as individuals of general competence in public affairs (about two to one). In any case, this particular strategy was not judged to be especially fruitful for the study of opinion leaders.

Another strategy for defining and locating opinion leaders focused on "specific influentials." This procedure was based on information provided by the two separate interviews with the 800 respondents, in June and again in August. Again using the area of public affairs as an illustration, the women's opinions on nine specific topics of current interest were recorded during the first interview. On the second interview, any *changes* in those opinions were noted. Once these changes had been verified, careful probing was undertaken to determine with whom the respondents had discussed these issues, and if those discussions had been influential in modifying their opinions. This proved to be a fruitful strategy, and some 619 verified opinion changes were identified. The "specific influentials" who had played a key role in each change were nominated by the respondents, providing both empirical instances of personal influence and the names of the opinion leaders. Again, family relationships were paramount, and males played a predominant role.

The third technique that was tried for studying opinion leadership was a somewhat less complicated effort to identify the "everyday contacts" of the respondents—people with whom they usually talked things over, regardless of the direction of influence. This approach was not particularly fruitful because only about half of the women could identify someone with whom they usually talked things over. Those that did usually nominated a member of their family.

The final technique was *self-designation*. This procedure was the one actually used to generate the main body of data that made up the research report. Self-designation means that the women interviewed were asked whether they had recently been influential to others. This line of questioning was used in both the first and second interviews. For example, the following question was posed for each respondent: "Have you recently been asked for your advice about (one of the four main topics: marketing, fashions, movies, or public affairs)?" If the respondent answered "yes," detailed information was collected regarding who asked for advice, about what, and so forth. In other words, the respondent was asked to identify the exact individual, by name and address, with whom the interaction took place. In this way, instances of opinion leadership were identified both in terms of the persons involved, the direction of the process, and the topic of influence.

The obvious problem with self-designation as a means of identifying and studying opinion leaders and their influence is that it views the process from only one end. There is, in other words, a problem of *validity*. If a person claims to have talked to and influenced another, how can such a claim be verified? Because the researchers had asked their respondents for the names and addresses of those whom they claimed to have influenced, one possible means of verification was to go to those designated and ask for confirmation. In fact, the investigators did obtain some 1,549 designations of persons who had sought advice from 693 of their 800 respondents. The intention was to contact all of those designated in order to view the influence process from their end. Unfortunately, many were unavailable during the study period (out of town and so on). However, some 634 were contacted. Of these, two-thirds confirmed the contact and the topic of the conversation. A fourth could not recall the claimed contact. Between nine and ten percent denied that the conversation ever took place. Overall, then, the question of validity was never answered in a rigorous manner, but at least some confirmations were made, and the researchers were satisfied that self-designation was a realistic strategy for the study of personal influence. The main subjects for the analysis, then, were the 693 "self-detected" opinion leaders.

After looking at all of the types mentioned—the generally influential, specific influentials, everyday contacts, and self-designations, the researchers narrowed their conceptualization of opinion leadership and personal influence. Opinion leaders are people recognized by their peers as having some special competence in a particular subject. People turn to opinion leaders for advice about a specific topic but usually do not seek them out for their opinions on a range of issues. Personal influence, then, takes place between people in face-to-face settings and concern rather specific topics.

***Opinion Leadership versus Other Influences.***    A major difficulty in studying the impact of opinion leadership on decisions is to sort it out from other sources of influence. For example, we are all influenced to an unknown degree by mass media advertising in our purchasing consumer goods, household products, or even food at the supermarket. For women, salespeople may play an influential role in the purchase of cosmetics or fashionable clothing. Newspaper ads for movies may be a factor for all of us in selecting a film to attend. In other words, opinion leadership is only one influence in a context of many. Identifying which influence played a predominant role in any particular decision may not always be possible, even for the person who made the choice.

Still, most people can recall whether or not they talked to someone else about a new brand of household cleaner, a new nail polish, or the merits of a particular movie before attending it. They can also assess to a reasonably accurate degree the extent to which these contacts influenced them to adopt the product in question.

The researchers made an extensive study of the comparative impact on such decisions by personal contacts versus media advertising and salespeople. In the area of marketing, for example, personal contacts with opinion leaders were substantially more effective in prompting marketing shifts that were advertisements in news-papers, radio, or magazines. Salespeople played an even smaller role. But for selecting a motion picture, newspaper ads had a much greater effect than personal contacts. In the world of fashion, by contrast, personal influence played an especially powerful role, although salespeople and magazine ads were also important.

Generally, in the areas of marketing, fashions, and movie selection, the impact of personal influence on people's decisions to change patterns of use, or to adopt something new, was greater than that of the formal media. There were many exceptions to this generalization, and there are undoubtedly many reasons why this tendency was found. Also, opinion leadership does not occur in a vacuum. A person may be exposed to media advertising, the blandishments of salespeople, *and* personal influence from a trusted source. Nevertheless, the data clearly supported the conclusion that opinion leaders were one of the more powerful influences on people's decisions in the marketplace of either consumer products and services or of ideas.

## The Characteristics of Opinion Leaders

Who were these 693 "self-detected" opinion leaders?[15] That is, how did they fit into the social life of Decatur? The researchers identified three significant dimensions in the lives of their respondents that were related to the opinion leader role. These factors played a central part in determining *if* a woman was likely to influence others, and if so, with respect to *what*. These dimensions were (1) position in the "life cycle," (2) position on the community's socioeconomic ladder, and (3) the extent of the individual's social contacts. These three factors provided a convenient framework within which to describe and analyze the flow of interpersonal influence concerning the four topics under study.

*Position in the Life Cycle.*   The classifications used to describe this dimension identify clusters of variables that change as the individual moves from one position to another. For example, younger, unmarried women have greater knowledge concerning fashionable clothing, hairstyles, and cosmetics than those whose lives are more centered on homemaking and raising children. By contrast with both groups, older women, whose children have grown, and who have a wide circle of contacts within the community, can be expected to know more of public affairs and community issues. Position in the life cycle, in other words, raises the probability of being knowledgeable about some topics but not others. Familiarity with a topic, and possession of the skills to deal with it effectively, are the foundations of the capacity to exercise personal leadership and be perceived as an effective opinion leader.

The investigators identified four life-cycle classifications into which they could categorize the opinion leaders identified in their sample (see Table 9.1). Consistent with the language of their time, they used the term *girls* to designate younger women. If a researcher did that today, he or she would be severely criticized.

*Socioeconomic Status.* People at distinctive levels in a community are characterized by differences in education, prestige, and income. These may be important factors in determining whether or not they will be sought out as sources for interpretation and advice. An important question for this research on opinion leaders was whether personal influence travels up, down, or laterally among such community social strata. To address this issue, the researchers divided their sample into three categories—high, middle, and low status—with about one-third in each. This was done on the basis of years of education and amount of rent paid (as an indicator of economic level).[16]

*Social Contacts.* The woman with limited social contacts has few opportunities to exercise personal influence. The one who regularly interacts with many people will have more opportunities to serve as an opinion leader. To test this idea, the researchers constructed a simple index of *gregariousness*. It was based on (1) the number of persons in the community the subject claimed to be "friendly with and talk with fairly often" and (2) the number of organizations and clubs to which she belonged.[17]

Information on these kinds of social contacts provided a relatively simple classification pattern. A subject who claimed seven or more friends and belonged to at least one organization was placed in the high category. At the other end, a subject with no organization memberships and few friends was placed in the low category. These subjects were then cross classified into the four categories shown in Table 9.2.

**TABLE 9.1**  Distribution of life cycle types in the sample

|  | (%) |
|---|---|
| *Girls* (single women, under 35) | 12 |
| *Small-family wives* (married, under 45, with one or no children) | 26 |
| *Large-family wives* (married, under 45, with two or more children) | 25 |
| *Matrons* (married, over 45, most of whose children are older that 15) | 37 |
|  | 100 |
|  | N = 693 |

SOURCE: Elihu Katz and Paul F. Lazarsfeld, *Personal Influence: The Part Played by People in the Flow of Mass Communication* (Glencoe, Ill.: Free Press of Glencoe, 1955), p. 225.

**TABLE 9.2**  Distribution of sample by social activity

|  |  | Number of Friendships | |
|  |  | High (%) | Low (%) |
|---|---|---|---|
| Number of organizations } | high | 27 | 14 |
|  | low | 31 | 28 |

SOURCE: Elihu Katz and Paul F. Lazarsfeld, *Personal Influence: The Part Played by People in the Flow of Mass Communication* (Glencoe, Ill.: Free Press of Glencoe, 1955), p. 228.

These three factors—life cycle, socioeconomic status, and gregariousness—were found to be related in many complex ways among the women in the sample. Summarized briefly, the more important of these relationships were as follows:

1. High gregariousness increases with life-cycle progression.
2. Girls (as defined by Katz and Lazarsfeld) tend to score medium in gregariousness. They belong to fewer organizations but have many friends.
3. Women of lower socioeconomic status tend to be low in gregariousness.

The significance of these three factors appears to lie in their power, either singly or in combination, to shape a woman's interest in certain life areas. They place her at different points in the social structure and limit or expand her contact with others in the community.

## THE FINDINGS

The four topics of personal influence chosen for study were everyday concerns in the life of Decatur: what to buy for the family, how to select from the world of fashions, what movie choices to make, and what to believe or decide regarding public events and issues. The three characteristics discussed in the previous section were used as a framework to follow the flow of personal influence from different types of opinion leaders to those who sought their advice and interpretation on these four topics.

### Marketing Leaders

The researchers found that the women in their sample often consulted each other for opinions about new products, the quality of different brands, and shopping economies. In fact, about half of the respondents interviewed in the June and August efforts reported making some kind of change to something new from a product or brand that they had regularly used. Opportunities for personal influence in this area were abundant. The task was to study how this influence flowed from one type of person to another. The analysis of who influenced whom in marketing decisions was made in terms of social status, life cycle, and gregariousness, in that order.

***The Horizontal Flow of Marketing Leadership.***    There was little reason to assume that women of higher social status were more skilled at marketing. A "trickle-down" effect was a possibility, with higher prestige making advice seem more significant. However, an examination of the proportion of the women at each status level who claimed to have provided marketing advice did not support the trickle-down concept. Marketing opinion leaders were found more or less equally at all status levels: Among the high-social-status women, some 27 percent claimed to have given marketing advice; the figures of middle- and low-social-status respondents were 24 percent and 21 percent, respectively (differences not statistically significant). In other words, high status did not seem to increase a woman's chances to serve as an opinion leader in any significant way. Generally, according to Katz and Lazarsfeld, the flow of marketing influence was *horizontal*. They explained it in the following terms:

> . . . it is more reasonable to expect that marketing influence is confined within the boundaries of each of the several social strata than it is [to assume] a random exchange conducted without regard for status differences. Seeking out a woman of like status for advice means seeking out a woman with similar budgetary problems and limitations. That is one major reason why we may expect that traffic in marketing is a status-bound activity. Secondly, since stores and shopping centers are likely to cater somewhat more to women of one status than another—by design or because of location or the like—women are more likely to encounter status peers during their marketing activities than to encounter status unequals.[18]

This generalization was confirmed in some degree by comparing the status levels of both the giver of advice and the receiver in those cases where both could be established. Unfortunately, such information was available for less than half of the cases where follow-up interviews were attempted to verify the self-designations of opinion leaders (see p. 198). Although these data have many limitations, they appear to show that "influences turn to influentials of their own status level much more often than they turn to those of other statuses."[19] Where crossovers in status levels did occur, they were just as likely to go up as down. In short, personal influence in marketing appears to take place horizontally, in other words, between people at the same general status level.

***Life Cycle and Marketing Leadership.***    The researchers anticipated that position in the life cycle would be an especially important factor in marketing leadership. Unmarried, younger women with no children would be unlikely sources for consultation about products related to family meal preparation, child rearing, or household domestic tasks. Older women, most of whose children had grown, might have had years of experience in marketing. However, their current responsibilities are more limited. Therefore, they were not expected to be the dominant category. The category with the heaviest current responsibilities and daily experience in marketing matters would be *large-family wives,* and the data strongly supported the speculation that they would be most sought for advice. In fact, 38 percent of the large-family wives claimed that they had served as marketing opinion leaders. The comparable figures were 23 percent for small-family wives, 20 percent for "girls," and 16 percent for matrons.

A second question is whether these large-family wives mainly influenced each other, or whether their personal influence flowed disproportionately to the other categories. The study provided only limited data on this issue. Katz and Lazarsfeld were able to conclude only that women of age 25–44 seemed to influence women somewhat younger or somewhat older than themselves. This included both small- and large-family wives. While not conclusive by any means, such information offers minor support for the conclusion that active homemakers offered marketing influence disproportionately to younger single women and older matrons.

***Gregariousness and Marketing.***    Here the findings were very clear. At all status levels and in all life-cycle positions, the women with more social contacts were the most influential in marketing. Among those classified as high in gregariousness, 33 percent had offered marketing advice. The corresponding figures for the other categories were 25 percent for those of medium gregariousness and 13 percent for those classified as low. These are statistically significant differences, and they imply a clear positive relationship between gregariousness and marketing leadership.

## Fashion Leaders

Fashion is an area of constant change. Keeping up with change in just the right sequence is the essence of being fashionable. Some two-thirds of the women in the sample had made some sort of change in fashion between their two major interviews. The problem was to discover what the role of opinion leaders of various kinds had been in influencing those changes.

***Fashions and the Life-Cycle Position.***    The factor that proved to be most important in fashions was life-cycle position, the same factor that had played a central role in marketing. In fashions, however, it was the "girls" who provided the greatest amount of influence. In terms of the four life-cycle categories, there were considerable differences in the proportions who claimed to have offered advice to others on fashions (see Table 9.3). Clearly, fashion leadership declined with each step in the life cycle. The authors explained this progression in terms of a rather traditional interpretation of women's roles:

> According to this view, marriage, as the realization of one goal of fashion participation, would be associated with a decrease in fashion

activities and leadership; motherhood, as a competing interest and activity, would also be accompanied by a further decrease in such fashion leadership; and matronhood, which for most women involves a withdrawal from youth-oriented competitiveness, should be associated with least fashion advice giving.[20]

In other words, Katz and Lazarsfeld saw attention to fashion as a means of catching a man. Once a male was landed, however, women were likely to forget fashion matters increasingly and concentrate more on their children. Later, they would lose even the little interest they might have left. This is obviously a very old-fashioned view by today's standards but probably correct at the time.

Whatever the reasons, the younger single women were the most active as opinion leaders in the area of fashion. The "girls" were well ahead of the others in such matters as cosmetics, hairstyles, and fashionable clothing. They had made more purchases and showed a considerably greater propensity to change. They were also the greatest "exporters" of fashion advice; that is, they not only talked to each other about fashion matters but were the strongest influences on the other categories of women.

***Gregariousness and Fashion Leadership.*** As was the case in marketing, gregariousness was an important factor in fashion leadership. In fact, there was a very similar pattern of positive association between gregariousness and influence. For the high category on gregariousness, 29 percent claimed to have offered fashion advice. The corresponding figures for the medium and low categories were 23 percent and 15 percent, respectively. These different rates appear to have occurred for much the same reason in fashions as they did in marketing: The socially active have more opportunities to offer advice to a broader range of recipients. Also, gregarious women at all social levels and in all life-cycle positions were more *interested* in fashion matters than their more reclusive counterparts. Presumably, then, there is a link between more intensive social activity and more intensive interest in fashion, leading to offering more advice, regardless of other life circumstances.

**TABLE 9.3** Percentage who offered fashion influence by life-cycle position

|  | (%) |
|---|---|
| Girls | 48 |
| Small-family wives | 31 |
| Large-family wives | 18 |
| Matrons | 14 |

SOURCE: Elihu Katz and Paul F. Lazarsfeld, *Personal Influence: The Part Played by People in the Flow of Mass Communication* (Glencoe, Ill.: Free Press of Glencoe, 1955), p. 248.

***Status and Fashions.***    Most people assume a relationship between being fashionable and being high in socioeconomic status. The stereotype of the wealthy and glamorous woman is well established in our culture. This, however, was not what the investigators had in mind when they probed into a possible link between social status in Decatur and the role as a source of advice on fashions. They anticipated that there would be a positive relationship between the two variables but not a concentration of leadership at the top.

What they discovered was that there was no such concentration. There were as many fashion leaders among the women of middle status as among those at the high level. On the other hand, women low in status played a much more minor role in distributing fashion advice. For example, among those in the high category, 26 percent claimed to have served as sources for influence on fashions. The middle category claimed the same figure, 26 percent. Only 16 percent of those in the low category claimed to have offered personal influence on fashions.

To summarize the flow of fashion influence, it is dependent most of all on life-cycle position. The younger, single women were much more active as fashion opinion leaders. Gregariousness was also important. Status made some difference, if one was low in this factor. It was the young, socially active women with middle or high status that had the most influence. Older women who were less active socially and of low status had virtually no influence on fashion at all.

## Public Affairs Leaders

Katz and Lazarsfeld made their analysis of opinion leaders in public affairs on the basis of several assumptions about the role of women in such matters:

> Without endangering their self-respect or the respect of others, women can, to a greater extent than men, get through life without participating in, or having opinions about, public affairs. Much more often than men, women express ignorance about current national and local events and issues; they talk less about these matters, and, when asked directly about their interest in politics and specific political events, they claim less interest than men.[21]

In other words, women of the time tended to be seen but not heard. Obviously, times have changed, but these conditions appear to have been present in Decatur at the time of the study in the immediate postwar years. Thus, findings in this area need to be interpreted within such a framework. In any case, the three factors—social status, gregariousness, and life-cycle position—once again provided the principal framework for analysis.

***Status and Public Affairs Leadership.***    The investigators reasoned that the factors that would lead their subjects to participate actively in the arena of public affairs would be contacts with politically active people (mainly males), level of education, and enough leisure time to pursue extrahousehold activities. These are obviously associated with high social status in a community like Decatur. For this reason, the researchers hypothesized that there would be a positive association between socioeconomic status and opinion leadership in the area of public affairs.

Their prediction was clearly supported. First, there were fewer women who were opinion leaders in public affairs that in the other areas studied, and those women tended to be concentrated in the high social status level. Among high status women, 19 percent claimed to have provided personal influence on some aspect of public affairs. For the middle and low status categories, the figures were 12 percent and 6 percent, respectively.

Following up their assumption that women were generally inactive in public affairs, the authors asked women who had been influenced to identify their sources of influence. Generally, the answer that they received was *men:*

> Unlike marketing and fashions, the public affairs arena is one in which men play an important role in influencing opinions and attitudes. Almost two-thirds of the persons named by the respondents as having influenced their opinion changes were men.[22]

These influences from men were likely to come from members of the family. In other words, husbands and fathers were the principal public affairs influentials for these subjects rather than other women.

***Gregariousness and Public Affairs Leadership.***   There is little doubt that women who have numerous social contacts offer more advice on public affairs than those who are less gregarious. Among those classified as high on this factor, 20 percent claimed to have offered personal influence on some aspect of public affairs. Among the medium category, the figure was 11 percent, and among those low in gregariousness, only 4 percent claimed to have been influential.

Gregariousness and status level were found to be associated, and both were factors in predicting opinion leadership. However, statistically controlling for gregariousness in the analysis did not account for the variations in the proportion of public affairs leadership at each status level. In other words, gregariousness and status were independent variables, but gregariousness was the more important.

***Life-Cycle Position and Public Affairs.***   Katz and Lazarsfeld noted that women who are busy with housekeeping and child rearing may not be active in public affairs. This would suggest a dominant role for the "girls." On the other hand, younger people generally take less interest in public affairs than those who are more mature. This meant that there were contradictory factors at work, making prediction difficult.

The data showed a rather weak association between life-cycle stage and public affairs leadership. The proportion who claimed to have influenced others on public issues declined somewhat with each stage: For "girls," the figure was 17 percent; small-family wives, 13 percent; large-family wives, 10 percent; and matrons, 8 percent. Such a trend suggests an inverse relationship between age (and life-cycle stage) and informal influence in public affairs.

In summarizing the flow of influence on public affairs, the authors noted the following: The public affairs leaders among these women were different from those who were influential in marketing or fashions. Life cycle was somewhat less important. On the other hand, social status, which is almost unimportant in marketing leadership, and which is only marginally related to fashions, is a key factor here. Gregariousness is also related to being influential. Generally, the most influential women were the better educated and more affluent, who had many social contacts in the community. Even so, most personal influence on public affairs issues came from men.

## Movie Selection Leaders

At the time the data were gathered, Americans went to the movies far more often than they do now. Television had not yet entered every home. Some 60 percent of the respondents said that they went to the movies at least once a month. The analysis of personal influence on movie selections was confined to this segment of the total sample.

From their earliest days, movies have had a special appeal to youth. This was certainly true in Decatur: Among the youngest category or subjects (those under 25), two-thirds went to the movies once a week of more. About half of those 25–34 went to the movies once a week or more. For those 35–44 the figure was about one-third. Among those 45 or older, less than a fifth went that often. In other words, moviegoing was clearly related to age, and it was far more popular than it is now.

These data led the investigators to anticipate that it would be the younger women in their sample, the "girls," who would be highest in opinion leadership in movie selection. We will see that this was clearly the case. However, gregariousness and socioeconomic status offered further guides to understanding the findings.

*The "Youth Culture" and Movie Leadership.*  The influence of life-cycle position on this form of opinion leadership was especially clear. This reflects the central role of motion pictures in the lives of the young people of the time. Among the "girls," 58 percent claimed to have influenced others on movie choices, a very high figure. For small-family wives, the figure was 23 percent; for large-family wives, 27 percent; and for matrons, 16 percent. For the single women, then, movies with friends were an important form of recreation and dating.

*Movie Leadership and Gregariousness.*  Here, a pattern emerged that was rather distinct from those of other areas. It was not those with the largest number of social contacts that were most influential. There was no clear relationship between gregariousness and personal influence on movie choices. Those subjects classified as medium in gregariousness claimed to have provided the most opinion leadership (32 percent) on movie selections. Those who were high and low were quite similar, with 26 percent and 24 percent, respectively.

The investigators tried to interpret these findings by noting that going to the movies is an activity that is almost always shared by others. People go to the movies with friends and members of their families but seldom alone. The selection of a movie takes place within a complex social process involving other people, namely family and friends. Whether one belongs to clubs and has a wide circle of acquaintances may make little difference on how a motion picture is selected.

***Socioeconomic Status and Movie Influence.***    As in the case of gregariousness, status did not seem to be a factor in providing personal influence on movie selection. This was probably the case because people at all levels in Decatur went to the movies rather frequently. About 25 percent of the women at each level claimed that they had offered advice to others regarding a movie. Within each of the status levels, however, it was the young unmarried women who played the dominant role.

In summary, moviegoing in Decatur was an important part of the youth culture. At all status levels and among shy as well as socially active people, it was the young single individuals who gave the most advice.


## CONCLUSIONS AND IMPLICATIONS

The two-step flow hypothesis, first identified as a result of the study of the 1940 presidential election, provided an important turning point in the development of theory and research in mass communication. The hypothesis as first formulated said merely that "ideas often flow *from* radio and print *to* opinion leaders and *from* them to less active sections of the population."[23] In retrospect, this seems like a simple idea; yet it was overlooked for more than a decade. However, when attention was finally focused on this secondary movement of information and influence through interpersonal networks between members of the audience, it changed thinking about the process of mass communication forever. No longer could mass communication be thought of solely in terms of a stimulus-response framework in which the media were on one side and members of the audience on the other, with little in between.

This new way of thinking was badly needed at the time. The accumulated findings of mass communication research at the time of the Decatur study were not providing support for the idea of simple, immediate, and direct effects that were produced by stimulation from mass-communicated messages. It was time to look for more indirect effects that were produced over a longer span of time by more complex processes. It was *Personal Influence* that opened up this avenue of research. It tried to explore "the part played by people" in the social flow of information and influence from media to mass.

The Decatur study can be faulted on many grounds if the standards of contemporary research are imposed. Its measurements, statistical analyses, sampling techniques, and verification procedures have clear limitations, to say the least. In addition, the goals of the research were never made clear from a conceptual point of view. For example, although much was made of the "flow" idea, the study did not trace the actual movement of ideas from the media to those who were identified as opinion leaders and on to the individuals that they influenced. Katz and Lazarsfeld appear to have set out to do this, but they had to give up (mainly for lack of resources). Thus, when one woman in their sample claimed to have influenced another about nail polish, canned soup, or an issue in the community, it is not at all clear that this actually represented some type of flow from a mass medium to an audience. The strategy of interviewing in April, then returning some months later to look for changes, was not adequate to the task. The researchers should have focused on specific media content (e.g., advertising messages or public affairs presentations) and then traced them from opinion leaders through interpersonal networks to study the two-step flow as it actually took place.

In spite of these criticisms, based on 20/20 hindsight, the Decatur study is one of the milestones in mass communication research because it represents a pivotal point of redirection. Earlier research had concentrated on individual differences characterizing the people who made up the audiences for mass communication and how those differences shaped their psychological and overt responses to the media. A little later, there was a shift to the study of social category memberships among members of the audience and how these influenced patterns of attention and response. *Personal Influence* represented the first clear and intensive focus on social relationships and their role in the mass communication process. The ties between people were seen as the most important factors, rather than the structure of the message stimulus, the perceived characteristics of the communicator, or the psychological makeup of the receiver, in significantly shaping the mass communication process.

We noted earlier that in its analysis of the findings from small-groups research of the time, the research report clearly identified the meaning functions of primary groups, an idea that is an important part of the meaning theory of mass media portrayals that has only recently moved to center stage in thinking about media effects.[24] More important, the Decatur study, and the two-step flow idea generally, set off significant new directions of research in the adoption of innovation, the diffusion of the news, and the study of distortions in interpersonal communication.

Perhaps most important of all, the influences of the media studied in *Personal Influence* seem a far cry from the powerful effects feared by those who saw the media as the ultimate agents of evil—or for that matter, the powerful effects of those who thought the media would be the means of salvation of modern democracy. The influences investigated were minor, difficult to detect, and completely nonthreatening. The study not only failed to confirm the validity of the idea that mass communications should be feared; it went a long way toward making the idea look quite unrealistic.

## NOTES AND REFERENCES

1. Charles Horton Cooley, *Social Organization* (New York: Charles Scribner's Sons, 1909), pp. 80–90.
2. Joseph T. Klapper, *The Effects of the Mass Media* (Glencoe, Ill.: Free Press of Glencoe, 1960).

3. Bernard Berelson, "The State of Communication Research," *Public Opinion Quarterly* 1 (Spring 1959): 1–17.
4. Elihu Katz and Paul F. Lazarsfeld, *Personal Influence: The Part Played by People in the Flow of Mass Communication* (Glencoe, Ill.: Free Press of Glencoe, 1955).
5. Cooley, *Social Organization*, pp. 23–31.
6. Fritz J. Rothlisberger and William J. Dickson, *Management and the Worker* (Cambridge, Mass.: Harvard University Press, 1939). See also Elton Mayo, *Human Problems in an Industrial Civilization* (New York: Viking Press, 1966); first published in 1933.
7. W. Lloyd Warner and Paul S. Lunt, *The Social Life of a Modern Community,* vol. I, Yankee City series (New Haven: Yale University Press, 1941).
8. Samuel A. Stauffer et al., *The American Soldier: Studies in Social Psychology in World War Two,* vols. 1 and 2 (Princeton, N.J.: Princeton University Press, 1948).
9. Kurt Lewin and Paul Grabbe, "Conduct, Knowledge, and Acceptance of New Values," *Journal of Social Issues,* 1(3):53–64 (1948).
10. Melvin L. DeFleur and Everette E. Dennis, *Understanding Mass Communication,* 5th ed. (Boston: Houghton Mifflin, 1994).
11. Katz and Lazarsfeld, *Personal Influence,* p.133.
12. Ibid., p. 137.
13. Ibid., pp. 335–338.
14. Ibid., p.335.
15. The exact number of the original interviewees who served as opinion leaders is a bit difficult to pin down. The figure 693 is the largest $N$ of the tables appearing in the analysis (ibid., p.225). In other places, different and smaller $N$s are given.
16. No indication was given as to how homeowners, who pay no rent, were handled.
17. Ibid., p. 227.
18. Ibid., p. 236.
19. Ibid.
20. Ibid., p. 248.
21. Ibid., p. 271.
22. Ibid., p. 276.
23. Paul F. Lazarsfeld, Bernard Berelson, and Hazel Gaudet, *The People's Choice* (New York: Columbia University Press, 1948), p. 151. This is an earlier report than the one cited in chapter 4.
24. Katz and Lazarsfeld, *Personal Influence,* pp. 53–56.

# chapter 10

# Project Revere: Leaflets as a Medium of Last Resort

$A$s the 1950s began, it became increasingly clear that World War II had not resolved the major political differences among the powerful nations of the world. If anything, the defeat of Germany and Japan had simply moved forward in time the point at which the political philosophies of the Soviet Union and China would confront those of the United States and its Allies in a global struggle for power, even though they had all fought together to defeat the Axis powers. In the end it led to the cold war and the possibility of nuclear holocaust. Thus, the first half of the twentieth century ended with an uneasy confrontation between democracy, communism, and the remnants of fascism. But for the ordinary people in the United States, there was no such global perspective—only a frustrated feeling of *déjà vu* as once more American soldiers battled an Asian enemy.

The Korean conflict was very different from World War II in a number of respects. It had not caught the nation off guard and unprepared militarily. The United States had a large fleet left over from the earlier war. It had an adequate number of well-trained combat divisions equipped with modern weapons. Above all, it had a large and aggressive Air Force. The country had emerged from World War II as the most powerful nation on earth, and it took on a peacekeeping mission that was worldwide in scope. Its so-called containment policy, forged by John Foster Dulles, was to keep the Soviet Union and China, as well as their satellite countries, surrounded by coalitions of Allied forces. Therefore, when North Korea invaded South Korea and challenged that policy, President Truman felt that intervention was essential.

But whatever their causes or labels, wars are not won by force of arms alone. In every war, ancient or modern, the beliefs, attitudes, and loyalties of the participants—whether military or civilian—have had a critical role in the outcome. Such factors have strong influences on motivations, decisions, and actions that can sometimes shape victory or defeat. Military leaders understand these issues very well, and they try to use whatever persuasive communications they can to shape people's behavior to the best advantage. The use of propaganda in wartime can be clumsy and a waste of time. However, if on occasion propaganda can reduce the efficacy of the enemy by only a fraction of 1 percent, it can be effective. Under the right circumstances, the right message delivered to the right people at the right time can profoundly alter the course of history.

It was with these purposes in mind that from 1952 to 1954, a team of sociologists with substantial funding from the U.S. Air Force studied the airborne leaflet as a kind of communication medium of last resort. It was thought to be the only way to get messages to large numbers of people when other, more normal, channels of communication were not available. The assumption made by the research team was that this medium would have its main use in times of war, such as in Korea where cities and industries had been disrupted by dropping leaflets warning of forthcoming bombing attacks. Or they had frequently been used to deliver propaganda messages to various kinds of populations.

It was not known to the team at the time, but evidence that came to light many years later strongly suggests that it was not really the Air Force that was behind the study and that goals other than use in situations such as the war in Korea were at stake. The new information makes it seem very likely that Project Revere was actually funded by the CIA as part of a larger series of social and psychological studies.[1]

Although anything associated with the CIA sounds sinister to many people today, the reasons for funding research of this type by such an agency during the time were both prosocial and in the national interest. The probable covert reasons for the study did not become clear until the Freedom of Information Act of 1966 made it possible for the public to obtain certain previously secret CIA files.

We now know that at the beginning of the 1950s, the American military and intelligence communities were deeply concerned by the fact that the Russians had developed a substantial lead in the design and production of intercontinental ballistic missiles capable of delivering nuclear bombs to certain cities in the continental United States. It was the first time that such a threat existed for the country, and the United States did not have the means either to prevent such strikes or to retaliate effectively. In other words, certain areas of the nation were vulnerable.

The American public was not aware of either the details of this "missile gap" or its military implications. It was not the kind of thing to inspire either stability or confidence. But, given those conditions, there was an urgent need to develop and understand ways of communicating with large populations scattered into the hinterland from cities that would become targets if the unthinkable happened. It was not the kind of research that could be conducted openly by the military without important questions being raised. Doing it through a university research group, however, right out in the open, and under the auspices of the Air Force that had a natural interest in airborne leaflets for propaganda purposes, gave it a less ominous look.

Final answers as to who funded the Mark-Ultra Mind Control Project and exactly why are still impossible to obtain, but if the information gleaned from old CIA files many years later is correct, then Project Revere had a greater significance than was realized at the time. In any case, it did provide at least some important information on the effectiveness and limitations of airborne leaflets as a communication medium vital to the management of disrupted populations. People under such circumstances have to be given instructions as to where to obtain food, medical help, shelter, and so on. The problem is, how well does it work?

## LEAFLETS AS A MEDIUM OF LAST RESORT

Leaflets are pieces of paper containing print, photographs, or drawings. They are a primitive device for communicating to people, but if they can be delivered in large numbers with messages that can be readily understood by the recipients, they can provide a significant channel for communication. Leaflets have been used for as long as the printing press has been around. They have a long history in politics as well as in war. They remain a significant medium in countries that control their media as a means of limiting dissent, and they are being used every day in countries around the world for a variety of reasons and causes, especially where power and authority are being challenged.

American forces distributed about 3 million leaflets during World War I. This figure rose to about 3 *billion* during World War II. Additional billions were used during the Korean conflict. They have been used in all subsequent military operations, including Desert Storm, Somalia, and others. One of their more effective uses in wartime settings has been in the form of "surrender passes" for enemy troops who want to give up but are afraid of being killed. The official-looking "passes" delivered over enemy areas in large numbers can be effective, on occasion, in triggering surrenders. Leaflets have had other successes. In 1945, airborne leaflets delivered on a massive scale to the Japanese population, in conjunction with both conventional and atomic bombing, probably shortened that war somewhat by convincing people that further resistance was unrealistic. In spite of their occasional successes, leaflets have clear limitations. If other, more usual ways of communicating are available, almost any other medium would probably be more efficient. Still, when other channels are *not* available, as in wartime or during periods of political repression, this primitive device may be the only means by which information can be delivered to large numbers of people.

A major problem with leaflets as a medium is that their limitations and capacities are poorly understood. Almost no scientific research has been done on their effectiveness as a communication medium. Controlled studies of communication to hostile populations are not possible during wartime. Impressions of their effectiveness can sometimes be gained by interviewing prisoners who have seen propaganda leaflets or who have used surrender passes. However, these impressions are limited at best. What is needed is more systematic information about who will pick up leaflets and under what conditions, and who will read them, pass on their messages to others, or comply with requests for action. These questions need to be answered not only for war but also under more peaceful conditions. Generalizations are needed about how leaflets can be used to provide vital information in *any* situation where the normal channels of communication are not available.

With this lack of knowledge in mind, the U.S. Air Force (apparently fronting for the CIA) made a decision to learn more about the communication efficacy of airborne leaflets as a mass medium. It sought a research contractor who would design and conduct investigations into the use of airborne leaflets as a means of communicating simple messages to civilian populations: a contractor who would not necessarily answer all possible questions about leaflets when used under all possible circumstances, but who would at least provide a beginning point, seeking basic generalizations about the advantages, capacities, and limitations of leaflets when studied under controlled conditions.

Responding to this challenge was a group of sociologists at the University of Washington under the leadership of Stuart C. Dodd. This group agreed to make the studies over a three-year period. The overall program was called Project Revere (after the well-known American patriot). It is a series of studies conducted between 1951 and 1953. The series had the common purpose of investigating some aspect of the problem of disseminating information by airborne leaflets, including the spread of information from these printed sources by word of mouth to other segments of the population who did not directly see them firsthand.


## PROJECT REVERE

The climate of opinion on American campuses during the early 1950s concerning the merits of the military establishment, and the wisdom of responding to its research needs, was far different from the case during Vietnam years. In the early 1950s, large numbers of World War II veterans were in school because of the GI Bill. Many were working on graduate degrees. These young scholars respected the military services, thought that they were important, and felt it was patriotic to assist them. It was in this climate of opinion that Project Revere was designed and conducted. Those responsible for specific studies in the series had all seen active service in the Navy, Army, or Marines. The military-related research appeared to them an opportunity to conduct studies on complex communication issues and to help their country at the same time.

The Air Force laid down few restrictions on what should be done, and their emphasis was on basic research rather than practical problems or wartime applications. The fact is, the Air Force left it to the research team to formulate the problem, design the means of addressing it, and sort out the implications of the findings. The only requirement was that the researchers try to find out more about leaflets as a device for communication. In an era before large-scale federal government grants had become widely available, the third of a million dollars allocated to the research provided an almost unprecedented opportunity. The researchers noted this at the time:

> To social scientists characteristically working on meager budgets it seems somewhat incredible that a group of researchers would have placed at its disposal almost unlimited funds for the purpose of deliberately conducting research into basic problems of communication without the insistence that practical problems were of importance. Yet, this is the context within which the present research was carried out. The United States Air Force felt that a truly practical research program into communication problems would be one that had long range aims. They recognized that the development of a full understanding of communication procedures requires first of all a good understanding of fundamentals.[2]

The research program was complex and included many separate studies. These investigations were completed in settings that included towns, grade schools, universities, colleges, large urban centers, housing projects, boy's camps, small groups, and communities struck by disaster. The central objective in these wide-ranging investigations was to gain knowledge about the leaflet as a medium of communication.

Leaflets can be delivered in a number of ways, openly or clandestinely, depending on the situation of the area. Most frequently in modern times, large-scale leaflet operations have depended upon distribution from aircraft. Airborne delivery is, of course, a chancy proposition at best. In addition to the vagaries of the elements—wind, weather, terrain—it is difficult to predict who will pick up a leaflet and what they will do with it once they have it. With luck, the leaflet will arrive at the relevant site in good condition, be picked up by a member of the intended audience, read, and passed on to other appropriate individuals. With even more luck, this will stimulate some form of desired action.

Sometimes the process works; usually it does not. In some respects, this is a problem with all mass-communicated messages. Newspapers, magazines, film producers, and broadcasting stations have only limited control over their intended audiences. Exactly who will receive what and how this will influence them remain questions for every attempt at communication, no matter what the medium. The unknowns, however, seem far greater for leaflets than for other kinds of media.

The only advantages that leaflets have over other media were noted earlier. They can be distributed to target populations under circumstances where other media do not exist, are inoperative, or are forbidden. And in spite of their small size, they do provide a permanent record that can be read or reviewed in secret and at the reader's own pace. With the use of pictures, maps, cartoons, diagrams, or symbols of authority, a leaflet can deliver both verbal and nonverbal messages in a relatively straightforward manner.

Under some circumstances, leaflets can stimulate significant action. For example, under wartime conditions leaflets have been used to warn civilian populations of forthcoming heavy bombing raids on particular targets. This has sometimes resulted in mass evacuations, with consequent disruption of the enemy's transportation routes and production facilities. In nonwar settings, leaflets can be used as an emergency medium to warn people of hazards, provide directions, indicate safe evacuation routes, or indicate that help is on the way. In a situation of political repression or occupation by hostile forces, even crudely printed leaflets delivered by any means possible can provide a last-resort medium of communication. In spite of their simplicity, then, leaflets can be a significant medium under certain circumstances.

The use of leaflets in Project Revere was in the context of civilian populations and their role in emergency conditions. No attempt was made to use leaflets to communicate propaganda messages in the usual meaning of that term, or to use them under the stress of wartime or during politically disruptive conditions.

## The Coffee Slogan Experiment

The investigators quickly became aware that research on the spread of a message through a population via leaflets involved the study of two distinct processes. The first was getting the message designed, printed, and delivered into the hands of at least some segment of the intended audience. The delivery would presumably ensure that at least some part of the relevant population had read and understood the message. The second process was to get the initial receivers not only to read the message but to give leaflets to others, or at least to *tell* others what they had learned—to get the initial receivers, in other words, to pass on the message by word of mouth. Broadly speaking, these two processes can be thought of as *message delivery* (to the target population) and *interpersonal message diffusion* (through the target population).

To provide initial information on message delivery, 55,000 airborne leaflets were dropped on Salt Lake City, Utah. Both face-to-face and telephone interviews were conducted in the drop zones to determine what kinds of people and how many had received a leaflet and if they had understood its message. A mail-back postcard questionnaire was attached to each leaflet. The purpose was to try out the mail-back request to see how compliance was related to a list of social and demographic factors. A similar but much larger study was then conducted in Birmingham, Alabama, where 326,000 airborne leaflets were dropped. The purpose here was to study the mail-back procedure more closely and to try to gain further information on what kinds of people would learn the message, pass on a leaflet to others, or mail back a completed postcard questionnaire.

While much was learned in these preliminary studies about dropping leaflets and assessing the degree to which people obtained information from them, it became increasingly apparent that getting subjects to pass on messages by word of mouth was entirely another matter. Generally, it appeared, people would do so only under rather special circumstances that provided adequate motivation. In fact, it became increasingly vexing and frustrating for the researchers as attempt after attempt failed to get people to pass on oral messages.

After a number of abortive attempts to stimulate spontaneous oral message transmission through several different kinds of groups, it was realized that special efforts would be needed to get some sort of message started through an actual community so that its routes by word of mouth could be traced. To achieve this objective, and to generate the data needed to identify and study the problems and dimensions of person-to-person message diffusion in a natural (community) setting, a rather elaborate experiment was conceived. The purpose of this unusual experiment was to stimulate a high level of social transmission of a simple message through a community, strongly motivating its residents to pass it on. This would make it possible to study the message's speed, accuracy, and extent of penetration as it spread through the community's word-of-mouth networks.

***Stimulating Interpersonal Diffusion.*** A small and relatively isolated rural community in western Washington State was chosen as the research site. It was a town of just over 1,000 inhabitants, with 249 dwellings included in its city limits and immediate environs. The community was carefully mapped, with the location of every dwelling and place of business plotted. The immediate goals were to start a short message with a sample of the residents, to motivate them strongly to pass the message on to others, and to encourage those who did *not* know the message to learn it. The research team planned to return several days later and interview every household in town. The long-range goal was a detailed study of the social routing through which the message had traveled as it diffused through the community. In other words, the experiment would permit a study of the extent, accuracy, and directions taken by a message started with a limited number of people and spread solely via interpersonal diffusion.[3]

A major problem was to design a simple message that could be easily spread and later traced as it moved from person to person. Another problem was to provide some sort of "cover" for the experiment so that the community residents would see what they were doing as natural and not as part of some study of "human guinea pigs." There was also the problem of motivation; an effective reward had to be attached to the acts of learning the message and passing it on to others.

A happy, if unusual, solution was found to this set of problems. A wholesale coffee distributing company was located that wanted to promote its house brand, called *Gold Shield Coffee*. The company was intrigued with the idea of working with the researchers on the message experiment. Its directors agreed to donate several hundred pounds of their product as rewards in exchange for the advertising exposure they would receive. The researchers and company officials made up a simple six-word slogan: "Gold Shield Coffee; Good as Gold!" This was the message to be passed along.

To stimulate people to learn this message and pass it on to others, the investigators and their interview team posed as representatives of the coffee company. They called upon a carefully selected sample of households in the community, representing 17 percent of the dwellings. Each subject interviewed of these households was given a free pound of coffee and was informed that the company was "trying out a new advertising slogan to see how it would catch on." Each recipient of the coffee read the six-word slogan from a printed card and then repeated it back. These respondents were to serve as "starters" of the message. They were told that the "advertising team" would return in three days with additional coffee to call on *every household in town*. Those that knew the slogan, the interviewers made clear, would receive a free pound of coffee. This would include the starters who were originally taught the slogan, provided that they could remember it three days later.

The coffee reward and the advertising cover turned out to be fortuitous selections. The price of the product had risen sharply about a month before the experiment, and many people in the area were deploring the situation. The free pound of coffee was gratefully received, and the prospect of an additional gift three days later was keenly anticipated. This advertising venture seemed to make sense to the subjects. They had long since become accustomed to both free samples and the sometimes curious antics of the advertising world. The entire community seemed eager to spread the slogan. (Indeed, in many cases, while the interviewer was departing the front door of a dwelling, the householder could be seen running out the back door to spread the word to a neighbor.)

Nevertheless, the investigators were determined to use every means to get people to pass on the message to others, and accordingly they had prepared an additional way of stimulating interest and providing motivation to spread the message. Late in the day of the first interview, 30,000 airborne leaflets were distributed evenly over the community by a low-flying light plane (with official clearance). These leaflets informed the members of the community about the slogan-spreading venture (but did not reveal the slogan itself). They pointed out that "one out of every five housewives in town already knew the message." The reader was informed that the "advertisers" would return in three days to every household, and that a free pound of coffee would be awarded at each dwelling where the slogan was known. (It should be know that the news media serving this community had agreed to avoid mentioning the study until after it was completed. This cooperation was excellent.)

With these steps completed, the community was left to its own devices for a three-day period. During this time, the people of the town became very active in spreading the message. The leaflets were widely picked up and distributed, raising curiosity about the mysterious message. The starters were in a position to reward others by passing on the slogan, and they did so with enthusiasm. When the researchers returned three days after the initial contacts, they found an eager community waiting to tell them the message and get their reward. Often, the interviewer was confronted in the street before he or she could even call on the householder. After it was over, it was found that some 84 percent of those interviewed had a recognizable version of the original slogan. A number of others reported incorrect or badly garbled slogans, but they received coffee in any case. In fact, several hundred pounds were given away. The householders were pleased with their rewards; the coffee company was delighted with the relatively inexpensive product exposure; and the Project Revere researchers obtained their badly needed data.

*Tracing the Social Pathways.*    The interpersonal networks through which the slogan spread were carefully traced. This was possible, if laborious, through the use of the aerial photographs, the maps of the dwelling places, the questionnaire data, and the addresses of the respondents. A person who received the message from a starter was identified as being in the *first remove* (from the starter); one who was two stages away from a starter was in the second remove, and so forth. By this means a total of 92 interpersonal networks were reconstructed. (There were 64 two-stage networks; 18 with three stages; 5 with four stages; 2 with five stages; and finally, 1 complex network involving 18 people and six stages.) These networks represented first tellings only; many people in town told the slogan to people who already knew. Overall, during the three-day period, the message traveled repeatedly through the social structure—up, down, and sideways. The only people who *didn't* know the message were social recluses, people who had been out of town, and a few who were retarded, senile, or too ill to be involved.

## The Patterns of Message Distortion

It should be emphasized that a major reason for choosing a simple six-word slogan with most words of one syllable was to minimize distortion as the message moved from person to person. One goal in studying the data was to reconstruct the curve showing the proportion of the population that knew the slogan at different points in time. Thus, it was anticipated that distortion of the message would pose few problems, and people who knew the message could easily be distinguished from those who did not.

In spite of these hopes, many inaccuracies crept into the message as it moved along the interpersonal networks of the community. In fact, it soon became apparent that message distortion was a major problem and that the emerging patterns of distortion resembled closely those that had been identified by students of the "rumor" process, for instance, Barlett in the 1930s and Allport and Postman in the 1940s.[4] In other words, as the number of stages or removes through which the information passed became greater, the message became less and less like the original. It became noticeably shorter; extraneous words crept in; new ideas replaced the original content; and contents from the surrounding culture of the subjects were incorporated. These changes constitute the *embedding pattern* that has been widely found in laboratory-type studies of serial message retelling.[5] The key concepts in these studies are *leveling, sharpening,* and *assimilation.* These patterns described the distortions that occurred in the slogan unusually well.

*Leveling.*    The six-word slogan was frequently shortened as it passed from person to person. Figure 10.1 shows that a fairly high degree of accuracy was retained through the first two removes from the starter. After that, the message deteriorated; the number of words declined sharply. These results raised serious doubts about the accuracy of interpersonal networks as communication channels. Due to the short message that the starters received, and the fact that they were carefully taught its content, the pattern of leveling in this community experiment was not

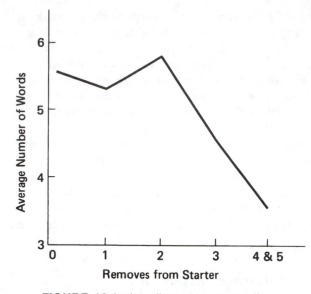

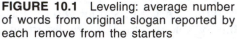

**FIGURE 10.1** Leveling: average number of words from original slogan reported by each remove from the starters

SOURCE: Melvin L. DeFleur, "Mass Communication and the Study of Rumor," *Sociological Inquiry* 32 (Winter 1962): 63.

as dramatic as those obtained from laboratory experiments that provide the starters with a wealth of detail, a long message taxing the memory, and freedom to construct the meaning as the individual starter sees fit. Even so, the simple message was leveled to a considerable degree.

*Sharpening.* Sharpening in rumor experiments occurs when certain details of a message are retained and emphasized as the message is passed along. These details then become the central core of the surviving message in serial retelling. Two somewhat different types of sharpening were noted in the respondents' versions of the six-word slogan. The first can be called *sharpening by selection.* This pattern of message distortion is what Allport and Postman referred to when they defined sharpening as "the selective perception, retention and reporting of a limited number of details from a larger content."[6] In the present situation, it means that certain words in the original slogan were retained to become its central ideas, whereas others were selectively dropped out as the message moved from person to person. Specifically, the last three words of the slogan, *Good as Gold* tended to survive the retelling process better than the first three. The words *Gold Shield Coffee* frequently dropped out during the leveling process as the number of removes increased. In addition, another form of sharpening identified as selective emphasis was given to certain parts of the message. This was termed *sharpening by intensification.* It is illustrated by the fact that some respondents in their enthusiasm intensified the basic idea of the slogan and reported that (the coffee) was "better than gold," "finer than gold," "pure gold," or even a "pot of gold." The sharpening pattern, then, was one where the last half of the slogan tended to survive, and in some instances to become intensified by exaggeration as the message diffused through the interpersonal networks. The brand name of the product, and the word *coffee* itself, were both essential to the original idea of the slogan. Nevertheless, they were frequently omitted as the message moved along its social pathways.

*Assimilation.*     Investigators of rumors in laboratory settings have uniformly noted that messages undergoing serial retelling tend to become distorted in accord with interests, attitudes, cultural norms, or stereotyped expectations of the subjects. Collectively, such forms of distortion are referred to as "assimilation." In other words, extraneous meanings or content are assimilated into the message as it is passed along. The instances of assimilation that occurred in the slogan study were essentially of three types. First, many respondents introduced a word or two into their version of the slogan to make it conform more closely to their verbal habits or to common modes of English speech. Thus, words such as *is as, it's as,* or *is just as* were variants of this practice of adding words to the middle of the slogan. This type of *linguistic* assimilation is frequently found in laboratory studies of serial retelling. For the most part, the proportion of respondents distorting the message in this minor way increased during the first two removes and declined sharply when the slogan became much shorter in the later removes (where such extra words were not relevant).

A second, and more important, type of assimilation is illustrated by respondents who altered the slogan conceptually by substituting or incorporating ideas that they obtained from the culture around them. For example, one person reported that the message was "The coffee that is good to the last drop" (the slogan of another brand). Another individual reported that the message was "The coffee that is *so* good" (an advertising claim of yet another brand). Another form of such *conceptual* assimilation occurred when respondents incorporated into their versions of the slogan ideas commonly associated with the word *gold.* Such words as *pot* and *pure* are frequently used in connection with the term *gold* and were thus assimilated to the concept. This type of distortion appeared to be more frequent in later removes.

Finally, another source of distortion was called *assimilation to logical source.* While not strictly a change in message content, it is illustrated by respondents who claimed to have obtained the slogan via the regular mass media or from some other source. Several persons claimed to have heard it on the radio. Others mentioned newspapers or television. One person reported reading it on a can of coffee. These claims were, of course, without foundation. The only possible source for learning the slogan was other people in the community.

What did these findings imply for the study of leaflets as a means of communicating to large numbers of people? While the results were in no way definitive, they indicated that even a very brief message, diffused under motivational conditions stressing accuracy, became substantially distorted as it moved from person to person. The resulting embedding pattern included leveling, sharpening, and assimilation in a manner closely resembling results obtained from typical laboratory research on rumoring. If the results of this community diffusion experiment can be interpreted as a reasonable guide to what can be expected to happen to information as it moves through the interpersonal networks involved in the "two-step flow" of communication (from a mass medium to a secondary audience), then several implications follow. Those people who are informed by others, as opposed to those who receive direct exposure to the medium, are likely to be poorly informed indeed. The farther they are removed from the person who had direct contact with the medium, the more inaccurate the information they receive is likely to be. The individual at the end of a chain of tellers and retellers is likely to receive a version of the message that is substantially shorter, and which has been selectively edited and distorted in accord with prevailing verbal habits, cultural themes, and stereotypes.

When mass communication depends heavily upon word-of-mouth diffusion to extend its range of contact, a low degree of fidelity to the original content is likely to prevail. These truncated or highly distorted messages are likely to be of limited utility in attempts to achieve propaganda goals or even to transmit simple instructions in times of emergency. What this social diffusion experiment told the researchers of Project Revere was that the *firsthand contact with the medium itself is essential in achieving accurate communication*. It was for this reason that further experiments were deemed necessary to find the most effective way to get leaflets directly into the hands of their intended recipients. In other words, interpersonal message diffusion was undoubtedly important, but direct message delivery—getting a leaflet to its intended audience member—was even more important.

## THE REPETITION EXPERIMENT

A major experiment was designed to try to determine how to use leaflets efficiently. Stated simply, how many leaflets per person in the intended audience does it take to ensure that the message will be learned by a given percentage of the recipients? Obviously, using too few would not result in a satisfactory level of communication. On the other hand, oversaturation might have various negative effects and achieve less in getting the message across than an optimum number. Although in the Project Revere research this issue was studied in the context of airborne leaflets, it is clearly a problem with many kinds of communications. For example, how often should an advertising message be repeated in order to maximize its influence on a given category of consumers? How often should a charity appeal be presented; or how frequently should an idea be presented in an educational setting? There are obviously a host of other considerations in these questions; the personality characteristics of the receivers, their cultural milieux, and the relationship between the factors and the content of the message remain paramount. But no message, no matter how closely related to the interests, values, and motivations of its audience, can achieve its effect if it is not perceived accurately and fully by the largest proportion of its intended recipients.

Instead of proceeding blindly by trial and error to study the question of message repetition versus level of response, the Project Revere researchers felt that it would be better to develop a *formal theory.* It was hoped that a formal theory would predict the relationship between the frequency of message presentation and the proportion of the intended audience who would learn its content.

The basis for a formal theory was found in the much-studied relationships between stimulus intensity and response from the field of classical psychophysics. Work on this problem began during the mid-nineteenth century. The purpose was to understand the relationship between the external world of stimuli and the internal or subjective world of sensations. For the purposes of developing the needed theory, it was postulated that any message transmitted over any medium can be regarded as a *stimulus* intended to elicit some form of desired *response.* This stimulation can be presented to a responding audience in varying intensities, either by presenting it more frequently or in greater volume. In the case of leaflets, increasing the sheer number dropped on a given group can be regarded as one method of increasing the intensity of stimulation toward the desired response of knowing the message or taking some action proposed by it. The development of an equation, a formally derived hypothesis, stating this relationship between communication stimulus intensity and amount of group response was the next step.

## Stimulus Intensity versus Response

There had been little systematic investigation dealing with quantitative stimulus-response relationships in leaflet communication. Martin F. Herz had summarized problems of measuring response to propaganda leaflets during wartime, but this literature was of little help.[7] A review of literature for the 25 years prior to Project Revere revealed a few studies of other media where variations in stimulus intensity were studied in relation to response, but most of these dealt with advertising messages and were characterized by contradictory findings.[8] In other words, it was necessary to begin from scratch.

Any discussion of stimulus intensity and response automatically brings to mind the sensory psychology studies of the last century, which resulted in the much-tested Weber's law. A voluminous literature was available on this generalization concerning variations in sensations that result from quantitative alterations in the intensity of stimulation. Weber's law is an equation (actually developed by Fechner) relating magnitudes of response—used as an index of sensation—to various magnitudes of stimulus intensity. Fechner wrote the *fundamentalformal,* the basic equation, after integration, in the following form:

$$R = a \log_e S + b \qquad (10.1)$$

The equation can be explained rather simply: $S$ is the level of stimulus intensity, whereas $a$ and $b$ are constants of proportionality and integration, respectively. Even if one is not familiar with mathematical representations, the idea is not very complex. The equation describes a *curve* showing that when stimulus intensity ($S$) is increased by a given amount, the response of the subject ($R$) will also increase by a regular and predictable amount. The pattern of the curve is one of *diminishing returns,* and this shape is set by the other terms in the equation. What it all boils down to is that doubling the intensity of a stimulus will not double the sensation felt by the subject (measured by some form of response). In fact, as stimulus intensity is increased, it takes larger and larger increases to elicit increasingly smaller increments of sensation (response). This relationship has been supported by numerous experimental studies conducted over many decades.

This psychophysical formulation was used as a basis for developing a parallel "law" (actually a formal hypothesis) to describe the relationship between stimulus intensity and response in leaflet communication. Specifically, the more leaflets that are dropped on a community, the greater will be the response of learning the message. However, this was expected to occur in a *pattern of diminishing returns.* In other words, the increments in response, when one increased the number of leaflets per person in the target population, were expected to become smaller and smaller as ever larger numbers of leaflets were used for each inhabitant. This general idea was tested in a preliminary study that used varying ratios of leaflets per person.

*The Pilot Study.*    An investigation was conducted to test the diminishing returns idea and to train the research team. Four small communities were used (whose populations ranged between 969 and 1,175). These communities were carefully selected for their similarity. All had the same type of economic base, none were satellites of an urban area, and all had similar population compositions. A ratio of 1 leaflet per person was used on one community, 4 per person on two others, and 16 per person on the other community. This provided three points along a possible curve, showing what proportion of the population in each community had learned the message.

The experiment was carried out in cooperation with the Washington State Office of Civil Defense, and the leaflets stated: "One visit from an enemy bomber could send evacuees pouring into your town!" It went on to ask recipients to consider, if such a disaster occurred, "how many refugees they could take into their home." The leaflet was signed by the state Civil Defense director, and it indicated that a Civil Defense representative would soon call at each home in the community to get their answers. The "representatives" were, of course, interviewers from the Project Revere team. Careful preparations had been made with aerial photographs and maps for each community, and interviews were conducted at every household. Once again, local media cooperated by refraining from mentioning the leaflet drop. The study was a training exercise for the larger experiment to come, but a considerable amount of useful data were obtained on interpersonal diffusion, time-growth patterns of the message, and other issues.

The civil defense theme provided an excellent cover for the experiment. The civil defense authorities were delighted with the information the researchers provided, and the townspeople found it to be a realistic issue, much on the minds of people during the time.

The data showed that using one leaflet per person resulted in 18 percent of the residents learning the message by the end of the first day. A fourfold increase of the ratio of leaflets per person (four for each inhabitant) nearly doubled the proportion who learned the message: 32 percent. Another fourfold increase, 16 leaflets per person, resulted in 55 percent of the population learning the message. When plotted on a simple graph, these three figures imply a curve of diminishing returns. Clearly, however, three points are insufficient to test the idea that this regularity will hold over a large number of cases. Nevertheless, the results of this pilot study were most encouraging, and the investigators decided to plan and conduct a more definitive test of the diminishing returns relationship. The first task in planning the study was to develop the hypothesis into a statement of greater precision.

***Formalizing the Hypothesis.***    In the discussion below, the manner in which the formalized diminishing returns hypothesis was derived in equation form is explained. For the reader who is not familiar with this type of mathematics, it is not essential to follow the formal derivation to understand the experiment and its results. The present section provides a verbal explanation of what the formal hypothesis was about. The mathematical derivation is presented in the section that follows. In nonmathematical terms, then, the general idea was to come up with an equation that described a curve of diminishing returns predicting how much communication would take place with the use of a given level of stimulus intensity (in this case, a given ratio of leaflets per person). Even if one does not follow the mathematics, it is important to see that it is possible (1) to begin with a specific set of assumptions, (2) to translate these into a formal mathematical statement, and then (3) to derive a testable hypothesis. Such a hypothesis has the advantage of specifying in the clearest possible terms the kinds of data that are needed for the test and the design of the experiment that will be required. We can assume that a community consists of many individuals interacting. We will further assume that the relationship between the intensity of a communication stimulus and the collective response of such a "subject" will show some similarity to the diminishing returns pattern described by Weber's law. (The pilot study data seemed to suggest that such an assumption had merit.)

A range of stimulus intensities is needed against which to check the corresponding degrees of response that are to be elicited. But the same subject (community) cannot be used over and over, because each succeeding leaflet presentation and response measurement would contaminate the experimental situation for the next. An experimental design is required in which a number of communities, selected carefully for their similarity, are exposed to different degrees of message stimulus intensity and in which comparable measures of response are obtained from each.

Given these circumstances, one can define a set of stimulus intensities that start at some arbitrary lower limit and increase by some power, say *two*, by doubling each preceding intensity. A suitable set of intensities for the leaflet experiment would be to begin with one leaflet for every four people. This can be doubled to one for every two people, redoubled to one per person, two per person, and so on. If this is carried through eight steps of doubling and redoubling, the following set of leaflet intensities would be obtained: 1:4, 1:2, 1:1, 2:1, 4:1, 8:1, 16:1, and 32:1.

Given such a range of stimulus intensities, response measures must also be specified. These can be defined as the proportion of a community's population that performs an observable act as a result of the message stimulation. This act could be learning the message, of course, but it could also be some other form of response, such as passing a leaflet on to others or filling out and mailing back a postcard questionnaire attached to the leaflet.

With these measures of stimulus intensity and response defined, we can state the hypothesis (in verbal terms) that the increase in response from one community to the next—where the next higher intensity is used—will be directly proportional to the change in stimulus intensity and inversely proportional to the previous stimulus intensity. We are stating, in effect, that a version of Weber's law will hold not only for individual stimulation but for the collective case when a community is stimulated to give some form of response, even though that response may depend upon social processes and the individual actions of many persons in the collectivity. (*At this point nonmathematical readers may wish to turn to the section on Experimental Procedures on p. 230.*)

***Deriving the Equation.***     To formulate our hypothesis into a mathematical expression suitable for testing, let $p$ denote the proportion of the population who respond as defined, and $r$ denote the measure of stimulus intensity. With a constant of proportionality, $a$, the above diminishing returns hypothesis can be stated in mathematical form as:

$$\Delta p - \frac{a\Delta r}{r} \tag{10.2}$$

Since stimulus intensity increases in powers of two in the series of leaflet ratios chosen, the above can be written:[9]

$$p_{i+1} - p_i = a \tag{10.3}$$

The solution to equation (10.3) can now be written as:[10]

$$p_{i+1} = p_i + ia \tag{10.4}$$

However, for the present development, it will help to express $p$ in terms of $r$ rather than in terms of $i$. Thus, for $i$ equal to or greater than 1, $r_i = 2^{i-3}$, which may be written as:

$$i = 3 + \log_2 r_i \qquad (10.5)$$

We may put this into equation (10.4) to get:

$$p_{i+1} = p_1 + (3 + \log_2 r_i)a = a \log_2 r_i + 3a + p_1 \qquad (10.6)$$

Equation (10.4) expressed $p_{i+1}$ in terms of $r_i$, but it is more desirable to express $p_{i+1}$ in terms of or $r_{i+1}$. This may be accomplished by recalling that each stimulus intensity will be just one-half the next greater one—that is to say, $r_i = \frac{1}{2} r_{i+1}$— and with this we can now write:

$$\log_2 r_i = \log_2 \frac{r_i + 1}{2} = \log_2 r_{i+1} - \log_2 2 = \log_2 r_{i+1} - 1 \qquad (10.7)$$

If we put this result into (10.6), we get:

$$p_{i+1} = a \log_2 r_{i+1} + 3a + p_1 = a \log_2 r_{i+1} - a + 3a + p_1 \qquad (10.8)$$

This gives a prediction of the extent of response for the $(r_{i+1})$th stimulus intensity. This can be labeled the typical case and designated as the $i$th case, rather than the $(i + 1)$th, allowing for the simplification:

$$p_i = a \log_2 r_i + (2a + p_i) \text{ valid for all } i \geq 1 \qquad (10.9)$$

The expression we are seeking comes out when equation (10.9) is further simplified by letting $2a + p_i = b$. Thus, we get the formal hypothesis:

$$p_i = a \log_2 r_i + b \qquad (10.10)$$

It can be noted how similar this is to Weber's law. As we noted on page 225, Fechner integrated his *fundamentalformal* to the expression:

$$R = a \log_e S + b \qquad (10.11)$$

This similarity of form is to be expected. However, equation (10.11), our formal hypothesis, avoids the assumptions involved in infinitesimal calculus (which would be difficult to justify in this case) and was derived from a different equation. In any case, equation (10.10) predicts values of response level for the communities that will get each leaflet ratio in the doubling and redoubling series defined earlier.

Ordinary statistical methods can be used to evaluate the differences between the predicted values and the values actually obtained from conducting the experiment. In the present case, chi-square provides a simple procedure for evaluating the goodness of fit between the observed and theoretical data. Note that equation (10.10) is not confined to leaflet communication specifically. It can be advanced as a testable hypothesis for any medium where measures of stimulus intensity and a level of community response can be obtained.

## Experimental Procedures

To test the formal hypothesis stated in equation (10.10), the researchers designed a rather elaborate field experiment around the series of leaflet ratios indicated earlier (p. 228). Eight small communities in western Washington State were chosen as sites for the test. Each was to receive a different leaflet ratio, and interviewing in each town would determine the proportion of the population who had learned the message (or made some other response) within a specified period of time. The actual results obtained can be compared to the theoretical proportions predicted by equation (10.10).

The communities were selected to be as much alike as possible. Their populations ranged between 1,015 and 1,800. They were relatively stable; all had similar climates and economic bases (lumbering and agriculture); and none was a suburb or bedroom community for a large city.

These eight "subjects" were assigned "treatments" by an elementary randomization procedure. These treatments were, of course, the leaflet drops, using the different ratios described earlier. Table 10.1 shows the ratio assigned to each community.

As in earlier Project Revere experiments, extensive preparations were completed before the leaflets were dropped. Town authorities were contacted; the cooperation of relevant news media was solicited; maps and aerial photographs were prepared; reconnaissance flights were made over the community to plan the best drop patterns; questionnaires were pretested; and interviewers were carefully trained. All went well. The nine newspapers, three radio stations, and one TV station serving the area agreed to the plan. Town officials were most cooperative. The interviewer teams had been thoroughly briefed, and all other details had been taken into account.

**TABLE 10.1** Ratios of leaflets per person assigned to the eight towns

| Leaflets per Person | Town | Population | Number of Leaflets |
|---|---|---|---|
| 1:4 | Orting | 1,299 | 325 |
| 1:2 | Sequim | 1,096 | 548 |
| 1:1 | Poulsbo | 1,306 | 1,306 |
| 2:1 | Oak Harbor | 1,475 | 2,950 |
| 4:1 | Ferndale | 1,015 | 4,060 |
| 8:1 | Arlington | 1,800 | 14,400 |
| 16:1 | Darrington | 1,052 | 16,832 |
| 32:1 | McCleary | 1,175 | 37,600 |
| Total number of leaflets | | | 78,021 |

SOURCE: Melvin L. DeFleur, "A Mass Communication Model of Stimulus-Response Relationships: An Experiment in Leaflet Message Diffusion," *Sociometry* 19 (March 1956): 18.

The leaflet used was a simple one. It combined the civil defense theme used in the pilot study with the mail-back postcard questionnaire developed in earlier research. The leaflet informed the reader that

> One raid from an enemy bomber could paralyze radios, telephones, newspapers. *In such a disaster* . . . leaflets like this could be dropped from airplanes to give official instructions. *You* are part of this scientific test to find out how effective leaflets are for spreading vital information to everyone.

The reverse side of the leaflet contained an appeal to "Be a Modern Paul Revere" and pass on extra leaflets to others to "help spread the word." It also asked the recipient to fill out and mail the (self-addressed and postage-paid) questionnaire attached to the leaflet in the form of a small postcard. The purpose of the postcard was to provide a measure of *compliance* with the request for a specific action.

All leaflet drops occurred on a Wednesday, commencing promptly at noon in each community. Skilled pilots and crews made sure that the leaflets were spread evenly over each site. Three days later, beginning at 9 A.M., face-to-face interviews were conducted in every other household in each community. (Previous Revere studies had shown that three days were ample for the message to spread.) The exact person in the household to interview was selected by a special method (often used by the U.S. Census).[11] The data gathering was designed to determine if the respondents had learned the message, and if so, *how* they learned (via social diffusion or directly from a leaflet); *when* they learned; and what subsequent *action* they had taken on the basis of the requests on the leaflet. Cooperation by the townspeople was excellent in every respect. After the experiment was concluded, local news media described the leaflet drops and their purposes.

## The Hypotheses versus the Data

To determine if a given respondent knew the message on the leaflets, his or her verbatim reply to the question "What did the leaflet say?" was carefully recorded by the interviewers. These replies were then independently reviewed by two judges who used previously established criteria to make their decisions as to whether or not a subject should be classified as a "knower" or a "nonknower." The procedure worked well, and interjudge reliability was $r = .94$.

The proportion of those interviewed who were classified as "knowers" was plotted by leaflet ratio as shown in Figure 10.2. By the method of least squares, the curve described by equation (10.10) was fit through the resulting points. This means simply that the curve predicted by the theory (equation [10.10]) goes through the observable data points in the manner that minimizes the distance between the empirical data and the points predicted by the curve. The whole idea is shown graphically in Figure 10.2

By using chi-square to compare how much the observed data differed from the predictions provided by the hypothesis (equation [10.10]), a test of good fit

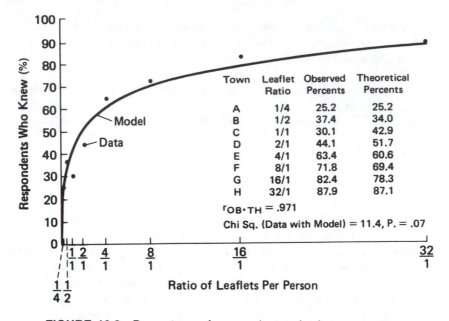

| Town | Leaflet Ratio | Observed Percents | Theoretical Percents |
|------|---------------|-------------------|----------------------|
| A | 1/4 | 25.2 | 25.2 |
| B | 1/2 | 37.4 | 34.0 |
| C | 1/1 | 30.1 | 42.9 |
| D | 2/1 | 44.1 | 51.7 |
| E | 4/1 | 63.4 | 60.6 |
| F | 8/1 | 71.8 | 69.4 |
| G | 16/1 | 82.4 | 78.3 |
| H | 32/1 | 87.9 | 87.1 |

$r_{OB \cdot TH} = .971$

Chi Sq. (Data with Model) = 11.4, P. = .07

**FIGURE 10.2** Percentage of respondents who know message for each leaflet ratio

SOURCE: Melvin L. DeFleur, "Mass Communication Model of Stimulus Response Relationships: An Experiment in Message Diffusion, *Sociometry* 19 (March 1956): 21–22.

was provided. Visual examination of the graph shows that the fit of the theoretical curve to the observed data was, on the whole, quite good. The probability value associated with chi-square indicates that the observed and the hypothesized (theoretical) percentages do not differ significantly. The differences between observed and theoretical values could easily have occurred by chance in a universe of such data described by the model. Stated more simply, the curve apparently fits the data, and the outcome supports the formal hypothesis.

A similar test of equation (10.10) was made with the data shown in Figure 10.3 obtained from the leaflet postcards that were mailed back. In this case, the curve fits the data pretty well, except in the case of the town that received eight leaflets per person. Here, the mail-back compliance was especially high. It was discovered that in this particular community, an active voluntary civil defense group took it upon themselves to see that the "civil defense test" was a success, and these public-spirited citizens made sure that as many people as possible completed the questionnaire and mailed back the postcard. Aside from this understandable aberration, the formal hypothesis seemed to predict this form of compliance behavior rather well.

The conclusion of this study was that the formalized hypothesis (equation [10.10]) provided a good description of the relationship between the specified stimulus intensity measures and the amount of communication that took place.

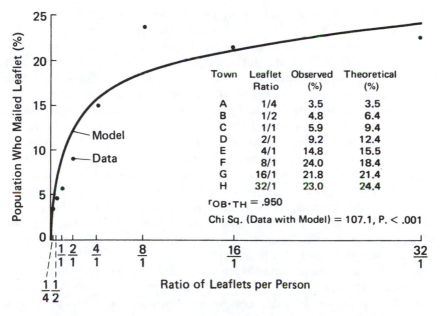

| Town | Leaflet Ratio | Observed (%) | Theoretical (%) |
|------|---------------|--------------|-----------------|
| A | 1/4 | 3.5 | 3.5 |
| B | 1/2 | 4.8 | 6.4 |
| C | 1/1 | 5.9 | 9.4 |
| D | 2/1 | 9.2 | 12.4 |
| E | 4/1 | 14.8 | 15.5 |
| F | 8/1 | 24.0 | 18.4 |
| G | 16/1 | 21.8 | 21.4 |
| H | 32/1 | 23.0 | 24.4 |

$r_{OB \cdot TH} = .950$

Chi Sq. (Data with Model) = 107.1, P. < .001

**FIGURE 10.3**  Percentage of town's population who mailed in leaflet postcard for each leaflet ratio

SOURCE: Melvin L. DeFleur, "Mass Communication Model of Stimulus-Response Relationships: An Experiment in Message Diffusion, *Sociometry* 19, (March 1956): 21–22.

With the exception of the one deviant case with the active civil defense group, the formal hypothesis also did well in describing the relationship between stimulus intensity and compliance. This version of Weber's law, in other words, seemed to apply in this communication setting.

## Message Diffusion and the Social Structure

These results of the stimulus intensity experiment indicated clearly that the frequency or redundancy with which a message is presented to a target audience is a vital factor in determining the eventual level of communicative and compliance outcome. But a message brought to the attention of the audience will also travel through social channels, as was demonstrated in the coffee slogan experiment. The significance of social diffusion had originally been suggested by *The People's Choice* research (see chapter 4), which resulted in the discovery of the "two-step flow" of communication. However, at the time of the Revere studies, little was known of the pathways through the social structure that a message would follow as message diffusion took place. The eight-community experiment not only provided data on the Weber's law hypothesis but also yielded abundant information on what kind of people passed on the message to what other kind of people. In other words, it was possible to sort out the *social itinerary* followed by the information as it moved through interpersonal networks.

One clear pattern that became apparent was that in a situation of relative *scarcity,* with fewer leaflets available per person, a larger proportion of those receiving the message learned it through social means. When leaflets were relatively *abundant,* on the other hand, that proportion dropped and more people learned by direct contact with a leaflet. For example, among those classified as "knowers" of the message in those four communities with lowest ratios of leaflets per person, 62.9 percent learned by social means. In the four communities with the highest leaflet ratios, the comparable figure was 47.8 percent (a significant difference). It should not be forgotten, however, that in absolute numbers, there were considerably larger numbers of knowers in the high-ratio communities. The implications of this pattern are of pragmatic interest in that learning by social means tends to result in relatively inaccurate communication. Therefore, if the intent of the communicator is to reach as many people as possible, high redundancy (stimulus intensity) is required.

The knowers of the message were not evenly distributed throughout the various social categories and subgroups in any of the communities. Under both high and low stimulus intensity conditions, both *age* and *family size* were significantly related to the probability of learning the message. Children were more likely to know the message than were adults; and adults from large families were more likely to know the message than adults from small families. This suggests that an important aspect of the dynamics of social diffusion (at least in this research) was that a flow of information took place *from children to adults.* More specifically, this flow tended to be from children to their parents. (An analysis of differences by sex showed no significant patterns). Children, then, were more active in picking up the leaflets, learning their content, passing on the message to others, and passing on leaflets to adults in particular.

Further analyses showed that family and friendship ties were important in the process of social diffusion. Among adults, transmitting or receiving the message by any means tended to take place more within the family than among neighbors, acquaintances, or strangers. This was not the case with children, who both learned and transmitted the message more with others outside the family. This was especially true in the case of oral transmission, as opposed to passing on a leaflet. Table 10.2 summarizes the relevant data.

How can we interpret these findings concerning the penetration of this particular message into the social structure of the communities involved? The following generalizations describe what happened: The leaflets appeared to have a special appeal to children, who picked them up, told other children, or passed on leaflets to their friends, parents, adult neighbors, or acquaintances. This in turn appeared to lead adults to discuss the leaflets and their message with other adults, or to take the requested action and comply by mailing back the postcard. Thus, children were, in a sense, *neutral transmitters* of the oral message, or of the leaflets. The principal role of children, then, was to obtain leaflets, bring them home, pass on the message to others, and thus stimulate action by adults.

**Table 10.2**  The flow of information from various categories of leaflet recipients to children and adults

| Identity of Message Transmitter | Age Status of Message Recipient | | | | | | | |
|---|---|---|---|---|---|---|---|---|
| | Pass-on-Diffusion | | | | Oral Diffusion | | | |
| | Adults | | Children | | Adults | | Children | |
| | (*N*) | (%) | (*N*) | (%) | (*N*) | (%) | (*N*) | (%) |
| Family member | 142 | 49.8 | 12 | 22.7 | 21 | 35.6 | 1 | 3.7 |
| Neighbor | 61 | 21.4 | 13 | 24.5 | 17 | 28.8 | 3 | 11.1 |
| Acquaintance | 75 | 26.3 | 28 | 52.8 | 21 | 35.6 | 23 | 85.2 |
| Stranger | 7 | 2.5 | 0 | 0.0 | 0 | 0.0 | 0 | 0.0 |
| Total | 285 | 100.0 | 53 | 100.0 | 59 | 100.0 | 27 | 100.0 |

Pass-on: For 3*df*, $X^2$ = 19.0, *P* < .001.
Oral: For 2*df*, $X^2$ = 18.2, *P* < .001.

SOURCE: Melvin DeFleur and Otto N. Larsen, *The Flow of Information* (New York: Harper and Brothers, 1958), p. 178.

## CONCLUSIONS AND IMPLICATIONS

The airborne leaflet is obviously a highly specialized medium of communication. As was pointed out, its significance today is as a medium of last resort—as a means by which audiences can be reached during emergencies, wartime, or times of political repression when no alternative channels remain open. Sadly, such situations are as frequent in contemporary times as they were in earlier periods. However, because of the unique qualities of leaflets as a medium it is appropriate to raise questions about the "generalizability" of the Revere findings to other media and other situations. Would they apply, say, to newspapers, radio, or television? In addressing this question, one can focus on the differences between these media and wonder if they share *any* common principles. Each conveys its message in a different manner and is attended to as a result of different needs and for varying gratifications. Yet, in spite of these differences, even a moment's reflection confirms that there *are* common principles underlying the process of communication when any of these media are used. Each involves an attempt on the part of communicators to achieve some form of change in their intended audiences. Each depends upon processes of perception and learning. And each is dependent upon the cultural rules of language usage to bring about some parallelism between the intended meanings of the communicator and the interpretations of the recipient.

Beyond these considerations is the fact that communication by any medium includes the two major stages through which information flows from media to audiences, first described as the "two-step flow communication" in *The People's Choice* (see chapter 4). This work became available to the academic community at large in 1948. By the time Project Revere began some three years later, little was known about this form of secondary communication other than the fact that it had been discovered somewhat serendipitously in the Erie County study. Later research on the two-step flow helped fill this gap. It focused on the *people* involved and the *roles* that they played in this form of interpersonal transmission of information and influence. Thus, studies of "opinion leaders" were undertaken, including studies of who their followers were and what topics were involved in such influence (see chapter 9). In contrast, the Revere studies concentrated on the *quality of the information* that was spread by word of mouth through interpersonal networks.

The most significant conclusion from such studies as the coffee slogan experiment was that the person-to-person flow of information resulted in message incompleteness, inaccuracy, and distortion. The implications of this were considerable: The Revere study showed the applicability of the *embedding pattern,* found earlier by social psychologists who had studied "rumoring" by use of the serial retelling strategy, to the word-of-mouth movement of information in the two-step flow. The complex processes of leveling, sharpening, and assimilation were found in the social diffusion of a message through a community. In other words, considerable doubt is cast on the importance of the secondary stage of the two-step flow as a process by which the meanings intended by a mass communicator can be paralleled in the interpretations of the audience toward whom the communication is directed. This issue is even more serious when it is recalled that the message under study was only six words and included only one word of more than one syllable!

The problems posed by the Revere research on message distortion also have a bearing on another line of research that became popular during the mid-1950s and later. The interpersonal diffusion of the news began to be studied intensively by researchers in journalism and communication. Dozens of studies traced time patterns in the spread of important news stories (e.g., Senator Taft's death, Alaska's statehood, the Kennedy assassination) as they moved from the media to the secondary stage of the two-step flow. Such time patterns were investigated as part of the Revere studies and were among seven doctoral dissertations and numerous articles in professional journals that appeared during or immediately following the project.[12] However, the significant factor here is that when the news is transmitted from person to person, it is likely to be badly distorted, no matter how fast or slow it moves, or how extensively it penetrates the population by word of mouth.

If social diffusion is not accurate and reliable, the importance of *direct* contact with the medium by every member of the audience is obvious. At least this was clearly the case with the relatively simple medium used in the Revere studies. This need for direct contact meant that it was important to understand the stimulus intensity issue. How often should the message be presented, and with what level of redundancy, to ensure that a given level of the intended audience *would* have direct contact with the message? The formal hypothesis based on Weber's law was an attempt to answer this question. The answers found and the diminishing returns relationship that emerged from the study may have been less important than the opportunity to conduct such research at a level of considerable precision. The mathematical model and its derivation were at the level of formal theory construction not often found in mass communication research, at least up to that time. The large-scale investigation, with eight separate communities carefully surveyed, and with the entire effort aimed at supporting or rejecting a formal mathematical model, was also unusual for the time. In fact, it is not at all clear that research in mass communication has increased its level of precision and theory construction beyond that achieved in Project Revere, even at present.

## NOTES AND REFERENCES

1. Melvin L. DeFleur and Otto N. Larsen, *The Flow of Information* (1958; reprint, with preface, New Brunswick, NJ: Transaction Press, 1987). (This book reports a number of the Project Revere studies. See preface for information regarding the role of the CIA.)
2. Ibid., p. xiv.
3. Melvin L. DeFleur, "Mass Communication and the Study of Rumor," *Sociological Inquiry* 32 (Winter 1962): 51–70.
4. F. C. Bartlett, *Remembering* (Cambridge, England: Cambridge University Press, 1932); Gordon W. Allport and Leo Postman, *The Psychology of Rumor* (New York: Henry Holt and Company, 1947).
5. Allport and Postman, *Psychology of Rumor,* pp. 75–115.
6. Ibid., p. 86.
7. Martin F. Herz, "Some Psychological Lessons from Leaflet Propaganda in World War II," *Opinion Quarterly* 13: 471–486 (1949).
8. Melvin L. DeFleur, "A Mass Communication Model of Stimulus-Response Relationships: An Experiment in Leaflet Message Diffusion," *Sociometry* 19 (March 1956): 12–25. (See n. 3 in this article.)
9. That is, if $i$ denotes the $i$th increase in stimulus intensity, then $r = 2^{i-3}$ because the lowest intensity ratio in the proposed set was $^1/_4$ or $2^{-2}$; in the next higher, $r = ^1/_2$ or $2^{-1}$; and so on through the fourth, $r = 2$, the sixth, $r = 2^3$, and so on. In the $i$th increase, then $r = 2^{i-3}$; and since $\Delta r = r_{i+1} - r_i = 2^{i-3}$ also, then $\Delta r$ must equal $r$. This being the case, $\Delta r/r = 1$, yielding equation (10.3).
10. The expression $p_{i+1}$ merely denotes the response of the community receiving the $(i + 1)$th stimulus intensity. But, if $p_{i+1} = p_i + a$, then it also equals $p_{i-1} + 2a$, $P_{i-2} + 3a$, and so on. By continuing this process we could express $p_{i+1}$ in terms of $p_i$ plus a certain number of $a$'s. If we want to express $p_{i+1}$ in terms of $p_i$, it is obvious that one must be added to the subscript of the latter, and it will also be noted that this is precisely the number of $a$'s that must be added to a $p$ to get $p_{i+1}$. In general, the number of $a$'s that must be added to a given $p$ to get $p_{i+1}$ is the same as the difference between their subscripts. Thus to $pi_1$ we must add $ia$'s to get $p_{i+1}$. This situation is summarized in equation (10.4).
11. Leslie A. Kish, "A Procedure for Objective Respondent Selection within the Household," *Journal of the American Statistical Association* 44: 380–387 (1949).
12. See pp. 285–293 in DeFleur and Larsen, *The Flow of Information,* for a list of publications and dissertations resulting from Project Revere studies, with special reference to the work of William Catton, Melvin DeFleur, Richard Hill, Otto Larsen, Ørjar Øyen, and Gordon Shaw.

chapter **11**

# Television in the Lives of Our Children: The Early Years

**W**hen the movies grew rapidly as a mass medium early in the century, one of the first concerns of the American public was their impact on children. In some ways, the mushrooming growth of television in the immediate postwar years followed a similar pattern. However, its adoption by the public was even more rapid, almost catching everyone by surprise. Suddenly, there was a remarkable new box in everyone's living room, with moving pictures as well as sound. The incredibly rapid pace of the adoption of this device, as well as people's growing alarm over its possible effects on the young, were factors that helped shape the earliest research directions designed to discover television's role in the expanding system of mass communication.

The television industry exploded across the American landscape during the 1950s; no other mass medium had ever grown so quickly. The extent of this expansion becomes evident when we consider a few facts. In 1948, there were fewer than 100,000 television sets in the United States; one year later, a million sets were in use in American homes—and that was only the beginning. Indeed, by 1959, more than 50 million television sets had been placed in American homes, and approximately 88 percent of U.S. households were the proud owners of television receivers. This was a dramatic turnaround from the beginning of the decade, when only about 6 percent of American households had even one set. Thus, in less than ten years, television had become a pervasive aspect of American life.[1]

Possession of a TV set quickly became a status symbol in the early years of television's diffusion through the American population. Families who could ill afford such a luxury sometimes cut corners on necessities in order to purchase one. Many acquired their sets through installment purchases—the "easy payment plan." In some cases, the urge to own a television and to be identified as an owner was so strong that families were said to have bought and installed antennas in conspicuous locations long before they purchased the sets to hook up and watch. This emergence of television as a status symbol led to occasional public outrage when it was discovered that some people receiving public welfare or other forms of relief possessed sets. Apparently the experiences of those who had lived through the depression years had been forgotten; at that time, radio sets were welcomed as extremely comforting to people trapped in trying economic circumstances (see chapter 3).

Television sets might have become a common household item even sooner if it had not been for the intervention of World War II. The technology of television broadcasting had been developed during the 1920s and 1930s, and by 1939, network TV broadcasts were already being made in the United States. The World's Fair that year featured demonstration of that latest scientific marvel, television. President Hoover had experimented with broadcasts, and President Roosevelt even delivered a speech over the new communication medium. The speech's broadcast audience, however, consisted of only a handful of people because commercial manufacturers had not yet begun to mass-produce sets. The Federal Communications Commission approved home television in 1941, on the eve of America's entry into World War II, and the communications industry had already begun to work out plans for its development. At that time, there were approximately 5,000 sets in private hands, mostly around New York City, and several small private stations were broadcasting regularly for two or three hours a day.[2]

World War II, however, abruptly altered this development and postponed the general availability of television until the war had ended. This hindrance to commercial development may account, in some respects, for the extremely rapid growth in both TV broadcasting and manufacturing when the country returned to a peacetime economy. For one thing, communications executives had the plans well laid for their expansion into television. In addition, electronics manufacturers had developed new techniques of production during the war that aided the industry in overcoming the problems of mass-producing television receivers. Besides all this, the prewar economic depression had finally ended. In fact, wartime rationing had created an immense pent-up demand for consumer goods and services. Americans, with jobs and money in their pockets, went on a buying spree. With minor fluctuations, the United States entered a period of unprecedented economic growth that was uninterrupted for more than two decades. With this prosperity came an increase in purchasing power. The purchasing power of the average American family rose to the point that TV ownership was within the means of all but the poorest.[3]

By 1960, 150 million Americans had acquired sets and rearranged their lives to accommodate the schedule of TV programs presented on their living room screens. This rearrangement appeared to be most striking in homes with children; such homes were more than twice as likely to have a set than homes that did not have children. Television had become the single greatest source of children's entertainment; it had displaced radio, comic books, playmates, and babysitters by a wide margin. However, the public knew very little about the effects of this new medium; the legacy of fear persisted among many Americans, and there was growing concern about what television might be doing to their children. Would the new medium stunt or stimulate their mental growth? Was it going to create armies of juvenile delinquents? Would it turn children into passive robots incapable of intellectual creativity? Would it propel children into an adult world of sex, liquor, and violence for which they were unprepared? American parents were deeply concerned about television's effects on this crucial segment of the population—from toddlers to teenagers.

The few research projects that dealt with the effects of television in the early 1950s provided no assurances to allay the fears of the public. A series of surveys by the National Association of Educational Broadcasters in 1951 discovered that crime and horror stories comprised 10 percent of the programming time in four American cities.[4] While by today's standards this might appear to be a small proportion of the shows, at the time it appeared to be excessive. Other investigations by social scientists revealed that watching television had reduced the amount of time that children spent playing—both indoors and outdoors. Viewing also reduced the amount of time that children devoted to helping out with household chores, such as cooking and cleaning. Children who watched television also spent less time listening to the radio, going to movies, and reading books.[5] Television viewing cut into all of the activities of daily life. No one knew, however, whether television could change attitudes or values. It was unknown whether television could create passivity or aggression, or whether it would enlarge or limit children's intellectual boundaries. Exactly what *was* happening to the tender minds tuned in to the electronic Pied Piper? Clearly, more research was needed to find out television's effects, particularly research focusing on children. In this setting, Professors Wilbur Schramm, Jack Lyle, and Edwin Parker undertook the first large-scale investigation of the relationship between television and children in North America. It is to that investigation that we now turn.

## THE RESEARCH PROGRAM

The results of the first major study of the effects of television on North American children were reported in *Television in the Lives of Our Children*. It presented the findings and conclusions from 11 investigations carried out between 1958 and 1960 in ten communities in the United States and Canada. The focus of the project was on the *uses and gratifications*—that is the functions—of television for various categories of children rather than simply on a straightforward analysis of "effects." The authors believed that the term *effects* was misleading in that:

> . . . it suggests that television "does something" to children. The conno-
> tation is that television is the actor; the children are acted upon.
> Children are thus made to seem relatively inert; television relatively
> active. Children are sitting victims; television bites them.[6]

Schramm and his colleagues argued that nothing could be further from the truth. Children were not, they emphasized, passive entities being acted upon by television. To the contrary, children were *active agents* who selected material from television that best fit their interests and needs. It was children who used television, not television that used children.

According to Schramm, Lyle, and Parker, children used television to gratify some need. They drew an analogy between television and a "great shiny cafeteria." From television, as from a cafeteria, children selected only what they wanted at the moment. It was conceded that television's bill of fare contained many dishes heavy in fantasy, that there were large slices of violence, and that there was less variety in the menu than some of the patrons might prefer at any one time. But, like the cafeteria, children took and consumed only what they wanted from television. Thus, it was argued that in order to understand television's effects, it was necessary to understand a great deal about the lives of children. We needed to know what it was in their lives that made them reach out for a particular experience on television. Only then could we know how their lives interacted with, and were influenced by, television. This was exactly what they proposed to do.

## Research Design and Methodology

As previously noted, Schramm and his associates conducted 11 separate studies between 1958 and 1960. The first study was funded by the San Francisco school system to gain information about the use of television by children in grades one through six. On the basis of the results obtained in the first study, subsequent funding for additional studies was provided, mainly by the National Educational Television and Radio Center. The scope of these studies is briefly summarized below:

### Study 1: San Francisco, 1958–1959

In the initial study, the researchers used a total of 2,688 children chosen to serve as representatives of grades 1 through 6, and of the eighth, tenth, and twelfth grades of the public school system. Some of the children were interviewed directly. Many of them, however, completed questionnaires and tests administered in their classrooms. Several hundred students kept diaries. In addition, data were obtained on some of the younger children through questionnaires completed by their parents. The study also included data from questionnaires completed by 1,030 parents, in which they described and reacted to their children's television behavior. The information gathered on each child varied somewhat according to the age of the child, but the researchers tried to learn as much as possible about each child's mass media behavior. Schramm and his associates were interested in what children used the different media for and what the media meant to them. In addition, they examined what the children knew about public affairs, science, popular and fine art, and other parts of the world. They also learned something about the children's family lives and their relations with children their own age. The research included measures of some of their psychological characteristics, their mental ability, the use they were making of it in school, and so on. In addition to all of this information gathered directly from the children and their parents, the researchers also talked to teachers, school officials, and other knowledgeable persons.

### Study 2: San Francisco, 1958

Interviews were conducted with 188 *entire families, as families.* The researchers talked to the parents and the children together so that the subjects could check up on one another and also so that the researchers could observe their interactions. The families were asked chiefly about the use of the media different members of the family made, and what part the media played in family life. In all, 188 mother, 187 fathers, and 502 children were interviewed.

### Studies 3–7: Rocky Mountain Communities, 1959

The entire sixth and tenth grades—or where necessary, an adequate sample of them—were interviewed in five communities in the Rocky Mountain area of the United States. In three of these communities, the researchers also included the first grade. In most respects, the information sought about each child paralleled that which had been obtained in San Francisco, although the questionnaires had been expanded and sharpened as the work progressed. In the case of the three first-grade cohorts, for example, the researchers administered vocabulary tests to the children. The total sample from the five towns was 1,708 children and 284 parents. As before, local teachers and officials were also consulted as a check on the information.

### Studies 8–9: Canada, 1959

Two communities in Canada were studied which were comparable to each other in most respects, except that one of them did not have television. Data were gathered in each community from the first, sixth, and tenth grades using the same materials developed for the Rocky Mountain towns, except that the materials had been improved through use, and somewhat expanded to take into account special characteristics of Canadian mass communication. Again, the first grades were given vocabulary tests. In all, 913 children and 269 parents were interviewed, and as before, the researchers consulted with local teachers and officials.

### Study 10: American Suburb

The researchers examined in detail the TV behavior, program choice, and time allocations of all of the elementary school children in one school. Data were gathered on a total of 474 children. Again, parents and teachers were consulted.

*Study 11: Denver, 1960*
This final study examined 204 students in the tenth grade in order to test several hypotheses developed from the results of the previous studies. The information obtained here dealt with the students' media behavior in relation to mental ability and social norms.

To summarize, a total of 11 studies were conducted. Overall, the researchers collected data from 5,991 students, 1,958 parents, and several hundred teachers, officials, and other knowledgeable persons in ten communities in the United States and Canada. These communities were chosen to be representative of North America and included isolated areas, metropolitan areas, cities, and towns of various sizes. The sample also included industrial, agricultural, and residential communities, and the level of the development of local television ran the gamut then existing in North America—from no television to highly developed, multi-station broadcast areas.

## The Functions of Television

Schramm, Lyle, and Parker offered their readers an explanation of *why* children watched television. They began with the functionalist assumption that every item in a culture exists because it is useful for the members of that culture. Therefore, they reasoned, TV viewing must be useful for children. And for it to be useful, it must be meeting certain needs, and it must be the *best* way of meeting those needs among the known and available alternatives. What were those needs? The authors posited three primary reasons why children watched television: (1) for entertainment, (2) for information, and/or (3) because of its social utility. Each of these reasons will be discussed below.

*Entertainment.* The most important and most obvious reason why children watched television was to enjoy the passive pleasure of being entertained. They enjoyed escaping from real-life problems and from boredom, and the children enjoyed identifying with exciting and attractive people. And TV programming was aimed more at escaping problems than it was at solving them. Watching television is an essentially passive behavior; it is something that the children surrendered themselves to; it is something that they did not have to work for or think about.

*Information.* Most children, when questioned, acknowledged that they learned from television. In many ways the medium served them as had the movies, as reported in Blumer's study (chapter 2). Girls said that they learned something about personal grooming—how to wear their hair, how to walk and talk, how to choose clothes—by observing the well-groomed mannequins on television. They also learned some of the details of contemporary manners and customs; for example, whether passengers are expected to tip the stewardess on an airplane. Some of the boys said that they learned how other young men dressed in New York or California. Others said that they learned a great deal by watching the performances of good athletes. More than one parent told of a child who learned to swing a baseball bat by watching professional stars on television and as a result became playground sensations until they began to imitate their young friends instead of the TV performers. Typical comments children made about television were: "It helps me to know how other kinds of people live"; or "The news is more real when you have seen where it happens." Many children said that television helped them in school by giving them ideas for themes or topics to discuss.

*Social Utility.*    Another attraction television had for children was its social utility. An example of this utility is that, among teenagers, watching television became a social occasion. It provided a handy excuse for boys and girls to enjoy each other's company; it gave them something convenient and inexpensive to do on dates; and it furnished them with a ready-made excuse for sitting close together. In addition, even when they did not watch television in the company of their peers, the previous evening's programs provided a common ground for conversations at school and on dates. If teenagers were not able to discuss these programs, they became out of step with their peers. Hence, watching television had a direct utility in their social lives.

Schramm, Lyle, and Parker reported that some children appeared to be quite compulsive about television. Such children were vaguely ill at ease when they missed a favorite program, or when their set was broken, or when some program or performer they particularly liked was off the air. Some children felt uneasy when they were away from television on a summer vacation. When asked to explain this feeling, one girl responded, "It's just as if they were your friends or your family. You miss them when you don't see them." Some children explained that they felt they were missing something, that they were out of step and were not in touch with what their peers were doing. It is evident, then, that watching television was functional for these children beyond the specific benefits of learning and entertainment.

The authors reasoned that any particular TV program might serve all three purposes for a child. A crime program, for example, would be likely to entertain many children. At the same time, however, it might teach some children specific skills and convey information about "what the world is like." In addition, the program provides the child with something to share and discuss the next day. It should be noted, however, that different children might view the same program in different ways. To one child, a news story about a murder trial might be a "whodunit" entertainment program. To another, it might be a commentary on conditions in the real world. For a third child, it could provide a way of learning how to commit murder. The message the child receives from the TV show can thus depend upon what the child brings to the TV set—that is, it depends upon the child's personal, social, and psychological characteristics.

Overall, the authors considered the use of television for entertainment and for information to be the most important uses. They argued that the chief needs that children gratified with television were those for both *fantasy* and *reality* experiences. Schramm and associates distinguished between fantasy content and reality content in the following manner:[7]

| *Fantasy Content:* | *Reality Content:* |
|---|---|
| invites the viewer to take leave of his problems in the real world; | constantly refers the viewer to the problems of the real world; |
| invites surrender, relaxation, passivity; | invites alertness, effort, activity; |
| invites emotion; | invites cognition; |
| works chiefly through abrogating the rules of the real world; | works chiefly through realistic materials and situations; |
| acts to remove, at least temporarily, threat and anxiety, and offers wish-fulfillment; | tends to make viewer even more aware of threat, perhaps more anxious, in return for better view of the problem; |
| offers pleasure. | offers enlightenment. |

It was thought that the predominant gratifications that television provided for children were for fantasy rather than reality needs.


## THE FINDINGS

The more quantitative and detailed findings of these 11 studies are too numerous and varied to be discussed in any detail. They can, however, be placed into five general categories: (1) how and when children used television, (2) children's learning from television, (3) reality seeking and social norms, (4) television and social relationships, and (5) the effects of television. Each of these sets of findings will be discussed in turn.


### How and When Children Used Television

The first direct experience that a child had with television typically came at age two, although it could not be said that most of the children were "users" at that age. Typically, such children "dropped in" on a program that someone else was watching. Soon after, they began to explore the world of television, and by the age of three, many children were making regular use of the medium. In fact, when asked, they were able to name their favorite programs. Figure 11.1 represents graphically the percentage of children using television between the ages of two and nine.

As can be seen, 37 percent of the three-year-old children were regular viewers, compared to 82 percent of the five-year-olds, 91 percent of those age

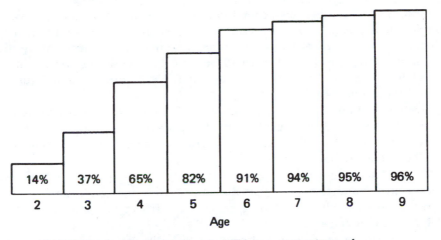

| 14% | 37% | 65% | 82% | 91% | 94% | 95% | 96% |
| 2 | 3 | 4 | 5 | 6 | 7 | 8 | 9 |

Age

**FIGURE 11.1**   The beginnings of TV use; percentage of children using it by age

SOURCE: Wilbur Schramm, Jack Lyle, and Edwin B. Parker, *Television in the Lives of Our Children* (Palo Alto, Calif.: Stanford University Press, 1961), p. 27.

six, and 96 percent of the nine-year-olds. Thus, by their ninth birthday, only 4 percent of the children could be considered nonusers.

But how much *time* did these children spend in front of the TV set? The "average" three-year-old spent about 45 minutes a day watching television. By the age of five, however, viewing time had increased to a little more than two hours per day. Between their sixth and tenth birthdays, children's viewing time slowly increased to about two and one-half hours each day. When the children reached 11 or 12, viewing time suddenly jumped to three or four hours daily; at this point, however, it began a slow, steady decline that continued throughout adolescence. It should be noted that these figures were for weekdays. Weekend viewing averages were higher, ranging from a half hour to an hour longer. In addition, the authors cautioned that their figures were conservative. Yet they also noted the cumulative situation: They observed that "from ages three through sixteen children spend *more total time* on television than on school. In fact, they are likely to devote more time to television than to any other activity except sleep"[8] (emphasis added).

We have indicated that age was an important factor in determining overall viewing time, and that the heaviest period of children's viewing usually came sometime between the ages of 11 and 13. But other factors, especially mental ability and social class background, were also important in determining the viewing habits of children.

The relationship between mental ability, as measured by IQ, and viewing time presented a rather dramatic picture. In the early school years, the children with high IQ scores tended to engage in high levels of TV viewing. However, sometime between the tenth and thirteenth years, a notable change occurred. The more intelligent children deserted the ranks of heavy viewers. The authors presented interesting data regarding this generalization. In the Rocky Mountain towns, for example, there was no relationship between IQ scores and viewing time among sixth-grade students. However, by the time the children had reached the tenth grade, most of the low-IQ children had become high viewers, whereas most of the high-IQ scorers had become low viewers. The data presented in Figure 11.2 illustrate these findings.

The chart shows that the percentage of light viewers increased generally between the sixth and tenth grades, but the chief increase was among those in the high-IQ group. Data from the other regions paralleled the conditions in the Rocky Mountain towns.

Why did the brighter children stop watching so frequently? Schramm and his associates found that television no longer presented a challenge to those children. Most of them were finding greater rewards in the print media and in social and school activities.

Social class background was also found to be important in determining the amount of time spent viewing. Children of well-educated parents tended to watch less than other children, following the example set by their parents. Children of working-class parents, however, were likely to watch more. The authors speculated that this difference in viewing time between social classes could be attributed to a difference in class norms. The middle-class norms of work, activity, and self-betterment influenced the viewing patterns of the middle-class youngsters by giving them incentives to engage in other activities, thereby reducing the time available for viewing.

**FIGURE 11.2** Percentage of children who are heavy viewers of television, by grade and mental level

SOURCE: Wilbur Schramm, Jack Lyle, and Edwin B. Parker, *Television in the Lives of Our Children* (Palo Alto, Calif.: Stanford University Press, 1961), p. 34.

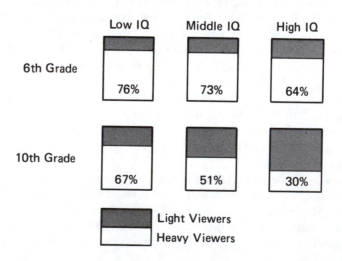

Schramm, Lyle, and Parker did indicate a note of caution, however. They pointed out that these general patterns did have exceptions, and that there were enough exceptions to lead them to believe that some of the most important factors in determining viewing habits must have been missing from their list. They felt that there was something beyond age, intelligence, and family that was affecting the children's viewing patterns. They believed that the missing elements were the child's social relationships and some of his or her personal characteristics.

Social relationships were indeed found to influence a child's use of television. The researchers discovered that children who had unsatisfactory relationships with their families, and/or with their peer groups, tended to retreat from those social interactions into TV viewing. When watching television, they could leave real-life problems behind them, at least for a time, and possibly reduce the tension in their lives. The more conflict there was in these children's lives, the more they watched television. It was evident, then, that problems with either the family or the peer group were clearly related to escapist fantasy seeking, and that children with such problems turned to television to escape.

***What Children Watched.*** Typically, the first programs that most children identified as their favorites were programs that the broadcasters referred to as "children's programs." The central characters of such programs were usually animals, animated characters, or puppets (e.g., Donald Duck, Huckleberry Hound, Howdy Doody, Rin Tin Tin), although sometimes the children themselves took the role of the sympathetic character. The programs were presented in story form and were full of action, often with a heavy component of slapstick humor. Such programs were traditionally aired in the late afternoon, after school, or on Saturday morning. Programs of this type monopolized the viewing time of preschool children, and their dominance persisted well into the elementary school years, although often in somewhat more mature forms, such as "Lassie." By the time the child was well settled in school, however, a new lineup of favorite programs had been established. These consisted of a number of program types created especially for children but modeled after adult programs: children's variety shows, children's adventure programs, children's science fiction, and children's westerns. The Walt Disney programs are examples of the "children's variety shows." The format varied widely, offering cartoons, adventure stories, legends, history, and nature stories; many programs contained a mixture of presentations. The authors offered "Zorro" as an example of "children's adventure programs." In these stories, the tale is told of a simple, strong, "good" hero. This hero is the master of his own fate in spite of the perils he faces in his adventures. The children's "science fiction" and "western" programs were both costume dramas—one set in the future and the other in the past or near past. The stories and characters were uncomplicated and featured adventure and excitement.

Such programs dominated the children's early school years, but soon two new types of programs became increasingly important in their viewing—the crime program and the situation comedy. The crime programs were only a short step from the adventure sagas, where the hero righted wrongs by his own strength, skill, and daring. The detective also solved crime through the use of skill, strength, and daring. Although these programs were generally scheduled during the "adult" programming hours, children usually began watching them in their early school years. The programs' largest juvenile audience, however, was teenagers.

As the children entered adolescence, another type of program became important in their viewing, the popular music variety show. The girls discovered these programs earlier and watched them faithfully, but such programming eventually became part of most teenagers' viewing. At this point, we have almost the entire line-up of programs watched during the teen years. The crime dramas became more absorbing, and the children's westerns were replaced by adult westerns such as "Gunsmoke." Programs like "Disneyland," "Zorro," and "Superman" faded in popularity. Much of the teenager's viewing time was now spent watching crime dramas and popular music shows. By now, little time was devoted to traditional "children's" programs. Interest in public affairs programming came late in this hierarchy. In fact, any use of media other than for entertainment was unusual. Figure 11.3 summarizes the general pattern that Schramm and his associates described in the growth of the children's program diet. As can be seen, the children learned to watch adult programs very quickly. For example, by the time the children were in the first grade, they were already devoting 40 percent of their viewing time to the kinds of programs that most viewers would term "adult." Moreover, sixth-grade children were devoting 79 percent of their viewing time to adult programs and were watching nearly five times as many adult programs as children's programs. This finding led the authors to caution that

**FIGURE 11.3**   Periods in childhood and youth when different program types are most important

SOURCE: Wilbur Schramm, Jack Lyle, and Edwin B. Parker, *Television in the Lives of Our Children* (Palo Alto, Calif.: Stanford University Press, 1961), p. 39.

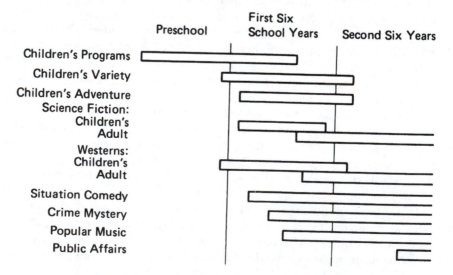

"networks which believe that they are producing programs for adults might do well to take another look at the age of their audience."[9]

***Predicting Children's Taste in Programming.***   It should be made clear that not all children preferred to watch the same types of shows. What were the factors associated with different program preferences? From our previous discussion, it is evident that one important factor was the age of the child. If it was known that one child was 9 and another 14, other things being equal, it was possible to predict that there would be certain differences in program preferences between them. For example, the younger child would be likely to prefer more traditional children's programs, such as Walt Disney, whereas the older child would likely have more interest in popular music shows and crime dramas. Another important factor was the child's sex. Differences in program preferences between boys and girls were apparent even as early as the first grade. Little girls preferred popular music shows, whereas boys preferred westerns and adventure programs. This pattern continued throughout the school years—girls preferred 'feminine" programs built around marriage and romance (e.g., situation comedies, popular music) and boys preferred "masculine" programs of excitement and adventure. The authors offered one explanation for these differences: Girls developed an interest in adolescent and adult roles at an earlier age than did boys.

Mental ability was again found to be an important factor. Schramm, Lyle, and Parker found that brighter children tried different things earlier. They began watching television earlier and more frequently; then they took the "hard steps" to serious programming sooner, such as watching news programs, educational shows, and documentaries. It was found, for example, that about twice as many of the brighter eighth-grade students were watching TV coverage of the 1958 congressional elections, when compared to lower intelligence groups. Moreover, of those who viewed this program, it was the brighter ones who most enjoyed it. The high-IQ scorers were also the ones who were chiefly able to identify faces that had appeared on television for public affairs reasons rather than for entertainment reasons. These patterns of viewing news programs, public affairs commentary, and so on began earlier with the brighter children. They were the first of their age group to turn away from the western and situation comedy shows.

In general, the brighter teenagers were being attracted away from television. Homework and their social lives kept them busier and they had less time for television. In addition, they were becoming more critical and discriminating in their choices of programming, abandoning those offerings which seemed to have less durable value for them. Both the high-IQ scorers and the low-IQ scorers were settling into adult viewing patterns. Thus, the high-IQ category used television less often and more selectively, and turned to print media for much of their serious informational needs. the lower IQ group, on the other hand, tended to use television more and printed media less. As their teenage behavior suggested, they used television heavily for crime mysteries, situation comedies, westerns, comedy, variety, and popular music programs. In short, sex, age, and mental ability were found to be related to program preference.

*Attitudes Toward Television.*    It is not surprising that Schramm and his associates found that most children regarded television with both affection and respect. What is surprising was that they were not alone. Their parents also showed similar attitudes toward television. When the authors conducted interviews in San Francisco with 188 families, each questioned together as a family unit, they asked each member of the family which of the media they would miss the most if they had to do without it. The overwhelming response was television—for the whole family. Overall, television was the most likely to be missed by parents and children alike; and television was the medium mentioned more frequently at every age, even though its relative importance declined during adolescence.

The children were generally enamored of television. When asked, they could find nothing they would change in its content, except that they wanted *more of the same.* Preteen girls, for example, requested more popular music shows and family situations. Boys in the same age groups wanted more war stories, sports, crime shows, and comedy. It was not until the children reached the late high school years that they became critical of television, and even then it was chiefly the brighter children. Those older children who were critical did not have major complaints. Some thought that there were too many commercials; others thought that some TV personalities were unpleasant; and a few thought that programming was too repetitive, that it was all the same.

When it came to the parents, however, it was a different story. Overall, they had definite ideas about changes they wanted. Most of them were clearly concerned about the amount of crime and violence on television. This was especially true for the better-educated parents with white-collar jobs. When parents from blue-collar families expressed concern, they tended to be more disturbed about sexual content in programming. In general, however, blue-collar parents were much more likely to express gratitude for television—it kept their children "out of mischief" or "off the streets," or it was an inexpensive babysitter.

## Incidental Learning from Television

The authors argued that most of a child's learning from television was *incidental learning.* Such learning was defined as "learning that takes place when a viewer goes to television for entertainment and stores up certain items of information without seeking them."[10] In their view, children learned while being entertained; however, the children did not seek out television strictly for informational purposes.

A number of conditions were found to be important in determining when incidental learning took place. These included the child's ability to learn, the child's needs at the moment, and what the child paid attention to. The ability to learn was looked upon pretty much as a matter of intelligence. Schramm and associates stated that "bright" children learned more from television. Indeed, such children learned more in any learning situation. Other factors, related to attention and needs, were found to be important. For example, children were more likely to pay attention to and learn some particular behavior if it was new to them.

The researchers discussed, as an example, the impact of a Hopalong Cassidy (a popular cowboy character) film in one of their studies. The show produced a considerable amount of learning on the part of younger children but had very little impact on the older ones. The difference between the two groups was accounted for by the fact that the film was a new kind of experience for the young children but "old stuff" to the older ones. Because the older children had seen such films many times before, this one did not command their close attention, an effect of familiarity. As children become more familiar with the subject matter, they learn to sort out the material. They note familiar things and set up a pattern of expectation that keeps them from having to pay too much attention to them. In any event, it is the new things, the ones that are not too familiar to them, that they single out for their attention and storage.

On the basis of this familiarity principle, Schramm and his associates posited that the greatest amount of learning from television occurs between the ages of three and eight, when most of the experiences are new to the children. At those ages, those experiences would be especially absorbing to the child. There is, however, another reason why television is an especially effective agent of incidental learning when the child is young. The reason is that television seems very real to them. A number of observers have commented that mass media content had greater impact on children if they believed that it had "really happened." The younger children are more likely to think that the events taking place on the picture tube in front of them are real.

The amount of identification that a child has with a TV character is another factor that affects the amount of incidental learning that takes place. All parents have observed their children galloping imaginary horses or acting out an adventure the way their favorite hero would play it. Girls copy the current romantic heroines—mimicking their entrances, their mannerisms, and their seductive manner in love scenes. Many researchers have written about children's identification with characters. "There is no doubt that a child can more easily store up behaviors and beliefs which he has imaginatively shared with a character with whom he identifies."[11]

A child is also more likely to pick out and remember something from an entertainment program if it is clearly useful to him or her. In this respect the child's needs become important. A girl, for example, is more likely to remember an attractive hairdo, whereas a boy is more likely to remember the techniques a third baseman used when he charged a bunt. If the child notices something he or she can tell to friends, then there is ample reason to remember it—especially if it can evoke laughter. Such "little bonuses" occur all the time in the course of entertainment. Something comes to the child's attention as the program progresses, he or she sees a use for it, and stores it away for the future.

In addition, there is reason to believe that the child will more likely learn and use something when he or she thinks that it will work. When a TV character fails at something, it is unlikely that the child will try it. But if the behavior appears to be both rewarding and socially feasible, there is more incentive for the child to store it away and then try it when the proper occasion arises.

Schramm and his associates believed that watching television contributed to a fast start in learning but that the advantage children gained did not last. They felt that children who viewed television would start school with larger vocabularies than nonviewing children of the same age. Likewise, the authors argued, child viewers would be more familiar with wider worlds and know more (at an earlier age) than nonviewers about adult life, sex, crime, and social problems. In order to test these hypotheses, however, the researchers had to compare two Canadian communities because they could not find an American community that did not have television. As expected, they found that first-grade children with television had higher vocabulary scores than similar children living in a community without television. By the sixth grade, however, the difference disappeared. Thus, the advantage gained from watching television did not last. It came as no surprise that IQ scores again emerged as an important factor. Remember our earlier discussions, which revealed that brighter children watched more television during their early years but then deserted the ranks of heavy viewers as they grew older. Such factors interact with exposure to television and must be taken into account when we observe that the advantages of TV viewing disappear. Schramm and associates referred to this interaction pattern as the "principle of maturation." According to this principle, when children mature to a certain point television becomes less attractive and rewarding to them. As a result, they increase the attention they pay to reality-oriented media material, or "material which is at least as useful for its information content as for its entertainment content, if not more so."[12]

## Social Norms and Social Relationships

The maturation principle held true for most children, but not for all. While most children decreased their TV viewing time considerably during their high school years, others decreased their viewing only slightly or not at all. Why did this happen? First of all, the pattern of fantasy seeking and reality seeking differentiated the children's media behavior more than anything else. Those children who were seeking knowledge or information turned more of their media attention to newspapers, quality magazines, and books. On the other hand, those children who primarily sought entertainment and fantasy/escape remained high users of TV fantasy, as well as other media with high fantasy components (e.g., comic books).

*The Importance of Social Norms.*     To understand why these patterns of reality seeking and fantasy seeking emerged, the researchers divided children into four groups according to the amount of their use of television, books, and magazines. The first group was fantasy-oriented; it was composed of children who were high users of television and low users of print media. The second group, on the other hand, was reality-oriented; it was composed of children who were high users of print and low users of television. The third group was referred to as the "high users" group. It consisted of children with high use levels of both print and television. The fourth group, the "low users" group, consisted of children who were low users of both print and television. In the sixth grade, membership in the reality-oriented group was very small, but by the tenth grade it had grown a great deal. Children who were members of this group differed from the members of the other groups. They had internalized the norms of the upwardly mobile middle class—norms of activity, self-betterment, and deferred gratification. At the beginning of adolescence, there was a turning point for a considerable number of children. They left the universal pleasure norm of their childhood for these middle-class norms. It was those children, if their mental abilities were sufficient, who became the chief users of print media and educational television. They were also the viewers more likely to select reality programs from commercial television. Social norms, then, had a great deal to do with what kind of use the child made of television.

*Television and Social Relationships.*   Another factor that determined how a child used television was social relationships. In general, it was found that children who had unsatisfactory relationships with their families or peer groups tended to retreat to television where they could escape from their real-life problems. However, when we examine some other variables, the relationship is no longer so simple. For example, when children of high intelligence and high social status encountered problems in their social relations, the amount of television they used went up, as expected. Such children turned to television for fantasy and escape, rather than seek reality in print media, as would be expected from them if their social relationships were satisfactory. But when children of low intelligence and low social status faced similar problems in their social relations, the result was not more use of television. If anything changed, there was less use of television.

The quality of the child's home and peer-group relationships did help to determine the amount of television he or she saw, but also much more. The child who came to television filled with aggression because of the frustrations of these poor social relationships was likely to seek out and remember the violent content of television. Schramm and associates concluded that if the child sought violence in answer to his or her own social needs, then he or she was likely to remember and resurrect such violence when real-life needs called for aggression. "In other words, parents, friends, schools have it is in their power to make significant contribution to the healthfulness of a child's use of television by giving him a warm and loving home, and helping him to normal and satisfying friendships with children his own age."[13]

## The Effects of Television

The relationship between television and a child can be understood only in terms of the characteristics of both. We have already discussed what a child brings to television (i.e., IQ, social norms, social relationships, and the needs and experiences for which age and sex are partial indicators). Now we turn to the question of what television brings to the child. To examine this, Schramm and associates monitored and analyzed a week of television in late October 1960, from 4 P.M.

to 9 P.M., Monday through Friday. Figure 11.4 summarizes their findings. It can be seen that commercial television brought to children fast-moving, exciting fantasy, with broad humor and a considerable amount of romantic interest. The authors considered the content to be "extremely violent." Shootings and sluggings were frequent; in fact, more than half the program hours consisted of programs in which violence played an important part. The researchers, it should be pointed out, did not take all of the violence seriously.

For example, the cartoons and slapstick films they deemed were intended to by funny, rather than exciting, were disregarded in the analysis. Nevertheless, in the hundred hours analyzed there appeared:

12 murders

16 major gunfights

21 persons shot (apparently not fatally)

21 other violent incidents with guns (ranging from shooting at but missing persons, to shooting up a town)

37 hand-to-hand fights (15 fist fights, 15 incidents in which one person slugged another, an attempted murder with a pitchfork, 2 stranglings, a fight in the water, a case in which a woman was gagged and tied to a bed, etc.)

1 stabbing in the back with a butcher knife

4 attempted suicides, three successful

**FIGURE 11.4**  Content of commercial television over 1.0 percent during the "Children's Hour"—4 to 9 P.M., Monday through Friday, late October 1960.

SOURCE: Wilbur Schramm, Jack Lyle, and Edwin B. Parker, *Television in the Lives of Our Children* (Palo Alto, Calif.: Stanford University Press, 1961), p. 138.

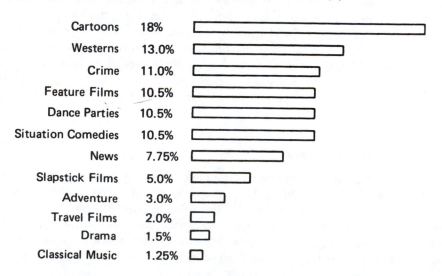

| | | |
|---|---|---|
| Cartoons | 18% | |
| Westerns | 13.0% | |
| Crime | 11.0% | |
| Feature Films | 10.5% | |
| Dance Parties | 10.5% | |
| Situation Comedies | 10.5% | |
| News | 7.75% | |
| Slapstick Films | 5.0% | |
| Adventure | 3.0% | |
| Travel Films | 2.0% | |
| Drama | 1.5% | |
| Classical Music | 1.25% | |

4 people falling or pushed over cliffs

2 cars running over cliffs

2 attempts made in automobiles to run over persons on the sidewalk

A psychotic loose and raving in a flying airliner

2 mob scenes, in one of which the mob hangs the wrong man

A horse trampling a man under its hooves

A great deal of miscellaneous violence, including a plane fight, a hired killer stalking his prey, 2 robberies, a pickpocket at work, a woman killed by falling from a train, a tidal wave, an earthquake, and a guillotining.

This picture of the adult world was heavy in violence, light in intellectual exchange, and deeply concerned with crime. Half of the characters in the stories were either involved in enforcing the law, breaking it, or both. There were 16 detectives, 16 sheriffs, 9 police officers, and an assortment of other law enforcement officials. In general, the detectives were more successful than the sheriffs, and the sheriffs were more successful than the police. But despite the presence of all these lawmen, a large part of the crime detection and enforcement had to be carried out by amateurs with steely nerves and a quick draw.

The picture presented of family life was mixed. In some programs, a tolerant, good-humored relationship was shown among the members of the family. Other programs showed conflict, screaming, distrust, and violence within the family. Little attention was paid to how the characters earned a living, so the child seeking career information got little instruction from commercial TV fare—that is, unless he or she wanted to be a "private eye," a western sheriff, or a crook. On the other hand, some of the programs, particularly situation plays, went out of their way to offer morals to their stories. Typical examples are: "Don't undervalue your real friends"; "What comes easy, goes easy"; "Don't always believe what you hear."

What kind of variety was there for the child to choose from? About 22 percent of the time a child could have found a reality program other than news somewhere on the four available commercial stations. But for more than half the time, the choice was strictly between different types of fantasy: for example, two crime shows, a cartoon, or a western. This, then, is what television brought to the child.

Television's effects are the result of an interactive process between the characteristics of television and the characteristics of its users. Different children could watch the same television content and the effects could be different. For example, Schramm and associates discussed a study done by Fritz Redl, who compared the reactions of disturbed children and normal children to selected TV fare. He found that "ordinary" children would avoid extremely violent and frightening TV content. Such was not the case, however, with the problem children. They sought to avoid the "nice" and "sweet" programs that showed loving parents and warm friendly relationships. Those kinds of programs, Redl argued, were likely to cause the disturbed children to lie awake or to have bad dreams because they reminded the children of what was lacking in their own lives. From this evidence, Schramm, Lyle, and Parker concluded: "Thus what would have been soothing (or at least innocuous) for most children was traumatic for these children because of their particular needs and background."[14]

The researchers then presented their "inventory" of the effects of television. They felt that they could now discuss the nature of these effects because they had studied the ways in which television entered the life of the child. They placed these effects in the following categories: (1) physical effects, (2) emotional effects, (3) cognitive effects, and (4) behavioral effects. We will briefly discuss what they concluded about each of these effects.

*Physical Effects.*   Schramm and associates found that the physical effects of television were not very important. Television caused no special eyestrain (when compared to reading) *if* the children viewed under the proper conditions. On the other hand, eyestrain was likely to occur if the child sat too close to the set, looked up at it, and/or viewed it in a dark room. In addition, the authors found little evidence of any serious loss of sleep as a result of TV viewing. The average difference in bedtimes between TV and non-TV homes was 15 minutes later for those who watched TV.

*Emotional Effects.*   Television's emotional effects were less innocuous. A TV program frightened almost all of the children at one time or another. What chiefly disturbed the children were situations where harm threatened some character or animal with whom they identified. It was particularly acute when the harm involved cutting or stepping into a trap—that is, nonritual violence. The children were frightened when they viewed such violent and stressful programs at too early an age, and many became particularly frightened when they viewed television alone or in a dark room.

In general, the children liked and sought excitement, on the television as well as in real life. However, they did not like the excitement to spill too far over into fear. Children engage in "thrill play" because they seek such excitement, and it has a parallel in television. The researchers raised serious questions, however, about the possible effect of the high level of excitement in television, a level that they saw as rising. They questioned what the effects of this excitement would be on the children's perceptions of reality. Would it take the edge off the actual experience and lead children to demand something of real life that it cannot give to them? The researchers saw signs that this was happening, but felt that the answer could be found only through long-term research.

*Cognitive Effects.*   Television probably helped some children more than others to grow into better-informed adults. It specifically helped those children who chose some of the reality experiences of television. Those children heard important people discuss current issues; they watched demonstrations of the arts and of science. They were "on the scene" in foreign places and observed great events. On the other hand, television was more effective, in all probability, in stimulating interest in the children and contributing to already existing interest, rather than in stimulating creativity or activity. There were cases where television did stimulate some children to read books that had a relation to some program. However, Schramm and associates cautioned that the most frequent kinds of activities resulting from TV viewing involved either mimicking fads (such as wearing the Davy Crockett hat) or adopting details that fit into an already existing interest—for example, a boy who changes his batting stance following the viewing of a major league game on television.

Some people had hoped that television would raise the level of children's tastes; they wanted television to bring more "highbrow" culture into their lives. There was little sign that this had happened, however. Indeed, there were indications that it was creating a level of taste in children based upon its own common denominator. The researchers were particularly disturbed by their finding that children learned to like the programs available to them, even though they would not ordinarily have selected them. Equally disturbing was television's treatment of adult life. They found that television was portraying a "markedly erroneous" picture of adult life. This, they reasoned, was not a positive contribution to the child's socialization process and might require some very tough adjustments later in life. Moreover, such portrayals of life, especially the depiction of sexual behavior and violence, could lead to "premature aging" and even cause children to fear the process of growing up.

***Behavioral Effects.***    The possible behavioral effects of television were the ones that had caused the most concern to both parents and researchers, yet Schramm, Lyle, and Parker indicated that they were in almost every case controllable through the non-TV life of the child. The researchers addressed the question of whether or not TV viewing made children too passive. They concluded that in *some cases* it did and suggested that long-term studies were needed to determine the magnitude and lasting quality of such effects. They also argued that "the way to avoid an excessive passivity in our children is not to give them television as a mother substitute early in life; rather to make them feel loved and wanted at home, and so far as possible to surround them with friends and activities."[15]

The most common and most feared charge leveled against television was that it taught delinquency and violent behavior. The researchers argued that it was a contributory cause in some cases. For example, some children confused the rules of the fantasy world with the rules of the real world. The researchers explained that a child who wanted to put the ground glass in the stew to see if it worked as on the TV program was merely experimenting in the real world with the tools of the fantasy world. They found too that children who brought aggression to television were more likely to remember aggressive acts portrayed there. The children wanted to be like the successful characters, whether those characters were good or bad. The researchers cautioned, however, that little delinquency could be traced directly to television. "Delinquency is a complex behavior growing usually out of a number of roots, the chief one usually being some great lack in the child's life—often a broken home, or a feeling of rejection by parents or peer groups. Television is at best a contributing cause."[16] Schramm, Lyle, and Parker concluded that overall, the effects of television pointed as much to the parents as to television. Parents who provided their children with warm, secure relationships and an interesting home life had little to fear from television.

## CONCLUSIONS AND IMPLICATIONS

*Television in the Lives of Our Children* was the first major North American study investigating the effects of television on children and the only large-scale investigation available on that subject until the Surgeon General's Report on Television and Social Behavior in 1972 (see chapter 14). The basic strength of this milestone is the exhaustive research upon which its findings were based. In many ways it resembled the earlier movie study (chapter 2). As we have seen, the researchers' investigations and findings included a fascinating comparison of children in communities with television and without it, an analysis of the influence of fantasy and reality in the content of programs, a detailed discussion of what children learned from television and the conditions under which they learned it, figures bearing upon homework habits and bedtime hours, a report on the program choices of children, and an exploration of the potential physical, emotional, cognitive, and behavioral problems among children that might result from viewing television. It explained in detail that children exhibited several different patterns in their use of television—patterns that changed as the children grew older. Thus, there were considerable differences between the children in their use of television, and these differences did not result simply from age but also varied in accordance with the child's sex, mental ability as measured by IQ, social class background, and the quality of each child's social relations, both with parents and/or with peer group(s). Moreover, the researchers found considerable interaction between these five factors. For example, socioeconomic class and social relations appeared to interact. On the one hand, middle-class children who were frustrated by their parents were likely to watch television more than their middle-class peers, other things being equal. In addition, they watched television for its fantasy experiences. On the other hand, working-class children who were similarly frustrated by their parents were likely to watch television less than their peers. Thus, differences in social class background altered the children's reaction to difficulties in their social relations.

Schramm, Lyle, and Parker suggested, by their very choice of title, that their approach to communication research focused more on the *uses* and *gratifications* of television for various categories of children rather than on actual direct effects. (The uses and gratifications approach, it might be noted, gained increased popularity in the 1970s and 1980s.) Indeed, a leitmotiv that reappears repeatedly in their discussions is: "In order to understand television's impact and effect on children, we have first to get away from the unrealistic concept of what television does to children and substitute the concept of what children do with television."[17]

The researchers did note, however, that it was the possible behavioral effects of television that had aroused the most concern in the public. Was television harmful to children? Was television turning children into delinquents? Or, conversely, was it making them too passive? Schramm and his associates pulled their findings together in the following widely quoted, but decidedly less-than-precise, statement:

> For *some* children, under *some* conditions, *some* television is harmful. For *other* children under the same conditions, or for the same children under *other* conditions, it may be beneficial. For *most* children, under *most* conditions, most television is probably neither harmful nor particularly beneficial.[18]

They also reassured us, more than once, that if a child was given love, security, and healthful activities in his or her non-TV hours, then there was little chance that television would have negative effects on the child. This assumed, of course, that the child was a normal middle-class child who had been properly socialized into the Protestant ethic. Their statements should have been quite comforting to middle-class parents, the principal audience of the book. For children of dysfunctional families, however, television influences were not so clear.

Theoretically, the research was very diverse. While uses and gratifications were the central perspective, the researchers used the theory of selective influence. For example, when they stressed the importance of mental ability in determining the effects of television, they implied selective influence based upon *individual differences*. A major emphasis of the work, however, was on selective influence based upon *social categories* and *social relationships*. Social categories such as age, sex, and social class all played a role in determining the ways in which children used television and therefore determined how children were influenced by viewing this newest medium. Social relationships, however, were found to be crucial in determining the influence of television on children. Poor family relationships and/or poor peer group relationships could send a bright middle-class child to the tube for fantasy/escape experiences. In many ways, then, social relationships took precedence over social categories in determining the influence of television on children.

The researchers also made use of the main tenet of contemporary meaning theory when they discussed the ways in which television could modify children's perceptions of the world. This influence, however, was mediated through such factors as IQ, age, sex, social class, and social relations.

There were methodological problems with this research, although such a statement could be made of practically any large-scale project. Part of the difficulty seemed to lie in the basic design of the research. Schramm, Lyle, and Parker conducted cross-sectional surveys in several communities, but with a variety of goals in mind. Thus, their findings were not always comparable. In spite of this, they attempted to make cross-community comparisons, and the validity of some of their conclusions can be questioned. Overall, this problem points out the difficulty of executing research designs under ever-changing conditions. It should also be noted, however, that this piecemeal approach to planning the research also had a definite advantage, an aspect of the problem that the researchers fully utilized. They analyzed the early studies first, then built new measures into the subsequent inquiries to test hypotheses formulated from the results of the earlier segments of the research. This approach allowed them to make more refined theoretical generalizations than would otherwise have been possible. Thus, we can see that a trade-off must sometimes be made to achieve research ends. In this case, the researchers traded complete comparability between the various communities surveyed for increased theoretical depth of analysis and for hypothesis testing.

One problem that could have been more easily addressed is the sophistication of the data analysis: it was much too simple. The parts written for general audiences were presented in basic understandable terms, but the sections of the book intended for more technically sophisticated readers generally did not go beyond simple tabular presentations (although more detailed) of the categories and frequencies of the occurrence. An example of such simplicity is the frequent mention of interaction effects between certain variables (e.g., age, IQ, social class, etc.). Yet these interaction effects were neither systematically investigated in the researchers' analyses of the data, nor were they spelled out in any great detail; we were simply informed that there was interaction between the variables.

Beyond the questions about data analysis techniques, however, is a deeper theoretical problem. Schramm, Lyle, and Parker consistently made many arguments and drew conclusions about developmental changes in children based upon cross-sectional data. They did *not* examine the changes in a group of children over time. Instead, they compared differences between various age-groups surveyed during the same time period and inferred that changes in the young children by the time they reached the age of the older ones would account for the differences. Strictly speaking, these inferences are not appropriate. In order to make such generalizations, they needed longitudinal data—measures of the same groups over time. The researchers never cautioned the readers about this; they accepted the differences as developmental differences. In fact, they *assumed,* rather than discovered, a "maturation effect."

Another difficulty in evaluating this research is the researchers' desire to go beyond their own data and to present a total picture of the state of the knowledge in the field. In effect, the book becomes, in its conclusions, self-contradictory. At times, the writers appeared to place great importance on the role of television in the lives of children. They informed us that television occupied more time in the first 16 years of the child's life than anything except sleep. They also indicated that it played a "major part in socializing children" and that it was the "greatest source of common experience in the lives of children." In addition, they believed that television distracted children from the "solution of real-life problems." Yet, in spite of these statements, they also concluded that for most children "television is probably neither harmful nor particularly beneficial." In a similar vein, they argued that television played at most a reinforcing role rather than an initiatory role in the various social ills that popular discussion had linked with it.

In short, some children could be "damned" by exposure to television. They did not indicate who they were. Those who could be "saved" were those who enjoyed the WASP world of love, security, and middle-class values. These were the simple solutions to the potential problems of television.

Considering their often quoted final conclusion about the effects of television ("*some* children *some* of the time," etc.), it was not surprising that many researchers interpreted this work as supporting the minimal-effects hypothesis. Yet the public was not satisfied. Perhaps it was the conflicting conclusions that bothered many people. How could something that occupied so much of their children's time and was so important in their socialization be so innocuous? In any event, the legacy of fear remained alive because in reality the "big" questions about television and its effects on children remained unresolved.

## NOTES AND REFERENCES

1. Wilbur Schramm, Jack Lyle, and Edwin Parker, *Television in the Lives of Our Children* (Palo Alto, Calif.: Stanford University Press, 1961), pp. 11–12.
2. Melvin L. DeFleur and Sandra Ball-Rokeach, *Theories of Mass Communication*, 3d ed. (New York: McKay, 1975), pp. 97–99.
3. Ibid.
4. Eli A. Rubinstein, "Television Violence: A Historical Perspective," in *Children and the Faces of Television,* ed. Eli A. Rubinstein (New York: Academic Press, 1981), p. 114.
5. Eleanor E. Maccoby, "Television: Its Impact on School Children," *Public Opinion Quarterly* 15: 421–444 (1951). See also Paul I. Lyness, "The Place of the Mass Media in the Lives of Boys and Girls," *Journalism Quarterly* 29: 43–54 (1952).
6. Schramm et al., *Television in the Lives,* p. 1.
7. Ibid., pp. 63–64.
8. Ibid., p. 30.
9. Ibid., p. 95.
10. Ibid., p. 75.
11. Ibid., p. 78.
12. Ibid., p. 98.
13. Ibid., p. 173.
14. Ibid., p. 143.
15. Ibid., p. 174.
16. Ibid.
17. Ibid., p. 169.
18. Ibid., p. 13.

chapter **12**

# The Agenda-Setting Function
of the Press: What to Think About

Early in the 1960s scholars were rejecting the idea that the media had powerful and immediate effects on their audiences. While some of the earliest research had seemed to point to that conclusion, the large-scale studies of the 1940s and 1950s had not supported such a view. The accumulation of research seemed more consistent with a minimal effects interpretation. At the same time, sensitive observers of the media and their audiences continued to feel that people were influenced in their beliefs and actions because of repeated exposure to the content of mass communications. Such influences might not show up in the kinds of research studies that had been conducted. It was entirely possible, it was felt, that the influences were long-term, subtle, and difficult to pin down by the experiments, survey studies, and other research efforts that had been in vogue. It was time, many communication scholars believed, to look in new directions.

But how could such subtle influences be studied? It was clear that the answer would not be found entirely by following sophisticated theories derived from psychology and sociology. They had not been particularly helpful during the previous 30 years in isolating the effects of the mass media on their audiences. Perhaps it was time to return to the obvious facts about the mass media themselves and how they functioned within the contemporary society. Such a new start might provide clues to the existence of long-term influences.

One obvious fact about the media in modern society is the constant flow of *news*. Another obvious fact is that large numbers of people read their newspapers and listen to news on radio. Some citizens rely more on television for their news; still others have little interest in daily events. Nevertheless, the mass media still are a significant source of detailed information about what is going on for very large numbers of people.

Another obvious fact is that the news industry seems more interested in some events than in others. It is widely understood that the material presented by the press is *selective*. That selectivity stems from its limited capacity to provide total surveillance, from factors imposed on those who do the gatekeeping, and from the financial limitations placed on media that must survive as profit-making business enterprises. Such variables go a long way to account for the manner in which the press decides which stories to select, follow up, emphasize, interpret, and present in particular ways.

But the essential point is that there is a constant flow of information from the press to its audience. Day after day, week after week, newsmedia provide their audiences with information on a list of topics and issues that seem important to those who manage those media. That information, selective or distorted as it may be, provides the most basic source for millions of people about what is taking place in their society. It seemed inconceivable to many media scholars that such a flow of information simply had no effect on those who received it. The idea that the news media powerfully controlled people's attitudes, beliefs, and behavior might not hold water, but the press obviously brings to their attention a selected agenda of topics and issues to respond to and think about.

From that starting point, pieces of the puzzle began to come together. For example, early in the century, Walter Lippmann had noted that since people had only limited opportunities to observe important events in a firsthand manner, they were dependent upon the press to provide them with information on what those events were like. The role of the press, he observed, was to provide us with views of "the world outside" from which we can form "pictures in our heads."[1] Lippmann understood very well that there was often a significant gap between the accounts of the press and what had actually taken place. But aside from the problem of outright distortion, the essential theoretical question that would eventually emerge from such considerations was whether the topics selected by the press to represent the "world outside" limited the kinds of events about which people could form interpretations of what was happening. Furthermore, if the press implied in some way by its presentation of topics that one event was *more important* than another, did readers come to believe that this was how it was *in reality?* In other words, were the "pictures in our heads" (whatever their nature and dimensions) ranked in our personal assessments of significance in a manner parallel to the way in which they were covered and differentially emphasized by the press in the daily flow of news?

These questions address subtle and long-term influences of the news media, and they are not readily reduced to hypotheses that can be tested in a short-term experiment or a one-time survey. In addition, such questions did not leap fully formed from the analysis of a single scholar or from any specific research study. In fact, they emerged from a complex background of ideas that brought together conclusions from both ancient and modern sources.

The conviction that communication shapes ideas is indeed ancient. Philosophers had long been concerned about the nature and sources of human understanding. In the seventeenth century, John Locke had outlined the relationship between the process of communication and the development of the human mind.[2] As the twentieth century began, the key role of language in human mental activities became a central focus in various branches of anthropology, social psychology, and sociology. Theories in those fields stressed the social sources from which people drew their meanings for the events in the world that surrounded them. The Sapir-Whorf hypothesis from anthropology was grounded on the fact that the languages used by different societies had great differences in structure. Those differences led the people who used them to see, interpret, and understand both the physical and social world in quite different ways.[3] The symbolic interactionism paradigm from social psychology was developed to show the relationship between the internal psychological organization of the individual processes of human communication and the organization of social systems.[4] Sociologists routinely assume that the conceptions of reality (meanings) people hold as individuals are socially constructed through a process of communication using shared language.[5]

In more recent times, these broad theories and propositions were brought very specifically into the study of the influence of the press—that is, the news media. An important clue as to what kind of influence such media might have on their audiences came from a comment made in a book by Bernard Cohen in 1963. He noted that "the press may not be successful much of the time in telling people what to think, but it is stunningly successful in telling its readers what to think about."[6] This rather simple, and widely quoted, generalization provided an important element in the ideas that would come together into the hypothesis that the press had an important *agenda-setting function.*

A number of scholars in other disciplines were also thinking along the same lines, and they provided additional elements. For example, sociologists Kurt and Gladys Lang observed that while there was considerable doubt that the press had great power to change people's attitudes, the media did provide an immense quantity of information from which people learned about the important issues of the day. Furthermore, the Langs noted, people seemed to learn about such matters as campaign issues in direct proportion to the emphasis placed on them by their manner of presentation in the media:

> The mass media force attention to certain issues. They build up public images of public figures. They are constantly presenting objects suggesting what individuals in the mass should think about, know about, have feelings about.[7]

What was needed was someone who could synthesize these various elements into a systematic and researchable hypothesis and test that hypothesis against carefully gathered empirical data.

## THE DEVELOPMENT OF THE HYPOTHESIS

In the mid-1960s, a small group of journalism researchers at the University of California at Los Angeles began to notice that whenever a news story that conceivably could have been a major one was played down, its impact on public opinion seemed to be greatly dissipated. The opposite also seemed true. Maxwell McCombs and his colleagues had recently read the Bernard Cohen book, plus other relevant literature, and they were fully aware of both Walter Lippmann's pioneering suggestions of how the press was related to public opinion and the social science background on the social construction of reality generally. The group was increasingly convinced that such influences of the press had to be studied in a long-term perspective.[8]

In 1967, Professor McCombs moved to North Carolina and met Donald Shaw. Together they undertook a program of research on various cognitive effects of the mass media. The research was given financial support by both the National Association of Broadcasters and the University of North Carolina. The concept of the agenda-setting function of the press was not the initial thrust of the research, but within a short time, they decided to study it as a major hypothesis in connection with the 1968 presidental campaign (Hubert Humphrey versus Richard Nixon).

## The Exploratory Study

To find out whether there were any grounds for assuming an agenda-setting function of the mass media, a study was designed that would compare media content with voters' beliefs about the presidential campaign. More specifically, the research compared what a sample of voters (in Chapel Hill, North Carolina) *said* were the key issues of the presidential campaign with the *actual content* of the news media to which they were exposed during the campaign. It was a simple design; essentially it was an exploratory effect to see if the agenda-setting hypothesis had any future. It was not a particularly large study. It focused on political news concerning the candidates and issues presented by television, newspapers, and newsmagazines concerning the candidates and issues over a 24-day period in the fall of 1968. This ended early in October, shortly before the election. It also probed the beliefs of 100 respondents concerning the relative importance of the issues of the campaign.

These respondents were selected randomly from lists of registered voters in five of the precincts in the community. These five were used to try to make the sample reflect the economic, racial, and social makeup of the community. A further factor in the selection of the final sample was that it included only voters who had not yet definitely decided how to vote. The grounds for this was the assumption that it was this category that was still open or susceptible to the influence of campaign information. Thus, it was a purposive rather than a random sample, concentrating only on undecided voters. This meant that broad generalizations to the community as a whole, or even to other types of voters, would be unwarranted. Nevertheless, for exploratory purposes, this was an appropriate strategy. If there was no agenda-setting effect among this "most susceptible" category of people, then the whole idea would seem to have little merit.

These respondents were asked to explain what they saw from their own personal perspective as the key issues of the campaign, regardless of what particular candidates happened to be saying at the moment. These were the main data used for comparison with the relative emphasis given the issues by the news media.

The media studied included five newspapers, two network TV news broadcasts, and two weekly newsmagazines that reported on the political campaign to the residents of Chapel Hill. Careful definitions were provided to identify what was and what was not a "major" or "minor" report in these media on some aspect of the campaign. For television, a major story had to be one of at least 45 seconds or more in length, or one of the three lead stories in a particular broadcast. A major story for newspapers was defined as any that appeared on the front page or any that appeared under a three-column headline in which at least a third of the story (and a minimum of five paragraphs) was devoted to political news. For newsmagazines, a major story had to be more than one column or any item that appeared in the lead at the beginning of the news section of the magazine. Minor items in these media were stories of a political nature that were smaller in time and space, or less prominent in positioning than the major items.

## Refining the Hypothesis

The findings showed that even among the major stories presented in the media, much of the news about a presidential campaign has little to do with the issues. A lot deals with the candidates themselves and assessments of who might win or lose. Nevertheless, an abundance of issue-related news information was provided to the community under study, and it was possible to sort out the relative emphasis given to such topics as foreign policy, law and order, fiscal policy, public welfare, civil rights, and so on. A rank order of emphasis of these topics was worked out for the various candidates and for the political parties. Thus, the manner in which the issues of the campaign had been presented by the news media in both major and minor stories was relatively clear, and a rank order of relative emphasis could be made with some precision.

When the judgments of the sample of voters as to the order of importance of these issues was compared to the relative emphasis given to them by the media, a startlingly high relationship was found. In fact, the correlation between relative media emphasis and voters' beliefs about the importance of the same list of issues was +0.976! Few correlations of that magnitude are found in social research. McCombs and Shaw concluded from their data that

> In short, the data suggest a very strong relationship between the emphasis placed on different campaign issues by the media (reflecting to a considerable degree the emphasis by the candidates) and the judgments of the voters as to the salience and importance of various campaign topics.[9]

There was, in other words, a close correspondence between the world outside, as constructed by news media, and the pictures in the heads of the sample of voters studied. Furthermore, the representation of that world outside (the actual emphasis given to the issues by the candidates) was not particularly distorted. There was clear evidence of an agenda-setting function of the news media. They had not indicated *what* the voters should think about the issues, but they did indicate which issues were to be thought *about* and which were given the greatest *emphasis* by the candidates. The voters themselves perceived those issues in that rank order and adopted it as their own.

In interpreting this extraordinary correlation, one must keep in mind the sampling conditions of the exploratory study. If respondents had been selected on a random basis from the community, the politically inactive would have been included as well as those who had bothered to become registered voters. Furthermore, as we saw in *The People's Choice* (see chapter 4), there are abundant grounds to assume that large proportions of voters make up their minds for whom they will vote early in the campaign. An agenda-setting effect would be much less likely among such citizens. The citizen who refrains from a choice until all the issues have been carefully examined (via news reports) is in a minority, but the sample in the exploratory study attempted to focus on just such individuals. Therefore, the significance of the impressive correlation for the larger population remained to be determined. It was clear to everyone concerned that additional research would have to be completed. In any case, there were certainly adequate grounds for hypothesizing that an agenda-setting effect of some kind would be found.

## THE CHARLOTTE STUDY

Four years after the 1968 election, Americans were faced with another national campaign to select a president. This time it was the incumbent Richard M. Nixon who was being challenged by the liberal Democrat George McGovern. The 1972 election provided an important opportunity to follow up the exploratory study on agenda-setting. In the fall of 1971, a series of workshops to design new studies were held at the University of North Carolina under the leadership of Donald L. Shaw and Maxwell E. McCombs.

These researchers were convinced that the most appropriate strategy for the accumulation of scientific knowledge in the field was *programmatic* research; that is, one study on a particular topic should lead to another that pushes the frontiers beyond those revealed by the first. In this way, the development of knowledge will be both accumulative and increasingly sophisticated. That was never the pattern in the pioneering efforts in mass communication, as researchers jumped from one topic to another, depending on a variety of factors. In more recent years, with more sources willing to provide funds, programmatic research has been on the increase, and the Charlotte study of agenda-setting provides an excellent example.

Essentially, Shaw and McCombs brought together a research team that designed and completed a panel study that focused on both media presentation of the political issues and voter perceptions of the significance of those issues. Thus, it was of a larger scale than the 1968 Chapel Hill study, but its central focus remained on the agenda-setting functions of the news media during a presidential campaign. This provided continuity with the exploratory study, but at the same time, it provided a number of new perspectives on this kind of influence of mass communication. The nature of the study, its overall objectives, research strategies, modes of analysis, and findings are set forth in a book published in 1977. This work, *The Emergence of American Political Issues: The Agenda-Setting Function of the Press,* prepared by Shaw and McCombs in association with seven other members of their research team, was the first book to attempt to formulate systematically and present extensive data on the agenda-setting hypothesis.[10]

## The Research Objectives

Like most of the complex studies reviewed in early chapters, the Charlotte study had multiple objectives, although each was related to the underlying process of agenda-setting. In order to understand the various analyses and the results obtained, each of these research goals needs to be understood. The paragraphs below provide a brief overview of the objectives, and each will be discussed in more detail as the findings are summarized.

*Defining the Concept.* One problem was to refine the definition of the concept and state the relationships between independent and dependent variables more formally. Up to this point, it had been a rather loose generalization indicating that correspondence could be expected between the relative emphasis given to a set of issues by the press and the personal salience assigned to those same issues on the part of voters. That idea was certainly supported by the Chapel Hill data, but the agenda-setting needed to be explicated—that is, systematically examined—with every aspect made explicit and clear.

*Information Sources for Personal Agendas.* An important objective was to try to understand better where people actually obtained information so as to decide on a rank order of salience of the issues of the campaign. Obviously, they obtained much of their information from news and political advertisements presented by the media. But in addition there was the question of other people. That source had emerged in an unexpected manner in *The People's Choice,* when it was concluded that there was a two-step flow of information and influence from the media to opinion leaders and then on by word of mouth to other segments of the population who had little firsthand exposure to the political campaign. Was that also the case for agenda-setting? Did political discussions with friends, family, or neighbors form or modify a voter's conceptions of the salience of the issues? Gaining an understanding of the role of interpersonal communication about the issues was a major objective.

*Sequencing over Time as a Major Variable.*    The influence of time sequence on personal agenda setting as a dependent variable was still another. In other words, does the order of importance of issues suggested by the news media at one point in time have a continuing influence so that it shapes voters' beliefs about the importance of those issues at a later time? Modern correlational techniques can provide answers to such questions, and unraveling time relationships was one of the objectives of the Charlotte study.

*The Personal Characteristics of Voters.*    What kind of people are most influenced in the agenda-setting process, and why do some more than others turn to the media for information about a presidential campaign? Are those with high levels of uncertainty about the issues, plus a need for orientation, most likely to give close attention to the campaign? If so, will they be most influenced by the media in forming their personal rankings of the importance of the varied issues? There is also the question of influence on actual voting behavior. It is one thing to form a hierarchy of importance that one attaches to the campaign issues, but it is another to be motivated to go to the polls because some of those issues are seen as critical. Finally, there was a special question of the young voter in the 1972 campaign. The voting age had just been lowered from 21 to 18. How many younger voters actually turned out, and how did they feel about the issues? These questions of individual needs, motivation, and age were all personal characteristics explored in the Charlotte research.

*Politics and Agenda Setting.*    Finally, when all the data are in, what is the overall picture? How important is agenda setting in the American political process? Is it another of those negative effects about which we should be concerned, or does it provide benefits to individuals and society? Is it a process that is independent of other social and personal influences of the media, or is it a part of larger and more general relationships that exist between the media and society?

Each of these objectives provides a focus for understanding why the particular data of the study were gathered and examines the implications of the results. But before those tasks can be undertaken, it is necessary to look at where the research was done and among what kinds of subjects.

## The Research Site

Charlotte, North Carolina, was selected with specific criteria in mind. For one thing, it is located some distance from major metropolitan communities. It is about halfway between Washington, D.C., and Atlanta, Georgia. At the time, this meant that it was served by a restricted number of media that could be effectively monitored during the research period. In fact, there were only two newspapers and the usual three TV networks. With its 1970 population of 354,000, it was large enough to be diverse but small enough so that samples could be drawn of the entire population of voters.

For another, Charlotte was not a sleepy Southern town. During the previous decade, many changes had occurred: It had grown rapidly, and indeed, a substantial proportion of its population were transient. Average family income had risen sharply, and many new businesses had made the city their regional headquarters. People moved in and out as young families came in from the countryside and as workers and executives took and left jobs in local branches of national companies and industries. At an earlier time, it was mainly a city of single-family dwellings, but by the early 1970s, a third of its inhabitants lived in apartments.

Finally, unlike many areas of the South, Charlotte was not a Democrat stronghold. In fact, during the previous 20 years, the entire county had generally gone Republican. In the election under study, President Nixon won easily over his challenger.

## The Panel Design and Sample

The agenda-setting hypothesis assumes that there is some causal relationship between the selective emphasis given to a list of issues by the media and the development of corresponding audience beliefs about their hierarchy of relative importance. The nature of this influence is not understood, but there is clearly a time factor involved. The media must do their part first, and the influence on the audience comes later. It was for this reason that a panel design was selected for the Charlotte project. Panel designs are based on the idea that a sample of respondents will be interviewed at one point in time and then interviewed again later, perhaps repeatedly. Earlier research (*The People's Choice*) had convincingly demonstrated that fears about a Hawthorne effect were without foundation. That is, the fact of being repeatedly observed had little influence on the behavior of those under study.

The original sample was selected from the official voter registration rolls of Mecklenburg County, in which Charlotte is located. The Board of Elections supplied tapes containing more than 150,000 names, and a computer program was used to select those to be included in the study. As is frequently the case, problems were encountered with this sampling frame. Murphy's Law dictates that if something can go wrong, it will. The law prevails in research as elsewhere. Some people on the list had died, and others had moved away, but these changes were not reflected in the voter registration records. Thus, the transient character of the city prevented the researchers from developing a truly random sample of registered voters.

The plan had been to interview the panel of respondents in June and then interview the same people again in October, shortly before the election. Still a third rather brief interview by telephone was scheduled just after the election was over. But when it came time to actually contact the people whose names were in the sample for their first interview, many could not be located. Aside form those who had died or moved, some were simply never home. A few refused to participate. But in spite of these commonly encountered problems, a total of 380 voters were successfully interviewed in June.

When the interviewers went back again in October, Murphy's Law struck again. An unusually large number of people had moved away. In fact, only 230 of the original 380 could be found. This was a loss of 39 percent, which was serious indeed. The researchers discovered furthermore that only a small number of black voters were included in their original sample (there was no way of knowing this ahead of time, as the official list had no racial identifiers). Therefore, before the October interviews, 41 black voters were added to the panel and interviewed with the June as well as the October questionnaires. About half of these (24) were included in the postelection interview. Generally, then, the basic analysis of the Charlotte study was based on 227 registered voters who were interviewed three times, plus 24 black voters who were added in October and also contacted in November. For many of the analyses of findings, the panel of 227 that was interviewed all three times provided the basic data on the agenda-setting role of the mass media.

The researchers were very much aware of the limitations of their sample and did not regard it as representative of either the community as a whole or the population of registered voters that remained in the county. Furthermore, they were concerned about the effects of the attrition on the characteristics of the sample between interviews. To see if this attrition had introduced serious biases, they made a systematic study of the percentage distributions within those who were interviewed on all three occasions. As it turned out, there were only trivial differences between the percentages who were in various categories of age, sex, race, income, education, and political party affiliation. In other words, in spite of Murphy's Law, their final panel design survived and yielded useful data, even though generalizations to larger populations would have to be limited.

## Findings

The objectives of the Charlotte study have already been set forth in summary. That overview provides a convenient framework for discussing the results that emerged from the research findings. The presentation of those findings in *The Emergence of American Political Issues* was made in ten chapters, each devoted to particular issues, and each prepared by one or two of the nine members of the research team. To bring these complex data into a simplified framework, the sections below attempt to summarize those findings and many of their interpretations within the five research objectives set forth earlier.

***Objective 1: Clarifying the Definition.***   In some ways it would be appropriate to address this objective last, as the data from the Charlotte study undoubtedly provides for sharpening and explicating the agenda-setting hypothesis. But since this objective served as a bridge between the earlier formulation of the hypothesis, developed mainly within the context of the Chapel Hill study, and prior, less focused research, it is appropriate to address the issue of clarification first.

It is in the first two chapters of their book that Shaw and McCombs demonstrate their commitment to a programmatic approach and systematic theory development in their study of the influence of mass communication on personal and social life. They set the study of agenda setting within a framework of accumulating, changing, and evolving theories of mass communication. They make note of the view that continues to dominate the thinking and fears of the public— that the media are very powerful. They then review the major changes in thinking that have characterized media theorists and researchers who had to interpret the findings of their investigation during the late 1940s and the 1950s. As we have noted earlier, they did not confirm the existence of powerful effects. Thus, there was a transition from a belief in all-powerful media to one of minimal consequences. This interpretation of media effects was well entrenched by the beginning of the 1960s.

Shaw and McCombs point out the (widely accepted) conclusion that the earlier research led to a belief in minimal effects because of its strategies of investigation and because of its commitment to a particular conception of the manner in which mass communication presumably achieved its influences on people's behavior. In brief, the commitment of many earlier mass communication theorists was to try to understand the influence of the mass media (particularly in the area of political effects) as generated by the following sequence: First, the media provoked among its audiences an *awareness* of the issues. Second, it provided a body of *information* to the members of that audience. Third, this information provided the basis for *attitude formation or change* on the part of those who acquired it. And fourth, the *attitudes shaped behavior* among those involved in the sequence.

Much of the earlier research, Shaw and McCombs noted, had bypassed the first two steps in this sequence and had focused on the attitudinal and behavioral influences that were presumed to take place. When it began to be clear that those kinds of influences were very limited, the baby almost got thrown out with the bath. Instead of advocating that researchers go back to study more intensively the awareness and informational effects of the media, those theorists who subscribed to the law of minimal effects simply declared that the media had virtually no influence on people at all. Needless to say, they were wrong.

Although Shaw and McCombs do not discuss it, it can be pointed out that an important factor that misled earlier communication theorists was the great popularity of the attitude concept. It virtually dominated social psychology from the time it was introduced early in the century. In many ways it filled the theoretical vacuum left when the older instinct concept was abandoned. In particular, there was a firm belief that inner feelings dictated action—that there was a powerful correspondence between attitudes and behavior. In more recent decades, the relationship between attitudes and behavior has been shown to be far less certain. People often behave according to the requirements of a social situation and the expectations of people important to them rather than according to their private convictions.[11] Thus, the commitment of communication theorists to the attitude-behavior paradigm was doomed from the start. Even if the media *had* proved capable of changing attitudes, there was no assurance that people would obligingly alter their behavior.

Shaw and McCombs then place the agenda-setting hypothesis squarely in a cognitive rather than an affective framework. They note that the first two steps in the old awareness-information–attitude-behavior sequence are where research attention is likely to be most fruitful. The media *do* call our attention to events and issues via the flow of news. The *do* provide information about those matters. And people *do* learn about them by attending to the media. The question is not whether attitudes and ultimately behavior are then changed. One need not make such affective assumptions. The more significant question is what people *believe* to be true about those events in the news, with which they can seldom or never have firsthand experience. It is these beliefs about the nature of reality that will guide their actions. As W. I. Thomas pointed out in 1923, people act upon their "definition of the situation." If they believe a situation to be real, they will act as though it is real.[12] In fact, as was pointed out at the beginning of the present chapter, philosophers, sociologists, psychologists, and others have discussed that aspect of human behavior for a very long time.

From a general theoretical point of view, the insistence of Shaw and McCombs on a return to the cognitive issues centering on the awareness- and information-supplying functions of the media has an important consequence. It provides an effective explication and clarification of the broad theoretical paradigm in which the agenda-setting function of the media is located. It becomes one of the processes by which the media in modern society participate in the *social construction of reality* for the populations that they serve. As the authors put it:

> The agenda-setting function of mass communication clearly falls in this new tradition of cognitive outcomes of mass communication. Perhaps more than any other aspect of our environment, the political arena—all those issues and persons about whom we hold opinions and knowledge—is second-hand reality. Especially in national politics, we have little personal or direct contact. Our knowledge comes primarily from the mass media. For the most part, we know only those aspects of national politics considered newsworthy enough for transmission through the mass media.[13]

Thus, the study of the agenda-setting function as conceptualized by Shaw and McCombs returns research on the influence of mass media to the issues suggested by such pioneer public opinion theorists as Charles Horton Cooley, James Bryce, and Walter Lippmann. It focuses our attention on the process by which the media play a significant part in generating a common culture—in this case, a consensus of shared beliefs about certain political aspects of our environment that play a significant part in bringing us together at election time.

How, then, did Shaw and McCombs define agenda setting for the purposes of research? They suggested that until a body of research is generated to provide a much larger base of findings, it should remain as a *hypothesis.*

> This book examines that agenda-setting power of the press, the hypothesis that the press itself has some power to establish an agenda of

political issues which both the candidates and the voters come to regard as important.[14]

The hypothesis suggests an influence not only on voters but on the candidates as well.

In terms of independent versus dependent variables, the press is clearly seen in the causal role. Yet, this should not be taken too literally. The intention is not to portray those who rule the media as making calculated decisions to manipulate the public. The hierarchies of emphasis and importance attached to political topics and issues by the press are seen as an inevitable part of the daily processing and presenting of the news:

> Each day editors and news directors—the gate-keepers in the news media systems—must decide which items to pass and which to reject. Furthermore, the items passed through the gate are not treated equally when presented to the audience. Some are used at length, others severely cut. Some are lead-off items in a newscast. Others follow much later. Newspapers clearly state the value they place on the salience of an item through headline size and placement within the newspaper— anywhere from the lead item on page one to placement at the bottom of a column on page 66.[15]

Thus, the causal chain clearly includes the gatekeepers who make the decisions about giving greater relative emphasis to one story versus another.

But gatekeepers do not act in a vacuum. They process the news according to well-understood criteria that are related in part to their socially derived conceptions of the proper role of the press in society and to the practical necessity of attracting and holding their audiences. Thus, the causal chain becomes very complicated when one attempts to sort out the independent variables that result in the differential emphasis given to the news. In fact, gatekeeping, media agenda setting, and the construction of individual agendas by members of the public are part of a complex social system. That system includes at least three classes of variables: those that account for selecting a particular event as a news item; those that govern the processing and delivering of the news in a given pattern of selection and emphasis; and those that determine who will be exposed and how they will interpret the media content:

Key factors that shape the agenda provided by the media are the values and beliefs used by reporters as part of the surveillance process. What events should be considered news? The nature of the medium is another consideration. Newspapers can report in depth while television can devote only a few minutes at most to an important story. Editors provide another level of screening. They have to select from available stories what they can fit into the time or space that they have at their disposal. Sometimes they must cut a story or move it to a back page, even though they may regard it as important. Sometimes there just isn't enough news. This means that less important stories can come to occupy the front page or the first slot on the broadcast. Finally, conceptions of audience interest, profit making, and even the social organization of the news industry have been recognized as factors that shape content of the news and the levels of importance suggested by the media. Thus, the causal chain that sets the media agenda is a complex one indeed.

When the audience receives the messages contained in the news, the process of personal agenda setting results in the assignment or assumption of differential weights of importance. Those weights or degrees of salience are derived in part from the cues provided by the news media. If a story is the lead item in the broadcast, on the front page, or set off by conspicuous headlines, its degree of salience is probably perceived as high. If the cues have the opposite characteristics, the weights and level of salience are more likely to be low. Patterns of attention are subject to variation according to the audience member's needs for orientation, interest in given topics, and other individual characteristics.

One of the features of the agenda-setting hypothesis that makes it attractive as a research topic is that the independent and dependent variables stated in the hypothesis itself can be *measured.* This is not always the case when studying the communication systems that result in a social construction of reality. The cues assigned to a story by the media can be measured by content analyses, and beliefs about salience on the part of the audience can also be measured by appropriate questionnaires. This makes it possible to *test* the agenda-setting hypothesis in a relatively straightforward manner. The degree of correlation between the agenda produced by the media and that perceived by the audience provides the basis for deciding whether there has been such an influence.

Generally, then, agenda setting can best be studied as a hypothesis that relates specific independent and dependent variables. Stated in hypothesis form, it appears to be deceptively simple until it can be seen as a relationship embedded in a complex web of factors that produce both gatekeeping and audience response. Even more broadly, it can also be seen as one part of the social construction of reality or, more specifically, the social construction of shared meanings that takes place as a result of both interpersonal and mass communication in modern society.

***Object 2: Information Sources for Personal Agendas.***    The agenda-setting hypothesis began as a relationship between media presentations of the news and personal views of the importance of issues. This is still its central focus. However, there is also a need to consider another form of media content—political advertising by the candidates—as a source from which impressions of the relative importance of issues can be formed. In addition, there is the complicating factor of interpersonal communication. People talk to others about what they have read in their newspapers or seen on television about the campaign and the issues. In other words, news, advertising, and personal discussions are separate sources of ideas about the nature and salience of issues in a campaign. Each can be examined separately.

What were the issues that were presented via the news media in Charlotte? Actually, the specific list of issues and their relative emphasis differed somewhat for the various media. The *Charlotte Observer* presented and emphasized one agenda. Each of the three TV networks presented its own version. Yet each of these media offered at least some information on all of the principal issues that were discussed by the candidates during the campaign. The big issue was Vietnam. The war was constantly in the news during the entire campaign period. As in every election, the economy was important to the voters. A third topic of high news value during the time was the national controversy over school busing. This issue was important locally as the school system tried to work out an acceptable level of integration. Concern over youth-drugs-morals was also substantial. It was a time of communes, counterculture, youthful rebellion, and, for many young people, a sharp change in sexual mores. These matters were often distressing to the relatively conservative voters of Charlotte. Foreign relations was another important topic, especially with the Soviet Union and China. After decades, the Chinese were just beginning to reestablish ties with the West. It was also a time when Watergate was a national preoccupation, along with its implications of government corruption. Such matters were troublesome to voters in Charlotte. Finally, the environmental movement had blossomed a short time earlier, and a major issue was concern over environmental pollution.

These seven, then, were the official agenda that was identified as central to the media coverage of the campaign. There were other topics that were in the news, such as the personalities of the candidates, the events of the campaign itself, other kinds of international events, and an endless flow of general campaign analysis. If we leave these aside, the relative emphasis given to the seven main issues by the news media under study can be seen in Table 12.1.

Table 12.1 shows that there were substantial differences between the levels of emphasis given to the issues in the media agenda as it was offered in June and October. This is to be expected as the candidates worked out and presented their positions. However, the correlations between the media themselves are high

**TABLE 12.1** The media agenda: Percentages of campaign coverage devoted to various issues by network news programs and by a local newspaper during June and October

| Issue | ABC | | CBS | | NBC | | *Charlotte Observer* | |
|---|---|---|---|---|---|---|---|---|
| | June | Oct | June | Oct | June | Oct | June | Oct |
| Vietnam | 27.1 | 20.7 | 27.0 | 19.4 | 23.4 | 17.9 | 16.5 | 21.3 |
| Youth-drugs | 1.0 | 2.1 | 0.0 | 1.6 | 1.4 | 1.7 | 3.3 | 2.7 |
| Economy | 4.0 | 14.5 | 4.4 | 15.9 | 3.7 | 12.1 | 6.9 | 3.8 |
| Busing | 2.5 | 4.5 | 2.2 | 3.2 | 1.9 | 1.2 | 1.9 | 1.6 |
| USSR-China | 3.0 | 0.3 | 2.6 | 1.9 | 5.1 | 3.5 | 4.1 | 4.3 |
| Watergate | 2.0 | 9.3 | 1.8 | 6.5 | 4.7 | 8.4 | 1.9 | 9.4 |
| Environment | 4.5 | 0.7 | 4.0 | 1.0 | 2.8 | 2.6 | 6.2 | 4.7 |

SOURCE: This table is based on information from Table 3-2 from Donald L. Shaw and Maxwell E. McCombs, *The Emergence of American Political Issues: The Agenda-Setting Function of the Press* (St. Paul, Minn.: West Publishing Co., 1974), p. 38.

(Table 12.2). In other words, the media were presenting a fairly uniform agenda to the voters.

The agenda-setting hypothesis predicts that exposure to the news will bring some degree of correspondence between the levels of importance assigned to the issues during the campaign by voters and the levels of emphasis given to those issues by the media. This is presumably a long-range influence. However, the design of the Charlotte study provided for only a four-month period in which to observe such an effect. Nevertheless, correlations were calculated between the agenda set by the media versus that of the voters in June and again in October. Evidence for such agenda setting would be an increase in the media-voter correlation over the period. As Table 12.3 shows, by that criterion there was evidence of an agenda-setting effect. For the two TV networks, the data indicate that there was an increase in agenda correspondence between June and October. Furthermore, that correspondence was substantially higher for those who viewed television the most. The pattern is different for the newspaper, where correspondence correlations showed a mixed pattern.

The general weight of evidence suggests that the agenda emphasized by the news media became the agenda of importance among the voters. The larger increase in correspondence among those who used television the most supports the conclusion. On the other hand, the data for the newspaper are difficult to

**TABLE 12.2** Correlations between the agendas as presented by the separate media

| | June | | | | October | | | |
|---|---|---|---|---|---|---|---|---|
| | **ABC** | **CBS** | **NBC** | *Ch. Ob.* | **ABC** | **CBS** | **NBC** | *Ch. Ob.* |
| ABC | — | .96 | .57 | .90 | — | .89 | .64 | .64 |
| CBS | | — | .61 | .94 | | — | .75 | .64 |
| NBC | | | — | .45 | | | — | .93 |
| Ch. Ob. | | | | — | | | | — |

SOURCE: These Spearman Rank-Order correlations are from Table 3-3 in Donald L. Shaw and Maxwell E. McCombs, *The Emergence of American Political Issues: The Agenda-Setting Function of the Press* (St. Paul, Minn.: West Publishing Company, 1974), p. 40.

**TABLE 12.3** Correlations between media and personal agendas in June and October

| | CBS | | | NBC | | | *Charlotte Observer* | | |
|---|---|---|---|---|---|---|---|---|---|
| **TV Use** | **June** | **Oct** | **Change** | **June** | **Oct** | **Change** | **June** | **Oct** | **Change** |
| Great deal or some | 0.33 | 0.68 | +0.35 | 0.21 | 0.64 | +0.43 | 0.39 | 0.28 | −0.11 |
| Little or none | 0.41 | 0.60 | +0.19 | 0.05 | 0.20 | +0.15 | 0.63 | 0.23 | −0.40 |
| Difference | −0.08 | 0.08 | +0.16 | 0.16 | 0.44 | +0.28 | −0.24 | 0.05 | +0.29 |

SOURCE: This table is based on Spearman Rank-Order correlations from Table 3-5 in Donald L. Shaw and Maxwell E. McCombs. *The Emergence of American Political Issues: The Agenda-Setting Function of the Press* (St. Paul, Minn.: West Publishing Company, 1974), p. 47.

interpret. Even though there was an increase in agenda correspondence between medium and voters as a whole, the pattern between heavy and light users was the reverse of that for television.

Candidate advertising is another potential source for agenda information. Little is known about its effect. Paid political advertising on television by the candidates during presidential campaigns has been criticized since it began. No candidate feels that he can dare ignore it, but many are uncomfortable with the idea that it provides an emphasis on personality and image-building rather than an intelligent analysis of the issues. Critics agree and maintain that the candidate with the fattest pocketbook has the best chance of winning through the use of televised ads. Nevertheless, TV advertising has become a central part of presidential elections.

While candidates cannot control the manner in which the news media report on them and their discussions of the issues, they can control their advertising campaigns. Therefore, paid TV advertisements provide an index of the *candidate's* issue agenda. The degree to which these candidate agendas correspond with voter agendas can be assessed, and that correspondence can show if there is an agenda-setting effect brought about by the advertising. There is, of course, the problem of sorting out the influence of the ads versus that of the news media if both have similar agendas. Nevertheless, the content of all candidate advertising was analyzed for a three-week period in October during the time when the sample was being interviewed. The frequencies with which certain issues were discussed in both the Nixon and the McGovern ads were calculated so as to obtain candidate agendas for each. These candidate agendas were not identical with those presented by the news media, so the problem of overlap was minimized. The question is, To what degree did the issues emphasized in candidate advertising reflect the order of emphasis as perceived by the voters? In other words, did the advertisements influence voters in setting personal agendas?

One important condition is whether or not the voters actually saw the advertisements. Few people deliberately seek out political advertisement on television, so exposure was incidental to viewing for other reasons. As might be expected, those voters who used television a great deal for political news were more likely to have seen the ads than those who used it lightly or not at all.

Overall, the correspondence between voters' agendas and candidates' advertised agendas was low. For the Nixon ads it was +0.11 and for McGovern, +0.37. However, another kind of influence was observed. The advertisements tended to create "affect," that is, positive or negative feelings about the candidates. The numerous Nixon ads led some to such affective responses, but it was the McGovern ads that created the greatest amount of positive or negative feelings. In fact, the results indicated that many people became more negative toward the senator after viewing his ads. This may have been a factor in his defeat.

A third major source of information about a presidential election campaign is other people. From discussions about the candidates and the issues, it is possible to develop a personal agenda based on the interpretations provided by friends, relatives, and other individuals. This may or may not be identical to that supplied by the press.

Included in the interviews with the Charlotte voter sample were items probing how often and to whom they talked about politics. As it turned out, the respondents engaged in a considerable amount of political discussion with family members, friends, and others. Furthermore, as the campaign went on, the proportion who were involved in such interpersonal exchanges increased, from 40 percent in June to more than 60 percent by October.

The researchers found that people discussed politics more with members of their family than with friends or others. This was especially true of females. However, the category that was most involved in such discussions was younger males of higher income and education. Nevertheless, virtually everyone had some involvement in political conversations. Those who talked the most were also likely to be the highest users of both television and newspapers as sources of political information. There was, therefore, an overlap between the two communication systems—mass media and interpersonal contacts.

The findings on the influence of political discussions were mixed. There was an especially high correlation between the frequent talkers and the agenda provided by the newspaper (0.83). On the other hand, correlations with the agenda supplied by TV news were low. Therefore, in spite of minor support for the hypothesis that participation in discussions of politics is related to agenda setting, the evidence was ambiguous.

In summary, the major information source for personal agenda setting was the news of the campaign as reported by the TV networks and to some extent, the newspaper. Paid political advertisements on television may help voters develop feelings about the candidates as individuals, but they do not appear to have a strong influence in shaping personal agendas of the issues. Interpersonal discussions of the candidates and the issues may play a part, but the best conclusion is that the press plays the larger role. Shaw and McCombs concluded that ". . . both the press and other people help share our ideas. Only sometimes the press seems to shout a bit louder. Or perhaps it is only more repetitious."[16]

***Objective 3: Time Sequences in the Agenda-Setting Process.***    Agenda setting is defined as a process that takes place over time. The assumption is that after voters pay extended attention to the rank order of emphasis given to issues in the press, the agenda of the individual will increasingly resemble that rank order. This implies a causal process. However, as is perennially the case, showing mere correlation between press agenda and voter agenda at a given point in time does not allow a causal inference. It is entirely possible that the interests of the voters play a part in shaping what the press will emphasize. Thus, it is conceivable that the causal influence is in the opposite direction. Which is the chicken and which the egg? Does the press set the voter agenda, or does the voter agenda set that of the press? The fact that they are correlated is important, but it is not conclusive in understanding causal direction.

One way to unravel the chicken/egg question is to see what comes first and what seems to follow at a later time. A rather simple procedure called "cross-lagged correlation" can answer such questions. The idea is rather straightforward, and it can be illustrated by examining the times shown in Figure 12.1. Time 1 is June, when the first interviews were conducted and the newspaper's agenda was first analyzed. Time 2 is October, when the second interviews were completed and the newspaper's agenda was again assessed. As can be seen, the newspaper's agendas are correlated (0.43) across the two time periods. The agendas of the voters are even more correlated (0.94) between times 1 and 2. There are also correlations between media and voter agendas at each of the time periods (0.46 and 0.10, respectively). Thus far, these data do not provide for causal inferences.

The key to understanding the cross-lagged correlation as evidence of a causal relationship is to look at the two diagonals as well as the above correlations in a total configuration. It can be seen that the relationship between the newspaper's agenda at time 1 (June) and the voters' agenda at time 2 (October) is greater than that of the diagonal running the other way. The comparison is 0.51 versus 0.19, with a difference of 0.32. Statistically speaking, this means that the newspaper's agenda offered in June accounts for much more variance in the voters' agenda in October than does the reverse relationship. It is clear that the voters' agenda in June had little in common with the newspaper's agenda of October (little variance accounted for). Thus, there is no causal relationship implied between June voters' agenda and the later agenda of the newspaper. The reverse is true, as revealed by the other diagonal. Also, the 0.51 correlation in that diagonal is larger than either the 0.46 or the 0.10 relationship between newspaper and voters on either end of the diagram. The bottom line is that such a configuration of correlations provides evidence to infer a causal relationship

**FIGURE 12.1**   Cross-lagged correlations between newspaper's and voters' agendas

SOURCE: These Spearman Rho coefficients were obtained from Figure 6-1 in Donald L. Shaw and Maxwell E. McCombs, *The Emergence of American Political Issues: The Agenda-Setting Function of the Press* (St. Paul, Minn.: West Publishing, 1974), p. 91.

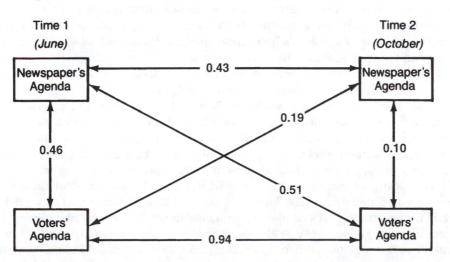

between media content in June and voters' ranking of the importance of the issues in October.

While the pattern of correlations shown in Figure 12. 1 shows rather clearly the influence of the newspaper on voters' agendas over the four-month period, the same pattern was not found for television. If similar diagrams were constructed for both CBS and NBC network news, the results would not show an agenda-setting influence across time. Thus, the newspaper appeared to play a clear role in shaping voters' agendas during the period studied, but television did not. This type of cross-lagged correlation has become one of the standard ways of looking at agenda setting at different points in time. In the Charlotte study, it is clear that each of the media did not have a similar effect.

***Objective 4: Personal Characteristics and Agenda Setting.***    In the search for psychological explanations of agenda setting, one of the immediate questions is, Why do some voters attend to media content more than others do? For the authors, it appeared that there were three major factors that influenced such different patterns of exposure. First was the voter's level of interest in the content, which is a function of perceived *relevance* to his or her concerns; second is his or her degree of *uncertainty* concerning the issues contained in that content; and finally, there is the matter of the *effort* required to locate a reliable source of relevant information. The first two of these factors—perceived relevance and degree of uncertainty—were incorporated into a concept that McCombs and his associates called *need for orientation.* Need for orientation, then, is a personality factor that presumably leads an individual to seek exposure to media content. The simple hypothesis can be formed that the greater such a need, the greater the attention. This, in turn, would lead to an increase in agenda-setting influences. The concept need not incorporate "effort," because mass media are so ubiquitous that this can be regarded as a constant that does not vary much from one individual to the next.

These considerations permit the development of a typology of patterns in the antecedents that lead individuals to have high, medium, or low needs for orientation. Figure 12.2 shows how these antecedents are related. Low relevance, for example, leads logically to a low need for orientation. High relevance and high uncertainty, on the other hand, lead to a high need for orientation. Moderate need for orientation has a high-low pattern of antecedents.

Data from the Charlotte study confirm that even when the relevance and uncertainty factors are measured in a variety of ways, differing levels of need for orientation are related to levels of exposure to media content and to the strength of the agenda-setting effect. The typology shown in Figure 12.2, in other words, provides a useful guide in predicting media usage and agenda-setting influences.

Five scales of perceived relevance of issues and four scales of uncertainty were used to measure these factors. Overwhelmingly, those voters with high needs for orientation ranked highest on media usage. These with moderate needs were, in turn, above those with low needs for orientation. The results were virtually uniform across all five scales. The scales also correlated in large part with

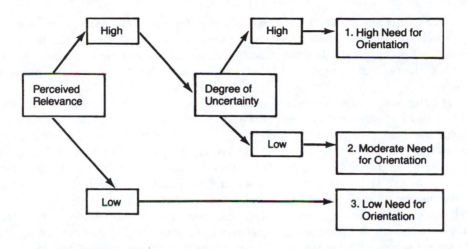

**FIGURE 12.2** Relevance and uncertainty as antecedents of need for orientation

SOURCE: This diagram is based on Figure 7-1 from Donald L. Shaw and Maxwell E. McCombs, *The Emergence of American Political Issues: The Agenda-Setting Function of the Press* (St. Paul, Minn.: West Publishing, 1974), p. 40.

the agenda-setting effect of the media, although the evidence was not as clear in every instance. The data on the 126 comparisons that were made for both the newspaper and television and for both June and October are too numerous to present in the present summary. However, the overall results present a substantial picture of support for the general hypothesis that need for orientation (combining perceived relevance of media content and degree of uncertainty) leads to media exposure and then to agenda-setting influences.

***Objective 5: Assessing the Political Role of Agenda Setting.*** The process of agenda setting was initially conceptualized, researched, and formalized within the context of election campaigns, voting, and mass media reports of political issues. The Charlotte study was a scientific effort designed to be programmatic— that is, to build upon previous research on agenda setting. However, in many ways its subject matter is uniquely traditional. It looks at the relationship between the Fourth Estate, those in charge of the political process, and those who are governed. Thus, agenda setting focuses on the venerable idea of the "power of the press" as an influence in politics—an old concept indeed. In fact, Shaw and McCombs suggest that our contemporary mass media, and specifically the news industries, play a dual role in shaping political activities:

> This means that the mass media are the major artisans of our popular political culture, of what the masses perceive to be political reality and the political concerns of the day. It also means that the mass media are major shapers of our elite political culture. Witness the role of the elite press as a source of information among major decision-makers.[17]

In other words, agenda setting is a part of the communication processes in society by which individuals develop and share political meanings. Specifically, it relates media and voters as the latter engage in the social construction of reality in the area of election campaigns, candidate images, and the dimensions of political issues.

At the same time, agenda setting does not define the media as passive transmitters of information conveying information about political events, candidates, and issues to a waiting public of voters. The media are formulators of meaning in their own right. They are active agents that select, screen, interpret, emphasize, and possibly even distort the flow of information from political events on one side of the system to voters seeking information on the other side. The press injects its own meanings into its reports before it presents them to its audiences. Its consumers, in turn, attend selectively and develop among themselves various shared interpretations ("popular culture") of what the campaign, candidates, and issues are all about. Furthermore, "major decision makers" are described as consumers of this socially constructed reality. The creations of the press become for them important sources of information upon which they base, to some unspecified degree, their political positions and policies. In other words, the press also shapes the "elite political culture."

If this conception of the role of the press is correct, it is a remarkably powerful medium. It shapes not only the public's political beliefs (and indirectly thereby their actions) but the nature of the political process itself by its influences on decision makers. With the press strategically in control of the high ground in the middle, it can exercise its power in both directions through the process of agenda setting. (Whether the press actually has this power to shape both sides of the political process remains to be seen.)

Meanwhile, several additional conclusions about agenda setting seem less open to controversy. These need to be summed up. From data presented by Shaw, McCombs, and their associates in various sections of their report, a number of generalizations appear to be more or less supported by the findings of the Charlotte study. While they do not list them in the following manner, it may be useful to do so because they seem to provide the beginning point for a more systematic theory of the juxtaposition of independent and dependent variables that are involved in the agenda-setting process:

1. Voters show increasing patterns of use of mass communications as the presidential campaign progresses.
2. Those patterns of increasing exposure to media content show variations between different types of voters characterized by distinctive personal characteristics and social category memberships.
3. Each of the media (newspapers versus television) plays a different role as an information source for various types of voters.
4. Increasing exposure to the media during a campaign appears to raise interest in politics among voters, and it helps define salient features of the campaign for them.

5. Because of increasing media use, interest, and salience, there is an increase in interpersonal communication about politics during the campaign.
6. Increasing media exposure and involvement in interpersonal communication leads to a rising need for information and orientation regarding politics during a campaign, which in turn stimulates more media exposure and interpersonal communication.
7. The influence of agenda setting on different categories of voters is, therefore, a product of exposure, type of medium, interest, salience, need for orientation, and interpersonal communication.

The researchers of the Charlotte study do not bring these several generalizations into an overall theoretical formulation. Indeed, given the pioneering nature of their study, it is not at all certain that they should have done so. Their task was to map out the major parameters that seem to play a part in shaping the agenda-setting process and not to test an explanatory theory in a definitive way. Nevertheless, the foregoing appear to represent the heart of the findings of the Charlotte study. Those propositions offered fertile ground for the growth of the research tradition that followed on the agenda-setting function of the press.

## CONCLUSION AND IMPLICATIONS

The study of agenda setting has now become a well-trodden path in the research territory of the communication scholar. The publication of the Chapel Hill study triggered a substantial interest in the process, and the publication of the Charlotte investigation reinforced that interest substantially. Today, dozens of studies appear every year in the journals devoted to communication specialties. In 1981, a much larger and more sophisticated study was completed by Weaver, Graber, McCombs, and Eyal. It was an analysis of the role of the press in agenda setting during the 1976 election. In terms of design, it was a much expanded version of the Charlotte study, and it probed many of the same issues in much greater depth.[18]

In spite of the wealth of studies focusing on the issue, many problems remain in developing an understanding of the process. Additional research is needed to explore the influence of different audience categories and individual characteristics, interpersonal communication, the duration of the effect, differential importance of issues, and above all, the unknown territory of how agenda setting is related to attitudes and behavior.

In many ways, the emergence of agenda setting as a central focus of communication research is a product of changes that have taken place in the field. As the present book has shown, the scientific study of the effects of mass communication began outside of journalism or related communication specializations. The Payne Fund studies (chapter 2) were undertaken by psychologists and sociologists in response to a public concern about unwholesome effects of movies on children. The milestones that followed (with the exception of the one study discussed in chapter 11) were also undertaken by social and behavioral scientists who were equipped to conduct quantitative research and reach findings supported by data. The central focus was on children and the potential harm to them that was created by the media. Social scientists have traditionally been disturbed by violence, the power of big corporations, and the exploitation of the underdog. As we will see in chapter 14, when the opportunity came to subject the media to intensive scrutiny concerning the stimulation of aggressive behavior among the young, and perhaps to lay the blame for violence in society at the door of the networks, social scientists almost trampled over each other in a rush to participate.

As schools of communication began to turn out research specialists trained in social science methodology, they tended to continue the same lines of investigation that had been opened by the social scientists who had blazed the initial trails in the scientific study of the media. Thus, Schramm explored *Television in the Lives of Our Children* (chapter 11), Gerbner pressed further into the relationship between violence and the media (chapter 13), and other communication specialists continued to study such traditional issues as needs and gratifications and the diffusion of the news, to mention only a few. Gradually, social scientists dropped out. For example, in sociology today the study of mass communication is regarded as a relatively obscure specialty. Much the same situation exists in psychology. From the 1940s through the 1960s, it was a thriving growth industry in those disciplines.

As mass communication educators increasingly turned out their own well-trained research specialists, it was inevitable that they would turn their attention away from the interests of sociologists and psychologists to find a topic more central to the basic interests of their intellectual heritage. The study of agenda setting is made to order for the communication researcher who looks back to the great traditions of journalism rather than to the founders honored by social and behavioral scientists. Agenda setting focuses on the classical topics—the Fourth Estate, political decision makers, voters, issues, and the power of the press in shaping our political destiny. These were the issues of James Bryce and Walter Lippmann, not those of the founders of sociology and psychology.

In short, the study of agenda setting may represent a major turning point in the scientific study of the effects of mass communication. It is clearly an effort to develop hypotheses and to assemble data regarding the classical questions concerning the relationship between the press and society. In that sense, it is a unique product of specialists in journalism, who now use the tools of the scientific method to understand better the workings of their venerable institution.

## NOTES AND REFERENCES

1. Walter Lippman, *Public Opinion* (New York: Macmillan, 1922).
2. John Locke, *An Essay Concerning Human Understanding,* ed. Peter Nidditch (Oxford: Clarendon Press, 1975), p. 402. First published in 1690.

3. Harry Hoijer, "The Sapir-Whorf Hypothesis," in *Language in Culture* (Chicago: University of Chicago Press, 1954), p. 94.
4. George Herbert Mead, *Mind, Self, and Society: From the Standpoint of a Social Behaviorist,* ed. Charles W. Morris (Chicago: University of Chicago Press, 1934).
5. Peter L. Berger and Thomas Luckmann, *The Social Construction of Reality* (New York: Doubleday, 1963).
6. Bernard Cohen, *The Press and Foreign Policy* (Princeton, N.J.: Princeton University Press, 1963), p. 13.
7. Kurt Lang and Gladys Engel Lang, "The Mass Media and Voting," in Bernard Berelson and Morris Janowitz, eds., *Reader in Public Opinion and Communication,* 2d ed. (New York: Free Press, 1966), p. 468.
8. Maxwell E. McCombs and Donald L. Shaw, "The Agenda-Setting Function of Mass Media," *Public Opinion Quarterly* (1972): 176–187.
9. This account of the development of the agenda-setting hypothesis and the early research is based on personal correspondence with Dr. Maxwell McCombs.
10. Donald L. Shaw and Maxwell E. McCombs, *The Emergence of American Political Issues: The Agenda-Setting Function of the Press* (St. Paul, Minn.: West Publishing Company, 1974).
11. These issues from the general standpoint of social psychology have been summarized from Alan E. Liska, *The Constituency Controversy* (New York: John Wiley & Sons, 1975).
12. William I. Thomas, *The Unadjusted Girl* (Boston: Little, Brown, 1923).
13. Shaw and McCombs, *American Political Issues,* p. 7.
14. Ibid., p. 86.
15. Ibid., p. 151.
16. Ibid., p. 86.
17. Ibid., p. 151.
18. David H. Weaver, Doris A. Graber, Maxwell E. McCombs, and Chaim H. Eyal, *Media Agenda-Setting in a Presidential Election: Issues, Images, and Interest* (New York: Praeger, 1981).

# chapter 13

# Violence and the Media:
# The Turbulent Sixties

America was bitterly divided in the late 1960s. The social fabric that had bound its people together was being ripped apart by forces that seemed to be uncontrollable on two fronts: The first divisive issue was an increasingly unpopular foreign war; the other was occurring in the streets of America's cities. Many citizens voiced their concern about the justifiability of the United States' involvement in the Vietnam conflict, but people also saw escalating violence at home. They feared rising crime, inner-city riots, campus disturbances, and other forms of civil unrest. In June 1968, President Johnson, in reponse to concerns about domestic violence and recent assassinations, created, by executive order, the National Commission on the Causes and Prevention of Violence. The commission was charged with investigating violence in America and making recommendations to the president for action. It was to examine "the causes and prevention of lawless acts of violence . . . the causes of disrespect for law and order, of disrespect for public officials . . . of violent disruptions of public order by individuals and groups,"[1] and other related matters the president might place before it.

Despite the often violent history of the United States, this domestic turmoil was relatively recent. Indeed, in 1960, sociologist Daniel Bell had commented about America in the 1940s and 1950s:

> A sober look at the problem shows that there is probably less crime today in the United States than existed a hundred, or fifty, or even twenty-five years ago, and that today the United States is a more lawful and safe country than popular opinion imagines.[2]

The country could not understand a few years later how the nation had lost this relative tranquillity.

The 1960s were years of sometimes violent street demonstrations for a variety of causes. Included among them were civil rights, inner-city despair, student activism, and the antiwar movement. Hundreds of people were killed in these confrontations, thousands were injured, and large-scale property damage was inflicted by vandals, looters, and arsonists.[3] In addition, the incidence of crimes unrelated to such disorders soared. The FBI recorded a 100 percent increase in reported violent crimes between 1958 and 1968. Major political assassinations took place, and the new crime of skyjacking literally took off with the times. The first skyjacking (more accurately, air piracy) that involved an American carrier took place on May 1, 1961, when a National Airlines aircraft was diverted to Cuba. Thereafter, such incidents occurred on the average of once a month, until 1968, when security systems became widespread. In most cases, the incidents involved persons who wanted to be flown out of the United States, usually to Cuba.[4]

The rising tide of the civil rights movement had begun to crest at the beginning of the decade. The pattern of response that this movement met was a prelude to much of what would later occur—nonviolent militant protest was followed by backlash, with the conflict finally forcing federal intervention when local officials were unable or unwilling to provide effective, equitable protection for the demonstrators. President Kennedy had been elected in an extremely close contest in 1960. He had overcome much latent anti-Catholic prejudice to reach the presidency, and he sympathized with the civil rights movement and took an interest in its goals. But, as a close advisor, journalist Ted Sorenson observed, "John Kennedy did not start the civil rights movement and nothing he could have done could have stopped it."[5]

A new era of "confrontation politics" had arrived on the American scene. Civil rights activists held marches, rallies, vigils, "freedom rides," "sit-ins," and "lie-downs"—often provoking violent reactions. In 1961, James Farmer led a group of followers on a historic journey from Washington, D.C., to New Orleans by bus. Their objective was to force integration of the transportation system, and they focused their attention on segregated bus stations. In Rock Hill, North Carolina, the bus was attacked; in Anniston, Alabama, its tires were slashed. Finally, in Birmingham the passengers were dragged from the bus into an alley and beaten. The group finally arrived in New Orleans, but they came by air. However, they arrived triumphant; they had faced and defeated the lion in the den. Similar confrontations with segregationists, varying in size, occurred all over the South, with consistent gains for the movement. In August 1963, 300,000 people joined Martin Luther King, Jr., in Washington, D.C., in a march for equality and freedom for all—and heard his stirring speech about his dream for democracy.

Political assassinations were a significant factor in the violence of the 1960s. The first jolted the nation on November 22, 1963. President Kennedy was shot as he visited Dallas, Texas. The vibrant young president had been struck down, and the effects were profound in all walks of life. Few who witnessed the funeral, either in person or on television, have forgotten the sights and sounds of the funeral procession—the flag-draped coffin, the riderless horse symbolic of the fallen leader, and the ceaseless deliberate cadence of the drums as the procession moved to Arlington Cemetery. Other prominent men also fell at the hands of assassins: Malcolm X, a black nationalist leader, was killed by gunfire in New York in 1965; Martin Luther King, Jr., was fatally ambushed in Memphis in April 1968; and finally, Robert Kennedy was shot in California in June 1968 as he sought the presidency. It seemed that no one in public life was safe from such attack.

Late in the summer of 1964, riots broke out in two black sections of New York: Harlem and Bedford-Stuyvesant. Six days of burning and looting followed. Similar riots and disorders occurred in over 100 cities during the summers of 1965, 1966, and 1967. Thirty-four people died in the Watts section of Los Angeles in August 1965 during a six-day riot. There were riots in Watts again the next summer, as well as in St. Louis, Chicago, Atlanta, and several other cities. In 1967, Newark and Detroit had major riots, and several other cities had disturbances attributed to racial grievances. Riots followed the assassination of Martin Luther King, Jr., in 1968.[6] Not only were lives lost, but the destruction of property and the cost to the nation were almost beyond calculation.

Campus protests for student rights and against the war in Vietnam also led to violent confrontations. Protesters at Columbia University and the University of California at Berkeley, led by the militant Students for a Democratic Society (SDS), were particularly effective in drawing attention to their grievances. A wave of bombings and other terrorist acts occurred during the later years of the 1960s, as disaffected groups adopted violent tactics. Groups like the Black Panthers and the Weathermen (a radical faction of the SDS) emerged to carry on the fight. They preached the use of violence in the service of their causes. Protests against the Vietnam war were particularly violent during and after the Democratic Convention in Chicago in August 1968.

While such riots, violent demonstrations, and militant organizations accounted for only a small part of the nation's overall crime, they attracted a great deal of media attention and generated considerable public concern. They were responsible for the enactment of tough anticrime legislation and for a number of police crackdowns. In late June 1968, shortly after President Johnson had created the Violence Commission, Congress passed and sent to him the Omnibus Crime Control and Safe Streets Act of 1968. In spite of his reservations about some of its provisions, Johnson signed it into law. The act was a policeman's program, toughening federal laws, and establishing the Law Enforcement Assistance Administration to provide support for state and local jurisdictions. The government was waging a war on crime.

Besides these new legislative measures, the government also sought to understand the root causes of crime during the 1960s. It searched for ways to deal with the problems of crime through a number of special commissions created to examine particular problems. In November 1963, the President's Commission on Narcotics and Drug Abuse proposed a strategy to control drug traffic and give treatment to drug abusers. The recommendations contained in their report provided the basis for most subsequent drug control measures taken by the federal government.[7] In February 1967, the President's Commission on Law Enforcement and the Administration of Justice submitted more than 200 recommendations that urged sweeping and costly changes in criminal administration. In February 1968, the President's National Advisory Commission on Civil Disorders, created following the Detroit and Newark riots, warned that America "is moving toward two societies, one black, one white—separate and unequal."[8] The report, which followed a seven-month study, placed much of the responsibility for the riots on a century of white racism and neglect. The commission felt that the deepening racial division was not inevitable, however, and that it could be reversed with a "massive and sustained" national commitment to act. Among the recommendations were sweeping reforms in federal and local law enforcement, welfare programs, employment, housing, education, and the news media. The commission indicated that implementation of these recommendations would be expensive but worth the price.

The final such report of the decade, *To Establish Justice, To Insure Domestic Tranquility,* was submitted by the National Commission on the Causes and Prevention of Violence in December 1969. The commission concluded after a year and a half of study that the time had come to reorder national priorities and make a greater investment of resources in the fulfillment of two of the national purposes of the Constitution—establishing justice and ensuring domestic tranquillity. They concluded that the cures to America's predicament of violence had to be based on two things—doubling the investment currently being made in the criminal justice system and restructuring urban life. Like the recommendations made by previous commissions, these measures could not be undertaken cheaply.

In addition to its final report, the Violence Commission issued a 15-volume series of reports from its seven task forces and five investigatory study teams. One of these reports, *Violence and the Media,* has become a landmark in the study of mass communication. It was indicative of the growing concern that the public had about the relationship between violence portrayed by the media and violence in everyday life.[9] We now turn to an examination of the contents of that volume.

## THE MEDIA TASK FORCE REPORT

*Violence and the Media* is a massive work. It contains more than 600 pages, including 19 substantive chapters and 18 technical appendices. The editors divided the volume into three parts: (1) "An Historical Perspective," (2) "The News Media," and (3) "Television Entertainment and Violence." Parts 1 and 2 contain the first nine chapters and seven appendices; the material in this part of the volume provides the groundwork and background for the Media Task Force–sponsored research and interpretation discussed in part 3. The volume builds upon the work done by other commissions and by individual scholars. It is well conceived and presented in an understandable manner by a well-qualified staff and a number of special consultants, many of whom were among the leading researchers in the field.

Part 1 of the Task Force report contains a summary of the philosophical and historical antecedents that underlie the American tradition of free speech, particularly as it is embodied in First Amendment rights. In part 2, the editors, Robert Baker and Sandra Ball, discuss the development, structure, and functions of the contemporary mass media. Among the topics discussed are the functions and credibility of the media, issues about access to the media, media coverage of civil disorders, and media practices and values. The report then draws a number of conclusions and makes recommendations to the government, to the media, and to the public. While limitations of space do not permit full discussion of all of the material presented in these first nine chapters, it is important that we know and understand the perspectives from which the Task Force research was undertaken.

## Perspectives on the Study

The Task Force report noted that much of our heritage regarding free expression stems from the struggle of the press against censorship and regulation. However, even though the press has functioned as reporter and critic for other social institutions, it has shown a marked reluctance to undertake self-analysis and criticism. Because of this reluctance, the Task Force rejected the argument that the government should not be involved in the study of the mass media. It is important, they argued, that we understand what forces shape the media, because the media touch the lives of Americans in ways that are both complex and intimate. Clearly, the Task Force felt that commercial pressures on the businesses that make up the communications industry did not ensure that, in the course of their doing business, the public interest was served. Thus, charges of infringement of free speech and of possible "chilling effects" that might result from government inquiry into media operations and practices did not deny government access to the information it needed to make reasoned judgments about the structure, functions, and possible regulation of the media. In the Task Force's view, it was more likely that public officials would be responsive to citizen need for access to the media channels than that the self-perpetuating corporate management of those media would answer this need. Such corporations already had acquired a highly concentrated ownership of those channels. As the Task Force observed:

> Clearly, then, the media merit study by anyone who would know more
> about the structure of American society. But when violence becomes the
> issue, the study is obligatory. For much of what we know of violence
> in all its forms we understand as observers and students of the mass
> media, not as participants.[10]

Since the influences of the media are so extensive, it is imperative that we understand how they are doing their job of informing the public. Because of their importance in shaping the public's knowledge and opinions of public affairs, the report focused its attention on media news functions.

## Mass Media and the News

When the Task Force turned to the functioning of the news media in American society, it focused particularly on the media's role in intergroup communication and the solution of social problems, particularly media effects on violence. The report, while highly critical of the practices and procedures of the news media, concluded that the news media could be an effective agent in reducing violence if they provided a true marketplace of ideas in which there was enhanced communication between groups. In addition, if they provided increased access to the media by minorities, there might be fewer confrontations that could produce violence in order to gain attention. The Task Force felt that the increased level of violence was due, at least in part, to the slow response of American institutions to demands for social change, and that an important part of this slow response was the failure of the news media to provide routine and peaceful access to new and different points of view. In its opinion, too many news organizations feared social ideas and social action. In addition, because of the failure by the media to report adequately the conditions underlying social protest, and because of their "action-oriented" approach to the coverage of conflict, the solutions that the media did offer to social problems, and even the media themselves, contributed to the widespread use of confrontation in the pursuit of social change.

The report concedes that some groups use violence to exploit press coverage, but such acts were not as common as popularly believed. Besides, the report maintained, violence was not necessary for a group to gain access—dramatizing the conflict was enough to focus attention on the issues. The message was not lost because of the media's tendency to focus on the violence rather than the issues that produced it. The Task Force also endorsed the Kerner Commission's criticisms of the media's handling of civil disturbances. In short, the report called upon the news media to provide the public with the information necessary to have effective democratic action. Journalists, it was felt, needed to reexamine their ways of doing things in order to see if the old ways met modern needs. New approaches were necessary; more emphasis was needed on analysis, opinion, and possible solutions to the problems, once the initial events had been reported. Thus, the news media, in pursuit of these goals, should try to provide a wide variety of such material as a matter of editorial policy. This material should include the full scope of approaches to the subject and should present the views of a wide variety of people. Both experts and nonexperts should cover the entire spectrum of opinion.

## THE RESEARCH FINDINGS

The third part of *Violence and the Media* is concerned primarily with television entertainment and the issue of violence. It contains a large number of papers, written by well-known experts in the field, that summarize past research dealing with the subject of violence and the mass media. The most significant presentation in this portion of the volume, however, is the section covering the new research that was prepared especially for the Media Task Force. Specifically, this new research consisted of: (1) a content analysis of portrayals of violence in prime-time television programs and (2) a nationwide survey of the actual violent experiences of Americans. Once these studies had been completed, a comparison of the two worlds of violence—television portrayals versus real-world experiences—could be undertaken and the accuracy of the media ascertained.

## The Content Analysis

The Media Task Force was concerned not only with the quantity of violence in TV entertainment but also its quality. In other words, how was violence portrayed? Who killed? Who was killed? Were the killings shown to be justified or unjustified? Were the aggressors in these situations rewarded or punished? The Media Task Force considered these inquiries and others to be important in addressing the issue of how violence was portrayed on television. To answer such questions, they contracted with Professor George Gerbner and his staff at the Annenberg School of Communication to do the content analysis. Gerbner, it should be noted, was then and remains a well-known expert both on the research technique of content analysis and the general area of the study of media violence.

The Annenberg/Gerbner content analysis of the TV world of violence examined the entertainment programs during prime-time viewing hours (4 to 10 P.M.) and Saturday morning viewing hours (8 to 11 A.M.) during the weeks of October 1-7, 1967 and 1968. The analyses were conducted by pairs of trained coders who viewed videotapes of the programs that had been supplied by the networks. A standard recording instrument for analyzing acts of violence was used by all analysts.

Gerbner and his staff had been given an important research goal: "To provide an objective and reliable analysis from which the Task Force could deduce the messages about violence which were communicated to the audience."[11] Since different individuals may perceive different messages from the same content, effects cannot be inferred directly from that content. However, knowledge of the content is a necessary starting point in the study of media effects. If certain messages are repeated over and over again, it was argued, they might be influencing a significant portion of the audience.

Since people do not agree on the boundaries of what constitutes violent behavior, it was obviously important that one and only one definition of violence be used in the content analysis. For example, while most people would agree that killing is an act of violence, many might not extend the concept to include verbal assaults. Therefore, violence was defined, in the Gerbner research, simply as "the overt expression of force intended to hurt or kill."[12] The Annenberg staff undertook the study with the understanding that they would produce a "bare bones" report; that is, they were to provide a report that contained little interpretation of the data. Later, the Media Task Force itself examined these data and provided further analysis and interpretation. Thus, the Task Force's treatment of the content analysis can be further divided into three sections: (1) the extent or quantity of violence on television, (2) the qualitative characteristics of television violence, and (3) the Task Force's interpretation of the content analysis.

***Extent of Violence.*** It was found that generally the network entertainment presented in 1967 and 1968 was filled with violence. Approximately 80 percent of all programs contained one or more violent incidents—for both years (see Table 13.1).

Furthermore, the total amount of violent programming on the three networks did not decrease between 1967 and 1968. The highest percentage of violent

**TABLE 13.1**  Programs containing violence (percentage of total programs presented)*

| | All Networks | | ABC | | CBS | | NBC | |
|---|---|---|---|---|---|---|---|---|
| | (N) | (%) | (N) | (%) | (N) | (%) | (N) | (%) |
| 1967 | ( 78) | 81.3 | (31) | 88.6 | (21) | 65.6 | (26) | 89.7 |
| 1968 | ( 71) | 81.6 | (20) | 90.9 | (27) | 77.1 | (24) | 80.0 |
| Total | (149) | 81.4 | (51) | 89.5 | (48) | 71.6 | (50) | 84.7 |

*N = Number of violent programs.
SOURCE: Robert Baker and Sandra Ball, eds., *Violence and the Media* (Washington, D.C.: U.S. Government Printing Office, 1969), p. 327.

programs (90.9 percent) was broadcast by ABC in 1968, and that network had ranked second highest in 1967 (88.6 percent). If a person who watched ABC wanted to avoid programs containing violence, it would have been difficult in 1967 but more so in 1968. CBS, on the other hand, had the lowest percentage of programs containing violence in both years, although the percentage increased from 1967 to 1968. Even though their programming ranked lowest in violence among the networks, a regular CBS viewer would have experienced difficulty finding programs that did not contain violence. NBC programming was the only network programming to register a decline from 1967 to 1968, from 89.7 percent of their programs to 80 percent. Nevertheless, a regular viewer of NBC programs who wanted to avoid violent programming during the prime-time hours was in a position comparable to that of the viewers of CBS and ABC.

On the other hand, if persons sought out violent programs, as was entirely possible, they probably would have been able to find them during all of prime-time television. In short, those who wished to avoid violent programming had an almost impossible task, while those who desired violence had little trouble finding it.

The researchers recognized that various types of programs would probably contain different kinds of violence and varying levels of violence; in some programs violent acts would appear more frequently than in others and might also be more brutal in nature. For the purposes of this research, the investigators classified each of the entertainment programs into one of three categories: (1) crime-western-adventure–style programs, (2) comedy-tone programs, and (3) cartoon-format programs. As we might expect, the crime-type programs were the most likely (96.6) percent) to contain violent incidents. Cartoon shows, however, followed closely (93.5 percent), whereas comedies were the least violent. Nevertheless, 66.3 percent of all comedies contained violence during the two years analyzed. Thus, the researchers concluded that not only was violence prevalent in crime-style programs and cartoons, but "violence plays a significant role in television comedy."[13]

Overall, the researchers examined 183 programs. The analysis of these programs included some 455 major characters—more than half of whom (241) were violent. In addition, a total of 1,215 separate violent encounters were recorded! It was clear that violent content was easy to find in the programs and extremely difficult to avoid.

*The Qualitative World of TV Violence.*   Most of the violent episodes were portrayed as serious in intent rather than as "funny." Humorous intent (slapstick, sham, etc.) was apparent in only two out of every ten violent acts. Violent acts were usually performed at close range, and more often than not, a weapon was used to inflict the pain. Typical weapons ran the gamut from knives and handguns to machine guns and explosives to elaborate devices for mass destruction. Portrayals of violence between members of the same family were rare (2 percent); more than half of the time, violence occurred between or among strangers.

The violence shown, however, produced little visible pain, and the gory details of physical injury (such as blood gushing from a wound) were shown in only 14 percent of all programs. In addition, the violence generally took an entrepreneurial form; in other words, it was undertaken in pursuit of some self-interest, often solely for personal gain rather than in the service of some (worthy or unworthy) cause. It is interesting to note that the "good guys" inflicted just as much pain and suffering as did the "bad guys," but the good guys usually triumphed in the end. Such good guys are, by definition, those who achieved a happy outcome. The losers (bad guys) came to an unhappy end. Generally, the good guy who was a killer did not suffer negative consequences for his acts of violence. Of the 54 killers who were major characters in the programs, 46 did not "pay" for their act with their own lives nor even suffer much punishment. Indeed, it is significant that the major characters who did die were all bad guys. Not one good guy character who killed was a victim of such violence himself!

While across all age groups at least one character in three was guilty of violent conduct, it was the young or middle-aged, unmarried male who was the most typical violent character. These characters committed more than their share of the TV violence; in nine out of ten cases, such characters were the killers, and in eight out of ten cases they were the fatal victims. Race and ethnic heritage also played an important part in the portrayal of violent behavior. Nonwhites and foreigners committed more than their share of violent deeds and were usually the villains. However, unlike their white American counterparts, for nearly every life taken, such killers paid with their own. Violence was observed between members of different races, nationalities, or ethnic groups in 28 percent of all violence episodes; in about another third of the episodes the violence occurred between opponents who shared the same ethnic background. However, such relationships could not be determined in the remaining incidents.

The police and other law-enforcement officials were portrayed in the crime shows to be nearly as violent as the criminals. There was, of course, one difference— violence by the police rarely cost them their lives. Police brutality was not usually portrayed; in eight out of ten instances, the level of violence employed by officers of the law was portrayed as no more than was necessary to get the job done. The problem was that the officers had to deal with "bad guys" who initiated violence. However, the law-enforcement officers were depicted as initiating the violence 40 percent of the time. The violent criminals were infrequently turned in for trial, conviction, and sentencing; the elements of due process of law were portrayed to be a consequence of violence in only 20 percent of the cases. Instead "shoot 'em up" solutions were the norm—with the bad guys losing.

The researchers pointed out that it was difficult to observe witnesses to crimes portrayed on television. "Frequent close-ups and medium shots tended to exclude them."[14] Even when witnesses are assumed to be present, showing them and their reactions adds to the cost of production and complicates the scene; it is therefore done only if showing them is necessary to make a specific point in the story. In half of the episodes where violence was shown, no witnesses appeared. When witnesses were shown, they were usually passive. In one-third of the violent episodes, witnesses were present but did not react to the violence. The witnesses assisted in or encouraged the violence in 9 percent of the episodes, and in only 8 percent did they attempt to prevent it. In general, violent behavior in the TV dramas was rarely overtly objected to by witnesses and rarely punished.

The historical period or setting of the drama was another significant factor in the violence. Seventy-four percent of all contemporary (in the 1960s) programs contained violence. However, this frequency paled when compared to those that were set in the past or in the future. Dramas that were set in the past contained violence 98 percent of the time, whereas those that were set in the future *always* contained violence. Overall, the researchers found that the TV dramas portrayed America as a violent country filled with many violent strangers. Indeed, America was shown as a nation with a mostly violent past and present but whose worst was yet to come; the future seemed likely to be totally violent.

***Interpretation of Content Analysis.***    The Media Task Force examined and interpreted the content analysis data, seeking to determine what messages were being broadcast over the airways to the viewing public. Once they had identified these various messages, the Task Force went beyond the data and inferred from them the social norms concerning the appropriate use of, and proper context for, violent behavior portrayed on television. The process they used for these inferences was one of identifying the substantive meaning of a televised event on the basis of incomplete information. As an illustration of the process, suppose that a boy had been turned down by a girl three consecutive times when he had asked her for a date. Might he not draw the inference that she was not interested in dating him? Although the girl had never come right out and said so, he could easily draw such a conclusion and stop asking her out. Thus, the boy "gets the message" and makes an inference based upon incomplete information.

The members of the Media Task Force argued that they used a similar procedure in deciphering the norms of violence implied in the messages contained in the TV programming. Their problem was to infer the substantive meaning of these violent messages (i.e., What were the television norms containing violence?). Since under these circumstances it was likely that more than one norm could be inferred from the same message, it was conceivable that one investigator's inference might not agree with another's. It was even possible for them to draw contradictory inferences. The fact that the inferences involved judgment meant that, within reasonable limits, two or more investigators could legitimately differ in their interpretations. To illustrate this, return for a moment to the boy-girl dating situation previously discussed. One inference that the boy who received three consecutive refusals could legitimately make was that the girl was not interested in him. However, based on these same facts, he could also have concluded that she was simply a very popular girl, and that if he kept trying, she might have time to fit him in. In this view, he would eventually get a date with her if he persisted. Remember, however, that practical factors limit the scope of such inferences. For example, the boy would not have been able to conclude, based upon these facts, that the young lady had been patiently waiting by the telephone for him to call, eagerly expecting a date with him. It is evident that, when the researchers of the Task Force interpreted the messages in the TV violence, their inferences were neither haphazard nor based upon whim. Their inferences consisted of a process of attributing meaning to events on the basis of factual, although admittedly incomplete, data, using logic and trained judgment.

Using this attribution process, then, the Media Task Force set forth a number of the norms concerning violence in television. Among them were:

1. Unmarried young and middle-aged males are more violent than others.
2. Violence can be expected more from nonwhites and foreigners than from whites and Americans.
3. Situations in which strangers are encountered at close range are particularly dangerous; violence is to be expected more from strangers than from family, friends, or acquaintances.
4. Middle-aged men and nonwhites are most likely of all groups to be killed when they become involved in violence.
5. Law-enforcement personnel are just as violent as the most violent citizens.
6. The past and present may have been saturated with violence, but the future will contain even more.
7. While the use of violence may lead to death, the inflicting of physical injury does not cause discomfort or pain.
8. Witnesses to violent behavior seldom intervene.
9. Persons who engage in violent behavior do not need to be concerned about punishment.
10. The use of violence is consistent with being a "good guy" because violence is a legitimate and successful means of attaining a goal. "Good guys" use violence just as much as "bad guys."

Overall, the report concluded that violence was a predominant characteristic of life in TV programming. Violence, as portrayed, was useful as a means of conflict resolution and to promote the achievement of personal goals. Violent behavior was a particularly successful means of reaching personal goals. especially when the individual had been cast in a "good guy" role, because that violence was not usually punished. On the other hand, alternative means of conflict resolution—such as cooperation, debate, and compromise—were notable for their absence in TV programming. Even when they were present, they were shown to be relatively ineffectual.

## The Violence Commission National Survey

The Media Task Force did not limit itself to an examination of the world of violence portrayed on television. They also investigated the actual world of violence as it was experienced by residents of the United States. There are two reasons why this examination of the real world was important. First, it was necessary for the Task Force to compare the fictional world of TV violence with the real world of violence—the major objective of the new research. Second, it was likely that persons who had experienced direct exposure to violence would be affected by exposure to TV violence differently than those who had not experienced it directly. Thus, the Task Force reasoned: "Experience with violence may be both an independent source of learning and an intervening factor between exposure to and the effects of violence on television."[15]

To examine this "real world" of violence, the Task Force contracted with Louis Harris and Associates, a well-known public opinion research firm. Harris and Associates designed and conducted a national survey using professional interviewers and an area probability sample to estimate the total adult (18 years of age and older) and teenage (14 to 19 years of age) populations of the United States. The area probability sampling procedure required a random selection of census tracts, of clusters within those tracts, of household units within the clusters, and finally of respondents within each household. In total, the samples consisted of 1,176 adults and 496 teenage respondents representing households within the United States. The respondents were considered representative of the total adult and teenage populations of the country.

The Louis Harris researchers collected detailed information about respondents' demographic characteristics in addition to the substantive information in three important areas: (1) the respondents' norms concerning violence, (2) the extent and nature of their actual experience with violence, and (3) the media habits and preferences of the respondents. Each of the areas will be examined and the major findings discussed.

*Norms about Violence.*    Norms set standards for behavior and define the limits of that behavior; they separate the acceptable and the unacceptable in social interaction. Moreover, norms have an explicit controlling function over behavior; conformity to them is rewarded but deviance is punished. Thus, it is generally assumed that most persons seek to act in accordance with established norms.

The survey sought to ascertain adult and teenage norms concerning violence. All respondents in both samples were asked to answer a series of questions that posed hypothetical situations. These items were intended to draw out their norms concerning the use of violence. In all, the respondents were confronted with 16 different situations, which involved eight different assailant-victim relationships and two levels of violence (minor violence and major violence). The eight different role relationships used in the hypothetical situations were

1. A parent and a child who was at least one year old and healthy.
2. A husband and a wife.
3. A wife and a husband.
4. A public school teacher and a student.
5. A male teenager and a female teenager.
6. A man and an adult male stranger.
7. A policeman and an adult male.
8. A judge and a citizen.

In each situation, the first party was the assailant and the second was the victim. The questions were administered in the following format, where situation A represented an example of minor violence, whereas situation B contained major violence.

A. Are there any situations that you can imagine in which you would approve of a policeman striking an adult male citizen?
   (1) Yes     (2) No     (3) Not sure
B. Are there any situations that you can imagine in which you would approve of a policeman shooting an adult male citizen?
   (1) Yes     (2) No     (3) Not sure

The findings were similar in both the teenage and adult samples, although the teenagers were more likely to approve of violence. The findings are presented in Table 13.2. As can be seen, only two role relationships won approval from a majority of the American adult population regardless of the severity of the violent act. These were a policeman and an adult male and a judge and a citizen. Thus, the police and judges may engage in minor and major acts of violence with the general approval of a majority of adults. Parents, teachers, teenagers, adult males, husbands, and wives, on the other hand, may engage only in acts of minor violence within these role relationships, with varying degrees of approval. Severe acts of violence, however, are disapproved within these role relationships by a majority of the adult population.

What distinguishes policemen and judges in these role relationships from the other characters studied is that they possess an institutionalized authority to engage in violence. For example, the police officer is authorized to use whatever force is necessary to apprehend lawbreakers, including violence. Judges, on the other hand, have the authority and responsibility of meting out punishments that are consistent with the provisions of the law. Such punishments may involve acts of violence: public whipping, the death penalty, and so on.

**TABLE 13.2** Adult responses to the general question, Are there any situations that you can imagine in which you would approve of X doing B to Y?

| | Percentage | | |
|---|---|---|---|
| | Yes | Not Sure | No |
| 1. Parent spanking his or her child, assuming the child is healthy and over a year old | 93 | 1 | 6 |
| 2. Parent beating his or her child | 8 | 1 | 91 |
| 3. Husband slapping his wife's face | 20 | 2 | 78 |
| 4. Husband shooting wife | 3 | 0 | 97 |
| 5. Wife slapping her husband's face | 22 | 2 | 76 |
| 6. Wife shooting her husband | 4 | 0 | 95 |
| 7. Public school teacher hitting a student | 49 | 4 | 47 |
| 8. Public school teacher punching or beating a student | 5 | 2 | 93 |
| 9. Policeman striking an adult male citizen | 73 | 5 | 22 |
| 10. Policeman shooting an adult male citizen | 71 | 5 | 24 |
| 11. Teenage boy punching another teenage boy | 66 | 4 | 30 |
| 12. Teenage boy knifing another teenage boy | 3 | 0 | 97 |
| 13. Man punching an adult male stranger | 52 | 5 | 43 |
| 14. Man choking an adult male stranger | 24 | 4 | 72 |
| 15. Judge sentencing a person to one or more years of hard labor | 84 | 6 | 10 |
| 16. Judge sentencing a person to death | 53 | 7 | 40 |

SOURCE: Robert Baker and Sandra Ball, eds., *Violence and the Media* (Washington, D.C.: U.S. Government Printing Office, 1969), pp. 343–344.

Interestingly, the role relationship in which the occurrence of violence is least approved is that of husband and wife. The vast majority of adult Americans disapproved of even the use of minor violence between spouses, no matter which of them was the instigator.

It should be noted that a small minority of both samples (less than 15 percent), adults as well as teenagers, gave general approval to use of high-level violence. The adults who were most likely to approve of high-level violence were male residents of metropolitan areas who were between 18 and 35 years of age and who had attained less than a college degree in their education. Among the teenagers who approved of high-level violence, the greatest proportion were black males between 16 and 19 years of age who lived in metropolitan areas.

Briefly stated, the major findings of the national survey were: Adult and teenage Americans approve of violence only when it is carried out by legally constituted authorities; that is, judges and police authorities may use a high level of violence when it is legally permitted. Low-level violence, however, is much more broadly approved of by the majority of both adult and teenage Americans. The only exception to this is the husband-wife relationship; there, even low levels of violence, such as slapping the spouse's face, is disapproved for either partner.

***Actual Experience with Violence.*** The survey respondents were also asked about their direct experience with violence. They were questioned about personal experiences with any of five violent encounters. Had they, the interviewer asked, experienced them as either the victim, the assailant, or an observer. The questions asked are presented below:

*Victim-Observer Questions*

Victim: Have you ever been
(repeated 1–5)

Observer: Have you ever seen
another person (repeated 1–5)

(1) slapped or kicked?
(2) punched or beaten?
(3) threatened or actually cut with a knife?
(4) threatened with a gun or shot at?
(5) choked?

First, the respondents were asked if they had been a victim, then if they had observed someone else being victimized, and finally, in a different series of questions, if they had been the assailant. Since it was strongly suspected that very few persons would willingly admit that they had committed a severe act of violence against someone else, a slightly different procedure was used to measure experience with violence as an assailant. Some of the questions were changed so that they implied self-defense rather than aggression. The questions about whether or not the respondents had used a gun or knife were placed in the context of self-defense in order to improve the willingness of the respondent to give an honest answer. It should be noted, therefore, that use of a knife or gun for reasons other than self-defense are not reflected in the answers to the questions.

*Assailant Experience Questions*

Have you ever (repeated 1–4)

(1) slapped or kicked another person?
(2) punched or beaten another person?
(3) been in the situation in which you had to defend yourself with a knife?
(4) been in the situation in which you had to defend yourself with a gun?

The data obtained from the responses to the experience questions are presented in Table 13.3. It is clear that for both adults and teenagers the most common experience with violence was as an observer. While low-level violence such as being kicked or slapped was a fairly common occurrence in their lives, more severe forms of violence were rarely observed, much less experienced, as either a victim or an assailant. Overall, the vast majority of Americans have not had direct personal experience with severe violence. The task force thus concluded: "Direct personal experience is not a source of learning about severe violence for the majority of the American adult and teenage populations."[16]

Who, then, were the "violents" in the actual world of violence? That is, who were the people who had experienced severe violence such as choking or threat

**TABLE 13.3** Adults and teens who have had experience with violence as the victim, assailant, or observer (%)

| Violent Acts | Adults | | | Teens | | |
|---|---|---|---|---|---|---|
| | Victim | Assailant | Observer | Victim | Assailant | Observer |
| Slapped or kicked | 0.54 | 0.30 | 0.57 | 0.72 | 0.49 | 0.83 |
| Punched or beaten | 0.30 | 0.16 | 0.45 | 0.42 | 0.38 | 0.64 |
| Threatened or cut with a knife | 0.13 | NA | 0.17 | 0.11 | NA | 0.19 |
| Threatened or shot at with a gun | 0.12 | NA | 0.16 | 0.06 | NA | 0.14 |
| Choked | 0.08 | NA | 0.13 | 0.16 | NA | 0.22 |
| Self-defense: Knife | NA | 0.05 | NA | NA | 0.03 | NA |
| Self-defense: Gun | NA | 0.09 | NA | NA | 0.01 | NA |

SOURCE: Robert Baker and Sandra Ball, eds., *Violence and the Media* (Washington, D.C.: U.S. Government Printing Office, 1969), p. 355.

with a knife or gun—as either victim, assailant, or observer? In the first place, it was found that a person who was a "violent" in one role was likely to be violent in the other two roles. That is, many of the violents in the victim role were also violent as assailants and as observers. Adult violents were mainly males between 18 and 35 years of age, who lived in metropolitan areas and who had obtained less than a college education. Although there were some variations among the teenage violents, the researchers concluded: "In general, both adult and teenage demographic subgroups with the highest proportion of violents are strikingly similar to the adult and teenage groups with the highest proportion of approvers of violence."[17] This fact, the Media Task Force argued, strongly supported the assumption that norms about violence are directly related to experience with it. They found further evidence of the relationship between norms and experience in the fairly strong statistical association between the two. In short, people who were violent in experience also tended to be approvers of high-level violence and vice versa. Thus, the Task Force argued that it had presented evidence that indicated that norms of approving violence was one factor related to the probability of actually experiencing violence.

***Media Habits and Preferences.*** The national survey conducted for the Violence Commission contained several questions dealing directly with the issue of the respondents' media habits and preferences. It was not surprising to learn that, for Americans, television was the medium most often used by both adults and teenagers for entertainment and relaxation. More interesting were the respondents' answers to the items relating to media preferences. One question, for example, inquired:

> How do you feel about the amount of violence portrayed in television
> programs today, not including news programs—do you think that there
> is too much, a reasonable amount, or very little violence?

Of those responding to this question, 59 percent said that there was too much
violence in TV programs, 32 percent indicated that there was a reasonable
amount, while only 4 percent thought that there was very little, with another 4
percent undecided. The Media Task Force concluded, on the basis of these data,
that "a majority of adult Americans think there is too much violence on television."[18]
Another question asked:

> Apart from the *amount* of violence, do you generally approve or disap-
> prove of the *kind* of violence that is portrayed on TV?

Only 25 percent of those questioned approved of the kind of violence portrayed
on television, while 63 percent disapproved, and 12 percent were not sure. On
the basis of these data, it was concluded that "Americans may not be getting what
they want in television programming when the issue is the kind of violence
portrayed."[19] Yet 25 percent of the adult sample indicated their approval of the
kind of violence shown on television. When we examine the characteristics of
these respondents, we discover that they are males between 18 and 35 years of
age who live in metropolitan areas and have attained less than a college education.
Thus, we can see that the demographics of those who approved of TV violence
were the same as those of the adult "violents" based upon actual experience. In
the teenage sample, 53 percent approved of the kind of violence portrayed on
television. And again the category with the greatest proportion of approvers was
black males between 13 and 15 years old who lived in metropolitan areas. In
short, there is almost a complete overlap between the "approvers" of television
violence and the actual "violents" in both the adult and teenage samples.

The limitations of such demographic data should be recognized. Even with
the substantial overlap between actual "violents" with respect to norms and
experiences, and the categories who approve of and prefer violent television
content, we cannot infer a cause-and-effect relationship. In other words, we
cannot conclude that viewing television violence causes violent norms and
behavior; nor can we say that having violent norms and experiences "causes" a
preference for violent shows. Because survey data are cross-sectional, they can
yield only correlations between characteristics; this allows us to speak of statistical
association between the characteristics but not of causality.

Another important limitation of the comparisons of these demographic data
is that the unit of analysis is a category, not an individual. It is not possible to
make reliable inferences about individuals from collective or central tendency
data. If a demographic category has a large proportion of its members classified
as "violents" and "approvers" of TV violence, it does not mean that all or even
most of the individuals who have the same demographic characteristics also have

the same norms, experiences, and preferences with respect to violence. The reverse inference would be equally untrustworthy. Unfortunately, those who prepared the report were apparently unaware of this non sequitur.

## Comparison of the Two Worlds

Thus far in our discussion of the content analysis and the national survey, the TV world of violence and the actual world of violence, respectively, have been described in terms of the extent and nature of their violence. When they are compared, however, the differences between the two worlds are quite noticeable. Clearly, the television world of violence does not accurately reflect the real world in many significant aspects. First of all, television exaggerates the probability of being directly involved in violent acts. Additionally, whereas in real life legality is a prerequisite for the approval of violence, in TV programs illegal violence is often approved. In real life, most violence occurs between family members, friends, or acquaintances, while in TV Land the majority of the violence occurs between strangers. In addition, the most frequent type of violence in the television world involves the use of a weapon. But the great majority of adult and teenage Americans have never experienced this type of severe violence. The most common role in the TV world of violence is the assailant, and the least common is the observer or witness. In real life, however, the situation is reversed; the observer is the most common and the assailant is the least common role. The TV world of violence is often set in a time and place other than contemporary America. However, no attempt was made in this study to demonstrate that TV programs accurately or inaccurately reflected the actual world of violence in the American past or the conditions in foreign countries.

It must be kept in mind when comparing the two worlds of violence that a major concern of the Media Task Force was to examine the kinds of implied norms that were depicted by television and the effects of such messages. The Task Force wanted to know if the norms of television modified or changed the actual norms of the viewing audience (especially its younger members) so that violence became commonplace or, worse, an acceptable method of obtaining a goal. What exactly were the audience members learning? The Task Force concluded that the high degree of overlap between preferences for violent media content and real-life violent experiences (coupled with norms in support of such acts) suggested that "the television world of violence has the capacity to reinforce the 'violents' in the belief and actions in the real world."[20] They further hypothesized that the long-term effect of TV violence on the "violents" would be in the direction of unrestricted approval of actual violence. They specifically argued that this group might be expected to act violently in conflict situations, when enforcing the law, and when attempting to achieve personal ends. The Task Force further cautioned that long-term exposure to the patterned world of TV violence could affect the norms and behavior of "normal" individuals: there would be an increase not only in the likelihood of their acceptance of violence but also in the probability that these individuals would use violence themselves. In short, the Task Force concluded that watching TV violence could both reinforce violent behavior and cause it.

## CONCLUSIONS AND IMPLICATIONS

The major conclusion of the Media Task Force was not particularly surprising. They found that TV portrayals of violence were "one major contributory factor which must be considered in attempts to explain the many forms of violent behavior that mark American society today."[21] While the research's concentration had been on TV programming, the Media Task Force did not let the other media off the hook. They too were guilty, but the Task Force believed that television, as the most popular medium, had the most powerful and hence most dangerous effects. However, all of the media had to share in the blame for helping to make American society into a more violent one.

Although the Task Force came to many specific conclusions concerning the effects of the media, these effects can, for convenience, be categorized as either short-term or long-term effects. Simply stated, the overall evidence from the many papers contained in *Violence and the Media* indicated that the major short-term effects were twofold: (1) Audiences that are exposed to mass media portrayals of violence learn how to perform violent acts; and (2) Audience members are more likely to exhibit that learning if they expect to be rewarded for violent behavior and/or encounter a situation similar to that portrayed. It must be remembered, however, that these conclusions about the short-term effects of media were derived from papers that summarized earlier research; the Media Task Force did not conduct research on the above issues. More important, it should be noted that the conclusions they drew concerning short-term effects were already well established in the scientific literature.

The Task Force's numerous conclusions about long-term media effects, however, contained many more new insights and in many ways anticipated research trends that would become prominent in the late 1970s and early 1980s. For example, the researchers stated: "Exposure to mass media portrayals of violence over a long period of time socializes audiences into the norms, attitudes, and values for violence contained in those portrayals."[22] They further added that the probability of such socialization increased as the age of the viewer decreased; the probability also increased as the number of alternative or competitive sources of socialization into violence decreased. The Task Force also noted that persons who had been effectively socialized in this manner by mass media portrayals of violence cold be expected to act in accordance with their beliefs. While this view has many implications, a few are quite blatant. First, these persons could be expected to resolve conflict in their lives through the use of violence; hence, the value of nonviolent means of problem solving would be diminished. Such persons would also be likely to use violence as a means to obtain desired goals, and when they engage in violence, would probably use a weapon. In addition to engaging in violence, they would probably observe passively when exposed to violence between others. Indeed, it is likely that individuals who have been influenced by the TV world of violence would develop the attitude that it is not the responsibility of individual citizens to help each other out of violent or violence-threatening situations. Thus, long-term exposure to mass media portrayals of violence might make members of the audience insensitive or emotionally neutral to real acts of violence.

Other important long-term effects were also discussed. They included

1. To the extent that mass media portrayals of violence contain rigid "good-guy"/"bad-guy," right/wrong, and either/or distinctions, young audiences are likely to develop and maintain psychological rigidity.
2. Inaccurate portrayals of class, ethnic, racial, and occupational groups in the mass media can be extremely damaging to communication between groups. When a group is portrayed as violent, members of the group may emulate the portrayal: nonmembers, however, may react to members with hatred, fear, or other emotions, creating additional intergroup conflict and violence. Such portrayals are especially potent if members have no personal contact with one another.
3. Both the extent and intensity of mass media portrayals of violence, especially on television, probably have the effect of creating and/or supporting a view of the world as totally violent. This worldview tends to promote widespread tolerance of violence, a feeling that is hopeless to try to control it, and the belief that individuals must be violent in order to survive in a violent world.

These major conclusions reached by the Media Task Force were marred by an important consideration: They were not inferred solely from the research and summary papers contained in the volume. The Task Force did a great deal of extrapolation and often outran the data; that is, there are many conjectures and suppositions in the conclusions. However plausible they may seem, it is difficult to separate them from the research findings. In short, the major conclusions of the study were not directly based on the research conducted, or even on the previous research summarized for the volume. This is the major flaw in the volume as a whole.

Nevertheless, important issues were summarized in the volume, and the research that was conducted did give concrete information concerning the violent content of television. The networks could now no longer delude us with claims that they had been reducing the violence in their programming, as they had said for years. The data clearly contradicted them. Additionally, the content analysis showed that the TV world of violence was a patterned one in which violence was portrayed in an unrealistic but potentially dangerous manner.

The Harris survey also added to our knowledge. We learned that a majority of Americans said that they did not approve of either the amount or kind of violence that was portrayed on television. The American public, it appeared, was not getting the type of programming it wanted. Moreover, it was clear that those persons who watched and approved of violent shows, and those individuals who were violent in actual behavior, shared certain characteristics. They were males between 18 and 35 years old who lived in metropolitan areas and who had an educational level of less than a college degree.

But what did these data really tell us that we did not already know at the time? Not much! As we discussed previously, we can infer no cause-and-effect relationships. We cannot draw reliable conclusions about individuals from grouped data. However, even if we were able to make causal statements about individuals from the survey findings, how much would we really learn? There was nothing new in the demographic descriptions of the "violents"—their characteristics had long been known. Perhaps the most important finding from the survey was that most Americans did not experience violence directly. For the most part, what Americans know about violence they learn from portrayals on television. Thus, the implications for television's role in providing constructions of reality and socializing the audience about violent behavior are truly significant.

Finally, the comparison of the two worlds of violence showed how different they were—and how unrealistically violence was portrayed on television. Yet the comparison raises the concern that if television can influence attitudes, values, and behavior, then the two worlds might one day be much more similar.

The editors, Baker and Ball, used a social learning theoretical approach to structure the interpretation of both the research conducted and the research summarized. However, it was not the simplistic stimulus-response assumption that characterized the old magic bullet theory. Indeed, they made this quite clear.

> Common sense and observation refute the claim that exposure alone makes all people think and act violently. We know that millions of adults and children are exposed daily to television entertainment programming but a majority of them do not espouse violent norms or behave violently.[23]

Although the volume discussed both short-term (direct) and long-term (indirect) effects, the editors emphasized the long-term and indirect effects. For example, they stressed the role that television may play in socialization. After all, their findings indicated that teenagers were more approving of violence on television than were adults. This is not surprising, given that the teenagers of 1968 had grown up with television, whereas the majority of the adults of that decade had not.

The editors also discussed the concept of identification and its relationship to social learning. "Identification occurs when an individual emulates another, seeking to be like that person in appearance and behavior."[24] By 1968, the importance of the process of identification for personality and attitude formation was already well established in scientific literature. Baker and Ball observed that in both the televised and the real worlds of violence, young and middle-aged males dominated the violence. Thus, they concluded that the potential for identification with characters in the TV world of violence was greatest for young males. They noted that a common problem in the maturation process of males is the establishment of a male identity. If the young males seized upon "violents" in TV portrayals in their search for masculinity, then they would be more likely to imitate the attitudes and behavior of the television world of violence, particularly if young males lack other role models.

Identification may act as an intervening factor between exposure to TV violence and the learning of violent attitudes and behavior from this exposure. Thus, young males are more likely than young females to learn violent attitudes and behavior from exposure to the TV world of violence. By stressing the long-term and indirect effects rather than the short-term direct effects, the editors were able to contribute to a theoretical approach that remains significant in the 1980s.

In terms of methodology, the research in *Violence and the Media* receives mixed reviews at best. Both the content analysis and the survey sampling were well done. However, in interviewing people in person, there are certain factors that become particularly important. One of these is the tendency for respondents to give socially desirable responses to sensitive questions. This could at least partially explain why a majority of respondents said they disapproved of violent shows while at the same time they watched them with pleasure. Asking respondents questions that required them to rely on their memory (e.g., "Have you ever seen . . . ?") can also be a problem. In addition, particularly in questions like those administered in this survey, there are problems of demand characteristics. That is, the respondent answers the questions in the way the interviewer seems to want it answered.

Moreover, the measurement of the role of assailant was not adequate. The questions concerning severe violence were conducted in terms of self-defense; the use of a knife or a gun for other reasons was never addressed. The researchers assumed that the respondents would not be honest about violent uses of guns and knives, so they did not bother to ask. Not measuring the assailant role is a major problem because we cannot make any assessment of the effects of behavior on norms and attitudes.

Additionally, the data accumulated by the Media Task Force were composed entirely of descriptive statistics. The content analysis and national survey were discussed solely in terms of frequencies and percentages, rankings, demographic groupings, and averages per program or per hour. Trends and tendencies were often noted simply by "eyeballing" the data. In short, the research analysis was descriptive; no inferential statistics were utilized. The discussions overgeneralized from the findings, particularly given the absence of inferential techniques. The analyses simply outran the data.

Yet, *Violence and the Media* has become a classic in the field of mass communication for several reasons. For a number of years (since the 1940 presidential voting study in Erie County, Ohio) many social scientists had argued that the primary effect of the media was reinforcement. In their discussions, reinforcement had taken on the unique meaning of "no effect." Thus, they argued that mass media presentations did not create attitudes, norms, and values among the audience but rather simply supported or reinforced attitudes, norms, and values already held. This was no effect? Indeed, even if the reinforcement effect *were* the only influence of the mass media, it would have to be viewed as extremely significant, given the widespread exposure that people have to the media in today's society. This was one of the major contributions of *Violence and the Media:* it forced social scientists to reevaluate the importance of the reinforcement effect. In addition, the work forced communication scholars to consider that the reinforcement effect and the "causality argument" go hand in hand. In other words, TV portrayals can both *create* and *reinforce* attitudes, values, and behavior. Indeed, a portrayal might do several things simultaneously. For some people it may reinforce attitudes, while for others it could help to form and shape attitudes and values, even if those attitudes and values differ from the portrayal. Because ours is such a heterogeneous society, different members of the audience can see different things in the same portrayal, perhaps focusing on different aspects of it and selectively ignoring others.

The public received only a superficial coverage of the research and conclusions. The media chose not to make this book and its contents a subject of public discussion. Nevertheless, *Violence and the Media* had an impact if only because it raised more questions than it answered. Furthermore, those questions were of deep concern to Americans. In fact, the clamor for answers on the issue of TV violence and its effects was to grow louder and louder until it could be heard even by politicians.

## NOTES AND REFERENCES

1. Executive Order 11412, in *To Establish Justice, To Insure Domestic Tranquility,* Final Report of the National Commission on the Causes and Prevention of Violence (New York: Award Books, 1969), p. vii.
2. Daniel Bell, "The Myth of Crime Waves," in *The End of Ideology* (New York: Collier Books, 1960), p. 151.
3. Robert W. Peterson, ed., *Crime and the American Response* (New York: Facts on File, Inc., 1973), p. 23.
4. Ibid., p. 74.
5. Theodore Sorenson, *Kennedy* (New York: Bantam Books, 1966), p. 528.
6. Peterson, *Crime and Response,* p. 23.
7. Ibid., p. 43.
8. Ibid., p. 45.
9. Robert Baker and Sandra Ball, eds., *Violence and the Media* (Washington, D.C.: U.S. Government Printing Office, 1969).
10. Ibid., p. 3.
11. Ibid., p. 312.
12. Ibid., p. 314.
13. Ibid., p. 328.
14. Ibid., p. 321.
15. Ibid., p. 341.
16. Ibid., p. 356.
17. Ibid., p. 358.

18. Ibid., p. 332.
19. Ibid., p. 333.
20. Ibid., p. 367.
21. Ibid., p. 375.
22. Ibid., p. 376.
23. Ibid., p. 375.
24. Ibid., p. 368.

# chapter 14

# The Surgeon General's Report: Television and Social Behavior

The ink was scarcely dry on the report of the President's Commission on the Causes and Prevention of Violence when a large-scale research program was funded by Congress to probe the issue of televised violence more thoroughly. The president's report had identified the relationship between violence in media content and violence in society as a potentially important and disturbing one, but available data on the role of media content left many questions unanswered. Meanwhile, by the late 1960s, the issue of violence in American society had reached new levels of concern: The urban riots had created confusion and anxiety; street crime had continued to rise sharply; and the nation's campuses were in chaos over the Vietnam war and related issues. Most of all, the assassinations of President Kennedy, his brother Robert, and Martin Luther King, Jr., continued to trouble Americans deeply. In the midst of all of these events, television became the nation's most widely attended-to medium. At the same time, the suspicion was well established in people's minds that the portrayal of violence in mass communication was a cause of violence in everyday life.

Political leaders are always alert to public issues that can have an influence on elections. Violence was just such an issue, and it proved to be a subject that linked research to politics. It was perceived by Senator John O. Pastore (Democrat of Rhode Island) as a problem that might be posing a "public health risk" for members of the American society. If TV violence prompted children to be more aggressive, he reasoned, some sort of political action might be required to modify the practices of the medium.

But what action might be needed? Outright censorship was out of the question, but careful research, showing the facts linking televised portrayals of violence to aggressive behavior, might be enough to change the programming of the industry. After consultation with the research community, it was clear that such facts were not yet clearly available. An impelling case could be made, therefore, that the federal government had a responsibility to provide the funds necessary to resolve the issue once and for all. It was this political situation that prompted the U. S. Congress to take a deep interest in research that could probe the linkage between violence portrayed in mass communication and aggressive behavior among its consumers. This interest led Congress to appropriate $1 million to fund research studies on violence portrayed on television and the behavior of children and adolescents.

After a massive research effort, five volumes of results (plus a summary volume) were published. Popularly (if incorrectly), they are collectively referred to as the "Surgeon General's Report." It is the task of the present chapter to review the highlights of these efforts and to place this massive project into perspective as a milestone in mass communication research.

The so-called Surgeon General's Report on Television and Social Behavior is a monumental collection of more than 40 scientific papers; it includes specially commissioned research in addition to extensive reviews of the relevant literature. Collectively, these independently prepared papers are referred to as the "technical report," and they are divided into five volumes according to their common subject matter and/or their empirical orientations.[1] In addition to these volumes of sponsored research, the Surgeon General's Advisory Committee itself prepared a report (*Television and Growing Up*), in which the committee states its conclusions about the relationship between viewing televised violence and social behavior. The committee's argument is that their conclusions were drawn from earlier research and from the papers and report contained in the five-volume "technical report." It is important to note that this summary volume, *Television and Growing Up*, was released weeks before the technical report and that the committee's conclusions in that volume were the ones that made headlines.[2]

In evaluating the committee's work, we should note that its title, the Surgeon General's Advisory Committee on Television and Social Behavior, emphasizes *more* than the issue of violence and the impact of televised violence on the attitudes and behavior of children. The issue of televised violence and its effects, was, however, the central focus of the research program, even though the research conducted for the program examined such diverse topics as TV advertising and viewer reaction to it, the amount of time spent watching television, activities displaced by TV viewing, the learning of specific information, and the comparative effects of black-and-white versus color television on the information learned from the TV program. A wide range of social science methods were used in these studies, including content analyses, laboratory experiments, field experiments, observation studies, and opinion surveys. Nevertheless, despite the diversity of topics examined and the multiple methods used, it is clear that the product of this research program does not cover the *entire* range of the subject of television and its influence on social behavior, nor was such a claim made by the committee.

As we noted, the impetus for the committee's work was provided by a request from Senator John O. Pastore, then chairman of the Senate Commerce Committee's Subcommittee on Communications. This committee provides legislative oversight to the Federal Communications Commission (FCC). In a letter of

March 5, 1969, to Robert Finch, then secretary of Health, Education, and Welfare, Pastore indicated that he was "exceedingly troubled by the lack of any definitive information which would help resolve the question of whether there is a causal connection between televised violence . . . [and] violence and antisocial behavior by individuals, especially children."[3] It was as though the recently completed review of the subject by the National Commission on the Causes and Prevention of Violence—both extensive and expensive—had never taken place.

Surgeon General William H. Stewart (on orders from President Nixon) announced on March 12, 1969, that his agency would immediately embark upon a study to "help resolve the question" and that a committee composed of distinguished men and women from appropriate disciplines would be appointed to study the issue. The job of the committee would be to establish scientifically, insofar as possible, what harmful effects, if any, violent TV programs have on children. Stewart also announced that a one-million-dollar budget was being assigned to the project from otherwise undesignated funds in the budget of the National Institute of Mental Health (NIMH), and a report was promised in approximately one year. In addition, NIMH provided staff for the work of the committee and was responsible for screening proposals, selecting those which would provide the most valuable data, and monitoring the implementation of the studies.

To aid in the selection of members of the advisory committee, the surgeon general sent letters to a variety of academic and professional associations, including the American Psychological Association, the American Sociological Association, and the American Psychiatric Association. He also wrote to the three major national networks: the American Broadcasting Company (ABC), the Columbia Broadcasting System (CBS), and the National Broadcasting Company (NBC). A letter was also sent to the National Association of Broadcasterers (NAB). All of these groups, as well as distinguished social scientists and government officials, were asked to recommend "knowledgeable scientists" for membership on the advisory committee.

A list of 40 "recognized experts" in the behavioral sciences and mental health disciplines was compiled by the surgeon general's office from the names received. Then, in a step retrospectively described as "it seemed like a good idea at the time," the surgeon general sent the list to the presidents of the three networks and the NAB asking them to indicate "which individuals, if any, you believe would *not* be appropriate for an impartial scientific investigation of this nature."[4] CBS declined to offer any advice, but ABC, NBC, and the NAB named seven persons on the list as unsuitable. Eleven members were chosen from the remaining names, and another member was chosen whose name had not been on the original list. The reason given for this addition was that representation in one of the scientific disciplines needed to be strengthened.


## OVERVIEW OF THE RESEARCH REPORTS

The committee began its work on June 16, 1969. The recent comprehensive examination of the existing evidence in the area of the televised violence made by the National Commission on the Causes and Prevention of Violence, and the reaction it received, reinforced the original decision to sponsor new research. Between August 1969 and April 1970, 40 formal research proposals were submitted and reviewed for possible funding. Those applications selected to receive financial support had to pass a formal review system similar to the one usually used by NIMH to evaluate research proposals. For the Television and Social Behavior Program, groups of four to seven senior scientists in the researcher's field of expertise met, on nine occasions, to review proposals. Each review committee consisted largely of social scientists in the field who were not affiliated with the Television and Social Behavior Program and senior staff members. In addition, one or two members of the Scientific Advisory Committee itself were present at most meetings. The committee as a whole did *not* select the research projects. In all, 23 independent projects were funded, providing a multidimensional approach to the assessment of television's effects. These 23 project—many of which involved more than one study and sometimes more than one report—form the basis of the technical report.

## Volume I: Media Content and Control

Volume I contains the results of six studies, although one of the studies incorporates the separate efforts of many investigators and is the object of discussion in five papers. Overall, a total of 11 reports and papers are contained in the volume, and they are all concerned with the *content* of television and how it comes to be what it is. These reports are *not* concerned with effects. The focus is almost exclusively on content intended as entertainment, rather that on news or educational programs: prime-time evening television and those programs designed specifically for children are dealt with extensively.

*Content Analyses of Televised Violence.*   Some continuity was maintained with earlier research. For example, in chapter 13, we noted the work of George Gerbner, who had done a content analysis for the National Commission on the Causes and Prevention of Violence; he did a similar one for the surgeon general's committee.[5] Gerbner analyzed one week of fall prime-time and Saturday-morning programming in 1969 and compared the results with the analyses done in 1967 and 1968. In all three studies, he used trained coders who enumerated and classified violent incidents by watching videotapes of selected network programs. He defined an instance of violence as "the overt expression of physical force against others or self, or the compelling of action against one's will on pain of being hurt or killed."[6] Note also that he was concerned not only with the quantity of violence but also with its quality or character.

   The overall results of the quantity of violence studies displayed, at best, a quality of irony. Killing, compared to 1967 and 1968, declined sharply. But the presentation of aggression, harm, and threat did not. These remained about the same throughout all three years. Thus, the *prevalence* of violence did not fluctuate much from 1967 through 1969. In fact, in each of the three years, eight out of ten dramatized entertainment programs contained violence; violent episodes occurred regularly at the rate of eight per hour. Therefore, overall—considering killing and other types of violence together—there was only a slight decrease in violence in prime-time television.

In children's cartoons, however, violence increased. The "children's viewing hours" were the *most* violent of all TV hours in 1969, and they were increasing their lead over other types of programs. Violence in cartoons did vary by network; CBS was always lowest. The three-year average was about the same for ABC and NBC, with NBC greatly increasing the level of violence in its cartoons during 1969. It is evident that any overall decline in violence over the three years is attributable to a reduction in violent programming aimed at *adults*. As Gerbner notes:

> It is . . . clear that children watching Saturday morning cartoons had the least chance of escaping violence or of avoiding the heaviest saturation of violence on all television . . . Of all 95 cartoon plays analyzed during the three annual study periods, only two in 1967 and one each in 1968 and 1969 did *not* contain violence. The average cartoon hour in 1967 contained more than three times as many violent episodes as the average adult hour . . . By 1969 . . . the average cartoon hour had nearly six times the violence rate of the average adult television drama hour. . . .[7]

As previously noted, the content analyses dealt not only with the quantity of violence but also with its quality or character—that is, when and where it occurs, who participates, and in what ways different kinds of people are involved. The major findings were: Violence was usually excluded from the familiar; it occurred with much greater frequency when the setting was the past (e.g., westerns) or the future (e.g., space adventure), rather that the present, and when the setting was remote or nonidentifiable. Violence was *least* common in urban settings, as compared to rural, small town, and remote settings. A particularly interesting finding was that, in 1969, violence was typically presented with an absence of suffering.

Violence, and TV action in general, tended to be the prerogative of males free of responsibilities. Roughly three-fourths of all leading characters were "male, American, middle and upper class, unmarried, and in the prime of life." Most male roles involved violence. In addition, most televised killings occurred between strangers or slight acquaintances, which is certainly not the case in the real world. Nonwhites, foreigners, and persons of low socioeconomic status, where shown, were portrayed as likely to become involved in violence; but they usually ended up on the "losing side." Women were depicted as lacking social power and influence and much more likely to be the objects of victimization. Between 1967 and 1969, female involvement (as the aggressor) in violence dropped sharply. In fact, this accounts for the slight overall decline in violence in prime-time television. Even though women characters were less violent, men were as violent as ever.

The discussion of the content analyses can be summarized best by noting that the most striking aspect of television violence is its unreality. People, relationships, settings, places, and times all depart from real life. Why is violence so portrayed in TV Land? Perhaps placing violence in such uncommon settings and involving people who are strangers is a device that makes violence itself less disturbing to the average viewer and hence more acceptable. In any event, two implications of these unrealistic portrayals can be noted: (1) The reflection thesis, which maintains that television simply mirrors the world as it is, receives little support; and (2) As a guide for attitudes and behavior, television cannot be said to provide much accurate information about real life.

*Interviews with TV Professionals.*    As part of the research, TV professionals were interviewed to gain insight into how TV content comes to be what it is. Two reports discuss these interviews; Muriel Cantor[8] interviewed 24 scriptwriters and producers involved in the production of children's programs, while Thomas Baldwin and Colby Lewis reported on the production of drama intended for adults.[9] While the two studies differ in many ways, the picture they convey is largely consistent.

TV professionals see violence as synonymous with action and hence as the best way of holding the attention of both children and adults. They claim to attempt to confine violence to situations where it is appropriate—essential to the plot or character. The TV professionals were generally unsympathetic with criticism of TV violence. They asserted that violence accurately reflects life (a contention that the content analyses did not support) and that it prepared the young for adulthood. They rebutted critics by citing influences on viewers other than television. They criticized parents for ignoring their responsibilities and argued that the high ratings of certain violent programs indicated parental support. Cathartic benefits of watching television were cited (even though the weight of the evidence did not support this theory).

The professionals *did* admit that television might adversely influence a "disturbed" viewer, but that they did not believe that the TV industry could be overly concerned with this segment of the population. They suggested that television might be a scapegoat when poverty, racial hostility, distrust of government, and alienation should be the true focus. They argued that on television, violent acts were shown as immoral unless they were in self-defense, or on behalf of national security or law enforcement. They argued that the heroes of violent programs used violence only when necessary and in accordance with the law. In sum, TV professionals generally believed that violence on the part of viewers was inhibited—either (1) because of cathartic emotional release or (2) because violence was always shown as either justified of punished.

Cantor found an overall indifference on the part of the producers regarding the possible harmful effects of television on children. "While the shows are in production, producers rarely consider the effects they may have on children; most believe those considerations are the networks' responsibility, or maybe the parents', but not theirs."[10] The creators of children's week-night programs expressed a similar indifference.

Those producing adventure stories deny that they are making shows for children, although these programs are categorized as children's programs by the National Academy of Television Arts. One producer, whose program's ratings and demographic survey data show a large number of children under ten as part of the audience, said, "We are not making a children's story. I don't think anyone in the business knows who their audience is. I think it is presumptuous of anyone to claim they know this. Kids don't know anything. They are not discerning. As long as we are on the air, I don't care."[11]

Networks, of course, do have broadcast standards departments. Each network has a director and about eight staff members who are collectively referred to as "the censors." The general attitude of the "censors" concerning the work of social scientists on the effects of TV violence is best summed up by the words of one chief censor: "We laugh at them. I don't see how the work accomplished so far by social scientists is of practical value."[12]

Many network people, in contrast to scriptwriters and producers, verbalized to the researchers interest in reducing violence, but the researchers felt that there was little chance that it could be substantially reduced given the methods of production. What else could be as popular and as effective as violence in holding the attention of both children and adults?

*Comparisons with Other Countries.*   Last in volume I is an interesting group of papers concerning the social processes and institutional structures through which TV content is organized and controlled in the United States, Great Britain, Israel, and Sweden. Michael Gurevich[13] compares these findings and notes that the proportion of violence in American entertainment programs is greater than that broadcast in any of the other three nations. Yet there is some tendency toward an Americanization of world television; a substantial proportion of the violence on the television of other countries is provided by American programs. However, the relative lack of governmental involvement in broadcasting separates the United States from other countries. In Great Britain, Israel, and Sweden, broadcasting is much more tightly controlled by governmental and other public institutions. In addition, in those countries broadcasters gain support either through subsidies or by the licensing of receivers. In the United States, govern-mental influence is minimal; broadcasters support their enterprise by the sale of advertising, and access is free once the viewer obtains a TV receiver. Thus, this report gives support to the view that TV violence is encouraged and perhaps made inevitable by the competitive economic structure of the American broadcast industry. For the future, however, perhaps public television represents a potential means of altering TV content in this country, since public television's content is not dictated by audience size.

## Volume II: Television and Social Learning

The second volume of the report consists of six papers: Two are essentially reviews of the literature while the other four report the results of experimental studies. The reports are organized around determining the nature of social learning and extent to which it occurs as a result of children watching television. More specifically, the reports are concerned with the nature of observational learning, or modeling; that is, the way in which the behavior of children changes as a result of observing the behavior of others. In this case, the children are observing the behavior of actors in television programs.

*Modeling and Observational Learning.*    Virtually all social scientists have acknowledged that attitudes, values, and behavior of any individual may be developed, at least in part, through observational learning. Research studies have shown that simple observation of others can be very effective in changing widely varied aspects of the behavior of children or adults. For example, children's observations of others in films, or on television, have been shown to produce an impressive level of learning of unfamiliar behavior, an increase in willingness among children to aid others and to share with others, and even a reduction of phobic reaction (e.g., seeing another individual pet a dog in a film may reduce the observer's fear of dogs). These are only a few examples from the impressive body of evidence that supports the conclusion that learning by observation is a critical aspect of the social learning process.

In discussing observational learning, a distinction must be made between *acquisition* of new behavior and *acceptance* of that behavior. In other words, we must distinguish between the ability to reproduce previously unfamiliar behavior (acquisition) and the actual performance of behavior that is the same or similar to that which has been observed (acceptance). A child may *observe and remember* novel behavior without necessarily performing that behavior. If the child can reproduce or describe the behavior he has witnessed (i.e., when asked to do so), the *acquisition* of new behavior has occurred.

The possibility that behavior can be acquired through observation and retained without necessarily being performed *immediately* (or ever) has important implications for our understanding of the effects of television. If a child has acquired some new behavior, he clearly possesses the potential to produce it, particularly if he finds himself in a situation in which such a performance might appear to be useful or desirable (for example, one similar to the situation from which he learned the behavior). Thus, although learning does not necessarily lead to action, it makes more probable the performance of otherwise unlikely responses.

The learning changes the potential range of behaviors a child may display when provoked or when under stress—especially in a new situation. Therefore, the process of observational learning can be seen to involve three stages:

1. The observer must be exposed to the behavior of another individual, either a "live" model (direct exposure to other persons) or a symbolic model (the behavior of others as observed in television and other media);
2. He must acquire and be able to reproduce what he has seen or heard; and,
3. He may or may not accept the model's behavior as a guide to his own actions.

Relating this to the viewing of televised violence, there is no doubt that children are exposed to violence (stage 1); nor is there any doubt that they can learn by viewing television (stage 2). What is missing is an adequate explanation describing the conditions under which an observer will accept a model's behavior as a guide to his own actions. Even today, the answer to this question remains an elusive one.

***Experimental Studies of Aggression.*** The experiments reported in this volume take as their starting point a study carried out by Albert Bandura in 1965; they represent variations and refinements of that classic work. In this project, Bandura had children watch a model perform a series of aggressive acts against a plastic Bobo doll.[14] One group of children observed the model rewarded for this behavior; another group observed the model receive no consequences; and a third group observed the model punished. When the children were subsequently placed in a play situation, those who had viewed the model rewarded or perform without consequences for the behavior showed a high level of direct imitation (i.e., they hit or kicked the Bobo doll in the manner the model had done). Not surprisingly, those who observed the model punished showed relatively few imitative or aggressive responses. Nevertheless, when the children in *all* groups were later asked by the experimenter to reproduce as many of the model's aggressive acts as they could—and were offered attractive rewards for doing so—all groups showed a remarkably *high and uniform* degree of learning.

Note that this evidence does not tend to support the argument advanced by network spokesmen that the depiction of violence has no harmful effects on young viewers so long as violent behavior is ultimately punished. We see that children learn the aggressive behavior and can reproduce it when the situation encourages such behavior.

One point should be clarified. The laboratory experiments concerned with the effects of violence or aggressiveness portrayed in films or on television have focused primarily on two different, although often related, kinds of effects: imitation and instigation. Imitation occurs when what is observed is copied or mimicked. This was shown in Bandura's study of the Bobo doll. There is no longer any doubt that a child may learn a new aggressive or violent form of behavior through observation and imitation. Bandura's work, in addition to the research of many other investigators, has thoroughly documented that fact. As previously discussed, the ability to imitate does not always translate into the performance of actual imitative behavior. Whether or not what is observed will be imitated depends upon a variety of situational and personal factors.

Instigation, on the other hand, occurs when what is observed is followed by a generalized increased aggressiveness. After viewing a boxing match on television, a child might exhibit increased aggressive behavior—some of which is the result of imitative behavior and some a result of instigation. In other words, the child's aggressive behavior after watching the TV program can be quite different in quality and character from the aggressive behavior displayed in the television program.

Since the fact of imitation was so well established, no research in the Television and Social Behavior Program was concerned solely with imitation. Instead, the research attempted to provide more precise and extensive evidence about the capacity of televised violence to *instigate* aggressive behavior in children. For the most part, these studies utilized the classic design developed by Bandura in studying imitation.

The study "Short-Term Effects of Televised Aggression on Children's Aggressive Behavior," done by Robert Liebert and Robert Baron,[15] is representative of this approach. The purpose of the study was to determine whether the willingness of children to engage in aggression against other children would be affected by the viewing of violent televised material. One hundred and thirty-six children (68 boys and 68 girls) participated in the study. Sixty-five children were five or six years of age; the remaining 71 subjects were either eight or nine years old. The children were randomly assigned to one of two groups. Both groups of children were shown brief excerpts from publicly broadcast TV shows. One group, however, observed the first three and one half minutes of a program from a popular TV series, "The Untouchables." The story line contained a chase, two-fisted fighting scenes, two shootings, and a knifing. In contrast, children in the control group viewed exciting, but nonaggressive, sporting events (e.g., hurdle races, high jumping, and so on).

After viewing one of these two programs, children in both groups were placed in a series of situations where they could either *hurt* or *help* another by pushing one of two buttons. The children were told that if they pushed the green button, they would help the other child win a prize; however, if they pushed the red button, they would hurt the other child's chances. They were also told that the longer they pushed the button, the more they helped or hurt the other child.

The results of this experiment are startling. Witnessing the aggressive episodes increased the willingness of the children to be an aggressor. But the primary effect of the exposure was that those who had observed the violent scenes pushed the red button for a significantly longer period of time than those who had observed the nonaggressive sporting events. It was the magnitude of the hurting response that was increased. It should be noted that *not all* of the young children became more aggressive. Yet the fact remains that most of these "normal" children acted in a much more aggressive manner after a very brief exposure to violence. We do not know how long such effects last, but we cannot overlook this evidence.

Liebert summarized the research reported in this volume and related it to 54 *earlier* experimental sudies.[16] His conclusion was that continued exposure to violence is positively related to the acceptance of aggression. Children who view programs or films in which aggression is rewarded are subsequently more violent in their own behavior. According to Liebert, the accumulated evidence shows that

> . . . at least under some circumstances, exposure to televised aggression can lead children to accept what they have seen as a partial guide for their own actions. As a result, the present entertainment offerings of the

television medium may be contributing, in some measure, to the *aggressive behavior of many normal children*. Such an effect has now been shown in a wide variety of situations. [Emphasis added][17]

In general, the studies contained in volume II were methodologically sound and generally consistent in their findings of a cause-and-effect relationship between viewing televised violence and subsequent aggressive behavior in children. The major criticism directed at these studies has been the fact that they were laboratory experiments. Laboratory experiments are probably the *most* efficient means of obtaining information, but critics charge that such studies represent an *artificial* situation that seriously restricts the possibility of generalizing the experimental findings to everyday life. Statistically significant effects may be obtained from events that occur in the laboratory, but will they, critics ask, have any relation to the behavior of young children in the "real" world *and* over long periods of time? Will aggressive effects that are present minutes after viewing the program persist one month or one year later? There is no doubt that laboratory studies do give us insight into cause-and-effect relationships that exist under *specified* conditions, but critics argue that laboratory studies are incapable of providing conclusive evidence about what happens in the "real-life" world. Questions about generalizing from laboratory experiments to the real world remain a subject of controversy.

## Volume III: Television and Adolescent Aggressiveness

The question of whether aggressive behavior by adolescents can be attributed in some degree, to viewing violent TV programming is the focus of the research reported in volume III of the technical report. Eight studies, plus review and commentary, all report analyses of the answers given by *adolescents* to questions asked of them in *surveys*. Note that the methodological focus shifts from small-scale laboratory experiments involving preadolescent children to field studies that examine the attitudes and behavior of adolescents in real-life settings. Thus, these studies address some of the questions of generalizability raised in objection to the experiments. It should also be noted that in some respects adolescents are easier to study than any other age group. One reason is that, unlike adults, they can be found in groups at schools rather than singly or in pairs at home. Moreover, as subjects they have a distinct advantage over children—they can usually understand and answer questions.

Generally, the studies in this volume all address three problems: (1) the measurement on adolescent TV use, (2) the measurement of adolescent aggressiveness, and (3) the correlation or association between viewing violence and aggressive behavior. Even with this common focus, however, the sophistication of the concepts, measures, samples, and modes of analysis vary widely among these studies.

*Adolescent TV Use.*    Three different measures of adolescent viewing behavior were used: (1) total time spent viewing television, (2) program preferences, and (3) frequency of viewing recurrent programs. Total time spent viewing was usually measured by asking the respondent to estimate how much time he or she watched television on an "average" day. Program preferences were usually measured by asking the respondents to list their favorite shows; this measure can also serve as an indicator of whether the individual prefers violent or nonviolent programs. Recurrent viewing was usually measured by providing the respondent with a checklist of recurring programs and asking how often he or she watched each. This indicator also served as a measure of how *often* the individual watched violent programs.

Although each of these measures has something in common, it is obvious that they are *not* measuring exactly the same thing. Therefore, they do not produce consistently similar results. While it might appear that adolescents who view television more frequently would also see more violence than those who view it less often, this is not always the case. An individual who watches a great deal of television may view only as much violence as another individual who watches less often overall but who has a distinct preference for violence.

The most general and consistent finding concerning adolescent use of television was that the amount of time spent watching *decreases* throughout adolescence. Children's viewing is the heaviest during the sixth grade; thereafter, the amount declines steadily. Many factors account for the diminishing of the "TV habit" during this age period. Generally speaking, teenagers increasingly discover other activities that compete with television for their time. Such a tendency is, in fact, particularly evident among those adolescents who have the greatest potential for involvement in other activities—the brighter and more socially skilled and members of more affluent social groups.

While age is indeed an important factor when considering viewing time, it appears *not* to be much of a factor when it comes to preference for violent programs. If there is any tendency, it is for older adolescents to be slightly more likely to name a violent program as their favorite. It is somewhat surprising, given the decline in viewing time among teenagers, that the average amount of time spent viewing by half of all American adolescents on a given day is *three hours or more.* While some do not watch at all, a substantial number watch twice that amount. Overall, a general impression is conveyed that many teenagers spend hours in front of a television set.

Another consistent finding was that of a negative relationship between TV use and mental ability. Almost all of the studies reported that intellectually brighter adolescents watched less television and, moreover, were less likely to prefer violent programs. A negative correlation between both IQ and/or academic performance and viewing time was obtained consistently. In addition, socioeconomic status also tended to be negatively related to the time spent viewing. Those adolescents whose parents' occupation and education levels placed them in the lower socioeconomic strata spent more time watching television than did those in the higher socioeconomic levels; they also indicated more of a preference for violence.

Adolescents saw the violent shows as being "highly realistic"; they thought they were even more realistic than news or documentary programs. Both boys and girls reported emotional involvement with TV violence. But the boys were more likely to identify with violent characters. It must be remembered, however, that the girls lacked aggressive female role models; this alone could explain their failure to identify with violent or aggressive characters.

***Adolescent Aggressiveness.***   Both the measures of aggression and the conceptualizations underlying it were numerous and varied in these studies. This is understandable, even defensible, in view of the fact that there is no simple or uniform consensual definition of aggression. For convenience, the measures of aggression can be placed into four categories:

1. Reports of aggression by others—usually parents, peers, or school officials
2. Self-reports of aggression and delinquent behavior
3. Self-reports of aggressive feelings and attitudes
4. Self-reports of cognitive and affective reactions to aggression

Some of the studies use a combination of these measures of aggression, whereas others do not.

The two most general findings about adolescent aggressiveness were: (1) Boys, not surprisingly, reported a higher incidence of aggressive behavior that did girls; and, (2) Aggressive adolescents were more likely to have come from low socioeconomic-status homes and to have received low grades in school.

***Relationships between Viewing Televised Violence and Aggressiveness.***   The studies in this volume were primarily concerned with the relationship between exposure to televised violence and aggressive tendencies. As previously discussed, some studies used total viewing time as an index of exposure; others employed preference for violent programs; and some used the amount of violence viewed. Most of the relationships obtained were positive but of low to modest magnitude. This is particularly true in regard to the strength of the relationship between both total viewing time and preference for violent programs, and aggressive behavior. Stronger relationships, however, were obtained between *amount* of violence viewing and aggressive behavior.

What do these correlations indicate about the relation between viewing televised violence and aggressive behavior? There are three general possibilities:

1. The viewing of violence leads to aggressive tendencies.
2. Aggressive tendencies lead to the choice of viewing violence.
3. Aggressive tendencies and the viewing of violence are both products of some third condition or set of conditions.

An example of the third alternative is a child who, as a result of certain personality characteristics, may be predisposed toward aggressive behavioral tendencies and toward a preference for violent programs. It should be noted, however, that these three alternatives are not necessarily mutually exclusive. The demonstration that one of the three processes exists would not preclude the occurrence of the others. Each may have an independent effect. In an attempt to find the most *plausible* explanation for the obtained correlations between measures of viewing and aggressive behavior, the study "Television Violence and Child Aggression: A Follow-up Study," by Monroe Lefkowitz and his associates will be examined in detail.[18]

The Lefkowitz study is somewhat unusual because it was a ten-year longitudinal study. Children in Columbia County, New York, were first tested in their third-grade classrooms (in 1959–60) and again ten years later as a part of the Television and Social Behavior Program. There were 436 respondents for whom both third-grade and "thirteenth-grade" data were available. The subjects were asked to respond to essentially the same questions on both occasions. The researchers had the children rate each other on aggression and then also interviewed their parents in order to establish aggressive tendencies both inside and outside the home. The subjects also made self-reports on their own behavior.

It was found that the popularity of an eight-year-old child in the third grade turned out to be a good predictor of that child's popularity ten years later. The child who is unpopular in the third grade tends to watch television more as he gets older and continues to be unpopular. More important, the TV habits that had been established by the age of eight were found to have influence on the boys' aggressive behavior throughout childhood and into their adolescent years. The more boys viewed violence in the third grade, the more aggressive their behavior was at that time and ten years later. In fact, the relation between third-grade TV watching and later behavior is even stronger than that between third-grade TV viewing and third-grade aggressive behavior. Lefkowitz and his associates thus argue that the effects of TV violence on behavior is cumulative. Since they also found that there was no relation between later TV preferences and earlier aggressive behavior, the authors also argue that this finding supports the claim that frequency of viewing violence is causally related to aggressive behavior ten years later. Although many of these same relationships were also found for girls, they were much weaker and less pronounced.

Another interesting finding was that the more an individual watched violent shows, the more likely he or she was to judge that the situations depicted in TV western and crime stories were realistic representations of life. Such a violent and hostile view of the world might lead these subjects to see their own aggressive behavior as normal and a perfectly proper method of solving problems.

Overall, Lefkowitz and his associates concluded that their findings, over a ten-year period, strengthened the conviction that there was indeed a real relation between viewing violence and behavior. Viewing violence *regularly* appears to lead to aggressive behavior. The significance of the studies in this volume was that they contribute to selecting between the three alternative explanations of the association between viewing violence and aggression. And there is considerably more support for the "viewing induces aggressiveness" position. If the association were due to the initially more aggressive youths preferring violent programs, then there would have been a stronger association between preference and aggressiveness than between exposure and aggressiveness, but this is not the case.

What about the third alternative? Is this relation between exposure to violence and aggressiveness due to some third set of conditions that affects both preference and exposure? When the researchers examined the relationship and took into account a variety of other variables, the relationship between exposure to violence and aggressiveness was not significantly diminished. Neither poor performance in school, nor low socioeconomic status, where norms of aggressiveness are more prevalent, explained any of the relationship. Nor did a variety of other additional variables. It should, however, be kept in mind that there is a multitude of additional factors that might account for the correlation. Noted communication researcher Steven Chaffee, however, concluded:

> There is clearly a preponderance of evidence in these studies to support the conclusion that adolescent aggressiveness and the viewing of violent television programs are statistically associated.[19]

He further clarifies this statement by pointing out that a significant positive correlation was found more often than not and that there was no negative correlational evidence. The correlation held up consistently in varying samples, with different sexes, age levels, and locations, and with a variety of measures of aggressiveness. It remained no matter what variables were controlled.

Yet overall, these correlations were of modest strength. What can we conclude from the studies we have reviewed in this volume? The best summary is probably as follows: Regular or frequent viewing of violent TV programs may cause aggressive behavior. This conclusion should not be surprising, since it would be terribly naive to expect that regular or frequent media experiences would have no influence on the social behavior of developing children. But TV violence is only one of many factors that lead to aggressive behavior. It cannot by itself explain aggressive behavior; but its influence cannot and must not be ignored.

## Volume IV: Television in Day-to-Day Life

The primary purpose of the 8 projects and 18 papers reported in volume IV was to provide a current picture of what kind of television people watched in the early 1970s. The projects included field studies, surveys, and laboratory experiments. Discerning these patterns of TV use is important, since most people have access to *at least one* TV set. The research contained in the volume dealt primarily with households containing children or adolescents; between 98 and 99 percent of these households reported that they had sets, with nearly half of those surveyed watching color sets.

In the early 1970s, television remained primarily a family experience where multiple family members viewed the same set. This was changing, however, because of the increasing number of multiset households. In homes with two sets, one was usually designated "the children's set." While having such a set reduced parent-child conflicts over program selection, it increased sibling conflict. It is not surprising that viewing time for both mothers and children was higher in multiset homes than in single set homes.[20] One study, however, did report that children influence their parents to watch the violent programs rather than the other way around.[21]

*Viewing and Age.*    Individuals follow an overall pattern of viewing consistent with their age levels. Children begin frequent viewing at about age 3, and their level of watching remains quite high until age 12, when it begins to decline. As people marry and begin having their own families, they again begin to spend more time viewing; the level stays rather stable throughout their early- and middle-adult years. After middle age, when the children have grown and left home, the level rises again.[22]

The studies in this volume reported that most children did watch television every day and that most watched for at least two hours. Many, of course, watched considerably longer. One study found that the viewing time of first-grade black boys varied between 5 and 42 hours weekly.[23] Another study, involving nursery school children, documented an average weekly viewing time of 34.55 hours for boys and 32.44 hours for girls.[24] This represented well over one-third of these children's *total waking hours* during the week. In yet another study, Jack Lyle and Heida Hoffman reported that "most elementary school pupils watch television before and after school as well as in the evening."[25] Older children (sixth grade and above) also watch through most of the evening prime time as well as during the earlier "family viewing" period. Children become purposive viewers long before they start school; they have regular viewing times and favorite programs. It is also interesting to note that sex differences in program preferences were evident by the time the children began school. Males showed a preference for violence; indeed, such violent programming, excluding cartoons, increased in importance as the children grow older. The children were found to be very consistent viewers; only 2 percent did not view on any given day.

Leonard LoSciuto reported that most adult Americans watch television daily and that they watched for at least two hours.[26] For adults, however, as much as 20 percent of the population did not watch on a given day. Women tended to watch more than men, probably because more women than men had the opportunity to watch during the day.

The studies in this volume clarified somewhat the relationship between viewing television and socioeconomic status. Before the television and social behavior program had begun, several studies reported that children of low socioeconomic status tended to spend more time watching television than did children of higher socioeconomic status. One study in the program supported this conclusion.[27] Lyle and Hoffman, however, in a replication of the classic study, *Television in the Lives of Our Children* (see chapter 11), found results reminiscent of the 1959 data reported by Wilbur Schramm, Jack Lyle, and Edwin

Parker: "At the sixth grade level, bright students tended to be among the heaviest viewers, but at the tenth grade level their viewing was more likely to be somewhat lower than that of their peers.[28] Overall, the viewing differences based upon socioeconomic status were not nearly as great as those found in 1959. It thus appears that there has been some leveling of comparative viewing among children. Several of the researchers (Lyle and Hoffman; Murray) suggest that the brighter children showed more variation in their program preferences. Such diversified program preferences were also related to higher socioeconomic status. Generally, children from higher socioeconomic groups and those who had higher IQs watched less violence than their age peers. This may not, however, have been their own choice, since their parents were also more likely to restrict program selection. For most children, however, there was little parental control of television viewing; indeed, despite what many mothers said, most children actually "viewed at will."

The data on adult viewing interestingly parallels that reported for adolescent audiences. Men watch more violence than women. Blacks watch more than Caucasians. The poor and less educated watch more than those who have gone to college. Male high school dropouts were reported to have a particularly high rate of violence viewing. This group is, of course, also higher than average in reports of actual violent behavior.[29]

***Family Patterns of Viewing.***   It should be pointed out that many of the studies in this volume made use of individual or family diaries. One member of the family, usually the mother, recorded for the whole family the amount of time spent viewing and the programs watched. LoSciuto,[30] for example, interviewed a national sample of 252 families and had them keep TV diaries. The study is interesting because of some of its peripheral findings indicating that only one-third of the programs watched were viewed all the way through by people who had tuned in. Two out of every five viewers reported that they had watched the program only because it happened to come on the channel they were watching or because someone else in the family wanted to see it. The diary records for the individuals showed a daily average of one hour, 59 minutes, but the respondents said that they watched three hours and 20 minutes on the average day. Other studies report the same discrepancy; the conclusion was reached that Americans consistently tend to overestimate generously the time they spend viewing and feel little social pressure to conceal TV viewing.

The obvious problem with diaries as a measure of viewing, however, is that people may neglect, for one reason or another, to record all of the programs viewed. This is especially true when one individual attempts to record the viewing of all family members, often with multiple TV sets. It is likely that some omissions will occur. This explanation was often given to clarify the discrepancy between recorded viewing time and verbal estimates of viewing time.

Another interesting study, conducted by Robert Bechtel and associates, examined the validity of such reports of viewing time. They wished to learn whether the viewing habits of individuals were more in line with what they say

or with what they report in their diaries. A small sample of 20 families participated in the project for a period of six consecutive days. Each household had a
camera installed so that actual behavior in front the set could be filmed. While
this is an intriguing idea, there is little doubt that the presence of the camera
affected the subjects' behavior and, in fact, several so reported. But whatever
effect the presence of the camera may have had, it recorded only three hours of
actual viewing time for every four hours' viewing reported by the same individuals
in a diary. This gives more credibility to the idea that Americans often overreport
their viewing time.

A more interesting finding was that the level of attention to the TV screen
was constantly varying. The researchers divided the activities they saw while the
TV set was on into six levels of attention:

1. *Participation* (actively responding to the set or to others regarding
   content from the set)
2. *Passively watching* (doing nothing else)
3. *Simultaneous activity* (eating, etc.)
4. *Positioned to watch* but reading, talking, or attending to something
   else
5. *In the viewing area* but positioned away from the set in a way that
   would require turning to see it
6. *Not in the room* and unable to see the set

Bechtel et al. indicate that as much as half the time the TV sets were on,
the viewers were doing something that placed them in one of the last three
categories. This means that they did not actually "watch," even though they may
have later reported that they watched the program. These researchers catalogued
an extensive list of activities in which the people who "did watch" were
simultaneously engaged. These ranged from eating and talking (the most frequent)
to activities such as sleeping, smoking, dancing, preparing meals, dressing and
undressing, doing exercises, and crawling.

The data presented by Bechtel et al. are important because they raise some
important questions about the nature of TV viewing. The most important question
is whether viewing time is restricted to "eye contact" time. The authors developed
their study from the standpoint of eye contact time, but is that necessarily
appropriate? Does a person who performs household chores with the television
set on, watching when something catches their interest, qualify as a viewer? The
results of the Bechtel study emphasize the problem of establishing the validity
of measures of viewing.[31]

Robinson advances this thesis a step further, arguing that viewer time is a
continuum of short periods of full attention interspersed with periods of non-
attention or only partial attention. The viewer is alerted to things of interest to
him or her by cues from the program itself. If Robinson is right, then the viewer
may see only small segments of a program. The viewer may see violence without
punishment, victims without criminals, as he or she tunes in and out of the
program. What can we say about the effects of portrayals of violence? Do those

who prefer violence see only the violent segments, while those who do not prefer it tune them out?

Considering all of the studies contained in this volume, it appeared that several changes had occurred during the 1960s in the public's attitudes toward, and use of, television. The evidence indicated that more time was spent in the company of TV sets than in the 1950s, but that the level of attention fluctuated greatly. Viewers were no longer "glued" to the set; in fact, it appeared that the set was often simply left on with the viewer tuning in and out as the programs changed. This raises the possibility that while television has become even more interwoven with our daily lives, its hold upon our attention has perhaps been reduced. Indeed, one might ask if the public's general affection for television has perhaps fallen despite apparent increases in "viewing time."

Moreover, the public has become more critical of television in one respect. The data gathered showed a high level of antagonism toward commercials. This antagonism was not only in regard to frequency but to their content. The public showed a strong tendency to reject them as deceitful, if not flatly untrue. And this antagonism was stronger among teenagers than among adults.

Overall, the new research indicated that while individuals do spend a great deal of time viewing television, they are primarily seeking relaxation. This in itself does not turn viewers into "escapists, social isolates, or deviants."

## Volume V: Television's Effects

The final volume of independent research prepared for the commission contained a mixed bag of 13 different papers and reports. Unlike the first four volumes, there was no common substantive theme that united the papers except that all of them were based upon ongoing research. The researchers cautioned that their conclusions were tentative, that the data presented were undergoing further analyses, or that follow-up studies were in progress. In all cases, the reports were not intended to be definitive.

Some of the papers did, however, explore the role of televised violence in some new and interesting ways. For example, Paul Eckman and associates[32] videotaped the faces of 65 five- and six-year-old children while they watched television (30 boys and 35 girls). The hypothesis was that the facial expressions displayed by the children while watching televised violence would reflect emotional reactions. The researchers also believed that certain types of facial reactions would be associated with subsequent behavior. They posited that child viewers whose faces expressed happiness or interest while watching violence would be more aggressive than children whose faces expressed sadness, disgust, or fear. Two different measures were used. The first involved a laboratory procedure where the children pushed "help" or "hurt" buttons in the manner previously discussed in the Liebert and Baron study (volume 2); the second was conducted in a more natural play situation.

The researchers found that facial expressions of emotions shown during the viewing of televised violence did indeed predict later aggressive behavior—but for boys only. They concluded, therefore, that it is not the mere presence of televised violence but the boys' emotional responses to it that predict later displays of aggression. However, the question remains, Why did the researchers fail to obtain the same success with girls? They speculated that the differences may have been due to the fact that the violence shown was male-oriented; in other words, it involved male actors and male roles. There were no female aggressors for the girls to identify with. In addition, we should also consider female socialization in regard to attitudes toward violence. Overall, the girls may have been more frequently censored or punished for approving of aggressive behavior whereas the boys were not. The authors concluded that more studies were necessary to test these possibilities—studies that should include female role models and take into account female socialization.

Another interesting and even more perplexing study was conducted by David Foulkes and his associates.[33] They examined whether presleep viewing of a violent program, in contrast to a nonviolent one, affected (reduced or increased) the vividness, pleasantness, aggression, or anxiety components of dream content. Each subject participated in two experimental sessions seven to nine days apart. After arriving at the sleep laboratory, they changed into bedclothes, had electrodes attached to their face and scalp, were exposed to either the violent or the nonviolent film, and slept. The experimental procedure was to awaken each subject after ten minutes of "Rapid Eye Movement" sleep. The subject was interviewed and instructed to go back to sleep after each awakening.

This study was repeated three times, with three separate groups of subjects. Different results were obtained each time. The results of the first experiment indicated that dreams recalled after watching violence were more exciting, more interesting, and more imaginative. There was *increased* general activation. The results from the first replication of this experiment, however, indicated that the exposure to the violent film produced less imaginative and exciting dreams. There was *reduced* general activation. Because of this conflict in results, a second replication was funded by the commission as a part of the Television and Social Behavior Program in an attempt to resolve the question. The results of this second replication indicated that there was *no difference* whatever in the content of dreams between viewing or not viewing one of the two films before sleep. The researchers indicated that follow-up studies were being planned to further clarify the issue.

The other studies reported in this volume were all projects "in progress," and the papers prepared for the volume were essentially progress reports on these continuing projects. Because of their in-progress status, those papers will not be examined.

## Summary Volume: Television and Growing Up

The report prepared by the Surgeon General's Scientific Advisory Committee, *Television and Growing Up,* contains a summary of the technical studies previously reported, recommendations for future research, and the committee's "definitive" statement about the relationship between the viewing of televised violence and aggressive behavior in children.[34] As previously noted, this volume was the one most often read by scholars and laymen alike; unfortunately, the five volumes of technical research are neither light reading nor, with rare exceptions, particularly enjoyable.

Since the technical reports have already been summarized above, we will turn our attention to the recommendations made by the surgeon general's committee. The committee qualifies its report at the outset by stating their unhappiness with the "narrowness" of the focus of the research program. "Exposure to violence," they argue, "does not exist in a vacuum." They further indicate that the narrowness of concentration "has severely hampered the interpretation of the results."[35] However, in any scientific investigation, narrowness of focus is somewhat mandatory. It is this approach that is taught to students in their courses on research methods. No social scientist has yet been able to study all influences on behavior simultaneously. Moreover, the investigators do manage adequate interpretations of their data. That the evidence is not clear, convincing, and irrefutable is not unusual—scientific answers are never absolute or final. A committee composed of "recognized experts" should have been cognizant of this, but they seemed not to be. Definitive answers can be sought as a goal, but such answers are unlikely to come out of a single series of investigations. In fact, it is widely viewed that definitive answers will perhaps never be found in social investigations. And it should be noted that most scientific studies have a more narrow focus than did the Television and Social Behavior Program.

The advisory committee recommended that future research concentrate on the following areas:

1. *Television should be studied in the context of other mass media.* The members of the committee argued that a positive relationship exists between an individual's use of television and use of other mass media. (This has not been found to be the case.) They thus believed that attempts to isolate the effects of TV exposure on social behavior resulted in "possible confounding of attributions."

2. *Television should be studied in the context of the **total** environment, particularly the home environment.* The question posed was: "To what extent does what the young viewer brings to the TV screen determine what he carries away—which is another way of asking where the television ranks among all other aspects of a child's environment?" The members of the committee indicated that they were particularly interested in identifying the predispositional characteristics of children who displayed an increase in aggressive behavior in response to televised violence.

3. *Studies should be conducted to distinguish between functional (useful) and dysfunctional (damaging) aggressive behavior.* The committee pointed out that the "realities of life require a certain set or readiness for aggressive behavior" and that the lines that distinguish

between aggression and vigorous competition are often blurred. Even in the early 1970s, most boys were being taught to "stand up for your rights and defend yourself." Thus, the argument is that the viewing of certain aggressive behavior (e.g., vigorous competition) may be beneficial for some viewers, especially perhaps for the shy, timid viewer.

4. *Modeling and imitation of prosocial behavior should be studied.* The committee argued that if children imitate aggressive acts, they may also imitate prosocial acts; furthermore, this imitation of positive prosocial behavior may balance any negative effects.

5. *We should examine the symbolic functions of violence on television.* Violent content in fiction may sometimes be a vehicle for presenting "messages" to a general audience about important social and cultural issues. Without the use of this violence, it may not be possible to examine these issues.

The advisory committee also called for a "more humane definition of violence." While violence was defined primarily in a physical sense in the research program, the committee argued that it should be expanded to include the "experience of [all its victims]." These victims include those who have been killed or disabled by unsafe drugs that have been approved for public use. (Prescribing birth control pills would thus be defined as an act of violence.) Pollution of the air and water, impure foods, the operation of a factory (if a death or disability occurs) are all violence. The committee goes so far as to say that the "casting of a vote in Congress, or the signing of an Executive Order" should be defined as violent when such acts have adverse effects "on a few people or a multitude of people." They then suggest that television should be used as a social force to modify society's definition and awareness of violence.

Finally, we come to the committee's conclusion concerning the relationship between viewing televised violence and exhibiting aggressive behavior. When the committee began its work in 1969, it took as the starting point the conclusions derived from a well-known 1961 study (which we discussed in chapter 11), *Television in the Lives of Our Children:* "For *some* children, under *some* conditions, *some* television is harmful. For *other* children under the same conditions, or for the same children under *other* conditions, it may be beneficial. For *most* children, under *most* conditions, most television is probably neither harmful nor particularly beneficial."[36] To see just how far we have come from these findings, the committee summarized its findings and conclusions:

Thus the two sets of findings (laboratory and survey) converge in three respects: a preliminary and tentative indication of a causal relation between viewing violence on television and aggressive behavior; an indication that any such causal operation operates only on some children (who are predisposed to be aggressive); and an indication that it operates only in some environmental contexts. Such tentative and limited conclusions are not very satisfying [yet] they represent substantially more knowledge than we had two years ago.[37]

It cost the American public $1.8 million to gain this "increase" in our collective knowledge. Such is the price of progress.

As a result of this report and the above conclusions and observations, the committee has been charged with having become an apologist for, and defender of, the broadcast industry. Given the industry's input into the committee's makeup, the charge is not surprising; the controversy surrounding the committee and its report will now be examined in detail.

## THE FIRESTORM OF CRITICISM AND THE SENATE HEARINGS

In many ways, the real impact of this research came not from the studies themselves but from the controversy that followed the publication of the committee's report. Even before the committee's work had been completed, the manner in which the advisory committee was selected became a topic of heated controversy.

The May 22, 1970 issue of *Science* magazine contained a report that publicized a previously little known fact: ABC, NBC, and the National Association of Broadcasters had blackballed seven social scientists distinguished for their past research and expertise on the subject (Albert Bandura, Leo Bogart, Leonard Berkowitz, Leon Eisenberg, Ralph Gerry, Otto Larsen, and Percy Tannenbaum). In response to this revelation, several members of the advisory committee threatened to resign but were persuaded to continue serving. This "purging" of respected scientists was understood from the outset in the academic community. It resulted in a number of scholars (including one of the coauthors of this book) refusing to take part in the NIMH project.

The notoriety prompted an explanation from Robert Finch, secretary of Health, Education and Welfare. He argued that the same procedure had been used with the earlier Advisory Committee on Smoking and Health. That is, the tobacco industry had been asked to approve the composition of that committee in order to forestall any subsequent charge that it had been biased against the industry. In both cases, Finch indicated, the purpose of seeking such advice was to enhance the committee's credibility and to secure the cooperation of the industry whose product was under scrutiny. What Finch neglected to note at the time was that in the smoking and health advisory committee, organizations on *both sides* of the controversy had been asked to identify unsuitable parties. Moreover, no individual had been allowed to serve on the committee if he or she represented any organization or group with an interest in the outcome.

The advisory committee appointed to investigate the TV question consisted of four psychologists, three sociologists, two psychiatrists, a political scientist, an anthropologist, and an educator. However, all three of the sociologists who served were affiliated with CBS! (Ira H. Cisin and Harold Mendelsohn were active consultants with CBS; Joseph T. Klapper headed the network's Office of Social Research.) Furthermore, two of the psychologists had network affiliations (Thomas E. Coffin was the research director at NBC, and Gerhardt Wiebe was a long-time research executive for CBS.) Not only was the broadcast industry given veto power over prospective members but it also placed five of its own people on the committee!

The reaction from social scientists was immediate and hostile. Leo Bogart's remarks are typical:

> The idea that an industry should not only be represented directly in a scholarly inquiry into its activities, but should also exercise a veto over the membership of the investigating panel, is too stupid and scandalous to escape commentary. It cannot be permitted again in future government-sponsored research on public matters that affect established interests."[38]

In addition to the five persons closely affiliated with the networks, four others were decidedly unfamiliar with empirical studies of communication effects, although each was well known and expert in his own field. This left only three persons (a political scientist and two psychologists) who could be said to both possess the necessary technical expertise and be free of affiliations with the TV industry.

Why was the committee so composed? The presence of the four members from outside disciplines was the result of a standard policy requiring heterogeneous representation in such panels. But their presence was compromised by the broadcast industry personnel whose participation was considered by many to be a simple function of the power of the industry and the hesitancy of the Nixon administration to offend it unnecessarily.

While the composition of the committee provided minimal affront to broadcasters, the shabby treatment of eminent social scientists shocked the scientific community. The blackballing of widely recognized experts *because of* their past work and professional expertise created a deep hostility among social and behavioral scientists. The irony was that it was the broadcasters who paid the price. The broadcast industry made a preemptive strike in a conflict that need never have occurred. In the end, it was the broadcasters who were bloodied.

In addition to the issue of committee composition and selection, the report issued by the advisory committee (*Television and Growing Up*) also sparked a controversy. Many of the independent investigators whose works were included among the papers in the technical volumes claimed that their findings had been "irresponsibly distorted" in the committee's report. Another charge was that "some highly pertinent studies demonstrating that violence viewing causes children to behave aggressively were not even mentioned."[39]

This storm of protest was the impetus for Senate hearings, chaired by Senator Pastore, March 21–24, 1972, before the Subcommittee on Communications of the Commerce Committee. It became clear from the testimony offered that the final advisory committee document reflected a considerable amount of drafting and redrafting, and this redrafting was largely the work of the two network research directors—those with the most at stake in the outcome. Indeed, one member of the NIMH staff testified that "as much as 90 percent of the report revision was made at the insistence of Klapper."[40]

Besides the more blatant errors and abuses, there are many statements in *Television and Growing Up* that were clearly misunderstood by those untrained in the social sciences. For example, in social science research a call for further study is almost always necessary—to confirm and elaborate findings. However, to reporters untrained in the social sciences this meant that the study failed to prove that violent TV presentations had harmful effects. And since *Television and Growing Up* was released prior to the technical reports, the conclusions contained in it were the ones that made news headlines. The *New York Times*, for example, ran a front page story under the headline: "TV Held Unharmful to Youth." Other newspapers and magazines reported the committee's findings under similar headlines. The cautious and carefully worded conclusions of the committee were reported in such a way in the news media that the meaning of the committee's language may have been distorted. The more cynical reader might infer that the carefully drafted wording was intended to mislead the technically unsophisticated.

Because of all the problems associated with the advisory committee report, Senator Pastore elected to bypass that report and to examine directly the five volumes of technical research during the hearings. The object: to arrive at an independent conclusion about the relationship between viewing televised violence and aggressive behavior. Before the end of the hearings, all those who testified before the Senate committee—even the presidents of three major national networks—agreed (although it must be admitted, some were under heavy pressure from the committee) that television violence had an adverse effect on children. No one who testified claimed that television violence was the sole cause of aggressive behavior. Indeed, many testifying wished to address other pertinent causes. However, Senator Pastore indicated that the issue was determining relationship between TV violence and aggressive behavior. He pointed out that no one was naive enough to posit a single cause.

The most definitive and incisive testimony given at the hearings was probably that offered by the surgeon general himself, Jessie L. Steinfeld:

> While the Committee report is carefully phrased and qualified in language acceptable to social scientists, it is clear to me that the causal relation between televised violence and antisocial behavior is sufficient to warrant appropriate and immediate remedial action. The data on social phenomena such as television and social violence will never be clear enough for all social scientists to agree on the formulation of a succinct statement of causality. But there comes a time when the data are sufficient to justify action. That time has come.[41]

Dr. Steinfeld might just as easily have said "Warning: the surgeon general has determined that viewing television violence is dangerous to your child's health."

## CONCLUSIONS AND IMPLICATIONS

What are we to conclude from all this? Can we, or should we, separate the research from the controversy surrounding it? The importance of the Television and Social Behavior Program obviously lies in the five volumes of technical reports and not in the advisory committee report. The most appropriate way of looking at that report is as the product of a three-way process of interaction—between government, the TV industry, and social science. From this perspective, what was studied and why becomes almost as interesting as what was learned. We can draw three main conclusions from the five volumes of research:

1. Television content is heavily saturated with violence.
2. Children and adults are spending more and more time exposed to violent content.
3. Overall, the evidence supports the hypothesis that the viewing of violent entertainment increases the likelihood of aggressive behavior. This evidence is derived from both laboratory experiments that permit causal inference *and* from surveys that provide evidence of real-life associations in everyday events.

Not all social scientists will agree with the third conclusion. It is easy to criticize most of the studies on an individual basis. For example, in some of the laboratory experiments, the samples studied were quite small. In many of the experiments and all of the surveys, there was an overconcentration on the more articulate and responsible older children and an underrepresentation of younger children (who appear to be especially susceptible to the influence of television). However, the methodological flaws of one study do not usually apply to another. Taken as a whole, the consistent accumulation of evidence allows us to feel reasonably comfortable with the conclusions reached.

The major problem of the Television and Social Behavior program of research is the way in which the research problem was posed. The advisory committee chose to frame the question in terms of direct effects: Does exposure to violence lead children to specific acts of antisocial behavior? As far as the broadcast industry is concerned, this is probably the most acceptable formulation. We must, however, consider the possibility, or probability, that television's most profound influences may be indirect. How does the presentation of life in TV programming alter the socialization process, if it does? Does it change the worldview of those who are regular viewers? Does it make violence a more common phenomenon in familiar contexts to more people and thus make it more acceptable? Or does the presentation of violence simply make for a more timid, fearful populace? How does the continual flow of violence in the media affect our beliefs, attitudes, and values, and the quality of life in our country? We do not really know what the long-term effects are for individuals or for society.

What, then, should be done about violence on television? Should it be eliminated? No, because violence *is* a part of life, and of art. Besides, the real issue is not the use of violence that honestly reflects the conflicts of the times, "the issue is the deliberate use of cliché violence, violence contrived to formula, violence as a commodity that can be packaged for sale."[42] When violence is packaged in an "acceptable" format, and is presented as real, it distorts reality, and it distorts the perceptions of those who must live in that reality. Violence contrived for the sake of violence—for comic effect, for amusement—without meaning or purpose, does no service to the viewer. It may beguile the audience, but in the end play may become real—and painful.

In conclusion, *Television and Social Behavior* has an assured place in the history of applied communication research. That place is secure not only because of the large budget and the controversy surrounding the project, but also because of the broad public and journalistic interest in the wider questions it raises. The reader should be cautioned that this chapter can only hint at the rich detail of the specific findings, theoretical insights, and heterogeneity of research methods and techniques employed. The *Television and Social Behavior* project remains one that is unique in its size, scope, and focus. In many ways, it is a noteworthy exemplar of mass communication research. Unfortunately, it is also a document that has been discussed much more often than it has been read.

## NOTES AND REFERENCES

1. *Television and Social Behavior*, vol. I, *Media Content and Control*, eds. G. A. Comstock and E. A. Rubinstein; vol. II, *Television and Social Learning*, eds. J. P. Murray, E. A. Rubinstein, and G. A. Comstock; vol. III, *Television and Adolescent Aggressiveness*, eds. G. A. Comstock and E. A. Rubinstein; vol. IV, *Television in Day-to-Day Life: Patterns of Use*, eds. E. A. Rubinstein, G. A. Comstock and J. P. Murray; vol. V, *Television's Effects: Further Explorations*, eds. G. A. Comstock, E. A. Rubinstein, and J. P. Murray (Washington, D.C.: U.S. Government Printing Office, 1971).

2. Surgeon General's Scientific Advisory Committee on Television and Social Behavior, *Television and Growing Up: The Impact of Televised Violence*. Report to the Surgeon General, United States Public Health Service (Washington, D.C.: U.S. Government Printing Office, 1971).

3. Ibid., p. 14.

4. Ibid., p. 15.

5. George Gerbner, "Violence in Television Drama: Trends and Symbolic Functions," in *Television and Social Behavior*, vol. I.

6. Ibid., p. 31.

7. Ibid., p. 36.

8. Muriel G. Cantor, "The Role of the Producer in Choosing Children's Television Content," *Television and Social Behavior*, vol. I.

9. Thomas Baldwin and Colby Lewis, "Violence in Television: The Industry Looks at Itself," in *Television and Social Behavior*, vol. I.

10. Cantor, "Role of the Producer," p. 19.

11. Ibid., p. 20.

12. Ibid., p. 21.

13. Michael Gurevich, "The Structure and Content of Television Broadcasting in Four Countries: An Overview," in *Television and Social Behavior*, vol. I.

14. Albert Bandura, "Influence of Models: Reinforcement Contingencies on the Acquisition of Imitative Responses," *Journal of Personality and Social Psychology* II: 589–95 (1965).

15. Robert M. Liebert and Robert A. Baron, "Short-Term Effects of Televised Aggression on Children's Aggressive Behavior," in *Television and Social Behavior*, vol. II.

16. Robert M. Liebert, "Television and Social Learning: Some Relationships Between Viewing Violence and Behaving," in *Television and Social Behavior*, vol. II.
17. Ibid., pp. 29–30.
18. Monroe M. Lefkowitz et al., "Television Violence and Child Aggression: A Follow-up Study," in *Television and Social Behavior*, vol. III.
19. Steven H. Chaffee, "Television and Adolescent Aggressiveness," in *Television and Social Behavior*, vol. III.
20. Jack Lyle, "Television in Daily Life: Patterns of Use," in *Television and Social Behavior*, vol. IV.
21. Bradley S. Greenberg, Phillip M. Ericson, and Mantha Vlahos, "Children's Television Behaviors as Perceived by Mother and Child," in *Television and Social Behavior*, vol. IV.
22. Lyle, "Television in Daily Life."
23. John P. Murray, "Television in Inner-City Homes: Viewing Behavior of Young Boys," in *Television and Social Behavior*, vol. IV.
24. Aletha Stein and Lynette Friedrich, "Television Content and Young Childrens' Behavior, in *Television and Social Behavior*, vol. II.
25. Jack Lyle and Heida Hoffman, "Children's Use of Television and Other Media," in *Television and Social Behavior*, vol. IV.
26. Leonard A. LoSciuto, "A National Inventory of Television Viewing Behavior," in *Television and Social Behavior*, vol. IV.
27. Jennie J. McIntyre and James J. Teevan, "Television Violence and Deviant Behavior," in *Television and Social Behavior*, vol. III.
28. Lyle and Hoffman, "Children's Use of Television," p. 138.
29. Harold Israel and John P. Robinson, "Demographic Characteristics of Viewers of Television Violence and News Programs," in *Television and Social Behavior*, vol. IV.
30. LoSciuto, "A National Inventory."
31. Robert B. Bechtel, Clark Achepohl, and Ronald Akers, "Correlates Between Observed Behavior and Questionnaire Responses on Television Viewing," in *Television and Social Behavior*, vol. IV.
32 Paul Eckman et al., "Facial Expressions of Emotion While Watching Televised Violence as Predictors of Subsequent Aggression," in *Television and Social Behavior*, vol. V.
33. David Foulkes, Edward Belvedere, and Terry Brubaker, "Televised Content and Dream Content," in *Television and Social Behavior*, vol. V.
34. Surgeon General's Advisory Committee, *Television and Growing Up.*
35. Ibid., p. 113.
36. Wilbur Schramm, Jack Lyle, and Edwin B. Parker, *Television in the Lives of Our Children* (Stanford, Calif.: Stanford University Press, 1961), p. 13.
37. Surgeon General's Advisory Committee, *Television and Growing Up*, p. 11.
38. Leo Bogart, "Warning, the Surgeon General Has Determined That TV Violence Is Moderately Dangerous to Your Child's Mental Health," *Public Opinion Quarterly* 36: 491–521 (1972).
39. Hearings before the Subcommittee on Communications, of the Committee on Commerce, United States Senate, March 21–24, 1972 (Washington, D.C.: U.S. Government Printing Office, 1972), p. 11.
40. Ibid., p. 41.
41. Ibid., p. 42.
42. Bogart, "TV Violence Is Moderately Dangerous," p. 519.

# chapter 15

# Television and Behavior:
# Ten Years of Progress

The year was 1977; the place, Miami, Florida. The occasion was the murder trial of Ronnie Zamora, a 15-year-old who was charged along with a companion with the killing of a helpless 80-year-old woman. The essence of the defense was that Zamora had learned from television that this was how people silenced those who threatened them. The elderly victim, his neighbor, had caught Zamora in an act of burglary and had threatened to call the police. But Zamora knew (allegedly from television) that "dead men can't talk." Ellis Rubin, the youngster's flamboyant attorney, introduced a novel defense, "television intoxication," arguing that it was watching violence on television that led Zamora to act as he did. The youth was portrayed as a TV *addict* who grew up on a viewing diet consisting mainly of violence and high-action drama. In Rubin's view, television, not Zamora, was the guilty party.

The jury disagreed and found Zamora guilty; watching television, they said, could not be used as an excuse for murder. Yet many people wondered if television had, in fact, played a role in Zamora's violent behavior. Indeed, were there other young Zamoras sitting in front of their sets consuming violence— human time bombs waiting to be set off? It was not a comforting idea. There were other TV violence cases that had captured the attention of the public. A group of teenagers in Florida had set homeless old men on fire after watching such a portrayal in a "Sunday Night Movie." A young woman in Boston had been the victim of a similar fate; she was dragged by a gang of violent youths to a vacant lot, beaten, and burned with gasoline. Her death occurred two days after the TV movie portraying such behavior aired.

Moreover, the level of violent crime remained high during the decade of the seventies, and little progress was apparent in solving the problem. While no one was blaming television solely for this social problem, the issue of televised violence and its link with antisocial behavior remained a salient concern with much of the public and with many media researchers.

By the 1980s, concern with television's effects was no longer focused primarily on the issue of violence; perhaps watching television was affecting our lives and those of our children in many other ways. Given that children spent so much time in front of the set, was television providing incidental lessons shaping many kinds of beliefs and actions? If so, what lessons were being taught and how did they influence youngsters? It seemed likely that there were many long-range effects. For example, seasoned teachers complained that the first generation of children who had television available all of their lives expected a level of humor, entertainment, and excitement in teaching that was quite different from that of earlier generations. Many parents were worried—how was television affecting their children's cognitive development? What about prosocial behavior, health, family activities, and other aspects of social life? It was within this atmosphere of concern that *Television and Behavior: Ten Years of Scientific Progress and Implications for the Eighties* came into being.[1]

## THE PROJECT AND THE ORGANIZATION OF THE REPORT

It was widely believed among both academics and the public that the ten years of progress report was simply an update of the information presented in the 1971 surgeon general's report, titled *Television and Growing Up,* discussed in chapter 14. Indeed, the 1982 report is often viewed as the "unfinished business" of the earlier project. That, however, is definitely not the case. The first report focused primarily (but not exclusively) on the issue of televised violence and its effects on children. However, in its summary of the 1971 report, the surgeon general's advisory committee recommended that other areas of television's influence be investigated. Of special importance to the committee were that (1) childrens' modeling of *prosocial* behavior be studied; (2) television influence be studied in the *home environment* (not in the laboratory); (3) the relationship of TV viewing to the *cognitive* and emotional development of children be examined; and (4) the ways television programming could be used to promote *good health* be considered. These were just a few of the committee's many recommendations for future research.

The scientific community responded to the committee's call; large numbers of research projects were undertaken, both in this country and abroad, which yielded an enormous amount of information. Indeed, in the decade following the publication of the surgeon general's first report, approximately *90 percent of all research publications on television's influences on behavior* (published by the end of the 1970s) had appeared. It was this body of evidence, consisting of more that 3,000 titles, that would be reviewed. Three-fourths of this massive accumulation of reports were published after 1975.

There was so much information available, and so little in the way of synthesis and evaluation, that Julius B. Richard, then surgeon general, suggested that a synthesis and evaluation of the scientific literature be undertaken by the National Institute of Mental Health (NIMH). That agency had provided leadership and had sponsored research in the area for more than a decade. Indeed, as discussed in chapter 14, it had directed research on a project, the results of which were published in *Television and Social Behavior* in 1971.

The new project began in early 1979. It was coordinated by Dr. David Pearl, chief of the Behavioral Sciences Research Branch, Division of Extramural Research Programs, at NIMH. Seven consultants were selected to advise and work with the NIMH staff on this project. Some of the consultants were media specialists; others were behavioral scientists, child development researchers, or mental health experts.

The advisory group played a key part in the entire review process. The nature of the report was influenced by several early decisions. First, because of the large body of existing literature, *no new studies would be undertaken* for the project. Instead, the project commissioned comprehensive and integrative *reviews of the existing literature* to present the state of the art in coherent and unified form. Second, it was decided to focus on a much broader spectrum of television and behavior than that which was offered by the 1971 report. Although the effects of televised violence on aggressive behavior among children would continue to be of central interest, it would receive less emphasis in the new project. The new report was to be given the lengthy title *Television and Behavior: Ten Years of Scientific Progress and Implications for the Eighties*. Decisions on areas to be covered and on the selection of scientists responsible for those areas were based on the recommendations of the advisory group.

Two volumes were prepared, both edited by David Pearl, Lorraine Bouthilet, and Joyce Lazar, all of NIMH. Volume 1 is a summary of the major conclusions of the report intended for public consumption, while volume 2 is a lengthy and detailed technical work intended for the research community. The latter consists of 24 separate reports prepared by independent researchers and 6 introductory papers prepared by the consultants, making a total of 30 reports and papers.

The independent researchers who prepared the comprehensive and critical syntheses of the scientific literature were among the most knowledgeable in communication research. Each prepared summaries in their own areas of specialization. The NIMH staff and consultants then provided comments and suggestions to the authors for revisions. However, the advisory group did not impose its opinions and values on the authors; it simply assumed an editorial function in regard to the clarity and soundness of each paper. Thus, the reports are independent products of the authors, representing their own surveys of the scientific literature as well as their evaluation, and in some cases, their own work. Even though no new research was commissioned especially for this project, research findings published for the first time are presented in some of the papers. The emphasis, however, is on review and evaluation of the existing relevant scientific literature.

It should be noted that much of the research reported was conducted with children and adolescent subjects; however, the 1982 report, unlike the 1971 version, is not limited to the influences of the medium on youth. The two reports do share an emphasis on entertainment programming. The rationale behind this focus is that such programs are those watched by most of the audience most of the time. Thus, TV news and news reporting are generally not covered. The same is true of public affairs programming. In general, then, the 1982 report covers seven broad areas of media research:

1. violence and aggression;
2. prosocial behavior;
3. cognitive and affective aspects of viewing;
4. television and health;
5. the family and interpersonal relations;
6. social beliefs and social behavior; and
7. television's effects on American society.

Because of the extensive nature of these reports, it was not possible to review all the findings of this massive project. Therefore, certain criteria were used in selecting which parts of the two volumes to cover. Generally excluded were sections devoted to complex methodological debates, topics of speculation that were not empirically investigated in depth, research studies dealing with topics that were current at the time but that in retrospect have little relevance for today (e.g., airplane hijacking to Cuba, debates about the war in Vietnam, and studies of specific TV programs that have long since vanished).

Generally, then, this chapter selectively emphasizes material closely related to the earlier surgeon general's report (chapter 14). Furthermore, the organization of materials in the original report was developed for needs rather different from those of the present book, and it was necessary to regroup the material into a somewhat different sequence. With those cautions in mind, the first issue to be discussed is further evidence on the topic of violence on television,

## TELEVISION VIOLENCE AS A CAUSE OF AGGRESSION

In general, the section on aggression and violence in volume 2 continues the long-term debate concerning the relationship between televised violence and aggressive behavior. What is new is that an attempt is made to settle the issue. The history of the violence controversy is reviewed in one paper, while another three focus on the following: (1) trends in violent content; (2) measurement of violence (neither of the two are discussed in the present chapter); (3) effects of TV violence; and (4) what processes produce the relationship between televised violence and aggression. The report on the fourth issue assumes that there is a positive relationship between televised violence and aggression, a conclusion that all the reports support, with one major exception.

## History of the Violence Controversy

Since the early days of television in the 1950s, the greatest single concern of the public about the medium has revolved around the issue of violence and its effect on behavior, especially with respect to children. Reviewing the issue once again, in the context of the 1982 project, yields the kind of feeling that baseball philosopher Yogi Berra called "déjà vu all over again." It is a perennial issue that remains to be resolved even today. Whether the cause-and-effect relationship between televised violence and behavior is ever proved to everyone's satisfaction—and more important, whether we ever collectively do anything about it if the causal links become clear—remains anyone's guess.

As discussed in chapters 13 and 14, two previous federal efforts were devoted to the investigation of the problem of TV violence. One report was by the National Commission on the Causes and Prevention of Violence and the other was by the Surgeon General's Scientific Advisory Committee on Television and Social Behavior. Both groups reported a suspected and probable link between TV violence and aggressive behavior. Yet the question of TV violence and its effect remained controversial. Perhaps some of the controversy resulted from the cautious conclusion of the surgeon general's committee (chapter 14, p. 336), which appeared to lead to different interpretations of the research results. As reported in the press, most newspaper writers and critics stated that television had no effect on aggressive behavior, whereas many (but not all) social scientists considered that a link between television and violence had been established.

> Most television researchers look at the totality of evidence and conclude, as did the Surgeon General's Advisory Committee, that the convergence of most of the findings about televised violence and later aggressive behavior by the viewer supports the positive conclusion of a causal relationship. A few researchers, looking at each piece of research individually and finding flaws in design and/or methodology, conclude that the case has not been made for a causal relationship.[2]

So, in fact, the question of the effects of TV violence remained unresolved in many people's minds, and it is likely that the public lost some confidence in the ability of social scientists ever to resolve the issue. Yet concern over the relationship between violence and TV viewing did not die.

The year 1975 brought several new developments. For one thing, Congress took up the question of violence on television along with its investigation of obscenity and sexual provocation and pressured the Federal Communication Commission to "do something." As a result, the FCC commissioners negotiated with the networks for the establishment of "family viewing hours" in the early evening. Writers and producers, however, challenged the arrangement on the grounds that it violated First Amendment rights and infringed on their right of trade. The courts ruled for the artists, but the networks continued the family hour (at least for a while) on an informal basis.

At about the same time, citizen groups began raising protests against some programming practices. Broadcasters should reduce the amount of violence, said the American Medical Association, because it threatened the social health of the country. The National Parent-Teacher Association began monitoring television content and sponsored public forums concerning its effects throughout the country. In addition, an activist group called the National Citizens' Committee for Broadcasting began linking advertisers with violent content. This resulted in some advertisers acting to reduce their association with violent programming. Additionally, a 1980 national survey indicated that violence on television continued to concern the American public; 70 percent of the respondents indicated that there was too much violence and that it was a "serious" or "very serious" problem.[3] As a result of this public concern and protests by citizen groups, all three major networks became involved in research on the social influence of the medium. Their approach, however, was in many ways reminiscent of the tobacco industry's efforts to solve their image problems through research. It was largely aimed at gathering evidence supporting their claims.

## Continuing Evidence on the Effects of Televised Violence

By the 1970s, most researchers seemed to agree that there was a causal relationship between televised violence and later aggressive behavior, although the evidence was by no means compelling. That conclusion was significantly strengthened by research in the decade following the publication of the surgeon general's original report. Indeed, in the following years, several important *field* studies found that televised violence resulted in aggressive behavior. The emphasis was on field studies, since the violence-aggression connection was well established in the laboratory, and according to researcher L. Rowell Huesmann, was "beyond challenge at this point."[4] Much more controversial were the data collected outside the laboratory, the argument being that if there is no effect in the "real world" (as opposed to a laboratory setting), then there is no major impact upon society.

*Studies Linking Violence Viewing and Aggression.*   J. L. Singer and D. G. Singer carried out two independent investigations that involved three- and four-year-old children over the course of a one-year period.[5] They carefully measured a number of variables at four different points in time. The Singers concluded that children's television viewing at home was definitely related to the various types of behavior they showed during free-play periods at day-care centers. They found consistent associations between heavy viewing of violent television programs and unwarranted aggressive behavior in the children's free play. Indeed, a variety of different multivariate analyses of their data all led to the same conclusion: "television viewing, particularly violence viewing, is a cause of heightened aggressiveness in children of that age."[6]

Another study of special significance was a five-year longitudinal study by E. D. McCarthy and associates.[7] In this research, data from 732 children were obtained that clearly supported the hypothesis that viewing TV violence is related to aggressive behavior, such as fights with peers, conflict with parents, and delinquency. They also found that the total amount of television viewed was positively related to aggressive behavior. This finding was particularly interesting because older studies (see chapter 14) had found no relationship between total amount of viewing and aggression. Moreover, several later studies reported the same findings.[8]

Another long-term study by researchers L. D. Eron and Huesmann collected extensive data on children in several countries.[9] At the time of the report, results were available for grade-school children in the United States, Finland, and Poland. As Table 15.1 indicates, in each of these countries significant positive relationships were found between television violence and aggression for *both* boys and girls. In earlier studies (chapter 14), the relationship was found only for boys. (Perhaps the appearance of more aggressive female role models for girls was a critical factor.) Additionally, the simple frequency of TV viewing also correlated highly with aggression.

One other study should be mentioned if for no other reason than that it was funded by the Columbia Broadcasting System (CBS). William Belson collected data on 1,650 teenage boys in London. Although his study was not longitudinal, he concluded on the basis of analysis of matched subgroups, that "the evidence . . . is very supportive of the hypothesis that high exposure to television violence increases the degree to which boys engage in serious violence."[10]

**TABLE 15.1**  Correlations between TV violence viewing and peer-nominated aggression

| | All Subjects | Males | Females |
|---|---|---|---|
| United States (*N* = 758): | | | |
| 1st grade | .212**** | .160* | .210*** |
| 2nd grade | .234**** | .204** | .245**** |
| 3rd grade | .232**** | .191** | .205** |
| 4th grade | .224**** | .184* | .260**** |
| 5th grade | .261**** | .199* | .294**** |
| | | | |
| Finland (*N* = 220): | | | |
| 1st grade | .141 | .026 | .139 |
| 2nd grade | .163 | .266* | .022 |
| 3rd grade | .257*** | .038 | .052 |
| 4th grade | .228* | .381*** | −.158 |
| | | | |
| Poland (*N* = 237): | | | |
| 1st grade | .227** | .296** | .070 |
| 3rd grade | .293**** | .259** | .236* |

*p* >*.05.          *p* >**.025.                    *p* >***.01                    *p* >****.005

SOURCE: David Pearl, Lorraine Bouthilet, and Joyce Lazar, eds., *Television and Behavior: Ten Years of Scientific Progress and Implications for the Eighties* (Washington, D.C.: U.S. Government Printing Office, 1982), vol. 2, p. 128.

*Conflicting Evidence.*     Not all people, even all social scientists, agreed that there was a causal relationship between televised violence and aggressive behavior. The whole issue of demonstrating causality has been the object of much debate and analysis in the social sciences. Because it is a complex concept, there is no single, unassail- able theory or approach; inferential errors may occur in either direction. In one case, a likely causal relationship may be rejected because the researcher employs too rigorous a standard of judgment. Likewise, a questionable relationship may be accepted because of a weak standard. In any event, much of the dispute about the causal implications of research on violence and aggression stems from such differences in judgment.

One major study that added fuel not only to the causality debate but also to the one over violence was by J. Ronald Milavsky and associates.[11] The results of this major study were first published in the report on ten years of progress, although a more detailed book appeared later. The Milavsky study was sponsored and carried by the National Broadcasting Company (NBC). In fact, all of its authors were employed by NBC's Department of Social Research. The study was designed as a panel survey covering a three-year period (1970–1973), and some 3,200 young people were interviewed as part of the project. Data were collected on elementary school boys and girls as well as teenage high school boys. The study focused on "purposive aggression," which was defined as "physical or verbal acts intended or known in advance to cause injury to others, rather than on rough play or accidents that might result in injury as an unintended or unforeseen consequence."[12] This definition is more restrictive than those used in other research. The researchers claimed that it was more realistic.

The researchers measured aggression in elementary school children six times during a three-year period; the high school boys were measured five times. These measures were "peer nominations" for the elementary students and "self-reports" for the teens. Both groups of students reported which TV programs they watched. However, for purposes of analysis, the investigators chose only those programs that they could classify as violent. The researchers obtained small positive correlations between measurements taken at the same time but none between those taken at different times. The findings of small correlations in same-time measurements are consistent with the results from other cross-sectional studies.

The investigators wanted to learn whether viewing TV violence had short- term effects or cumulative effects that produced consistent behavior patterns in real-world settings. The study, however, provided "no evidence that television violence was causally implicated in the development of aggressive behavior patterns in children and adolescents over the time periods studied."[13] Thus, while Milavsky and associates did not disagree that viewing violence on TV is associated with short-term aggressive behavior, they found no long-term cumulative relation- ship between viewing televised violence and patterns of aggressive behavior.

It is not difficult to predict that this study, with its wealth of data, would provoke much discussion. The study was carefully planned and methodologically sophisticated. It stood in opposition to a large body of evidence that indicated a relationship between televised violence and aggressive behavior. Even so, critics were quick to criticize the statistical model used to test the hypotheses. As Eli

Rubenstein argued: "Milavsky and his colleagues chose to establish causality in accord with a statistical model whose complexity and relative newness will permit honest differences of opinion about its appropriateness for this extensive set of data."[14]

Many researchers who had reached opposite conclusions continued to maintain that there is a *positive* relationship between viewing televised violence and aggressive behavior. For example, L. Rowell Huesmann concluded that:

> While the strength of all relation changes as a function of situational determinants, population characteristics, and measurement techniques, the evidence seems overwhelming that television violence viewing and aggression are positively correlated in children.[15]

## What Produces the Relationship?

Many researchers argued that rather than continue to gather evidence that there is a relationship between the viewing of televised violence and an increased possibility of aggressive behavior, researchers should move to the issue of what processes produce that relationship. Four different possibilities had been suggested: observational learning, attitude changes, physiological arousal, and justification processes.

*Observational Learning.*    According to the observational learning model, children learn to behave aggressively from watching violent actors on television just as they learn cognitive and social skills from watching parents, siblings, peers, and others. Bandura's original experiment (discussed in chapter 14) suggested the validity of the thesis and, although observational learning had been successfully demonstrated in the laboratory many times, questions remained about its role in field settings. Indeed, it was not until 1977 that the results of a longitudinal study were first published in the area. Its findings provided substantial evidence for observational learning as a plausible explanation for the link between televised violence and aggressive behavior. Since then, several other field studies concurred with those findings. These field studies clarified the way that observational learning may be linked to other factors. Some of the findings, for example, indicated that observational learning is most likely related to age; specifically, it is a significant factor for young children, but it loses some importance in adolescence. Research indicated that children as young as two years easily imitated televised behaviors; in fact, some imitation was observed in even younger children.

Some researchers attempted to tie observational learning more closely to cognitive-processing psychology. Researchers Tulving and Thompson's concept of encoding *specificity* in human memory seems particularly relevant. They argued that the likelihood of an item being recalled depends upon the specific encoding (acquisition) context being reproduced, including even apparently irrelevant aspects. The major idea was that forms of aggressive behavior can be elicited by the presence of specific cues in the environment—cues that are also present in televised violence. Indeed, in one study, a number of cases were analyzed in which juveniles seem to have imitated specific criminal acts portrayed on television; for example, the Boston incident in which a gang burned a woman to death.[16] In each instance, it was found that highly specific visual cues present in the TV program (e.g., a woman carrying a bright red gasoline can) were also present in the environment in which imitated behavior occurred.

Overall, the research on observational learning and cognitive processes suggested that children who watched large numbers of aggressive behaviors on TV programs may have stored, and at a later time retrieved and performed, those behaviors when appropriate cues (from the portrayals) were present. Even aspects of the scene that seem irrelevant (e.g., color) may have served as triggering cues. The recall of an aggressive behavior that provides a solution to a problem a child faces may lead to modeling of that behavior in the child.

*Attitude Change.*    Another area in which TV violence is thought to exert its influence on children (as well as adults) is their attitudes. Research indicates that the more televised violence a child watches, the more favorable the child's attitude toward aggressive behavior. Overall, attitudes of frequent TV viewers toward aggression tend to be more positive than those of less frequent viewers because the former perceive that aggressive behavior is the norm. In fact, it has been found that the more aggressive a subject is, the more likely it is that he or she thinks others are also aggressive.

A major study, using a longitudinal design, found that children's attitudes toward aggression could be changed if adults discussed the program with them.[17] Children who viewed frequently were selected and randomly divided into experimental and control groups. The children in the experimental group were exposed over the next two years to two treatments designed to mitigate the effects of TV violence. The first treatment was begun at the start of the second year; three small-group sessions were held in which the investigators tried to teach the subjects how unrealistic TV violence was. The children viewed brief excerpts from violent shows and participated in a highly structured discussion of the actors' behaviors. The control group viewed nonviolent educational excerpts, followed by discussion of their content.

In addition, the researchers used a more formal attitude change procedure at the beginning of the third year. They had each experimental subject write a paragraph on why TV violence is unrealistic and why viewing too much of it is bad. In two sessions, the children in the experimental group wrote the paragraph, received suggestions, and rewrote it. They were then videotaped reading their paragraphs, after which they watched the videotape of themselves and their classmates. The subjects were told that the tapes were going to be shown to school children in Chicago. The control group made a tape about what they did last summer.

Six months after the final experimental session, the last data were collected on all the children. The mean peer-nominated aggression score for the experimental group became significantly lower than the score for the control group, as indicated by Table 15.2. In addition, the viewing of violence was a much more important predictor of aggressive behavior for the control group than for the experimental group. In short, the experimental group was much less aggressive than the control group. Since the children were randomly assigned to each group, the researchers concluded that the changes in the children's attitudes were the result of their intervention.

While not every study published during the ten-year period found a positive relationship between viewing violence and positive attitudes toward aggression, it was concluded that *overall* the evidence suggested that TV violence can change one's attitudes toward aggression and that one's attitudes in turn influence one's behavior. At the same time, we should point out that the cognitive paradigm on which this type of interpretation rests has not been particularly fruitful in the study of the effects of the media.[18]

*Arousal Processes.* Some researchers hypothesize that arousal processes are the intervening factor between the viewing of violence and attitude change. However, there is a great deal of confusion about the nature of arousal. Some researchers argue that television is making children hyperactive by "overloading" them with stimulation, while others claim that television is "anesthetizing" children by the same overloading process. However, there has been a great deal of interest in what has been considered a major consequence of arousal—desensitization. For example, boys who regularly watched a great deal of violence on television showed less physiological arousal when they looked at new violent programs than did control subjects.[19] While such findings are difficult to replicate in field studies, it should not be a great surprise that emotional and physiological responsiveness to scenes of violence habituates in a manner similar to other responses.

*Lack of Evidence for a Cathartic Process.* In direct opposition to the previous approaches, catharsis theory predicts that aggression will be *reduced* after watching violence on television. It is an old concept with origins as far back

**TABLE 15.2** Effect of the intervention on mean level of aggression over the course of one year

| | | Mean Peer-Nominated Aggression (Peeragg) | |
| --- | --- | --- | --- |
| | | **Before (1978)** | **After (1979)** |
| Experimental Group (N = 59) | | 154.0 | 175.3 |
| Placebo Group (N = 58) | | 158.0 | 242.8 |
| **Analysis of Covariance** | **Source** | **df** | **F** | **Signif.** |
| Covariates | | | | |
| | Sex | 1 | 1.23 | — |
| | Grade | 1 | 0.00 | — |
| | Peeragg 1978 | 1 | 61.12 | .001 |
| Effects | | | | |
| | Group | 1 | 6.40 | .013 |
| Error | | 112 | | |
| Total | | 116 | | |

SOURCE: David Pearl, Lorraine Bouthilet, and Joyce Lazar, eds., *Television and Behavior: Ten Years of Scientific Progress and Implications for the Eighties* (Washington, D.C.: U.S. Government Printing Office, 1982), vol. 2, p. 133.

as ancient Greece. In any case, catharsis is a process that supposedly reduces or dissipates the need or desire to be aggressive as a result of viewing depictions of violent behavior. However, since almost all the evidence points to an *increase* in aggressive behavior rather than a decrease, catharsis theory is contradicted by the available data.

***General Conclusions about the Basis of the Relationship.***   Broadly, then, researchers moved beyond the question of whether there is a positive relationship between viewing TV violence and aggressive behavior and began seeking to explain why that relationship exists. The weight of evidence as of the end of the 1970s strongly suggested that observational learning and attitude change induced by TV violence contributed to the positive relationship. Meanwhile, the concept of arousal remained an attractive possibility. Finally, the available data convincingly contradicted the catharsis model.

## PROSOCIAL BEHAVIOR

During the 1970s, considerable research examined whether television content could produce prosocial behavior. After all, if viewing violence could produce aggression, then it followed logically that viewing altruistic, friendly, or cooperative situations should result in behavior approved by society. *Prosocial* was defined as that which is "socially desirable and which in some way benefits another person or society at large."[20] This definition obviously involves a value judgment based on the wider social context.

Observation learning theory, which as we have seen is often linked with the violence issue, was applied to prosocial behavior. According to the theory, television can have diverse effects, depending on the content of what is watched. Indeed, if one of the main ways in which people learn is by observing others, then it follows that people should learn a variety of behaviors by viewing others on television. As a contact for observational learning, television provides its viewers with access to a wide range of observational learning experiences.

Researcher J. Philipe Rushton has categorized TV content that is prosocial into four types: (1) altruism, which includes such behaviors as generosity, helping, and cooperation; (2) friendliness; (3) self-control behavior, which includes resisting temptations and delaying gratification; and (4) behavior that helps adults and children cope with fears. Rushton reviewed 42 studies. Some were laboratory experiments, while others were carried out in field settings. Nonetheless, results from both types of studies came to similar conclusions.

## Altruism

The studies that address altruism agree that children who watch this type of behavior on television become more altruistic themselves. For example, in a series of experiments, several hundred boys and girls from six to nine years old were shown five-minute videotapes in which a child played a bowling game and won gift certificates.[21] On one of the tapes, the character donated the certificate to charity; on the other, the character did not. Subsequently, the children were watched through a one-way mirror to see how much of their winnings they donated to a similar charity. The results showed that children were strongly influenced by what they had seen on television, and modeling of altruistic behavior was clearly demonstrated. Children who had watched generosity on the videotape gave more of their certificates to the charity than those who had watched selfishness portrayed.

Several other studies, using similar procedures, have yielded similar findings. One study found that children from five to seven years old were influenced by TV models to share both candy and money.[22] Moreover, these findings are not limited to American children. Another study showed that eight- to ten-year-old British children were influenced to donate tokens to a charity by watching TV models do so.[23] Critics, however, point out that these studies all took place in laboratory settings and that they are not like the typical television-watching situation. However, field studies have been carried out (eight such studies were reviewed by Rushton). While the results were not as clear-cut, they generally tended to support the conclusion that altruistic behavior can be learned by watching televised models who display such patterns.

## Friendliness

All of the seven studies of friendly behavior described in the report used nursery school children as subjects. Two laboratory and five naturalistic studies were included. For example, a 1976 study carried out in Canada investigated whether prosocial TV content could increase young children's friendliness toward ethnic minorities.[24] After viewing special "Sesame Street" inserts containing nonwhite children, a sample of children who were three, four, and five years old showed a strong preference for playing with minority as opposed to white children. Children who had not seen the special program inserts did not show such preferences. The subjects, all English Canadian, also watched inserts with a French Canadian boy and indicated an equally strong preference for him after seeing the special program inserts. The control group showed no such preference.

The goal of one very dramatic field study was to see whether TV programs could be used to enhance social interaction between nursery school children who tended to isolate themselves from their peers.[25] Thirteen extremely solitary children were selected for this study. One group of these children viewed a specially prepared film shown on television. The film portrayed several scenes in which children interacted in a nursery school setting and were rewarded for it. For comparison purposes, a control group of children watched a film about dolphins. The results were dramatic, to say the least. Children who viewed the televised scenes increased the number of their interactions with others from an average of 2 per day to an average of 12 per day. The control group, on the other hand, showed no increase in their interaction with other children. A follow-up at the end of the school year indicated that the changes were durable over time— the subjects were still interacting with other children.

## Self-Control

Most of the studies on the effects of showing self-control behaviors on television are laboratory experiments. However, some field studies have been done. One example is a 1972 study in which girls who were eight and nine years old were told the rules of an electronic bowling game. They were also told that they could win money by scoring high.[26] Before playing the game, the children watched a TV program in which they saw a young girl model playing the same game. Some of the girls, however, saw a film in which the model broke the rules in order to win money. The other girls viewed a film that was identical except that the model abided by the rules. The results were as expected: The girls who saw cheating on the film cheated twice as often as the other girls.

Some studies looked at a particular form of self-control, in the form of delayed gratification. For example, in a 1974 New Zealand study, 72 eight-year-olds were used as subjects to determine whether viewing television could affect patterns of delayed gratification.[27] The normal behavior of the children was established by asking then if they would prefer a small reward, such as money, immediately, or a larger one by waiting for seven days. Later, some of the children watched TV programs showing an adult female model engaging in delayed gratification behavior and explaining why she had acted in such a manner. The control group of children did not view such programs. The results showed that the children who had watched the examples of delayed gratification were subsequently more likely to choose to delay their gratification for a larger reward. Moreover, when the children were retested four weeks later, their behavior still showed the effects of the exposure to the TV films.

## Coping with Fears

Fourteen studies were included in the report that show the capability of televised presentations to modify people's fears. Some of the studies used adult subjects, while others worked with children. One pioneering investigation dealt with young children who ranged from three to five years old.[28] These children were all afraid of dogs. To determine which children were afraid of the cocker spaniel used in the study, the researchers measured their willingness to approach and play with it on several occasions. Then, over an eight-day period, some of the children were shown eight 3-minute films showing other children playing with dogs. A control group of similarly fearful children saw movies of Disneyland. The children were then given the chance to approach a live dog. Children who previously were afraid of dogs and who viewed the film with the dog were more likely to approach and play with the animal than were the subjects in the control group. In addition, the reduction in fear generalized to dogs that were quite different from those seen in the film, and the reduction remained when they were retested four weeks later. Similar results were obtained by other researchers using young children and a large German shepherd as the film stimulus.[29] Although both groups of children showed high levels of fear in the pretest, eight of the nine boys in a film group were subsequently willing to approach, pet, and feed the live German shepherd. In contrast, only three of the nine boys in the control group did so.

Bandura and his associates studied the influence of film programs on fear of snakes in adolescents and adults.[30] Only persons whose dread of snakes was so severe that it interfered with activities such as camping and gardening were tested. The subjects watched a 35-minute film in which children, adolescents, and adults interacted with a king snake. The results were clear: Those who watched the film were significantly less fearful. Indeed, the behavioral measurements of fear were stringent and involved actually holding a snake and allowing it unrestrained in their laps. These findings were confirmed by a similar experiment in 1973.

Another interesting study involved 60 children age four to six who were preparing to undergo elective surgery for hernias, tonsillectomies, or urinary-genital-tract difficulties.[31] The goal of the study was to reduce their fears about their forthcoming surgery. The children were divided into two groups and were shown either a film of a child being hospitalized and receiving surgery or an unrelated control film. The treatment film depicted various events that hospitalized children encounter. Although both groups received extensive preparation by the hospital staff, there was a significant reduction of fear in the experimental group both the night before the operation and during an examination three to four weeks later. The parents also reported more problem behavior in the children who had not seen the medical film.

It should be noted that although 14 different studies were reviewed regarding the use of TV or film presentations to help individuals cope with fear, many other studies dealing with the same subject were published during the 1970s. All reached the same conclusion: Such presentations have a clear therapeutic potential.

The general conclusions regarding television and prosocial behavior seemed reasonably clear. Forty-two studies, both laboratory and field, supported the same generalization: Television and film programs can modify viewers' behavior in a prosocial direction. Friendliness, cooperation, helping, generosity, observance of rules, delayed gratification, and reduction of unreasonable fears can all be increased by the use of televised materials. Rushton argues that these studies "suggest that television is an effective agent of socialization, that television entertainment is modifying the viewer's perception of the world and how to live in it."[32]

There seems little doubt that people learn from watching television and, more important, what they learn depends on what they watch. If viewers see prosocial behavior in TV programs, then this is what will be learned as appropriate, normal behavior. If, however, aggression and antisocial behaviors are shown, these may be judged as normative by viewers. If this seems like an extreme position, then one should consider that such a view is quite consistent with the logic behind the billions of dollars spent annually by advertisers. They believe, often correctly, that repeated exposure to their brief messages will change the behavior of the public toward their products.

This massive body of research clearly implied that television can no longer be viewed as mere entertainment. As a major source of observational learning experiences, it determines what people judge to be appropriate behavior in a variety of situations. Indeed, Rushton concluded that "television has become one of the most important agencies of socialization that our society possesses." And, as the studies in this section indicate, television can have beneficial effects for our society; it is a potential force for good. In short, television has the power to affect the behavior of viewers in a positive, prosocial direction.

## COGNITIVE ASPECTS OF TELEVISION

One of the key advances in research on television in the seventies was the recognition that the medium must be understood more broadly. In particular, its relation to the cognitive and effective development of children needed to be examined. Children begin to pay attention to the medium by the time they are six to nine months old. From that point on, television is an increasingly frequent intruder into the life of a child. Today's children grow up in an environment where television talks, entertains, and promotes products for their consumption. They must organize these experiences along with those of the physical and social environment.

### Cognitive Growth

Just how does television affect the cognitive growth of children who often spend more time watching television than they spend in school or in conversation with adults or siblings? Also, to what extent do the structural properties of television as a medium influence the way new information from other environments is processed? It may be that the very nature of thinking itself is being modified by the heavy visual stimulation that characterizes regular viewing. The broad field of television and its relation to cognitive and functioning includes such topics as cognitive processing and the effects of encoding TV scenes and programs.

Research in the area of cognitive processes blossomed during the decade of the 1970s. Approximately 75 major books and articles were published on the topic during that period. The research reviewed for the present chapter examined how individuals perceived, remembered, and comprehended what was seen and heard on television; almost all of the research subjects were children.

When a child lounges in front of a television set staring at it intently, what is attracting the youngster to the set and capturing his or her attention? In an effort to find an answer to these questions, researchers unobtrusively observed children in a playroom with the television on, usually through a one-way mirror. In addition to the TV set, the room had toys and games that might have distracted the children. The results of these studies were informative chartings of the attention paid by children to television as a function of attributes of the presentation, age, and individual differences.

One principle used to explain attention to television is called *attentional inertia.* It has been defined as "the longer people look at the television screen the greater the probability that they will continue to look."[33] Inertia also characterizes *not* looking. "The longer children have directed their attention elsewhere, the less likely they are to begin looking at television."[34] Attentional inertia has been found in children of all ages as well as among college-age adults.

The age of the child is, on average, directly related to the length of time he or she looks at the set. Six-month-old infants gaze only occasionally at TV programs, whereas at age one children actually watch about 12 percent of the time that a set is turned on. There is a dramatic jump in viewing between the ages of two and three years, rising from 25 percent to 45 percent of the time. By age four, children are watching about 55 percent of the time, even when they are in a playroom with many distracting toys.

Children were also attracted to television by specific features of programs. For example, their attention was obtained and maintained by women characters, women and children's voices, auditory changes, peculiar voices, activity or movement, camera cuts, sound effects, laughing, and applause. Negative attributes—those that terminated looks at television—included voices of men, extended zooms and pans, animals, and still pictures. Auditory cues were found to have strong effects in attracting attention. Apparently, children quickly learned which sights and sounds went together so that what may have appeared to be a peripheral background sound actually may have been an attention getter. For example, "chase" music implies a chase scene, which is exciting and fun to watch. Thus, children did not attend to just any content of television; rather they were psychologically active and selective, and they shifted their attention according to the sense and meaning of what they saw and heard.

When children are paying attention to the TV set, do they understand what is going on? Age is the single most important factor. Young children did not appear to understand much of television's offerings. However, young children frequently remembered discrete scenes or events (actions less than a scene). What they did not understand were relations between the scenes. But older children and adults typically "chunked" programs into larger units that encompassed several scenes.

One important implication of these findings pertains to the ways children come to like or dislike characters and, by inference, whether they imitate their behavior. For example, children do not like aggressive characters. But when they do not understand the relations between aggressive behavior and antisocial motives, they may like the TV character and even model the character's behavior.

## Influences of Encoding

Television is a visual medium in which encoding techniques that have no counterparts in the real world are used to produce a stream of constantly changing images. Special effects, such as camera cuts and slow motion, are used in unique ways—with sound effects, accompanying music, unusual cries and noises, canned laughter, and faceless narrators. During the decade of the 1970s, there was new interest in studying television's encoding conventions. One of the major reasons for this interest was the belief that television's effects may at least partly be the result of *form* as well as content. It may be that fast action, loud noises, and unusual camera effects are just as responsible for behavioral effects as is violent content. Obversely, the slow pace of some programs may be more important than content in producing prosocial conduct.

Two laboratory studies provided support for the idea that the formal features of television could instigate aggressive behavior in children, even in the absence of violent content.[35] The first showed three different kinds of programs: one high in both violence and action, one low in violence and high in action, and one low in both. It was not possible to find a program high in violence and low in action. The second study used advertisements with different levels of salient formal features—action, pace, visual special effects—in the commercial breaks of a nonaggressive program. There was no aggression in the program or in any of the commercials. In each study, pairs of preschool children were observed in a play situation containing a variety of toys before and after viewing the experimental programs.

In spite of the diverse content and formats of the programs and commercials, both studies came to the same conclusion: Children tended to be more aggressive after high-action programs than after low-action or no television programs at all. Interestingly, violent content did not add to the level of aggression produced by high levels of action alone. These findings support the hypothesis that the high-action format can lead to increased aggression without the modeling effects of violent content just as it aroused more attention with or without violence.

It is debatable whether form and content can be clearly distinguished, even though they may be defined independently. In practice, form of presentation and content of message systematically concur. Thus, the two effects are confounded in real-world situations, and all studies of content that attribute effects to one may also include the effects of the other.

## ADDITIONAL INFLUENCES ON INDIVIDUALS AND SOCIETY

During the late 1970s, research concerning the effects of television on viewers expanded to many kinds of issues. In large part, the earlier preoccupation with violence versus prosocial behavior, or even with cognitive versus emotional influences, represented attempts to determine to what extent television was the "bad guy" among the media. At times it seemed like there was a kind of determination to show that television's main influence was to create harm to those who attended. However, beyond those concerns were other, less explored questions, such as the possible influence of the medium on health, family life, gender roles, the status of ethnic and racial groups, and beliefs about the aged. Even broader questions were coming over the research horizon. What was the role of television in teaching about such matters as leisure, religion, and citizenship?

In other words, as research interests broadened, it was increasingly recognized that television had a potentially significant role in shaping people's interpretations—good or bad—in many areas of social life. The research community recognized that insufficient attention had been paid to that broader role as part of the general communication processes by which we collectively shape meanings.

For these reasons, the report on ten years of progress assembled research findings on a long list of topics.[36] While previous sections focused on studies dealing with violent, prosocial, cognitive, and affective aspects of behavior, the remaining parts of the chapter extend the list to include health, family issues, social beliefs, and behavior.

## Health

One of the recommendations of the original Surgeon General Committee on Television and Social Behavior was that we should "consider and stimulate television's health-promoting possibilities."[37] In 1971, virtually nothing was known about the portrayal of health-related issues in TV programming. Few answers were available as to what kind of health portrayals were available to viewers and whether or not such messages were likely to encourage healthy or unhealthy lifestyles. Media researchers were quick to follow up on this suggestion, and their zeal produced a plethora of published articles in the subsequent years.

Three lengthy summary articles in the report on ten years of progress review the status of health-related research. The first is concerned with the content of TV programs; it focuses on portrayals relevant to health and health-related behavior.[38] Another examines TV campaigns that were designed to promote better health;[39] the reasons for the successes as well as the failures of specific TV campaigns are reviewed. The final paper analyzes the use of television by persons in institutions (e.g., mental institutions, nursing homes), as well as its effects on such persons.[40]

***Portrayals of Health-Related Issues.*** One major paper in this section, titled "Programming Health Portrayals: What Viewers See, Say, and Do,"[41] reviewed the multitude of studies on health portrayals on television. Both direct and indirect health messages were included. Among the direct messages analyzed were the portrayals of medical conditions as well as physician and patient behavior in televised dramas. Indirect messages included an analysis of lifestyle behaviors, such as smoking, alcohol use, risky driving, or use of seat belts. The researchers pointed out that by the beginning of the 1980s, "lifestyle illnesses" accounted for about half of the deaths in the United States each year. Indeed, advances in medical sciences had led to a shift in the type of illness most likely to be fatal. Many acute infectious diseases had been conquered, whereas many chronic ones, in which lifestyle plays a major role, continued to take their toll. Nutrition and dietary patterns, smoking, and alcohol use were included in the risk factors for lifestyle diseases. Thus, their portrayal may have had some relevance to viewers' health-related practices, particularly if a consistent message was conveyed.

At the time of the project, the average viewer watched television about 30 hours each week (about 4.5 hours per day). During that time, he or she was exposed to health-related concepts and behavior many times in both programs and commercials. The nature of these portrayals, however, was (and still is) usually determined by dramatic or sales functions, rather than scientific or therapeutic criteria. In one study, health-related topics were found to occur in 7.2 percent of the total broadcast time.[42] Most of these appearances were in entertainment programs or commercials. There were few informational programs dealing with health issues.

In addition, 70 percent of the health information provided was considered inaccurate, misleading, or both, while only 30 percent was rated useful. Viewers were ten times more likely to see a message urging the use of pills than one concerning drug abuse. Some of the brief public service messages, including those on heart disease, smoking, and crisis centers, were considered useful and informative. But information about most major health problems, such as cancer, stroke, accidents, hepatitis, maternal death, malnutrition, and venereal disease, was virtually nonexistent. Thus, according to this survey, television was performing nowhere near its potential in offering health information.

Both prime-time (8 to 11 P.M.) and children's weekend-daytime (8 A.M. to 2:30 P.M.) network dramatic programs were dominated by themes involving action, power, and danger. Both also portrayed many acts of violence, which, as the researchers pointed out, is definitely related to health. Few accidental fatalities occurred in the world of prime-time television despite all the risky driving, fires, and explosions. In real life, automobile accidents were a leading cause of death for young adults in the United States. However, while automobiles and trucks were common on television, seat belt use was seldom seen. Indeed, one study found only a single instance of characters using seat belts, and even that depiction was followed by a wild driving stunt in which the driver did not use a belt.[43]

Prime-time characters were rarely shown to have any type of physical impairment; in fact, almost none even wore glasses. Only 2 percent of major characters were physically handicapped; they tended to be older, less positively presented, and more likely to be victimized, and they were almost never shown on children's programs. Characters suffering from mental disorders, however, did appear on prime-time programs with some frequency—abut 17 percent of prime-time programs involved a depiction or theme of mental illness. Moreover, about 3 percent of major characters were identified as mentally ill, and in the late evening programs, this percentage doubled. The mentally ill were also disproportionately depicted both as "violents" and as the victims of violence. Of the dramatic characters in prime-time programs, 40 percent of "normals" were violent compared with 73 percent for the mentally ill. Similarly, 44 percent of the "normal" characters were victims of violence, whereas the figure for mentally ill characters was 81 percent. No other group of fictional characters suffered, nor was shown to deserve, that fate so often. Those most likely to be portrayed as mentally unstable in TV programs were sales and clerical workers, manual laborers, criminals, and scientists. Those least subject to mental illness were policemen, owners and proprietors, farmers, and ministers. Overall, the portrayal of the mentally ill was very unrealistic; television was certainly not reflecting "reality" as far as this topic was concerned.

Another category of portrayals studied was nutrition and obesity. Eating and drinking occurred about ten times per hour. Moreover, 75 percent of all dramatic characters ate and drank or talked about doing so. In the portrayal of nutrition patterns in prime-time programs, eating was anything but balanced or relaxed. Of all eating-drinking episodes, characters "grabbing a snack" (39 percent) occurred nearly as often as breakfast, lunch, and dinner combined (42 percent). For children's weekend-daytime programming, the incidence of snacking rose to 45 percent, while regular meals declined to 24 percent of all eating-drinking episodes. In addition, the snack was most often a high-calorie, high-fat food; fruits were consumed only 4 or 5 percent of the time.

The beverage most frequently consumed on television was alcohol. In fact, the kinds of drinks consumed were inversely proportional to those in real-life settings. On television, alcohol was consumed twice as often as coffee or tea, 14 times as often as soft drinks, and 15 times as frequently as water. Indeed, alcohol was hard to escape in the late 1970s TV Land. One study found it shown or mentioned in 80 percent of prime-time programs (not counting commercials).[44] Moreover, a 1980 study reported that alcohol use was present in 12 of the 15 most popular programs.[45] It was estimated that the average child viewer would see approximately 3,000 drinking episodes a year! Furthermore, the drinkers were not the villains or the bit players; they were the good, steady, likable characters.

While obesity is a problem that plagues around 45 percent of the American population, fat people are rarely seen on television. In a study done in 1979, less than 6 percent of male characters and 2 percent of female characters portrayed on television were found to be obese. Not one of those was a leading character.[46] The results of another survey found that 11 percent of the characters were overweight, but none of the obese were children, teens, or young adults.[47] When fat people were portrayed, they were usually members of a minority group. Sixteen percent of the black and 80 percent of the Asian American characters were obese. On the other hand, the causes of obesity are seldom made clear. Many characters portrayed on television consume large amounts of snacks, sweets, and alcohol, but few have weight problems. They eat and drink but stay slim. Just what the effects of such depictions are remains unclear, but it is unrealistic, to say the least.

Smoking had become less common in TV portrayals during the 1970s, although it was still frequently seen in the reruns of old movies. An analysis of major characters found that few smoked—only 11 percent of the men and 2 percent of the women.[48] The highest levels of smoking occurred in dramatic presentations, but even there it was only 13 percent of the male and 4 percent of the female characters. In general, situation comedies had little smoking, whereas crime and adventure shows portrayed somewhat more. There were, however, no instances of TV characters expressing antismoking sentiments or refusing to smoke.

Of special interest were health portrayals on the daytime serials. They were so frequent in this kind of programming that they were worthy of special mention. Coping with illness and its effects is one of the major themes of the soap opera. Nearly half of all characters become involved in health-related problems. These include psychiatric disorders, heart attacks, pregnancies, automobile accidents, attempted homicides, attempted suicides, and infectious diseases, in that order. The major killers, however, were homicides, car accidents, and heart attacks. In spite of the fact that men were sick and got hurt more often than women, illnesses were more often fatal for women. Cardiovascular diseases claimed four times as many women characters as men. In addition, half of all pregnancies resulted in miscarriages, while 16 percent resulted in the death of the expectant mother. Mental illness also struck women more frequently and usually resulted from guilt, trauma, or the inability to cope with crises.

However, the world of the soap opera was a just one. While illness, like the rain, might fall on the good and the bad characters alike, it was the good people who were likely to survive. The bad deserved their fate. In another twist of facts, the extent of a person's suffering seemed to be related to their survival, except that unlike the real world, suffering seemed to enhance one's chances of recovery.

Not only were medical facts distorted in the daytime serials, but characters with professional occupations were greatly overrepresented. In fact, one study reported that more than two-thirds of all professionals portrayed were medical practitioners.[49] Another reported that about 80 percent of the men in the serials were doctors.[50] Finally, health was also found to be the most frequent topic of conversation among characters. This led the authors of this particular research summary to argue that "it may be that daytime serials comprise the most prolific single source of medical advice in America."[51]

How were medical doctors portrayed in prime-time television? Professionals played a disproportionately large role in the world of prime-time television, but doctors and nurses dominated. In fact, TV doctors and nurses were five times more numerous than they are in real life. Only police and criminals were more numerous than health professionals in the world depicted in TV programming. Most doctors and nurses were white, young, or middle-aged—and always attractive. As might be expected, nine out of ten doctors were male, whereas virtually all nurses were female.

Television doctors were "good guys." Fewer than 4 percent were portrayed as evil. That was half the rate for other professionals. In addition, they were smarter, fairer, and more rational than other characters, including nurses. In addition, TV doctors were symbols of power and dominance. However, they were portrayed as using their power carefully; they were ethical, kind, and willing to take risks to help their patients. Unlike businesslike physicians in the real world, television doctors thrived on private relationships with their patients. A full 61 percent of their work was done on house calls or in other field settings. But even with all these admirable qualities, doctors were seldom shown to have a personal life. That is, they were rarely shown at home with the family.

***Health Campaigns on Television.***    Douglas S. Solomon reviewed health campaigns on television and analyzed the reasons for their success or failure. "In a campaign, there is a deliberate effort to convey a particular message about health and to persuade the audience to heed that message."[52] This is, of course, very different from entertainment programs where any learning about health is only incidental. There have, however, been some health campaigns on daytime soap operas.

There is still debate about the ability of campaigns to change attitudes and behavior. Some communication researchers believe that most campaigns are ineffective; others believe that a carefully planned campaign can achieve the desired results. A number of campaigns have been conducted encompassing community mental health, drug abuse, smoking, use of seat belts, dental health, cancer, venereal disease, and alcoholism. For the most part, the results have been encouraging.

***The Stanford Study of Heart Disease.***    An interesting example of a televised health campaign is the Stanford Heart Disease Three-Community Study.[53] The program was conducted, beginning in 1970, by an interdisciplinary team of researchers. They explored the possibility of reducing cardiovascular risk in a community through education programs in the mass media. Two communities were exposed to intensive mass media campaigns in English and Spanish. The Spanish programs were not merely translations of the English but were specifically tailored to the Spanish-speaking community and its culture. One community also received face-to-face instruction for a small group of persons considered to be at high risk. A third community served as a control. People from each of the communities were examined for cardiovascular problems before the program began and twice thereafter at one-year intervals. They were also asked what they knew about cardiovascular disease and what they were doing about it. In addition, the researchers took physiological measures such as blood pressure, weight, and plasma cholesterol. After one year, the estimated risk of heart attack and stroke had been reduced only in the community receiving both the personal instruction and the televised programs. But by the end of the second year, the community receiving just the televised program had come down to the same level. In the control community, however, risk had increased. The researchers concluded that mass media campaigns could clearly be effective, but that more research was needed on how to refine the techniques and target the message. For example, ways to reduce smoking and to increase participation in physical exercise needed to be devised. Thus, the study used television to teach specific behavioral skills, and the evidence was clear that the program worked.

***Institutionalized Populations and Health Issues.***    The report on ten years of progress included a summary of the uses of television by persons in institutions. People temporarily in hospitals, elderly people confined to nursing homes, and psychiatric patients all rely on television to fill the hours.[54] There is evidence that having television available has a therapeutic effect. And since the chronically ill, geriatric patients, and the mentally ill tend to use television particularly heavily, there is a possibility that it might play a larger role in therapy if appropriate programming could be made available. Such research remains to be undertaken.

## The Family and Interpersonal Relations

Among the recommendations of the surgeon general's committee in 1972 was that future research on television be conducted "in the context of . . . the home environment." That recommendation was taken to heart by a number of investigators during the 1970s. The research conducted on the family can be divided into two broad categories: (1) detailed content analyses of the portrayal of families on TV and (2) television's effects on family and social interactions.

*Content Analyses of Television's Families.*   One of the dominant themes of TV programming has been the portrayal of family life. From 1946 through 1978, 218 fictional family series were broadcast as "prime-time, network shows in which the main characters in each episode are members of a family and in which the major proportion of interaction is among family members, usually in a home settin."[55] The rubric "family series" includes family dramas, family drama-comedies, serials, adventure series, and even some cartoons, such as "The Flintstones." Many of the TV families of the period became part of our collective history and culture. Millions of Americans fondly recall the families portrayed in "The Adventures of Ozzie and Harriet," "Father Knows Best," "Leave It to Beaver," "I Love Lucy," "The Honeymooners," "All in the Family," "The Waltons," "The Jeffersons," and so on. Moreover, in the decade that followed, family series experienced a resurgence in popularity led by "The Cosby Show," which according to Nielsen Ratings, led in program popularity through the 1980s.

   Researchers argue that by shaping our family-related cultural norms—and thereby our individual ideas, attitudes, and values about what kind of family life is desirable—TV families influence "real-life" families. We can judge our own family against the normative models offered by television. But how are TV families portrayed? Researchers Lynda Glennon and Richard Butsch conducted a content analysis of all 218 family series, with a special focus on the social class of the portrayed family.[56] Occupation of the head of the household was used as the indicator of social class. They found an overrepresentation of middle-class families and a corresponding underrepresentation of working-class families. Many of television's families were quite successful and glamorous. They lacked the mundane problems that most real families must face. Indeed, the middle-class families appeared to be quite successful economically. Many had servants, usually a maid. On the other hand, two dominant recurring themes emerged in portrayals of working-class life. One theme was the father and husband as inept, dumb, or bumbling (e.g., "The Honeymooners," "All in the Family"), a characterization that seldom appeared in middle-class family portrayals. The second theme was upward mobility. It was not always present and usually appeared only where the working-class family was given some dignity. Membership in the working class was presented as a one-generation phenomenon; it was portrayed as something to escape, and its desirable features were ignored, serving to weaken the legitimacy of the working-class family lifestyle. Middle-class families, on the other hand, were portrayed in two different ways. In one, both parents were superpeople who were able to deal effectively and rationally with any problem. However, in at least some shows the husband was intelligent, mature, and strong, but the wife was a giddy fool (e.g., "I Love Lucy"). The researchers suggested that working-class children might be left with the impression that their fathers were inadequate, inferior, and the laughingstock to the rest of the world. Also, the upward mobility theme implied that it was easy to attain success and to move almost without effort into the middle class. Furthermore, the idealized portrayals of middle-class families might lead viewers to question the adequacy of their own families. Indeed, it has been hypothesized that viewers learn family roles and ways to solve family problems by watching TV families.

Another family-related question addressed was whether parental intervention in the form of discussions about how unrealistic television is can diminish the impact of such programs. Some evidence indicated that actions by parents can diminish television's effects on children. For example, a 1974 study, using disadvantaged preschoolers, found that those children who viewed "Sesame Street" with their mothers, and discussed it with them, were more likely than others (who did not discuss the programs with their mothers) to increase their learning of cognitive skills.[57] In a similar study, parents of 276 grade-school children were asked to watch television with their child and explain the content of a Saturday morning newscast. This parental intervention did stimulate the child's attention to the newscast and also enhanced recall.[58]

## Social Beliefs and Social Behavior

Melvin DeFleur and his associates have formalized "social expectations theory," which predicts that TV viewers of all kinds learn the patterns of social organization of all kinds of groups—their norms, roles, ranking systems, and social controls—even if they have never been members or never will be.[59] But what evidence exists that television contributes to the learning of various social roles? Researchers in the 1970s studied portrayed patterns of expectations associated with gender, age, race, occupation, and consumer behavior. Did these portrayals lead viewers to stereotype role occupants in a manner consistent with the televised messages? And does the worldview of heavy viewers differ from that of light viewers?

No area of behavior has been as extensively analyzed by communication researchers as that of sex and gender roles. Indeed, in terms of the sheer number of publications, it is clear that there was massive interest in conducting content analyses on this topic during the 1970s.

Perhaps the single most important point developed from the content analyses was that men greatly outnumbered women on television. There were about three times as many males shown. Moreover, the number of men and women characters varied with the type of program. There were approximately equal numbers of men and women in situation comedies, family dramas, and soap operas; but men outnumbered women 5 to 1 in action adventure shows, and 4 to 1 in Saturday morning cartoons.

The men portrayed on television were employed in a wide variety of jobs One study of Saturday morning fare, for example, found men in 42 different jobs. Women, on the other hand, occupied only 9 different jobs.[60] Another study found twice as many women characters as men characters in low-prestige jobs.[61] The late 1970s brought the appearance of a few new programs in which females had difficult and demanding jobs. The women, however, were usually single, sophisticated, often divorced, and their work glamorous. Some analysts observe that such new roles were really not very different from past roles because the women usually depended on men, they were portrayed as more emotional than men, and there was more concern for their safety.

What personal traits differentiated men from women on television during the 1970s? In general, males were portrayed to be more rational, intelligent, independent, powerful, tolerant, and stable. Females, on the other hand, appeared warmer, more sociable, more attractive, more peaceful, and less competent. Moreover, women were often treated as sex objects and were more likely than men to use their bodies seductively. Yet by the late 1970s, this was changing in that men were being portrayed more frequently as sex objects, especially in the action-adventure programs, where they were often called upon to prove their physical prowess.

During the 1970s, there was an increase of sexually suggestive behavior and innuendo. However, by contemporary standards it was pretty tame stuff. There were few, if any, visual portrayals of explicit erotic behavior (bare breasts, nude people engaging in sexual unions) on commercial TV programming. However, there were numerous cues for the viewer about the events that presumably would happen or had happened off screen. For example, sexual intercourse was frequently implied (but not graphically shown). It is significant that most references to intercourse on television, whether verbally insinuated or contextually implied, occurred between unmarried partners. Indeed, this occurred five times as often as references to sexual activity between married couples. References to intercourse with prostitutes came in second. Together, these accounted for almost 70 percent of all allusions to intercourse on prime-time TV programs.[62] Sex was also commonly linked with violence. For example, most verbal references to sex in action-adventure (police) programs resulted from discussion of rape or other sex crimes. And even when they were not prostitutes or victims of sex crimes, women characters used their eroticism to entrap men.

In terms of television's effects on learning about sex roles, research during the period focused primarily on stereotyping. A 1974 study asked children three to six years old to indicate whether a woman or man would be in a certain occupation and found that children who were heavy viewers tended to stereotype men and women much more that children who were light viewers.[63] The same pattern emerged from several studies. That is, again and again the heavy viewers gave stereotypical answers as to whether males or females would be found in various kinds of work roles traditionally associated with one gender or the other.


***Race and Ethnicity.***   For the hundreds of thousands of Americans who live in sections of the country where few minority citizens reside, television's portrayal in news and fiction is the primary source of information about race and ethnicity. During the 1960s and 1970s, much attention was given to the portrayal of African Americans but little to Hispanics or any other group. In addition, the studies done (consistent with other areas of research) were generally content analyses rather than studies of effects on audiences.

The proportion of African-American characters on TV was about 10 percent during the 1970s, a near equivalent to their (12 percent) proportion in the population at the time. In contrast, during the 1950s only a few were shown, all of whom were classic comic stereotypes, like Amos and Andy. Few Hispanics were shown, reported as 2.9 percent (1970–1976) and 1.5 percent (1975–1977). Orientals comprised 2.5 percent between 1970 and 1976. Native Americans comprised less than 0.5 percent during the same period.[64]

Both African-American and Hispanic TV characters were found mainly in situation comedies. Approximately 41 percent of all black characters appeared in just six shows. The same kind of concentration was also found with Hispanic characters, with 50 percent in only four shows. During the 1950s and 1960s, blacks were overrepresented as criminals. This was no longer true in the 1970s. But blacks were less likely than whites to have jobs and, when employed, more likely to have lower status jobs.

An analysis of the occupation of Hispanic characters on television revealed a heavy emphasis on unskilled or semiskilled labor. Furthermore, of the 53 Hispanics found in three sample weeks, 22 were comic portrayals and 22 were either lawbreakers or law enforcers. Thus, there were three significant images of Hispanics: the clown, the criminal, and the cop.

Two important questions can be raised about the effects of minority portrayals on television: (1) Do the portrayals affect white children's attitudes and reactions toward those depicted? (2) Do the portrayals affect the self-images of minority children? Research indicated that white children who had little or no interaction with African Americans reported that television gave them information about their physical appearance, speech, and dress. Studies of "Sesame Street" gave evidence that white children who were regular viewers had more positive attitudes toward other races than children who had not been exposed to the programs. Additionally, a 1976 study with white nursery school youngsters manipulated segments of a program containing nonwhite characters. Only one-third of the control group (who viewed solely white actors) subsequently selected minority playmates from photos. However, more than two-thirds of those exposed to multiracial segments made similar choices.[65] Thus, it can be concluded that television was a factor in learning about race and ethnicity for many white children, especially those who have limited contact with minorities.

Researchers also studied the self-image of minority group children who watched programs such as "Sesame Street" and "Villa Alegre." In general, all of these public television shows had a favorable effect on cultural pride, self-confidence, and interpersonal cooperativeness of minority children. It was also found that movies depicting successful black athletes, entertainers, and others enhanced the self-concept of black children.

***Aging and the Elderly.***   The topic of television and aging was of particular interest for two major (but rather ironic) reasons. First, during the 1970s, people over 65 watched more television than any other age group—even more than children. (This is still true today.) There is virtually unanimous agreement that television is of utmost importance in the lives of many elderly people. It is their most frequently named activity. Second, older people were infrequently seen on television, but when they were shown, they were often portrayed in a negative fashion. It was not until the decade of the 1970s that researchers concerned themselves with the characteristics of the elderly shown on television.

A 1979 study analyzed the age of characters on prime-time programs for the years 1969–1978.[66] Of the over 9,000 characters that were portrayed, only 3.7 percent of major and minor characters were 65 or older. The elderly people that were shown were portrayed as comparatively unattractive and unhappy. Other studies reported even fewer elderly characters, usually only a little over 2 percent. Also, through stereotypical characterizations, television tended to perpetuate myths of old age. Prime-time television presented a picture of the elderly as being verbally hostile, cranky, ugly, sexless, senile, confused, helpless, stubborn, eccentric, and foolish. In sharp contrast, the daytime soap operas presented the older person as important, attractive, and independent.

Older men greatly outnumbered older women in prime-time television, even though in fact there are more older women than men. One researcher reported that a viewer could expect to see an old man about every 22 minutes on prime-time television, while one would see an elderly woman only every four or five hours. In addition, females were shown to age earlier and faster than males. In general, older women were portrayed in a more negative fashion than older men and were almost never portrayed as "successful." The exception again was the soap opera. Here, women's roles were stronger, and older women had very positive, serious roles.

What are the effects of such TV portrayals on the elderly population, and how do the portrayals of the aged affect other people's attitudes and reactions toward them? In a 1980 study, researchers examined the self-perceptions of elderly individuals and related this to the amount of television viewed.[67] They found that positive perceptions of TV portrayals of the elderly enhanced the self-concepts of older people. Likewise, negative portrayals lowered self-esteem. Also, frequent viewers, when compared to less frequent viewers, were more likely to view the elderly in general as hindrances to society.

Several other studies in the same series found that young people who were heavy viewers tended to stereotype the elderly much more than did young people who were light viewers. Specifically, among heavy viewers, the young were more likely to believe that older people were "not open-minded, not bright, alert or good at getting things done." Heavy television viewing also led to other inaccurate beliefs about old people, such as the idea that the number of elderly persons was decreasing or that old people did not live as long as they used to and, in general, were less healthy than had been the case 20 or 30 years ago.

***Responses to TV Commercials.***    Responses to advertising differ substantially across various social categories. Consumers can be categorized according to race, sex, socioeconomic status, and social context. The most crucial variable, however, is age, since information-processing abilities and product needs vary through the life cycle. Researchers in the area of consumer socialization have generally used three broad age categories: childhood (up to age 12), adolescence (12 to 17), and adulthood (18 and older).

Researchers concerned with the consequences of advertising for children pointed out that they were exposed annually to about 20,000 TV commercials. Saturday morning ads, in particular, were targeted to young audiences. Generally, young children (under 12) liked to watch Saturday morning commercials, whereas adolescents were undecided. The younger children enjoyed the humor and entertaining qualities of TV commercials.

Age was an important factor in children's belief in advertising claims. Young children usually believed the claims, but older ones were more skeptical. Trust by children was related to the product. They were more distrustful of claims made about toys they knew about than they were about medical or nutritional products. Heavy-viewing children were more likely to believe advertisements than were light viewers.

Some researchers tried to determine the role of TV advertising in the development of children's awareness of, and preference for, toys and food products. In some cases, they simply asked children or their parents where they learned about desired products. According to a 1977 study, mothers of young children ranked television first as a learning source for products in general, followed by friends and catalogs.[68] A similar study supported this conclusion; mothers and children both cited television as the most important source for cereal and toy information.[69]

Children often desired to have advertised products. Several studies found a high positive correlation between viewing commercials and liking frequently advertised foods. One study reported that children who saw an advertisement for a toy tended to prefer playing with the toy rather than with a friend. In fact, they would rather play with a not-so-nice friend who owned the toy than with a nice friend who did not.[70]

A significant finding with young children was that they often took advertisements literally. In a laboratory study, children aged four to seven were shown a commercial for Cocoa Pebbles (a popular breakfast cereal) in which cartoon characters Fred Flintstone and Barney Rubble claimed that the cereal was "chocolatey enough to make you smile." Among the reasons for wanting to eat the cereal, two-thirds cited the chocolate taste, but three-fifths wanted it because it would make them smile. More than half desired the cereal because Fred and Barney liked it.[71]

In another study, a commercial that showed a circus strongman lifting a playhouse and eating the cereal was presented to youngsters. When asked, nearly two-thirds of the four- to seven-year-old children thought that the cereal would make them stronger. One-third even said that the cereal would make them strong enough to lift really heavy objects.[72] Again, children who were frequent viewers of Saturday morning cereal advertising at home were much more likely to believe the strength claims than those who were not heavily exposed.

Several studies indicated that children did not evaluate food advertising critically. In fact, young children tended to accept as true claims made in four commercials identified by the Federal Trade Commission (FTC) as possibly deceptive. Again, a significant difference was found between the children who were heavy and light viewers. Heavy television viewers were less certain about the validiy of nutrition claims in food commercials and had lower nutrition knowledge.[73]

The report *Television and Behavior* included a number of sections dealing with broader effects of television on American society and its social institutions. These included religion, laws and norms, leisure, public security, and citizenship. Many of the issues and problems studied in this section were linked to specific topics in the news agenda of the period. These included airline bomb threats, comic books, decline of box office movies, radio's changing formats, problems of mass-audience magazines, hijacking of planes to Cuba, food tampering, the war in Vietnam, and politics of the period. These suggested interesting lines of research for the future but have lesser implications for today's influences of television as a medium than the issues addressed in previous sections.

## CONCLUSIONS AND IMPLICATIONS

The 1982 report on television and behavior is in essence a summary of 90 percent of the published research on the medium's influence on individuals and society at the time of publication. For the most part, it summarizes research published during the 1970s, although a few of the titles appeared in 1980. The fact that one decade could produce such a massive amount of literature accents the interest in the role of television in American society. If a single statement could epitomize what was found in this research summary, it is the following:

Almost all the evidence testifies to television's role as a formidable educator whose effects are both pervasive and cumulative. Television can no longer be considered as a casual part of daily life, as an electronic toy. Research findings have long since destroyed the illusion that television is merely innocuous entertainment. While the learning it provides is mainly incidental rather than direct and formal, it is a significant part of the total acculturation process.[74]

One of the most significant developments signaled by the NIMH report is that media research moved beyond the violence theme and started to investigate the possible interaction between the viewer and what is seen on the television screen. This was quite a departure from the surgeon general's first report.

The 1982 report also signaled another major development in media effects research. It reflected clearly the shift to a new theoretical point of departure for research—the meaning theory of media portrayals, emphasizing the role of mass communication in the social construction of interpretations of reality within our society.[75] It became clear to many researchers that among the potentially damaging influences of television is the way it may shape the viewer's understandings of the real world. As we have seen in this chapter, those concerns included health concerns, the portrayal of women and minority groups in stereotypical fashion, and the portrayal of family life and how that might affect social expectations of norms and roles (and even evaluations of our own family).

A major flaw evident in many of the research projects included in the report is that they present data from descriptive content analyses without documenting the effects of that content. A very real problem with content analyses based on samples of TV characters is that researchers show what they have found and then go on to draw inferences about the behavior of members of the audience. This is a flagrant non sequitur. Proof of influences on audiences is obviously much more tedious, qualified, and time-consuming than describing media content. Perhaps this is the reason why such documentation has not been pursued with vigor. At the same time, such research is not impossible. The meaning theory of media portrayals, generally speaking, predicts the type of effects a given content should have. It is now time to resist simply assuming effects from content and turn to demonstrating that they actually exist.

In addition, even the content analyses themselves are not without flaws. Obviously, it is important to know the nature of messages and meanings of TV programming. For that reason, content analyses should be rigorously conducted. Yet so many of them are based largely on simple frequency counts of a phenomenon portrayed. Moreover, it is often assumed that if people in a given social category, group, or role are omitted or neglected in portrayals by the medium, this condition will lead to a devaluation of such people in real life. This is another flagrant non sequitur. Such a proposition would be difficult to support with empirical evidence. For example, if Hispanics are not seen on television, some people may believe that it is because they are not worth seeing. But if few bankers or stockbrokers are seen, it is doubtful they will be devalued for that reason. All of the research based on content analyses must therefore be viewed as speculative as far as influences on audiences are concerned.

The most widely publicized finding of the 1982 report was its conclusions about televised violence. Various popular media (e.g., *Time, Newsweek*) uniformly highlighted the single conclusion that violence on television leads to aggressive behavior by children. From such media reports, one might have assumed that televised violence was the only concern addressed, insofar as all the other relevant issues and areas covered by the report were virtually ignored.[76]

As might be anticipated, the major TV networks issued statements calling the 1982 report "inaccurate," but they did not bother to identify the inaccuracies. The American Broadcasting Company (ABC) did publish a 32-page critique of the report titled " A Perspective on Television and Violence," but nothing in the critique refuted the major findings of the report.[77] Typically, only the question of televised violence was addressed. In addition, by calling the evidence "correlational," the networks' defense sounded remarkably similar to that of the tobacco industry after being confronted with evidence linking their product to lung cancer. It must be granted that the evidence concerning televised violence and aggressive behavior is complex; yet the convergence of that evidence from so many studies is compelling. Indeed, most social and behavioral scientists now accept the conclusion of the 1982 surgeon general's report that links televised violence to later aggressive behavior.[78] Since research has now demonstrated this association in both field and laboratory studies, most researchers have shifted the focus of their work beyond this issue to investigate what processes produce the relationship.

Another major finding regarding the link between televised violence and aggressive behavior is that the sole culprit may not be portrayed violence per se. Some research suggests that aggression can be stimulated by high levels of action, even without high violence content. Thus, television's form and codes may be partly responsible for aggressive behavior. Additionally, the 1982 report emphasized the concept of arousal and its relationship to aggressive behavior. Apparently, some TV viewing can heighten a state of general arousal. This increased level of excitement may then be channeled into aggression. Therefore, it is possible that exciting TV programming, regardless of content, may for a number of reasons induce aggressive behavior. Obviously, the well-documented link between televised violence and aggressive behavior is far from simple. In later years, new questions were constantly being raised regarding this perennial issue.

The topic of prosocial behavior also received considerable research attention. Overall, it was concluded that programming that provides prosocial portrayals can induce similar behavior in the viewer. Both laboratory and field studies consistently found that behavior such as friendliness, cooperation, delay of gratification, and generosity could be enhanced by exposure to appropriate TV content. Such findings support the general explanation that observational learning takes place when people view television. There now seems little doubt that individuals learn from viewing television and that what they learn depends upon the content that they watch. In short, television can no longer be dismissed as mere entertainment; it is a major source of observational learning for millions of people. In this role, it may be one of the most important agencies of socialization in our society.

Overall, *Television and Behavior: Ten Years of Scientific Progress and Implications for the Eighties* is a noteworthy document and a milestone in the development of mass communication research for several major reasons:

1. It shifts the focus away from the relatively narrow confines of violence on television to larger concerns with many other kinds of effects of the medium.
2. There is also a shift from examining short-term direct effects to searching for long-term indirect effects, which are, of course, more elusive and of considerably more importance to our society. This changes the focus to what DeFleur and Dennis have termed the accumulation theory of media effects.[79]
3. The above change was brought about by a shift from the cognitive approach on attitude change and the like to the meaning theory of media portrayals, which focuses on the role of communication in the social construction of reality.
4. The report promoted the view of television as an important educator, albeit an informal rather than a formal one.

Obviously, there are connections between these four reasons. Nevertheless, for many years, the high visibility and continued emphasis on televised violence has obscured other important issues. In particular, it is important to look at the totality of television viewing as a continuing form of informal education. The 1982 report gave us a clearer view.

## NOTES AND REFERENCES

1. David Pearl, Lorraine Bouthilet, and Joyce Lazar, eds., *Television and Behavior: Ten Years of Scientific Progress and Implications for the Eighties,* 2 vols. (Washington, D.C.: U.S. Government Printing Office, 1982).
2. Eli A. Rubinstein, "Introductory Comments," in Pearl, et al., eds., *Television and Behavior,* vol. 2, p. 104.
3. J. Immerwahr, J. Johnson, and J. Doble, *The Speaker and the Listener: A Public Perspective of Freedom of Expression* (New York: Public Agenda Foundation, 1980).
4. L. Rowell Huesmann, "Television Violence and Aggressive Behavior," in Pearl et al., eds., *Television and Behavior*, vol. 2, p. 127.
5. J. L. Singer and D. G. Singer, *Television Imagination and Aggression: A Study of Preschoolers' Play* (Hillsdale, N.J.: Erlbaum, 1980).
6. Ibid., p. 127.
7. E. D. McCarthy et al., "Violence and Behavior Disorders," *Journal of Communication* 25 (4): 71-85 (1975).
8. For a review of these studies, see Huesmann, "Television Violence and Aggressive Behavior," p. 128.
9. L. D. Eron and L. R. Huesmann, "Adolescent Aggression and Television," *Annals of the New York Academy of Sciences* 347 (1980): 319-331.
10. William Belson, *Television Violence and the Adolescent Boy* (London: Saxon House, 1978), cited in Pearl et al., eds., *Television and Behavior,* vol. 1, p. 15.
11. J. Ronald Milavsky, Ronald Kessler, Horst Still, and William S. Rubens, "Television and Aggression: Results of a Panel Study," in Pearl et al., eds., *Television and Behavior,* vol. 1, pp. 138-157.

12. Ibid, p. 139.
13. Ibid, p. 154.
14. Rubinstein, "Introductory Comments," p. 105.
15. Heusmann, "Television Violence and Aggressive Behavior," p. 105.
16. C. W. Turner and M. R. Fern, "Effects of White Noise and Memory Cues on Verbal Aggression" (paper presented at the meetings of the International Society for Research on Aggression, Washington, D.C., 1978).
17. L. R. Huesmann, L. D. Eron, R. Klein, P. Brice, and P. Fischer, "Mitigating the Imitation of Aggressive Behaviors," Technical Report, Department of Psychology, University of Illinois, Chicago Circle, 1981.
18. A long-standing debate in social science concerns the relationship between attitudes and behavior. It is very clear that they are not always correlated, because a person may have a particular attitude but choose to behave in an opposite way because of the social norms or social requirements of the situation. Such conditions sometimes cause people to act in a direction opposite that consistent with their internal attitudes.
19. V. B. Cline, R. G. Croft, and S. Courrier, "Desensitization of Children to Television Violence," *Journal of Personality and Social Psychology* 27 (1973): 360-365.
20. J. Philipe Rushton, "Television and Prosocial Behavior," in Pearl et al., eds., *Television and Behavior,* vol. 2, p. 249.
21. J. H. Bryan, "Children's Cooperation and Helping Behavior," in E. M. Hetherington, ed., *Review of Child Development Research,* vol.5 (Chicago: University of Chicago Press, 1975).
22. R. Elliot and R. Vasta, "The Modeling of Sharing: Effects Associated with Vicarious Reinforcement, Symbolization, Age, and Generalization," *Journal of Experimental Child Psychology* 10 (1970): 8-15.
23. J. P. Rushton and D. Owen, "Immediate and Delayed Effects of TV Modelling and Preaching on Children's Generosity," *British Journal of Clinical and Social Psychology* 14 (1974): 309-310.
24. G. J. Gorn, M. E. Goldberg, and R. N. Kanungo, "The Role of Educational Television in Changing Intergroup Attitudes of Children," *Child Development* 47 (1976): 277-280.
25. R. D. O'Connor, "Modification of Social Withdrawal through Symbolic Modeling," *Journal of Applied Behavior Analysis* 2 (1969): 15-22.
26. G. M. Stein and J. H. Bryan, "The Effects of a Televised Model upon Rule Adoption Behavior of Children," *Child Development* 43 (1972): 268-273.
27. G. C. R. Yates, "Influence of Televised Modeling and Verbalization of Children's Delay of Gratification," *Journal of Experimental Child Psychology* 18 (1974): 333-339.
28. A. Bandura and F. L. Menlove, "Factors Determining Vicarious Extinction of Avoidance Behavior through Symbolic Modeling," *Journal of Personality and Social Psychology* 8 (1968): 99-108.
29. J. A. Hill, R. M. Liebert, and D. E. Mott, "Vicarious Extinction of Avoidance Behavior Through Films: An Initial Test," *Psychological Reports* 22 (1968): 192.
30. A. Bandura, E. B. Blanchard, and B. Ritter, "The Relative Efficacy of Desensitization and Modeling Approaches for Inducing Behavioral, Affective, and Attitudinal Changes," *Journal of Personality and Social Psychology* 13 (1969): 173-199.
31. B. G. Melamed and L. J. Siegel, "Reduction of Anxiety in Children Facing Hospitalization and Surgery by Use of Filmed Modeling," *Journal of Consulting and Clinical Psychology* 43 (1975): 511-521.
32. Rushton, "Television and Prosocial Behavior," p. 255.

33. W. Andrew Collins, "Cognitive Processing in Television Viewing," in Pearl et al., eds., *Television and Behavior,* vol. 2, p. 10.

34. Ibid.

35. For a description of these studies, see Mabel Rice, Aletha C. Huston, and John C. Wright, "The Forms of Television: Effects on Children's Attention, Comprehension, and Social Behavior," in Pearl et al., eds., *Television and Behavior,* vol. 2, pp. 24-38.

36. Pearl et al., eds., *Television and Behavior,* vol. 1, p. 2.

37. Ibid., p. 87.

38. George Gerbner, Michael Morgan, and Nancy Signorielli, "Programming Health Portrayals: What Viewers See, Say, and Do," in Pearl et al., eds., *Television and Behavior,* vol. 2, pp. 291-307.

39. Douglas S. Solomon, "Health Campaigns on Television," in Pearl et al., eds., *Television and Behavior,* vol. 2, pp. 308-321.

40. Eli A. Rubinstein and Joyce N. Sprafkin, "Television and Persons in Institutions," in Pearl et al., eds., *Television and Behavior,* vol. 2, pp. 322-330.

41. Gerbner et al., "Programming Health Portrayals," p. 292.

42. F. A. Smith, G. Trivax, D. A. Zuehlke, P. Lowinger, and T. L. Nghiem, "Health Information during a Week of Television," *New England Journal of Medicine* (1972): 518-520, cited in Gerbner et al., "Programming Health Portrayals," pp. 291-307.

43. Gerbner et al., "Programming Health Portrayals," p. 297.

44. J. Dillon, "TV Drinking: How Networks Pour Liquor into Your Living Room," *Christian Science Monitor,* June 30, 1975, cited in Gerbner et al., "Programming Health Portrayals," p. 297.

45. E. Futch, M. J. Geller, and S. A. Lisman, "Analysis of Alcohol Use on Prime Time Television" (unpublished paper, State University of New York at Binghamton, 1980), cited in Gerbner et al., "Programming Health Portrayals," p. 297.

46. Gerbner et al., "Programming Health Portrayals," p. 296.

47. L. Kaufman, "Prime-Time Nutrition," *Journal of Communication* 30 (3): 37-46 (1980).

48. Gerbner et al., "Programming Health Portrayals," p. 297.

49. M. Downing, *The World of Daytime Serial Drama* (unpublished doctoral dissertation, University of Pennsylvania, 1975).

50. M. G. Perloff, "Television Soap Bubbles," *New Republic* 172 (May 10, 1975): 27-30.

51. Gerbner et al., "Programming Health Portrayals," p. 295.

52. Solomon, "Health Campaigns on Television," p. 13.

53. J. W. Farquar et al., "Community Education for Cardiovascular Health," *The Lancet,* June 4, 1977: 1192-1195.

54. See D. W. Jeffers, R. E. Ostman, and C. Atkinson, "Mass Media Availability and Use in a Mental Institution," *Journalism Quarterly* 56 (1979): 126-133; and R. E. Ostman, D. W. Jeffers, and C. Atkinson, "Madness and the Mass Media" (paper presented at the convention of the Popular Culture Association, Cincinnati, April 1978).

55. Lynda M. Glennon and Richard Butsch, "The Family as Portrayed on Television, 1946-1978," in Pearl et al., eds., *Television and Behavior,* vol. 2. p. 265.

56. Ibid.

57. G. S. Lesser, *Children and Television: Lessons from Sesame Street* (New York: Random House, 1974).

58. J. M. McLeod, Mary Anne Fitzpatrick, Carroll J. Glynn, and Susan F. Fallis, "Television and Social Relations: Family Influences and Consequences for Interpersonal Behavior," in Pearl et al., eds., *Television and Behavior,* vol. 2, pp. 272-286.

59. Melvin L. DeFleur and Sandra Ball Rokeach, *Theories of Mass Communication,* 5th ed. (White Plains: Longman, 1989), pp. 219-227.
60. L. Busby, "Defining the Sex Role Standard in Commercial Network Television Programs Directed Toward Children," *Journalism Quarterly* 51 (1974): 690-696.
61. J. McNeil, "Feminism, Femininity, and the Television Series: A Content Analysis," *Journal of Broadcasting* 19 (1975): 259-269.
62. For a discussion of this study and other similar ones, see Elizabeth J. Roberts, "Television and Sexual Learning in Childhood," in Pearl et al., eds., *Television and Behavior,* vol. 2, pp. 209-223.
63. A. Beuf, "Doctor, Lawyer, Household Drudge," *Journal of Communication* 24 (2): (1974) 142-145.
64. Bradley S. Greenberg, "Television and Role Socialization: An Overview," in Pearl et al., eds., *Television and Behavior,* vol. 2, pp. 179-190.
65. G. Gorn, M. Goldberg, and R. Kanugo, "The Role of Educational Television in Changing the Intergroup Attitudes of Children," *Child Development* 47 (1976): 277-280.
66. For a discussion of this study, see Greenberg, "Television and Role Socialization," pp. 186-187.
67. F. Korzenny and K. Neuendorf, "Television Viewing and Self-Concept of the Elderly," *Journal of Communication* 30 (1): (1980) 71-80.
68. T. Barry and A. Sheikh, "Race as a Dimension in Children's TV Advertising: The Need for More Research," *Journal of Advertising* 6 (1977): 5-18.
69. Charles K. Atkin, "Television Advertising and Socialization to Consumer Roles," in Pearl et al., eds., *Television and Behavior,* vol. 2, p. 193.
70. M. Goldberg and G. Gorn, "Some Unintended Consequences of TV Advertising to Children," *Journal of Consumer Research* 5 (1978): 22-29.
71. Atkin, "Television Advertising and Socialization," p. 191.
72. Ibid.
73. S. Sharanga, *The Effect of Television Advertising on Children's Nutritional Attitudes and Eating Habits* (unpublished doctoral dissertation, Cornell University, Ithaca, New York, 1974), cited in Pearl et al., eds., *Television and Behavior,* vol. 2, p. 197.
74. Pearl et al., eds., *Television and Behavior,* vol. 1, p. 87.
75. See Melvin L. DeFleur and Sandra Ball Rokeach, *Theories of Mass Communication Research* (White Plains: Longman, Inc., 1989), pp. 228-271.
76. Eli A. Rubinstein, "Television and Behavior: Research Conclusions of the 1982 NIMH Report and Their Policy Implications," *American Psychologist* (July 1983): 820-825.
77. Ibid.
78. Ibid.
79. Melvin L. DeFleur and Everette E. Dennis, *Understanding Mass Communication,* 4th ed. (Boston: Houghton Mifflin, 1991), pp. 560-561.

# chapter 16

# The Lessons of the Milestones

**I**t is obvious that the question to be asked at this point is, What have we learned from these 14 major research efforts? It is also obvious that the answer to that question will not be easy to formulate. From one point of view, the cup is at least partly full: an impressive number of concepts, hypotheses, empirical generalizations, methodological techniques, and research strategies were produced by these projects and programs. From another point of view, the cup is still partly empty: many aspects of mass communication remain to be discovered. Compounding the difficulty is the fact that it is not always easy to separate the achievements of the 14 efforts reviewed in the present book from those of numerous other investigations. In many cases, the latter were stimulated by the milestone studies. In turn, smaller scale efforts sometimes played a part in shaping the directions of the major projects we have reviewed. But in spite of these considerations, there are a number of identifiable contributions that either had their origins in the milestone projects or were greatly advanced by them.

A useful approach to bringing together a summary of significant contributions is to identify broad categories of findings that can provide a framework for interpreting the influence of these 14 projects on the study of mass communication in American society. For example, numerous *empirical generalizations* about media influences have been formulated on the basis of observational evidence obtained in each of these important studies. These are mainly descriptions of specific regularities, patterns, or relationships between variables that the original investigators observed in the behavior of audiences or other components that make up our system of mass communication. For example, the Payne Fund studies of the early movies showed that children often imitated actions that they saw on the screen (chapter 2). The study of the daytime radio serials showed that listeners often turned to the soap operas for advice about their own problems (chapter 5). How can generalizations of this kind be assessed? They appear to have been valid and reliable in their time, but do they still describe the process and influences of mass communications in contemporary society? Or has the situation changed so much that many such generalizations are obsolete? If so, are such generalizations without any value whatever?

A second issue is the current status of the focused theories of mass communication that describe and explain some limited aspect of the process or its effects on people. For example, a theory of the role of mass communications in the process of the adoption of innovation was an important result of the Iowa study of hybrid seed corn (chapter 6). The study of films used to persuade soldiers in World War II showed that such efforts produced only limited and selective effects (chapter 7). Theories focused on well-defined aspects of the process or effects of mass communication stimulate the research process to move forward on what is often referred to as a "cutting edge." Focused theories identify problems with known boundaries and set forth reasonably clear propositions that can be tested against well-defined data. It is in this category that some of the milestone studies have made very clear contributions. However, we must ask whether those theories remain applicable to contemporary society and our modern media system.

Finally, a very different set of issues related to the milestone studies are those pertaining to methodology. In what ways have these noteworthy projects shown us better ways to conduct research on the effects of mass communication? The question of applicability to contemporary society is less significant here. A more appropriate question is, How has communication science been enriched by the development of the measurement strategies, controls, research designs, or modes of statistical analysis used in the milestone studies? In some cases, those contributions were true innovations, in the sense that they had never been used before in any kind of social research. Their use in mass communication research was a contribution not only to the study of the media but also to social science as a whole. In other cases, techniques that had proved valuable for other types of research were borrowed, brought into the field, and adapted to the study of mass communication. Both sources of methodological innovations are important, as they add significantly to the tool kit of the communication researcher.

## LOOKING BACK: A REVIEW OF MAJOR FINDINGS

What can be said in overview about this legacy of research findings? Clearly, each of the milestone studies left its unique contribution to the developing area of mass communication studies. However, some were more important than others. Taken together, they provide an enormous amount of information about the effects of the media under study as they existed at various points in history and on the specific populations who made up their audiences at the time. Most broke new theoretical ground, opening pathways that are still being explored today. Some had their greatest impact on the general public, often confirming their fears of the new media among us. Several introduced valuable methodological techniques.

All were important in altering the perspectives of communication scholars concerning the role of the mass media in modern society and their impact on us as individuals.

## A Summary of What Was Found

Before attempting to assess the collective impact of this series of major studies, it will be helpful to review very briefly, one at a time, the salient conclusions that emerged from each. Therefore, the sections that follow provide a thumbnail sketch of their major goals, findings, and conclusions.

***The Payne Fund Studies: The Effects of Movies on Children.***    Of the 13 separate studies of this massive research program conducted between the late 1920s and early 1930s, we chose two to illustrate the range of research strategies and interests that were used in the series as a whole. One was the set of psychological field experiments conducted by Peterson and Thurstone to study the impact of exposure to one or more films on children's attitudes toward social issues. The other was the more qualitative approach to Blumer, who used a biographical technique to probe the influence of the movies on children's daily behavior, such as in their play, imitation of the actors, daydreaming, fantasy, and emotional life.

Peterson and Thurstone concluded that exposure to a single movie did little to shape children's attitudes toward racial and ethnic categories. However, two or three films on the same topic produced significant modifications. Furthermore, such influences tended to persist for long periods. These conclusions initially impressed behavioral scientists because they were based on an experimental approach that was favored by those who wanted to study human conduct within the (experimental) traditions of the physical sciences. Also impressive was the use of inferential statistics, a relatively recent innovation. Perhaps more than anything, the new attitude measuring procedures that Thurstone himself had pioneered seemed especially sophisticated.

Blumer's studies are undoubtedly more intriguing now than they were at the time. They were essentially qualitative rather than quantitative. Their lack of elaborate experimental designs and inferential statistics made them seem less scientific to the research community of the period that was enthusiastically converting to quantitative strategies. Today, however, when the limitations of experiments and surveys are more apparent, and when qualitative research has found an accepted role in scientific studies of human behavior, Blumer's project reveals a depth of sensitive insights and information on children's imitation of role models, adolescent emotional development, and the problems of young people interpreting the adult world. Children copied the speech patterns, hairstyles, and mannerisms of the stars; acted out the plots they saw on the screen; had a rich fantasy life related to the movies; and underwent profound emotional experiences while viewing. Many of these influences today would be discussed in terms of modeling (using the actors as models for personal behavior) and meaning (using the norms and shared interpretations provided by the movies as valid constructions of reality). Blumer's contributions to such issues were not recognized at the time because neither modeling theory nor the meaning theory of media portrayals had been developed. In retrospect, however, he pioneered the way.

Understandably, in the decade that followed, the Payne Fund studies fell into disrepute. As new and even more impressive methodologies were developed in the social and behavioral sciences, the Payne Fund research was found wanting by comparison. Critics pointed to their lack of control groups, problems in sampling, shortcomings in measurement, and other difficulties that placed technical limitations on their conclusions. The public, however, neither understood nor cared about such issues. To laypeople, the experiments seemed impressive and appeared to show that, just as had been feared, the movies were a bad influence on children. Such an interpretation was supported by the results of some of the other studies, which showed that the movies had unwanted influences on school attendance, academic performance, retention of factual material (such as ideas about tobacco, liquor, and sex), children's sleep, moral concepts, fantasy life, and juvenile crime. It was a damning list. The end result was to reinforce the legacy of fear concerning the mass media that was the result of their role in World Was I as instruments of manipulative propaganda.

Thus, in retrospect, the Payne Fund studies can either be denounced for their methodological shortcomings, applauded because they forced future researchers to use more refined methods, criticized because of their theoretical naïveté, or celebrated for their anticipation of concepts and theories that would be further developed in later decades. However, *they cannot be ignored;* their historical importance to the foundation of the field is indisputable.

### *The Invasion from Mars: Radio Panics America.*

A decade after research started with the Payne Fund studies, a new medium had successfully challenged newspapers and movies for the attention of Americans. Radio was a wonderful new source of information, entertainment, and news. It was glamorous and trusted. It was thought at the time to have great influence on its listeners. In October 1938, that aura of trust was rudely challenged by the now-famous broadcast depicting an invasion of hostile Martians. The conviction that radio could strongly influence its audience was forcibly reinforced: Of the 6 million who tuned in, a million were severely frightened or panicked.

The study conducted by Cantril illustrates an important feature of several of the early media studies. It was not actually conducted in an effort to understand the influence of the process or effects of mass communication in a direct sense. It was designed as a study of panic behavior. The fact that mass communication was the stimulus for the panic did not seem all that important. The entire situation simply represented an opportunity to learn more about a particular form of collective behavior of considerable interest to psychologists. This was a common early pattern. Many of the early contributors to mass media research conducted their investigations to probe issues of concern to their parent disciplines rather than to directly attempt to develop the study of mass communication as a research field in its own right. Thus, there was an accumulation of quite unrelated studies of such topics as public opinion formation and change, violence, political influences, panic behavior, and persuasion. All were done in a context of mass communication, but there was no systematic attempt to build later studies on the theoretical foundations of those completed earlier because of their great differences in disciplinary origin. In the Cantril study, the emphasis was on comparing the individual differences and social category characteristics of two types of listeners: those who discovered that the broadcast was a play and simply sat back to enjoy it and those who were terrified by their belief that the Martians had arrived to destroy us all. Data were gathered that had a bearing on the social aspects of listening, and they showed that social relationships had some bearing on response to the broadcast. However, the main effort was on the personal and social characteristics that led to a selective mode of response.

Methodologically, the study can be either denounced or praised. By contemporary standards of well-designed and meticulously conducted research, it was sloppy and naive in many respects. The number of subjects was small; they were not selected by a standard sampling design; and they were not interviewed immediately after the broadcast. Additional data were obtained in later surveys and content analyses, but it was the initial sample of 135 people who were the main focus of the research. However, the study had to be rushed into the field as soon as possible. There were no models to follow, and there certainly had been no opportunity for planning in advance for an invasion from Mars. The fact that the study was done at all is remarkable. While these problems do not erase its shortcomings, they make them quite understandable.

**The People's Choice: The Media in a Political Campaign.**     Few studies in the history of social science have had a greater impact on a field than did the study of mass media influences on voters in Erie County, Ohio, during the presidential election of 1940. First, it provided a long list of empirical generalizations that described the detailed attention of voters to mass communications during a political campaign of several months' duration. Second, it advanced a number of new concepts, measuring procedures, research strategies, and theoretical explanations of media influences on the voting decision. Finally, it prompted a fresh look at social relationships as an important part of the mass communication process—a set of factors conspicuously absent in any extended way from earlier research.

From a methodological standpoint, the panel design was both innovative and sophisticated. It provided an important set of controls that enabled researchers to assess the results of repeatedly interviewing the same sample. This brought a new kind of experimental logic into survey design. Panel techniques came into wide use in fields that involve polls and surveys.

The study of the voters in Erie County was also important for its focus on multivariate analysis. The techniques used for apportioning the influences of such factors as socioeconomic status, religion, occupation, urban-rural residence, and age seem crude by current standards. Today we can accomplish with statistical software and a few strokes of a keyboard what in the 1940s took months, even years, to do with only electric calculating machines based on nineteenth-century designs. Nevertheless, the logical foundations and worth of such analyses were demonstrated in an unusually clear manner in the Erie County investigation. The study also clarified the role of social category memberships in political pre-disposition and the influence of the mediated campaign in achieving activation, reinforcement, and (limited) conversion. But perhaps most important of all was the unanticipated discovery of the role of social relationships in the word-of-mouth diffusion of information. The "two-step flow" hypothesis stimulated research not only in mass communication but also in the diffusion of influence, information, and innovation in a number of related fields.

***Audiences for Daytime Radio Serials: Uses and Gratifications.*** This project brought together a massive amount of data on the uses and gratifications that women listeners derived from the popular daily radio dramas that came to be called "soap operas." Radio had arrived during the 1920s, and it became a popular medium during the 1930s. By 1940, virtually half of the adult women in the United States listened more or less regularly to one or more of the 40 daily dramas that were on the air. As it turned out, they were not socially isolated (as the magic bullet theory had suggested). Heavy listeners were, however, more limited in their intellectual range and interests. They had lower educational attainment and were less likely to vote in a presidential election. Those who listened regularly did so in part because they like radio programs in general, listening more often and later into the night than those who were not serial fans. The listeners gained emotional release from their experience. The dramas enabled them to engage in a great deal of satisfying wishful thinking. And finally, listeners felt gratified because the social depictions in the plays provided them with advice that they thought they could use in their own lives.

***The Iowa Study of Hybrid Seed Corn: The Adoption of Innovation.*** The role of mass communications in the adoption of innovation came to be better understood as a result of a small study of the process by which Iowa farmers began to use hybrid seed corn. It was an unlikely beginning for the development of a theory that would explain how people learned of and made decisions about new products and services from information obtained, in part, from the various mass media. The problem was to determine why it is that of many technological and other innovations that became available every year, only some are adopted and widely used by the public. Generally, those that are adopted follow a distinctive pattern as their use increases in a society. A curve of adoption is described as a few take up the innovation at the beginning and then more and more follow until the numbers of new users of the innovation starts to decline and then tapers off. In this way, an s-shaped curve of adoption is described as different kinds of people, exposed to different kinds of information, adopt at distinct stages along the curve. Understanding the adoption of innovation and the role played by mass-mediated information is important in an industrial society where an enormous flow of consumer goods is produced and the state of the economy depends on the levels of adoption of many kinds of new services, products, and technologies.

*Experiments with Film: Persuading the American Soldier in World War II.* Few researchers have access to as many subjects as they want, when and where they want them, and with the power to order them to cooperate fully. Just such unusual conditions prevailed for the behavioral scientists of the U.S. Army who studied the use of films for indoctrination and training during World War II. The main thrust of the research was to see if the films could change the beliefs and attitudinal orientations of new recruits. The most important of the films consisted of the *Why We Fight* series, prepared for the purpose of informing the men about the war—why it was being fought, the nature of the enemy, and what it would take to win. Their purpose was not only to provide factual knowledge but also to raise the morale and commitment of the recruits to the war effort. Other training films were also studied.

As it turned out, the films were not very effective, at least in the sense of achieving dramatic changes among those who viewed them. It was clear that the recruits did learn many important facts about the war, the enemy, and so forth. And because those facts were learned, many of the men formed more favorable opinions about a number of specific issues. Influences of this kind were most likely to occur among recruits with higher intellectual ability, who presumably could learn facts more easily. Thus, the comparison of audience members with distinctive patterns of individual differences guided much of the analysis. But there was little evidence of more dramatic results. The films were ineffective in improving certain attitudes, motivation, or morale.

At the time, the research team, the filmmakers, and the Army were disappointed and rather surprised that the series had such limited effects. While a number of interpretations and speculations were advanced as to why the results were not more significant, the findings did not fit well with the prevailing belief that carefully designed communications, with just the right content and structure, could achieve change in general attitudes and other dispositions—and presumably corresponding changes in overt behavior. But in spite of the lack of support of such cognitive assumptions, the finding of limited effects from the films was in the long run one of the important outcomes of the American Soldier studies. In time, the continuing failure of additional research to support a powerful effects cognitive model forced a search for new interpretations of the nature and influence of mass communication.

*Communication and Persuasion: The Search for the Magic Keys.* With the war over, there was much to do. For students of communication, there was basic research to be conducted to learn how to change people's beliefs, attitudes, and behavior—an essential task in building a better world free of the racial and religious horrors of totalitarianism. If a systematic theory of persuasion could be developed, the promotion of prosocial behavior might be effectively accomplished.

The goal was basic research that was supposed to lead to what we have termed the "magic keys" around which messages might be designed so as to alter beliefs, opinions, and attitudes, which would then achieve the desired changes in behavior.

The Yale Program of Research on Communication and Attitude Change focused on variables related to (1) the communicator, (2) the content of the communication, (3) the audience, and (4) actual responses made by members of the audience. The methodology was the controlled experiment. The settings were essentially stimulus-response situations in which little contact was allowed between members of an audience. Before-and-after assessments of each individual's beliefs or predispositions were completed; experimental conditions (or control conditions) of varying message content or structure were imposed; and the data were examined to see whether the message had achieved change.

Many empirical generalizations emerged concerning source credibility, one side versus both sides of an argument, and other aspects of message organization and content. The personality characteristics of the audience members were also discovered to be related to type and direction of changes in opinions and attitudes achieved by persuasive communication.

Did they locate the "magic keys" to persuasion that can serve as sure guides to the promotion of prosocial behavior? Not really. In retrospect, the Yale studies probably set too lofty a goal. While they were imaginative and thorough, the underlying idea that it is possible to discover ways to manipulate people through the systematic use of clever words and message structures according to a formalized theory of persuasion was simply too much to ask. However, while the Yale studies did not provide final answers, they did yield important clues and hypotheses to be pursued. Therefore, the significance of these experiments is that they developed an important foundation on which further research into the psychological and social dynamics of persuasion could be pursued.

***Personal Influence: The Two-Step Flow of Communication.***    Programmatic research, in which one study leads to another that pursues hypotheses or theoretical issues uncovered in the first, is common in the physical sciences. However, such linkages between studies are rare in the study of mass communication. The work of Katz and Lazarsfeld reported in this project was a notable exception to that rule. Here the research effort was focused on the phenomenon of social relationships between members of the audience that had been unexpectedly encountered while conducting the Erie County study.

The somewhat serendipitous discovery that the mass communication process seemed to involve a "two-step flow" of information and influence represented a rather radical change of thinking. Before 1950, those trying to develop theories of mass communication had given little thought to the idea that the kinds of social relationships described by the term *primary group* had anything to do with mass communication. Most previous research had been based on the assumption that members of an audience responded to the media as individuals. By the 1940s, communication theorists no longer saw as realistic the magic bullet theory, based on assumptions of uniformity among members of the mass society and their uniform modes of response. In its place came an emphasis on individual psychological and demographic factors that shaped the responses of members of the audience in selective ways.

In 1955, however, the publication of *Personal Influence* presented communication theorists with considerable evidence that close and intimate social relationships had to be presumed by the members of the audience. People not only passed on information that they had acquired from direct exposure to the media; they also influenced the opinions and decisions of those to whom the information was passed. An important new area of mass communication research, therefore, was to map out the interpersonal channels followed in two-step flow from media to mass and to identify what kind of people influenced others in the process.

**Project Revere: Leaflets as a Medium of Last Resort.**   A team of sociologists with substantial funding that they thought came from the U.S. Air Force studied the use of airborne leaflets. It was a medium of last resort that could get messages to large numbers of people when other, more normal, channels of communication were not available. It was not known to the team at the time, but evidence that came to light many years later indicated that it was not really the Air Force that was behind the study, and that goals other than military uses were at stake. As now seems clear, Project Revere was apparently funded by the CIA as part of a larger series of social and psychological studies called the Mark-Ultra Mind Control Project.

The American public was not aware of the details of the "missile gap" dilemma that apparently made funding available for this project. It was not the kind of thing to inspire confidence in the ability of one's government to protect citizens. But given those conditions, there was an urgent need to develop and understand ways of communicating with large populations scattered into the hinterland from cities that would become targets if the unthinkable happened. The problem was, how well would leaflets work for such a purpose?

One important consideration was the question of "how many" leaflets per person were needed to get a simple message across as to the availability of food, shelter, and medical attention. Relatively elaborate studies were undertaken to try to develop guidelines. As it turned out, it was possible to incorporate the concept of "repetition" into the study of this simple medium. This made possible the use of adaptations of classic theories from psychophysics and the development of mathematical models that would predict the amount of learning of the message that would take place under specific conditions of repetition. One of the clearest findings from this part of the research was the "curve of diminishing returns" related to message repetition. Geometric increases in the availability of the message did not result in corresponding gains in message learning. In fact, after a point, doubling or redoubling the repetitions had virtually no effect whatever in getting more people to learn the message.

From a methodological standpoint, the level of precision of these studies has seldom been equaled in communication research. The amount of funding for the studies was undoubtedly a factor, because each step and operation could be carried out with little concern for the costs of sampling designs, pretesting, control procedures, interviewer training, measurement, and statistical analysis. In addition, with notable exceptions, the use of mathematical representations of the theories being tested has not characterized more recent research on mass communication issues. The development and testing of such theories in Project Revere was at a very advanced level by comparison. Thus, the Revere studies remain a model of sophisticated theory development, systematic research strategies, and carefully conducted research procedures.

***Television in the Lives of Our Children: The Early Years.***    During the 1950s, America became a nation of television fans, almost overnight. Early in the decade, home TV sets were rare; by the end of the period, there was a receiver in the overwhelming majority of American households. The question was, What were the programs received by 150 million television sets doing to the nation? In particular, the recurring question that concerned American families was how this lively new medium was influencing children.

Schramm and his associates tried to answer that question by focusing on the uses children made of television, the functions if performed for them, and the satisfactions or gratifications they derived from viewing. Armed with theories of selectivity, they envisioned the new medium as a kind of cafeteria from which children chose content consistent with their interests. It was a conception of an active audience using a medium to meet its needs and to obtain gratifications rather than a passive one being acted upon.

The researchers concluded that children watched television for three primary reasons: to be entertained, to acquire new information, and to participate in social activities associated with viewing. The most significant were the entertainment and information functions. Like adults, children wanted to escape from boredom. Watching attractive people in exciting adventures was an enjoyable pastime. The acquisition of information was often not a deliberate goal. One of the important concepts that emerged from the study was that of "incidental learning." As in Blumer's early study of the movies, Schramm and his associates showed that children unwittingly learn many details about adult behavior and the world while being entertained. Today, this has become a very important idea.

While psychological factors were studied (e.g., intelligence and frustration) as variables accounting for selective viewing and influences, the major thrust from a theoretical point of view was on social categories and social relationships. Social class, age, and sex were seen to influence the selection of content. Similarly, the nature of the social relationships young viewers enjoyed with their parents and peers also shaped viewing patterns and influences.

In an analysis of the effects produced by the medium, there were no dramatic and disturbing findings. There were only minor physical effects (eyestrain), some emotional effects (fright), and numerous cognitive effects (learning new material and learning about the adult world). Overall, the study revealed a complex but not particularly threatening relationship between children and television. For most children under most condition, television seemed neither harmful nor beneficial.

Not everyone was happy with the results of this rather bland view of television in the lives of children. To critics of the medium, it seemed that it failed to prove what they already knew—that television was bad and harmful to the young. To those expecting more dramatic results of some kind, the work seemed to do little more than provide further support for a minimal-effects interpretation. It just seemed inescapable that an activity that occupied more time in the first 16 years of life than anything except sleep simply must have strong (and probably bad) influences. Thus, while many empirical generalizations emerged from the findings, this first major probe of the new medium did little to set aside the more political questions that were beginning to be associated with the (suspected) negative effects of television.

*The Agenda-Setting Function of the Press: What to Think About.*   In spite of the limited effects shown in much research on media influences, there remained a conviction that (1) the media could create significant effects but that (2) somehow some of their more important influences had not been uncovered by past projects. By the late 1960s, at least some communication scholars began to feel that another, and possibly simpler, approach might reveal more long-term media influences. One such group, led by McCombs and Shaw, was particularly interested in the influence of the press, that is, traditional newspapers and broadcast news programs. They decided to investigate the level of importance audiences attach to issues as a result of the way they are presented in the news.

It was a significant focus for research for two reasons. First, it was a modern counterpart of one of the oldest assumptions made by many nineteenth-century scholars who had studied the relationship between the press, public opinion, and politics. Since mass newspapers began, many political analysts have attributed to the press the power to influence the thinking and actions of the electorate regarding candidates and issues. McCombs and Shaw believed that only research could settle the question as to whether or not such influence actually exists. Second, issues that are seen as important or unimportant are probably evaluated and acted upon in different ways by voters who attend to the news. This seemed to be a logical point from which to begin their research. While judging issues to be more or less important does not imply approval or disapproval, such evaluations may form a framework for assessing the merits of particular political leaders or their proposed programs. Ultimately, such opinions and conclusions may be the basis for political action, such as voting for one candidate or another.

There are several obvious facts about the news media in American society that influenced researchers' formulation of their basic research questions. One obvious fact is that there is a continuing flow of news that reaches very large audiences. It is also obvious that the news is selectively prepared and presented by the press in such a way that a daily agenda of issues, topics, and items is placed before the public for their consideration. A third obvious fact is that the press does not treat all news items equally. Some are presented as leading stories; others are given minor recognition.

The effects of this differential emphasis on news stories might not be of the direct kind that had been looked for in media research on attitude and behavioral change, but there might well be long-term and indirect influences that could be uncovered. Therefore, while it might be true that the news media do not instantly shape our beliefs, attitudes, and behavior regarding the issues and topics they present, their daily agenda places before us a selective list of things to think about. By focusing our collective attention on that list, the media agenda provides the personal agenda of concern to members of the audience.

The 1972 study of agenda setting was clearly a milestone in mass communication research. Like many of the studies that break new ground, the work can be criticized in several respects. Certainly, it had methodological flaws. The researchers encountered numerous problems in designing their samples and in developing rigorous measurement techniques. However, the study made use of innovative statistical techniques, such as cross-lagged correlations, to study influences on voters' beliefs from one time period to another. But above all, both the first study and the second stimulated considerable interest in the way in which the press tells us daily what to think about.

*Violence and the Media: The Turbulent Sixties.*    Public discontent with the media, especially television, rose sharply during the 1960s. In part it was a response to the events of the times. The war in Vietnam not only set America against its military foes but also set its people against one another. Violence in the society escalated: a counterculture developed; crime rates rose; students protested; inner cities exploded in turmoil; there were frequent demonstrations; flags, draft cards, and brassieres were burned in public; drug use expanded as a problem; skyjacking began; and political leaders were assassinated. It was a frightening time.

Much of this activity was shown dramatically on television's evening news night after night. It was an ancient custom to kill the messenger who brought bad news. Apparently, a somewhat parallel association between the bearer of the news and the upsetting events grew during the 1960s. Americans loved television, but as the medium brought them daily portrayals of these mounting miseries, the legacy of fear returned in force, and suspicion grew that television was a major culprit, causing much of the nation's increasing violence, delinquency, and crime.

Politicians responded, as they frequently do, by appointing a committee. At the end of the decade, President Johnson appointed a National Commission on the Causes and Prevention of Violence. It appointed more committees. One was as Media Task Force to assess the role of mass communication in stimulating violence in the society. Their major concern was television. The Task Force report contains a major section devoted to the topic of violence and the media. Included was new research, including a content analysis of violence portrayed in prime-time TV programs.

The world of prime-time television was shown to be filled with violent action. Approximately 80 percent of the network programs studied during typical weeks during two consecutive years contained violent incidents. A rich set of conclusions and generalizations described the details of violence as they appeared in televised portrayals. The overall conclusion was that violence was a predominant characteristic of television programming, and it was used in the programs, especially by the "good guys," as an effective and approved means of conflict resolution. To the public, this was a disturbing report.

Other data showed that there was a significant difference between the norms and level of violence as shown on television and the same phenomena in actual daily life. This difference led the Task Force to conclude that television had to be considered a possible contributing factor in explaining why there were so many forms of violent behavior in American society. The report also emphasized the need for further study of the long-term effects of mass communication, especially television. It indicated the probability that as children see violence portrayed day after day, week after week, and on over a span of years, this would influence their attitudes and conceptions of norms toward violent and aggressive behavior.

Such a position was entirely consistent with Blumer's pioneering interpretations of media influences, Schramm and Parker's concept of "incidental learning," and DeFleur's "cultural norms" theory.[1] From such diverse sources, plus later research, emerged the contemporary meaning theory of media portrayals; that is, the media are seen as providing constructions of what society is like, the nature of its norms, and what behaviors are appropriate in various circumstances. Presumably, from media portrayals of social life, children internalize those conceptions as their own. Note, however, that in the actual Task Force report, the older cognitive assumption that media content shapes attitudes (which then shape behavior) was seen as the actual mechanism of influence.

***The Surgeon General's Report: Television and Social Behavior.***    Public concern with violence in American society rose to new heights during the last years of the 1960s. That concern had a realistic basis. Almost daily the news showed campus riots, assassinations and their aftermath, drugs, crime, and ghetto upheavals. The idea deeply established in public thinking—that the media were a causal agent in these troubles—and now reinforced by magazine articles, books, and other reports by media critics, provided an interpretive framework. It seemed to many people that mass communication, and especially television, was a cause of much of the violence in society. It was disturbing to think that if television were indeed the source from which children learned to be aggressive and solve their problems by violent means, then everyone was at risk whenever a child sat down in front of a TV set.

As always, when Americans need action on a social problem, they turn to the federal government for solutions. Increasing demands were made on Congress to "do something." Such widespread concern seldom goes unnoticed by political figures who want to be reelected. By 1969, Senator Pastore had convinced his colleagues to fund large-scale research on the relationship between the violence portrayed on television and the behavior of children and adolescents. The $1 million appropriated for the studies was something of a record. The management of the project was placed in the hands of the U.S. surgeon general and was coordinated and administered under his direction by the National Institute of Mental Health (NIMH). Once again, the principle that research is a political as well as a scientific process was confirmed.

The entire project created numerous controversies. After the dust had settled and the results of the 40 studies had been widely examined, it did appear that the research had advanced our knowledge about the effects of violence shown on television. The advisory committee summed up by saying that there was a tentative indication of a relationship between viewing violence on television and aggressive behavior among certain categories of children. They were careful to point out that this was a preliminary conclusion subject to further verification by additional research and that it certainly did not apply to all children. In fact, they noted that it characterized mainly those who were already predisposed to be aggressive and who were in particular environmental circumstances.

The careful and guarded, but scientifically responsible, conclusion pleased almost no one. It did, however, point to the importance of conducting further research, not only on the issues of the effects of exposure to portrayals of violence on television but also on the influence of other kinds of content. This may have been one of the most important outcomes of the project.

***Television and Behavior: Ten Years of Progress.***    Public concern with violence in American society remained high during the 1970s. Crime was still a very serious problem, with few signs of improvement. Public suspicion remained that television was a causal factor in violence and aggression. Indeed, as the decade moved to a close, there were several spectacular examples of teenagers imitating violent behavior portrayed on television—examples that did little to reduce such fears. For example, in a widely publicized murder trial, "television intoxication" was used as the basis for the legal defense of a youthful offender. The claim was that the client had seen so many murders on television that he could no longer distinguish between right and wrong regarding such activity. Fortunately, the legal strategy was unsuccessful, but the possibility that it could occur did little to calm the public. Generally, then, the legacy of fear was alive and well and clearly concerned with television as the society looked ahead to the 1980s.

At the same time, concern about the influence of television no longer focused on violence alone. Children were spending increasing amounts of time in front of their screens, but no one knew just what lessons were being offered or what was being learned. The concerns of both experts and parents ranged from alcohol and drugs to television's impact on cognitive development. Following the release of the 1971 Report to the Surgeon General, the scientific community took up research on various influences of television with considerable enthusiasm. Because of the richness of the new research base, no further studies needed to be commissioned by NIMH. To pull those more recent findings together into a new report on television and social behavior, 24 researchers in the field were selected by the federal agency and asked to prepare comprehensive and integrative reviews of the existing literature. These were published in the 1982 report of the NIMH monitoring team.

The report was in two volumes, and several of the summaries contained findings that had not previously been published. The final volumes covered seven broad areas. These were (1) violence, (2) health, (3) prosocial behavior, (4) cognitive and affective aspects of viewing, (5) the family and interpersonal relations, (6) social beliefs and social behavior, and (7) television's effects on American institutions.

When the findings and conclusions were released, the media predictably focused mainly on the issue of televised violence and aggressive behavior. The remaining six topics received little publicity. The media did not find to their liking the conclusion that portrayed violence tended to lead to aggressive behavior, at least among some categories of children, even though the case for television as a causal factor had become far stronger. Most of the participating researchers accepted the generalization, and the NIMH team interpreted the evidence in that manner.

Complicating this issue was the finding that the content of violent programming on television may not be solely responsible for the medium's part in stimulating aggressive behavior. New research found that aggression could be stimulated by high levels of action in a program, even without a substantial amount of portrayed violence. In other words, television's form as well as its violent content may be partly responsible for the link between violence and aggression. Thus, new questions were raised regarding this perennial issue.

On a positive note, it was found that TV content can produce prosocial behavior. What viewers learn from television depends upon what they watch. If they see prosocial behavior as a response to a particular situation, then they will learn that this is appropriate and normal. However, if aggression and antisocial behavior are shown as responses, then those forms will be learned as appropriate. Hence, television appears to have as much potential for "good" as for "bad."

Television's role as an informal educator was scrutinized with respect to a number of issues: minorities, women, drugs, alcohol, risky driving, and family life. Thus, the report contains numerous content analyses of the "lessons" taught on such topics. Unfortunately, content analysis does not reveal whether people attend to what is on the screen, and it certainly does not show how they interpret such content or how it influences their behavior, if at all. Thus, the classic error of content analysis was committed, as effects were simply assumed from the nature of what was portrayed.

## Explaining Mass Communication in a Context of Change

A number of the projects discussed in this book may appear to be of only historical interest to some, like looking at a silent film from days long gone. In fact, 9 of the 14 foundation efforts were conducted during the first three decades after scholars first turned to systematic studies of mass communication. But they are much more than just interesting artifacts from an earlier period. They are important for two reasons: First, they paved the way in pointing out the pathways needed to understand mass communication—routes that later researchers needed to explore in greater detail. Second, they yielded many empirical generalizations that provided the basis for a number of focused theories that explain various aspects of the process and effects of mass communication.

*The Significance of Pioneering Studies.*   As is the case in all fields of science, early and classic studies provide the broad map of the territory that needs to be explored as a new discipline comes into existence. For example, studies such as the presidential election in Erie County, the research on the spread of hybrid seed corn, and the investigation of the radio soap operas of the 1940s mapped out broad behavioral territories. The election study revealed for the first time a two-step flow of communication beyond mere direct exposure to media. The seed corn research uncovered a process of adoption of innovation in which media play a significant role. The radio serial study pointed to an active rather than passive audience who use media messages for their own purposes and gratifications.

These maps of needed research were extensively followed by subsequent waves of investigators who studied the behaviors revealed in greater detail, often formulating tentative explanations of these particular processes and effects. Such follow-up research is very important. It yields more refined understandings of the situations and causal sequences that the original studies seemed to reveal. As these become better understood, other researchers find additional avenues to explore.

In addition, the 14 studies or projects we have reviewed have yielded a substantial body of information about media effects that helps us understand them today. If we add the results of literally thousands of follow-up and other efforts that were addressed to similar issues during the same period, the size of the body of knowledge that could be traced to the milestones is impressive indeed.

On a less positive note, the conclusions about mass communication resulting directly or indirectly from the milestones discussed in the various chapters is by no means unified or systematic. It was assembled by scholars from various disciplines, working on many distinct aspects of mass communication, studying different media, and focusing on a variety of behavioral influences for many kinds of unrelated purposes. This diversity makes it especially difficult to synthesize and interpret what it all means. In short, the body of knowledge about the effects of mass communication revealed by the milestones discussed is both large and impressive, but also complex, uncoordinated, incomplete, and perplexing.

One way of trying to understand the implications that this body of knowledge has for the study of mass communication today is to look at two conceptually distinct but interlocking issues: (1) the status of the hundreds of empirical generalizations that have emerged from the first half century of research and (2) the question of the contemporary utility of the more limited number of focused theories that were formulated and tested in the milestone studies.

***Problems with Specific Empirical Generalizations.***    Those who try to develop valid and reliable generalizations to describe the effects of mass communication are confronted with a curious set of obstacles. Those obstacles are generated because of the ever-changing nature of what is under study. The media industries undergo virtually continuous change. The most obvious form of that change is in technology. Many media devices or situations that were state of the art only a few years ago now seem quaint and outdated—drive-in movies, vacuum-tube TV sets with rounded screens, eight-track cassette tapes, limited selection of television channels and so on. Constantly over the horizon are new technological marvels that promise to "reinvent" our media to bring us unbelievable richness in choices of entertainment and useful information.

Equally significant are social and cultural changes in the society as a whole. These continually reshape the nature and requirements of audiences as they collectively redefine their goals and priorities. Fads and fashions, along with new social movements and subcultures, constantly emerge in a dynamic and creative society. Changes in folkways and mores make new demands on the media as they alter the public's standards. This, in turn, determines what is politically correct in political ads, levels of violence, and depictions of religions, minorities, or sexual activities. For example, we now tolerate displays of nudity and sexual coupling on our home TV screens that would have driven earlier generations into a frenzy of enraged protest. In addition, formal norms that regulate our media also undergo change. Legal controls that restrict or foster media business organizations, or what can or cannot be printed, broadcast, or exhibited by whom. obviously come and go.

Still other changes are reflected in demographic indices. Our population is not only larger but also more complex than it was in earlier decades. Moreover, the composition of that population changes from year to year in terms of age, education, number of immigrants, rural versus urban residence, religious affiliation, and political orientation. Currently, Americans are getting older, better educated, healthier, more urban, less orthodox, and more culturally diverse. Such trends both create and reflect alterations in shared conceptions of what the media should offer and how their content should be evaluated.

This dynamic nature of society and the media systems within it influences the status of specific empirical generalizations derived from particular media research projects at particular points in time. What appears to be a completely valid generalization at the time it is published may be an outdated curiosity a few years later. For example, the generalizations that emerged from Cantril's study of the invasion from Mars broadcast would be unlikely to be found again if a similar broadcast occurred today. These inescapable facts of societal change, media system modification, and obsolescence of generalizations from mass communication research pose a very considerable restriction on the study of this subject matter. Put metaphorically, it is difficult to locate eternal verities about the process and effects of mass communication using the strategies of science while searching through the shifting sands of social, cultural, and technological change.

To some, the time-bound nature of many generalizations seems to pose insurmountable obstacles to the development of a body of reliable and valid knowledge concerning the effects of mass communication. Indeed, in recent years some scholars have given up on science—or perhaps they never approved of it from the start. In its place, they have attempted to substitute an alternative strategy. They declare that the only fruitful way to study mass communication is within a *critical cultural perspective*. This is a difficult position to define because there appear to be as many critical cultural perspectives as there are critical people writing about them. Basically, however, the central goal seems to be to look at the mass media in the United States (and elsewhere for that matter) and point out what is *wrong* with them and the cultural products that they produce. A common strategy is to complain about how they are owned and operated by a limited number of powerful corporations and conglomerates who use the media for their own profit and advantage. Such critics maintain that the media offer the public entertainment at a low level of taste in exchange for their accepting beliefs, ideologies, products (and even political candidates) that are often of great benefit to that same powerful elite. To many critics, this spells political and economic exploitation of the masses and the use of the media to maintain unfair control of the system.

If this sounds disturbingly familiar, one need only read Karl Marx. It is essentially the same kind of analysis but in modern dress. One need not strike out intellectually against such a position. It is entertaining to read, and it must be a lot of fun to blast the media, their content, and those who control them. Moreover, all sides of all debates should be heard. However, it has yet to be made clear how a critical cultural perspective offers much in the way of systematic answers and verifiable facts about the structure, functioning, and influences of mass communications in modern societies—the kinds of questions that have been addressed by the accumulated research of the past. That, as the milestones discussed in this book reveal, has been organized around the timeless framework provided many years ago by Lasswell, who stated that the proper study of communication was to find out "*who* said *what* to *whom* over what *channel* with what *effect*."

In spite of the problems of constantly changing media and society, as outlined earlier, there is little doubt that the methods of science can be used effectively by communication researchers to address Lasswell's questions by gathering and interpreting empirical evidence. In contrast to those who advocate a critical cultural approach, the research community has accumulated an impressive set of answers. Professional communicators have been studied; the content of the messages have been analyzed; the structures of audiences have been mapped; the ways in which distinct media influence the process have been investigated; and the influence of mass communication on both individuals and society has been a central concern. As a result, at least some relatively clear insights about mass communication are now available.

It is far less clear what has been accomplished by those who have chosen a critical cultural perspective. However, perhaps it is too soon to ask for an accounting in the manner of the present book. Hopefully, at some point is time, a treatise will be prepared that systematically reveals the milestones that have resulted from assuming a critical cultural perspective for the study of the process and effects of mass communication.

But where does all of this discussion leave mass communication research? It may be true that many of the specific empirical generalizations that emerged from its milestone (and other) studies are of the variety that is "true today but maybe not tomorrow." However, this need not be a total obstacle to the development of valid explanations of the various aspects of mass communication posed in Lasswell's definition. There are other sciences—meteorology and geology, for example—that deal with a changing universe of phenomena. Storm systems, highs, lows, rains, drought, and other events studied by the weather sciences present a constantly changing picture. Indeed, the pace of change can be swift. On a very different time scale, the geologist also faces constant change. Over eons, mountains thrust up only to be eroded away; layers are deposited over other layers to form complex stratified deposits; even the continents themselves, which seem so stable, are said to be roaming around on the surface of the earth. But in spite of these circumstances, both sciences develop explanations and predictions for the phenomena they study. What are they doing, and what lessons do they provide for the study of mass communication?

The critical feature that enables such fields to develop theories in spite of a disorderly universe is that they look beyond individual generalizations to search for patterns among them—configurations that when considered together suggest causal influences. By this means, they can develop *focused theories* of limited categories of phenomena. Such theories transcend the vagaries of shifts in the daily relationships between whatever elements they have under study. They focus on *underlying principles*. Thus, the fact that specific generalizations obtained from media research have a short shelf life need not pose an insurmountable obstacle if focused theories can be generated at the next level of abstraction.

***Inducing Focused Theories.***    As noted earlier in this chapter, a focused theory is one that describes and explains some set of events or phenomena that has clear boundaries. For example, modeling theory describes, explains, and predicts how particular kinds of actions are adopted and made habitual by people who observe others doing something. Agenda-setting theory describes and explains how the hierarchies of prominence set by those who design and transmit the news influence the personal agendas of their audiences. Thus, each of these theories is focused on a particular set of events or actions.

The way in which a configuration of specific empirical generalizations can lead inductively to a well-focused theory at a higher level of abstraction can be illustrated by the classic story of King Louis's clock. During the seventeenth century, Louis XIV of France was deeply interested in astronomy. It is a science where accurate measurement of time is crucial. A master clock was built in Paris to the most exacting standards available at the time (which were surprisingly good). Then, he had a second clock made whose works and pendulum were precise duplicates. It beat in perfect time with the master clock. It was possible to construct a second clock that was equally accurate because of a specific generalization learned earlier that the length and mass of the pendulum governed its oscillations.

Then, in 1671, in order to make certain astronomical observations, Louis sent Monsieur Jean Richter to the island of Cayenne, in French Guiana (which is close to the equator). The goal was to track the orbits of certain planets and stars from the two locations. Richter was given the second clock so as to be able to make observations of the same heavenly bodies at the second location at precisely the same time as was being done in Paris.

From the very beginning, nothing went right. In fact, the whole project was a disaster. Richter's observations seemed to be dreadfully in error. Then, to everyone's astonishment, it was discovered that his duplicate clock was losing almost precisely two and a half minutes per day! Eventually, it become clear that clocks with a given pendulum length beat slower at the equator than they do in Paris (an empirical generalization). Later it was noted that they beat at intermediate rates in between, depending on the distance from the equator (another empirical generalization).[2]

The only thing that could account for such a configuration of generalizations was the explanation (focused theory) that the equator was farther away from the center of the earth than Paris, and that the closer one got to the poles, the lesser the distance to that center. This meant that the force of gravity was not as strong at the equator as at the poles, and that it gets stronger as one moves from the equator toward the poles.

It was a remarkable insight. If the generalizations were true, a theory could be inductively developed that the world is *not actually a globe* but is squashed down at the poles and fatter at the equator! This theory of the world's shape turned out later to be completely verified by evidence derived from studies of Newton's famous laws of gravitation, and the mystery was solved.

The point is that a pattern of empirical generalizations provided a basis for inducing an explanation that was not present among any of the individual generalizations themselves. This same process of induction from configurations of empirical generalizations led communication researchers to formulate a number of focused theories that can both explain and predict what will happen in the American society under certain conditions of exposure to mass communications.

An example of a focused theory in mass communication that was induced from a number of generalizations was the *theory of limited and selective influences* of mass communication.[3] As the review of the milestone studies reveals, one of the first generalizations that became clear is that individual differences in such psychological factors as critical ability (chapter 3), needs for gratification (chapter 5), and prior beliefs (chapter 8), led to selectivity on the part of the audience. It also became clear that the social categories in which people could be classified led to selectivity. For example, rich Protestant farmers attended to news about the presidential campaign differently than poor, urban factory workers (chapter 4); younger working women sought different media content than matrons who were raising families (chapter 9); and children gathered and distributed more leaflets than adults (chapter 10). Then, another generalization was added as a basis for content selection by audience members. The role of social relationships between members of families and other primary groups was revealed (chapters 4, 6, and 9). That too led to selective attention to media content. Added to the configuration was the generalization that media messages had limited influence on those who attended, rather than the immediate and powerful effects that had been assumed before empirical research began (chapters 7 and 8).

Putting these generalizations together inductively yielded the theory that people who make up the mass society are very diverse in their psychological makeup and in their locations in the social structure. This diversity leads them to select some media content and ignore others; that is, people attend to, interpret, and respond to the content of mass communications selectively in ways influenced by their group memberships and social ties. Moreover, even if they do attend, influences are not particularly powerful. Thus, the theory both explains and predicts selective and limited effects among audiences. The inductive process of developing this theory from a configuration of more specific generalizations about factors leading to attention to media content revealed by research was no different from that in which generalizations about the accuracy of a clock led to a theory concerning the shape of the earth.

## FOCUSED THEORIES TO WHICH THE MILESTONES CONTRIBUTED

Focused theories, then, are an invaluable legacy from the milestones. Undeniably, the research summarized in previous chapters was not the sole basis for the various contemporary theories that have been formulated. However, the milestone projects clearly played a major contributory role. In retrospect, some of the theories derived from the accumulated research now seem more attractive, valid, or otherwise significant than others. Nevertheless, they have provided the guiding principles around which much research has been conducted and continues to be conducted today. Furthermore, an important point is that, with the exception of the magic bullet theory, none has been made obsolete by changes in media or society. A brief review of a number of such formulations can illustrate the idea.

### The Demise of the Magic Bullet Theory

As was discussed in chapter 1, the magic bullet theory was the earliest general theory of the influence of mass communication that was widely shared when empirical research began. It served as a kind of "jumping off" point for theoretical development in mass communication. It was based not on empirical generalizations derived from media research but on certain assumptions about human nature and the social order that prevailed at the end of the nineteenth century. At the time, social and behavioral scientists rejected interpretations of "rational" human beings and stressed the "animal" side of human nature. It was assumed, for example, that human beings are uniformly controlled by their biologically based "instincts" and that they react more or less uniformly to whatever "stimuli" come along.

This conception of the human condition had a strong influence on early thinking about the power of mass communications. It portrayed human populations as composed of irrational creatures that could be swayed and controlled by cleverly designed mass communications stimuli. This theory led people to believe that those who controlled the media could control the public. Thus, the magic bullet theory implied that the media have direct, immediate, and powerful effects of a uniform nature on those who pay attention to their content.

The Payne Fund project seemed to support this theory, at least at first. However, shortly after research began, it became clear that it rested on assumptions that were not viable; and as additional projects accumulated, they brought about a rejection of this formulation.

## Uses and Gratifications Theory

As the magic bullet theory came into question, it began to be replaced with explanations that described the nature and behavior of audiences in quite different terms. The research on radio serials provided an important foundation for this new perspective on the activities of audiences. The new theory addressed the important theoretical question as to why audiences deliberately seek out some kinds of media content and completely ignore others. That is, why do people intentionally buy a particular kind of magazine or book, turn first to a particular section of the newspaper, or scan the radio and TV schedules to locate certain programs? These goal-oriented forms of behavior indicate clearly that audiences do not simply wait placidly to receive whatever content happens to come their way. They seek content from the media that they anticipate will provide them with certain kinds of experiences. In other words, these are receivers who want to use the information in some way or to obtain satisfactions that they anticipate. This theory focuses on psychological factors—individual structures of interests, needs, attitudes, and values that play a part in shaping selections from the media.

One of the largest projects based on this approach was the study of *Television in the Lives of Our Children*. It showed that youngsters sought out and used what they found on television to fulfill a variety of needs. It did not show that the new medium provided harmful experiences; it did show the uses and gratifications TV viewing provided for children at the time.

## Agenda-Setting Theory

The works by McCombs and Shaw very clearly provided the empirical foundation on which this popular theory came into existence. It explains an important influence of the press in terms of how individuals come to regard some events and situations that they encounter through news reports as more important than others. According to the theory, those who control the news media make decisions about what should be reported to the public. This becomes the agenda of the media at any given time. As this agenda is presented to audiences, a high level of correspondence develops between the amount and kind of attention paid to a particular political issue by the press and the level of importance assigned to that issue by the people in the community who had received information about it from newspapers and other news sources. Thus, agenda setting implies a relationship between decisions about the treatment of an issue or event in newspapers and TV and radio news, and the beliefs about its importance or significance on the part of individuals who make up the news audience. This does not imply that the press tells people *what* they should think and decide about the issues. However, it does imply that the press tells people what they should think *about* and what issues were important enough to require their decisions.

## Adoption of Innovation Theory

In a changing society, there is a constant flow of innovations. Some are invented by members of the society; others are borrowed from other groups. These can range from the trivial, such as a new dance step, to the profound, such as a new political philosophy, such as communism or democracy. But whether invented or borrowed, every innovation is taken up by people in a particular society in a rather regular process that is well described by the theory of the adoption of innovation. That theory, initially formulated in the hybrid seed corn study, is important for the study of mass communication for two reasons: First, each of our major mass media was originally an innovation that had yet to be adopted and widely used. This is true of the mass newspaper (which began in New York in the early 1830's), the motion picture (beginning at the turn of the century), home radio (early 1920s), television as a mass medium (post–World War II), and so on. Each spread through the society following a curve of adoption. A second way that innovation theory is important to the study of mass communication is that the media are often largely responsible for bringing new items to the attention of people who eventually adopt them. This process is of great importance in a consumer-oriented industrial society, where getting people to purchase goods means jobs and economic growth.

## The Two-Step Flow and the Diffusion of Information

Beginning with the serendipitous discovery of the "two-step flow" of communication in the Erie County study, it has been increasingly clear that a large segment of the audience gets its news and information not directly from exposure to media messages but indirectly from other people. Thus, both information and influence diffuse through societies by word of mouth. The dynamics of the process were observed in both *Personal Influence* and *Project Revere*. The process is related to, but in many ways distinct from, the adoption of innovations. The innovation here is not some product or technological item, which requires a thoughtful decision as to whether to adopt and resources in order to do so. In the diffusion process, in which information moves from person to person to an audience beyond the media, that which spreads through the society is news. Or in the two-step flow of influence by opinion leaders, it is an assessment or interpretation of some item of information. Neither requires a major act of decision making or parting with resources on the part of those who receive it. Thus, even in our sophisticated "information" society, with its satellites, computers, and news media with worldwide reach, word-of-mouth communication is still a part of the mass communication process. Most of us can recall learning of some major news event this way, but modern research on word-of-mouth transmission of news has shown that it is not a very reliable or accurate system for moving information that includes many details. However, it does work well for short messages of a dramatic nature, such as "the space shuttle blew up," "the president has been shot," or "we won the big game."

## Limited and Selective Influences Theory

Evidence mounted from research on the effects of mass communication conducted during the 1930s and 1940s, that the influences of mass communication were quite limited. A number of the milestones (on films used by the Army, the daytime radio serials, the Mars radio program, the leaflet study, and others) showed these effects to be weak, not powerful. Moreover, as was explained earlier, three kinds of factors seemed to guide what people selected from the media. These were their individual differences, their social category memberships, and their social relationships with friends and family. The accumulation of research findings made it necessary to develop explanations that took into account the fact that different kinds of people selected different kinds of content from the media and interpreted it in different ways. Thus, by the time of the studies of violence and children, it came as no surprise that the effects of television in stimulating aggression were both difficult to demonstrate and by no means universal among all the categories of youth. In other words, the influences of television's portrayals of violence were both selective and limited.

## Modeling Theory

The mass media, and especially television and movies, present many depictions of people acting out patterns of behavior in various ways. These depictions can serve as "models" of behavior that can be imitated, and people who see the action depicted may adopt it as part of their own behavioral repertoire. This kind of influence was clearly apparent as far back as the studies of the influence of movies of the 1920s on children. Blumer noted the extensive imitation of actions and situations children saw on the screen. A more sophisticated version of modeling theory was derived from research findings plus a more general perspective called "social learning" theory originally formulated by Bandura. This theory provides explanations of the acquisition of behavior by seeing it performed by someone else, whether the media are involved or not. The reason that modeling theory is particularly relevant to television and motion pictures is that they actually *show* actions performed by persons (models) who in the course of various kinds of dramas or other content, can be seen behaving in various kinds of social settings. Thus, the modeled behavior is depicted more realistically than if it were only described in verbal terms, as would be the case with radio and print.

## Social Expectations Theory

Every human group has its own set of rules that must be followed—its customs and expectations for many kinds of social behavior. If the individual does not conform to these social expectations, he or she risks social criticism and even rejection. But what are the sources from which we acquire our knowledge about such social skills and learn the social expectations of others? The answer derived from mass communication research is that there are many sources. Obviously, we learn from our family, from peers, from schools, and from the general community. But in our modern world, by watching television or going to a movie, or even by reading, one can learn the norms, roles, and other components of social organization that make up the requirements of many kinds of groups. Such incidental learning was clearly demonstrated by many of the studies discussed in the report on ten years of progress that summarized research on various kinds of norms and roles. However, the theory extends beyond families and gender roles. There is an almost endless parade of groups and social activities, with their behavioral rules, specialized roles, levels of power and prestige, and ways of controlling their members portrayed in the media. There is simply no way that the ordinary individual can actually participate in most of these groups so as to learn by trial and error the appropriate forms of conduct. The media, then, provided broad if unwitting training in such social expectations.

## The Meaning Theory of Media Portrayals

One of the oldest explanations of human behavior—extending back to Plato's Allegory of the Cave—is that people act on the basis of what they believe to be real. Those beliefs are learned, remembered, and acted upon in terms of the words that make up their language and images derived from observing depictions of social situations. Even the early radio soap operas provided such portrayals. Contemporary media such as movies and television depict in detailed, dramatic and realistic ways almost every form of individual behavior and social situation that can be imagined. These depictions constitute "definitions of situations"—lessons in meanings, social implications, and personal consequences of the activities and social relationships that are portrayed. From such incidental portrayals, we can vicariously experience virtually any set of circumstances, from being in a submarine deep under the sea to traveling in a spacecraft to an alien planet. From this vast array of definitions of situations, people can select forms of action that seem appropriate when similar, analogous, or parallel situations arise in our own lives. That kind of influence of the media was shown as far back as the study of the daytime radio serials.

## Cultivation Theory

This perspective, which in many ways is a focused version of meaning theory, grew out of studies of media-portrayed violence and its influence on children. In particular, it was based on the work of George Gerbner in the Violence Commission's report. He began by tracking the amount of aggressive behavior shown on television. The major thesis of Gerbner's research is that people who are heavy viewers of television will see the world as a more violent and fearful place because of the high levels of violence shown on their TV screens. Conversely, those who are light viewers will see their neighborhoods and communities as less violent environments. The theory has been extended in an effort to move beyond the issues of violence to address the more general influences of television on human social life and personal beliefs.

As a last word, the above is by no means a complete inventory of the theoretical formulations to which the milestone studies contributed. They do, however, illustrate the point. Without that foundation of studies (plus literally thousands of others that followed up), we would know far less about the process and effects of mass communication and the role of the media in our society.

## NOTES AND REFERENCES

1. Melvin L. DeFleur, "The Cultural Norms Theory," in *Theories of Mass Communication* (New York: David McKay, 1970), pp. 129–139.
2. Arthur N. Strahler and Alan H. Strahler, *Modern Physical Geography*, 2d ed. (New York: John Wiley and Sons, 1983), pp. 5–6.
3. See Melvin L. DeFleur and Everette E. Dennis, *Understanding Mass Communication* (Boston: Houghton Mifflin, 1994), pp. 554–557.

# Index